Revisiting Education in the New Latino Diaspora

A Volume in
Education Policy in Practice:
Critical Cultural Studies Series

Series Editors
Edmund T. Hamann, *University of Nebraska–Lincoln*
Rodney Hopson, *George Mason University*

Education Policy in Practice:
Critical Cultural Studies Series

Edmund Hamann and Rodney Hopson, Series Editors

Praise for *Revisiting Educatiion in the New Latino Diaspora*

"Timely and compelling, *Revisiting Education in the NLD* offers new insight into the Latino Diaspora in the U.S. just as the discussions regarding immigration policy, bilingual education, and immigrant rights are gaining steam. Drawing from a variety of perspectives, contributing authors interrogate the very concept of the diaspora. The wide range of research in this volume thoughtfully illustrates the nuanced phenomena and provides rich descriptions of complex situations. No longer a simple question of immigration, the book considers language and legal status in schools, international adoption, teacher preparation, and the relationships between established and relatively new Latino communities in a variety of contexts. Comprised of rich, thoughtful research *Revisiting Education* provides a fascinating window into the context of Latino reception nationwide."

—**Rebecca M. Callahan,** Associate Professor, University of
Texas-Austin

"As the leader of a 10-years-and-counting research study in Mexico that has identified and interviewed transnationally mobile students with prior experience in U.S. schools, I can affirm that in addition to students with backgrounds in California, Arizona, Texas, and Colorado, migration links now join schools in Georgia, Minnesota, Oklahoma, Alabama, etc. to schools in Mexico. For that reason and many others I am excited to see this far-ranging, interdisciplinary, new text that considers policy implementation through lenses as different as teacher preparation, Latino adoption into culturally mixed families, the fate of Latino newcomers in 'low density' districts where there are few like them, and the misuse of Spanish teachers as interpreters. This is an relevant book for American educators and scholars, but also for readers beyond U.S. borders. Hamann, Wortham, Murillo, and their contributors should be celebrated for this fine new collection."

—**Victor Zúñiga,** Director/Dean, División de Investigación y
Extensión/Research and Extension

Revisiting Education in the New Latino Diaspora

edited by

Edmund T. Hamann
University of Nebraska–Lincoln

Stanton Wortham
University of Pennsylvania

and

Enrique G. Murillo, Jr.
California State University, San Bernardino

INFORMATION AGE PUBLISHING, INC.
Charlotte, NC • www.infoagepub.com

Library of Congress Cataloging-in-Publication Data

CONTENTS

SECTION III: EXISTING INFRASTRUCTURE RESPONDS

FOREWORD

Amanda Morales

You don't see me…. You see your idea of me…. As you evaluate my brown skin,
my long dark hair, and my ambiguous facial features, you say, "What are you?
I know you are something…."

As a young girl, growing up in an otherwise all-White German farming community in western Kansas, I embodied the identities of both my Mexican American father and my Irish and Native American mother. We lived on the edge of town, where the paved roads ended and the dirt roads crunched and crackled as the occasional truck drove by. My father, Francisco Silos Rodriguez, a native Texan, was born into a migrant farm working family, and spent the large majority of his childhood and young adult years traveling across the country, harvesting a wide variety of crops. From May to January, he and his family followed the harvest as far north as Washington State to pick cherries and as far west as Arizona to pick cotton. However, it was the sugar beets of Kansas that brought him and my mother together.

My mother grew up the daughter of an orphan from the "wrong side of town." As a fiery, strong-willed young woman, she met my father at a street dance. And at the age of 16, she was bound and determined to marry a tall, dark, and handsome Hispanic man. My father liked that idea too. So he and his brother (who later married her sister) became the only two Latinos within a 30-mile radius. Dad did everything with great passion and

Revisiting Education in the New Latino Diaspora, pp. xi–xv
Copyright © 2015 by Information Age Publishing
All rights of reproduction in any form reserved.

joy. He worked hard and loved to sing and play the guitar. He was a quiet and proud man, yet he did his fair share of fighting. He was a boxer and found great joy in the opportunity to "put folks in their place," especially when he was outnumbered.

Given the reputation of my father and my uncle in my hometown, my family's socioeconomic status, and my multiethnic background, social life in school was interesting. My identity was concurrently novel and inconsequential. I remember feeling that I was a little different, but not less than; a self-concept I developed primarily as a tribute to my mother. Because my father worked long hours as a laborer, she was my primary cultural influence. She raised my sisters and me to have faith and to value all aspects of our heritage.

Despite the rocky start my father had in the community (a rockiness I recognize more as an adult), most folks did their best to get along with my family. However, even though he applied for many positions within the community, my father was never able to get a nonlaborer or an eight-to-five job that would allow him to be home more often.

As the only children of color in the community, my family's cultural heritage was not understood or accommodated for in schools. As was common during the early 1980s, teachers in the High Plains rarely encountered families like ours, and as a result, we assimilated to the majority culture in many ways. I really did feel as though I fit in among my peers. This, coupled with the fact that I didn't have distinctly "ethnic" features, meant life for me in this small farm town was relatively typical.

I was a bit of a dreamer and a free spirit with little interest in rural life. Upon graduation, I took the giant leap to higher education, and enrolled at a community college three hours away. Despite the fact that I was overwhelmed with fear and doubt, I was determined to make my own way and to prove that I could be successful. With no vehicle of my own to get me back home, I felt like home was worlds away.

In what I can best describe as directionless serendipity, after completing my Associate's degree I enrolled at a state university and flourished with the support and mentorship of the McNair Scholars program. Then I married and moved to Texas after completing my BA. After a few years of coming "back home" for holidays and special occasions, including when 'going home' stopped being from Texas to my hometown and started being from Manhattan Kansas (where I had started a PhD program) to home, I began to notice some changes. With each visit, I saw more and more ethnic diversity. Changes in farming and industry in the area, particularly the expansion of the local feedlot, meant young faces of various shades joined the aging, all-White faces I was long accustomed to seeing.

I also heard stories of troublesome interactions that my little sister was having in junior high and high school. She described racial comments from some classmates and even a few teachers. Despite her being only 10 years younger than I, it was surprising how different her socialization and schooling experiences were from mine.

To be sure, a little of this may have been a product of our personalities. She was quiet and reserved, with the personality of my father. However, it was more than just a question of social adjustment; I think something more profound had changed. Instead of the local Latino community being just two "settled-out" sugar beet pickers (i.e., my dad and uncle) and their families, there were now more people who looked like us (i.e., the New Latino Diaspora) and there was more of a xenophobic response.

I share this short autobiography because I think it ties together so much of this book. In Chapter 1, Hamann and Harklau (reprising their chapter for the 2010 *Handbook on Latinos and Education*) acknowledge that in emphasizing the "new" of the New Latino Diaspora (NLD) the first edition of *Education in the New Latino Diaspora* (Wortham, Murillo, & Hamann, 2002) made invisible Latinos like my dad and uncle who, per the construct of the NLD, settled in Kansas earlier than the NLD narrative describes. Yet as the comparison of my northwestern Kansas childhood and my sister's illuminates, something did change back where I am from. There is a NLD, and there was a reaction to it by more established populations that also impacted how my family was viewed.

My autobiography has a minor echo in Bruening's chapter (Chapter 2). My sisters and I weren't English language learners (like the students Bruening describes) but we were part of a "low-incidence" population for which the rest of the community did not need to reorganize itself much, a point that changed when the Latino population grew. I'm not undocumented like the student who offers the poignant *testimonio* in Urrieta, Kolano, and Jo chapter (Chapter 3), but like that student, I don't like how my purported success (I earned my PhD from Kansas State University (K–State) in 2011) sometimes seems to excuse the system as fair and the way I am regarded and included/excluded as unproblematic. Though my K–12 experience did not match the disciplining and channeling of students of color into a school-to-prison pipeline (like what Raible & Irizarry describe in Chapter 4), that does not mean their account does not resonate with me. Now as a teacher educator at K–State and one long-involved with that university's BESITOS program (further described by Herrera & Holmes in Chapter 12), I have worked with first-generation Latino college students who have made it to campus almost in spite of what K–12 teachers and peers said of them, rather than because of the support of many. At K–State, I have also watched many close colleagues design teacher education travel-study efforts to Mexico and more recently Ecuador, as Mexico's drug violence has led our university to stop sending students to that country, which makes Chapters 15 and 16 (both accounts of NLD teachers' travel-study) sound quite familiar. I am committed to helping create a teacher workforce ready to be responsive to and supportive of the NLD, even as I concede that that remains an uphill battle.

In this volume, *Revisiting Education in the New Latino Diaspora*, Hamann, Wortham, and Murillo have once again, successfully drawn on the knowledge, expertise, and innovative work of a wide range of veteran and emerging scholars who speak passionately and authentically. The editors' dedication to understanding the nuanced experiences of Latinos living in the United States and Latin America and the complex social, economic, and political implications of the NLD is visible in both the breadth and depth of this volume. For example, I had never particularly thought about the in/appropriateness of Spanish as a foreign language teachers as intermediaries between schools and Latino families (Harklau & Colomer's Chapter 8), early childhood education in the NLD (Adair's Chapter 11), how policy could be more progressive than practice (as in Lowenhaupt's example from Wisconsin [Chapter 13]), how communities might try to recruit 'better' immigrants than Latinos (as Lynn achingly describes in Chapter 6), nor how teacher education challenges in Kansas have their echo in the Pacific Northwest (as in Contreras, Stritikus, Torres, & O'Reilly Diaz's Chapter 10 about Washington State). Nor had I thought about the particular lens of Latin American-descent adoptees being raised in mixed race families (Flores-Koulish's Chapter 7) or how indigenous populations from Mexico might have a different perspective on being part of the NLD than others encompassed by this label (see Leco Thomas' Chapter 5). Even as much of this volume seemed familiar, the descriptions and analyses kept drawing my attention to something new.

Broken into three sections, the authors set the context for this edition in the first section by providing a reflective critique of the 2002 edition and then by "whetting the appetite" of the reader for what is to come in the following two sections. The second section, "Actors and Improvisational Local Practice," engages the reader in authentic personal narratives and thought-provoking, historical and contemporary analyses of research in multiple contexts. Consistent with the education policy and practice book series' breach from traditional policy implementation studies, these chapters start with small cases, accounts, autobiographies, and so forth, and from there turn their attention to policy. In the third section, "Existing Infrastructure Responds,: the authors examine how the NLD fares and/or is conceptualized in formal education policy, particularly those concerned with teacher preparation, both in-service and preservice.

As a product of the early Latino diaspora of the 1970s in Kansas, I am able to see my family's experiences represented in many of the narratives and perspectives shared in this book. As a researcher and practitioner working in a NLD state, I feel this volume will be an essential addition to my library, as each chapter raises many critical points for consideration. As I think about K–State's challenges and opportunities as we work with schools and school districts, I suspect I will draw a lot from the chapters by University of Pennsylvania colleagues (Chapters 9 and 14) as we consider what the academy can and should do to support improved education in the NLD. As I think about the descriptive statistics shared in Chapter 17 about the NLD continuing to get larger and more established (even as new immigration tapers off) and in Chapter 1 that suggests Latino high school completion rates lag those of other populations in NLD states, I find myself concurrently both invigorated and angry. This matters for more and more kids and more and more places. It is not yet as good/successful as it needs to be. I don't say that purely abstractly, nor about some obscure population. I am a sister of a student who struggled in the NLD; I am the teacher of teachers who will or will not adequately understand and support NLD students and parents. And I am a mom who lives in Kansas. My children, my most sacred and intense connection to the future, are getting a public education as part of the NLD. I join the various authors here in declaring: "We have to get this right." You must see me.

REFERENCE

Wortham, S., Hamann, E., & Murillo, E. (2002). *Education in the New Latino Diaspora.* Westport, CT: Ablex.

DEDICATIONS AND ACKNOWLEDGMENTS

DEDICATIONS

Individually, we dedicate this book to: Susan, Megan, and Alex (ETH); Ben and Rachel (SEFW); and Maya and Diego (EGM). Collectively, we dedicate it to the rising generations in the New Latino Diaspora—to newcomers and those more established, to those well served by current school practice and those for whom schooling must become more responsive, to DREAMers and their allies. We hope our efforts contribute (in however modest a way) to making the world you're growing up in more inclusive, more responsive, more informed, and more just.

ACKNOWLEDGMENTS

The editors would like to thank George Johnson, Benjamin Gonzalez, Elisabeth Reinkordt, William England, Julie Feldman, Brittany Black, and Elias Arellano for their various contributions to the logistics, copyediting, design, translation, and other logistic tasks that have led to the creation of this volume.

SECTION I

INTRODUCTION

CHAPTER 1

REVISITING EDUCATION IN THE NEW LATINO DIASPORA

Edmund T. Hamann and Linda Harklau

This is an updated and adapted version of Chapter 9 of the *Handbook of Latinos and Education*, edited by Enrique G. Murillo, Jr. and published in 2010. That chapter (titled "Education in the New Latino Diaspora") pointed to gaps, visible in hindsight, in the original *Education in the New Latino Diaspora* volume (Wortham, Murillo, & Hamann, 2002) and, more importantly, laid out new directions for the topic area of both scholarly inquiry and activism. The volume you are now holding (i.e., *Revisiting Education in the New Latino Diaspora*) attempts to follow the agenda outlined in the 2010 piece. Additionally, we acknowledge the emergence of new issues (like the Obama Administration's Deferred Action for Child Arrivals [DACA] and the large-scale influx of violence-fleeing unaccompanied minors from Honduras, Guatemala, and El Salvador) that are important but not much further explored here.[1] To clarify which text is original and what has been added, new text is italicized (excepting this paragraph).

***

In 2002, Hamann, Wortham, and Murillo noted that many U.S. states were hosting significant and often rapidly growing Latino populations for the first time and that these changes had multiple implications for formal schooling as well as out-of-school learning processes. *They and the various contributors to their edited volume* speculated about whether Latinos were encountering the same, often disappointing, educational fates in communities where their presence was unprecedented as in areas with a longstanding Latino presence. Only tentative conclusions could be provided at that time since the dynamics referenced were frequently novel and in flux.

In this chapter we revisit that inquiry in light of 12 subsequent years of research and outcome data. We begin by defining and elaborating on the concept of "New Latino Diaspora" (NLD), tracing its origins, and noting the diverse populations and contexts it represents. Next we turn to an analysis of educational outcomes in new Latino diaspora communities in light of two competing hypotheses. The first would suggest that in areas where there has been little history of anti-Latino institutionalized racism and little record of Latino school failure (or success), educational improvisation might lead to better outcomes than in areas with long-established racialized patterns of weak Latino educational outcomes.

Alternatively, the second would suggest that racialized patterns of schooling and interaction for Latino communities in California, Texas, or Chicago are carried into and recreated in NLD settings, leading to similar or even poorer educational outcomes. We conclude with a review of emergent scholarship and suggestions for further work that might shed light on education in the new Latino diaspora and, in some instances, on Latino education more generally.

REVISITING THE CONCEPT OF A NEW LATINO DIASPORA

The term "diaspora" refers to "people settled far from their homeland" (Diaspora, n.d.) with the connotation of being forcibly expelled by religious, political, or economic forces (Brettell, 2006). It has become a key, if somewhat imprecise, construct in recent anthropological and sociological scholarship on global migration, transnationalism, and ethnicity (Brettell, 2006; Lukose, 2007). The term "new Latino diaspora" was first used in the late 1990s (see Murillo & Villenas, 1997). As Hamann, Wortham, and Murillo (2002) explain, the term denotes the fact that "Increasing numbers of Latinos (many immigrant and some from elsewhere in the United States) are settling both temporarily and permanently in areas of the United States that have not traditionally been home to Latinos—for example, North Carolina, Maine, Georgia, Indiana, Arkansas, rural Illinois, and near resort communities in Colorado" (p. 1). These locales mostly contrast with the nine states of the 'traditional' Latino diaspora—Arizona, California, Colorado, Florida, Illinois, New Jersey, New Mexico, New York, and Texas (National Taskforce on Early Childhood Education for Hispanics, 2007)—that have longstanding Latino populations as well as many newcomers, although the mentioning of Colorado and Illinois on both lists highlights some of the limitations of defining *new* and *traditional* using state borders.

The rise of the new Latino diaspora in the United States can be attributed to changing patterns of labor markets in the U.S. where several industries in particular are driving Latino immigration and in-migration to new, often rural areas, including agriculture, construction and landscaping, assembly and manufacturing, and poultry and meat processing (Kandel & Cromartie, 2004; *Marrow, 2011;* Schmid, 2003; Zuñiga & Hernández-Leon, 2005). No matter what the draw, these newcomers are more likely to be young and more likely to have children than existing residents (Schmid, 2003); hence, the character and quality of their educational experiences in the NLD become especially significant.

Compared to more established Latino communities, current "new" Latino diaspora locations tend to be characterized by higher proportions of Latinos who speak Spanish as a first language and struggle with English (Singer, 2004). They also have substantial numbers of undocumented parents (Pew Hispanic Center, 2006), although most children of undocumented parents are themselves documented (National Task Force on Early Childhood Education for Hispanics, 2007; Passel, 2006). *As Table 1.1 in Stacy, Hamann, and Murillo (this volume) demonstrates, in 2011, in the 22 NLD states where Latinos constitute at least 10% of the 18 and under population, in only one those of states (Maryland) was the majority of the Latino population foreign-born. Given that migration between the U.S. and Mexico is now essentially flat (i.e., roughly equal numbers in and out), Latino populations in the NLD, like in the rest of the country are likely to be increasingly U.S. born.*

Hamann et al. (2002) suggested that in the new Latino diaspora, newcomer Latinos were confronted with "novel challenges to their senses of identity, status, and community" (p. 1) and that responses by non-Latino established residents were improvisational, as local norms of inclusion/exclusion and assimilation/accommodation were lacking. In short, the new Latino diaspora was defined by **who** (Latinos), **where** (places were Latinos have not previously lived in significant number), and **encountering what** (improvised interethnic interaction). Each of these can be further considered.

While *who* gets counted as Latino (or Hispanic) is mainly a topic for other *publications*, it is worth mentioning four dynamics here. First, as Oboler (1995) noted in her study of Peruvian newcomers to the United States, newcomers from Latin America who come to the U.S. often arrive thinking of their ethnic identity in nationalistic terms (e.g., Peruvian) and are surprised by the racialized nature of the Latino/Hispanic identity in the

United States. The relatively small initial number of Latinos in NLD communities tends to facilitate the formation of a pan-ethnic Latino identity. Nevertheless, although members of the new Latino diaspora may embrace a pan-Latino identity, it is not automatic that they will, nor that, if they do, they will continue to feel a pan-Latino solidarity. Referencing a "new Latino diaspora" in some ways measures the semiotic taxonomies of the host society as much as the self-identity of the diaspora's ostensible members.

Comparatively, in most sites in the new Latino diaspora, those of Mexican descent form the majority of Latinos, and *Latino* verges on becoming a short hand for *Mexican* (Wortham, Murillo, & Hamann, 2002). Yet as large Dominican and Guatemalan populations in Rhode Island (Portes, Guarnizo, & Haller, 2002), large Salvadoran populations in metropolitan Washington, DC (Portes et al., 2002), and Central American populations in post-Katrina New Orleans (Campbell, 2005; Lovato, 2005) make clear, Mexicans are not always the dominant Latino group in new Latino diaspora settings. Moreover, who is Mexican can be a complicated question as non-Spanish-speaking or limited-Spanish-speaking indigenous Mexicans from Oaxaca, Chiapas, *Michoacán (see Leco Thomas, this volume),* and elsewhere make up a new portion of the transnational migration stream, including into new Latino diaspora locations like Hillsboro, Oregon (Zehr, 2002). (See also Villenas [2007, p. 421] for a discussion of nation-state identities, like Mexican and American, that obscure indigenous identities.)

Third, with relocation across the U.S. in connection with jobs becoming the norm for all, but particularly for educated professionals and the military, third- and fourth-generation Chicanos are now living in places that historically have had few Latinos. In 2001, for example, the U.S. military was 15.3% Hispanic and made up more than a fifth of all Marines (Pew Hispanic Center, 2003), so it follows that in communities with large military facilities a military-related Latino population exists. Counting Latino U.S. Marines' training in North Carolina as educational participants in the NLD seems to make sense. In 2011, according to an *NBCLatino News* story, 16.9% of all new U.S. military recruits were Latino (Sánchez, 2013).

More generally, it makes sense to count established Latinos (e.g., Tejanos) as part of the NLD when they are located away from the nine traditional Latino gateway states. At the same time, however, this discussion highlights the fact that up to this point new Latino diaspora locales have been of interest primarily because of their new immigrant populations whose linguistic and ethnic outsider status is clear. In a country with a powerful drive towards assimilation, the perceived linguistic, ethnic, and racial distinctiveness and thus diasporic status of third or fourth- or fifth-generation Latinos in their adopted communities is a much more open question.

Fourth, all the original cases in *Education in the New Latino Diaspora* (Wortham, Murillo, & Hamann, 2002) reference emergent Latino communities and presume that Latino children are growing up in Latino families. While this assumption is often safe, it is not always so. Transracial and transnational adoptions often locate Latino children away from Latino communities and reference points *(a point further explored by Flores-Koulish [this volume])*. According to a November 5, 2006 *New York Times* story (Lacey, 2006), Americans adopted 18,298 Guatemalan babies in 2005. When these babies end up with Anglo parents in Vermont, Kentucky or Maryland, should they be counted as part of the new Latino diaspora? Are these children treated as Latinos by their adoptive parents or siblings? By their larger communities? Villenas (2002) notes of Latina parenting in North Carolina, that Latina mothers raise them using **dichos** *(proverbs)*, tell them to be **al pendiente** *(vigilant)*, and hope that they **se comporten bien** *(carry themselves appropriately)*. If adoptive parents do not do that, should we talk about adoptive parent practices as part of education in the NLD?

Writing about Latinos in the Southeastern United States, Villenas and Murillo noted that in that part of the new Latino diaspora, "There is no Alamo to remember, nor occupied territories to claim, nor a legendary Aztlán to recreate" (as cited in Villenas, 2002, p. 30). As we consider *where* to locate the new Latino diaspora, is this paucity of a history and related claims to place and precedent important?

Answering "yes" would obviate at least some of the need for explaining the improvisation of inter-ethnic interaction and the intermittent resistance of the established non-Latino community. But if we want to also locate the new Latino diaspora in the Midwest, Great Plains, Northwest, and non-Mid-Atlantic Northeast where there are some Latino memories and histories, do we risk being complicit in established communities' erasure of Latino histories (an erasure that explains the surprised and improvised reaction to the newcomers) if we call these places "new"?

In her compilation of historic *corridos* (folksongs) created by Mexican migrants and immigrants in the 19th and early 20th centuries, folklorist Herrera-Sobek (1993) notes references in song to steel work in Pennsylvania and work with sugar beets in Kansas and Michigan. Likewise, McConnell (2004) traces the beginnings of recruitment of Mexican labor in the rural upper Midwest to the 1917 Immigrant Act that curtailed supplies of European-origin labor. While resulting Latino communities were disrupted by the depressions of 1920–21 and 1929 when many of those of Mexican origin left or were forcibly repatriated, recruitment and migration flows renewed during labor shortages in World War II and subsequent years. *(See Morales's Foreword [this volume].)*

Gouviea, Carranza, and Cogua (2005) proposed the phrase "re-emerging Latino communities." Acknowledging that Nebraska's Latino population was estimated at 125,000 in 2005, they also pointed out that Nebraska's 1980 Census Count tallied 28,000 Latinos (many third- and fourth-generation with ties to the railroad and/or sugar beet industries). Describing Nebraska's new demographic reality and the fact that in many communities Latino newcomer/established resident interaction has been improvised and tentative should not obscure the long-time presence of Latinos in that state. Does our desire to call these sites "new" obscure these histories? Yet would excluding them from our list, mean we overlook locations where there is now much improvised interaction (despite modest-sized antecedent populations)? *Bruening, Sawyer, Richardson Bruna, Herrera and Holmes, and Morales all write chapters (or the foreword) in this volume that further illuminate NLD dynamics in America's Great Plains Heartland.*

Conversely, in the original crafting of the concept of new Latino diaspora, it was not made clear whether the arrival of new Latino nationalities to a setting that has hosted other Latino groups should be included. Put tangibly, should the new arrival of a large Mexican-origin population in New York City be counted as part of the new Latino diaspora? There is not much of a history of a Mexican presence there, although there is long history of Puerto Ricans, Cubans, and other immigrant groups (from Latin America and the rest of the world). Clearly, Mexican newcomers are now an important population in New York, and the scholarship on their negotiation of this new setting includes the negotiation of schooling (e.g., Cortina & Gendreau, 2003). Does our desire to exclude New York because it is a traditional diaspora site limit a substantial piece of the "new" story?

Defining such a wide portion of the country as the new Latino diaspora may also obscure important regional differences in Latino educational enrollment patterns and their impact. In much of the new Latino diaspora, notably the South and Pacific Northwest, the growth in Latino populations is occurring concurrently with growth in the population generally, although not necessarily growth in student populations. In 1995–96 Virginia counted 1,079,854 students, of whom 34,597 were Hispanic. Washington State counted 956,572 students, of whom 74,871 were Hispanic (National Center for Education Statistics, 1998). A decade later in 2005-06, Virginia enrolled 1,193,378 students (+113,524), of whom 91,557 were Hispanic (+55,960). Washington's student population grew to 1,020,311 (+63,739) and its Hispanic population to 139,005 (+65,134) (National Center for Education Statistics, 2007). In other words, while increased Hispanic enrollment accounted for half the growth in Virginia's student population, it accounted for all of the increase in school enrollment in Washington. This was in spite of the fact that Washington's non-Hispanic total population grew in that period from 5.13 million (Campbell, 1996) to 5.73 million (U.S. Census Bureau, 2007).

These demographics also bring into relief another trend: Latino and non-Latino households increasingly differ in terms of the likelihood of including school-age children. Part of the educational reception of Latinos in the NLD is likely shaped by many non-Latino established residents not having children and a racialized aversion to paying taxes or otherwise supporting other people's children. (Lynn's chapter [this volume] includes some exploration of this dynamic.) In contrast, in Iowa recently, immigration is credited for being the reason that the state's total population is not declining even as non-Latino school enrollments fall substantively (Grey, 2006).

Thus the context for interethnic interaction in the NLD varies. *Lynn (this volume) considers this topic as well, noting how Korean newcomers were recruited to replace Latino workers in a Georgia poultry plant. In not-yet-published follow-up research carried out in 2013 in three of the six meatpacking communities raided in December 2006 by Immigration and Customs Enforcement (ICE), Hamann recorded that in each (Grand Island, Nebraska; Dumas, Texas; and Hyrum, Utah) schools had to negotiate a new postraid changes in demography as Somalis, Sudanese, Karen, and other refugee groups were recruited by the packers to replace detained Latino laborers (see Hamann and Reeves [2012]).*

In some places, growth of the new Latino diaspora helps explain the proliferation of classroom trailers (as existing facilities are inadequate for the growing enrollment) and the shortage of teachers, particularly those trained in TESOL. In other places, the growth of the new Latino diaspora is the reason that schools have not closed and that teaching lines have not been discontinued; they are the reason for the stability of the school (although they are not necessarily viewed as such).

Rural and metropolitan areas also vary in terms of how they have become part of the NLD. In many Southern and Midwestern small towns, the new Latino diaspora is characterized by very sudden and rapid increases in Latino school-age students (Kochhar, Suro, & Tafoya, 2005). Often these rural areas have not experienced such dramatic demographic changes since White settlers first entered the area (Hamann, 2003; Kochhar et al., 2005). In these settings, Latino immigration to the region has consisted primarily of first-generation immigrants who are more likely to be novice speakers of English (Kochhar et al., 2005).

In many cases, Latino students in new diaspora communities are encountering improvisational educational responses, particularly in regard to language issues. Many teachers in new diaspora communities are untrained in TESOL and home-school communication is hampered in many cases by a lack of bilingual educators or translators (Bohon, Macpherson, & Atiles, 2005). Dalla, Gupta, López, and Jones (2006) report, for example, that in 2004 of Nebraska's 22,000 educators, fewer than 200 were trained in TESOL. Even when TESOL programs and other pedagogical responses to newcomers exist, they may be thought of as "elaborate experiments" (Grey, 1993)—albeit experiments that suffer from a lack of a 'control' population. In other words, the improvisation of programs and teaching methods is applied to all. Grey (1993) also notes that these experiments are led or managed—particularly at the school and district administration level—by those untrained and unfamiliar with newcomers (i.e., educational leaders who do not know what they do not know). Some new Latino diaspora locations serve as reluctant experiments, resulting in inadvertent or even intentional flouting of educational laws set in place to protect the rights of language minority students (see Beck & Allexsaht-Snider, 2002) and half-hearted teacher professional development efforts (Zehr, 2005). *See Bruening (this volume) for an exploration of what happens when a school has limited English as a second language expertise and limited understanding of how best to deploy what it does have. See also Lowenhaupt (this volume) for consideration of when a state policy presumes more teacher capacity and inclination to work with Latino English language learners than was fully the case.*

Finally, we again face complications revisiting the "encountering what" dimension of defining the new Latino diaspora. While the notion of a new Latino diaspora might imply a blank slate for the local negotiation of inter-ethnic relationships and educational policies and practices, local interaction can never be entirely free of outside influence. Indeed, the general mobility of the U.S. population as well as a common pattern of secondary migration of Latino immigrants from established to new diaspora areas make it all but inevitable that some individuals will carry with them thoughts, scripts, and experiences that have been extant nationwide or in the traditional Latino diaspora. Moreover, even in the absence of interethnic contact, local communities are immersed in nationally circulating images of Latinos in mass media (Berg, 2002; Mastro, 2003; Mastro & Behm-Morawitz, 2005) as well as ideologies concerning linguistic and cultural diversity and educational policy (see Ricento, 2000). For example, national media coverage of California's Proposition 227 seems to explain why some educators in northern Georgia turned away from bilingual education although they had initially embraced it (Hamann, 2003).

More optimistically, traditional Latino diaspora locations have also exported more promising educational innovations. With support of the Bill and Melinda Gates Foundation, the Cassin Educational Initiative Foundation, and several other philanthropies the Cristo Rey High School model from Chicago has been or will be replicated in Baltimore, Birmingham, Indianapolis, Omaha, and Portland, among other cities. The original Cristo Rey is a bilingual Catholic high school in Chicago's Pilsen and Little Village neighborhood with dramatically reduced tuition that makes ends meet by having students work one-day a week as temp workers through a complex and highly successful internship program. Cristo Rey takes only low-income students. In Chicago this has consisted of 99% Latino enrollment *(Kearney, 2008).* In the new sites—where the internship model is being replicated but not necessarily the bilingual component—Latino and African American students are expected to be the main enrollees (Zehr, 2006).

Even with all these caveats, we hold on to all three words: new, Latino, and diaspora. It is still true that in large swaths of the United States interethnic interaction related to the education of Latinos is primarily a new phenomenon and the habits and expectations that will steer that interaction are still far from set. In these settings, people with ancestries tracing from Mexico, Central America, Puerto Rico, Ecuador, and the Dominican Republic, view themselves and/or are being viewed as belonging to a singular, inclusive pan-ethnic identity: i.e., Latino.

Capps, Fix, Murray, Ost, Passel, and Herwantoro Hernandez (2005, p. 8) noted that 55% of elementary school students with immigrant parents have parents who were born in Mexico (38%) or elsewhere in Latin America (17%). They then remarked (p. 13) that the states with the fastest growth between 1990 and 2000 in children of immigrant elementary students included:

1st Nevada (+206%)	6th Arizona (+103%)
2nd North Carolina (+153%)	7th South Dakota (+101%)
3rd Georgia (+148%)	8th Oregon (+96%)
4th Nebraska (+125%)	9th Colorado (+94%)
5th Arkansas (+109%)	9th Iowa (+94%)

Eight of these states (all but Colorado and Arizona) have not historically hosted a substantial Latino population. What else should they be called if not "new Latino diaspora"?

A look at the 10 states with the proportionally fastest growing Latino populations between 2000 and 2010 yields a different list (and shifts what is being counted). Just Arkansas (5th), North Carolina (6th), and South Dakota (9th) make both lists, but each of these are NLD states, as are the other seven: South Carolina (1st), Alabama (2nd), Tennessee (3rd), Kentucky (4th), Maryland (7th), Mississippi (8th), and Delaware (10th). Conceding that proportional growth is bigger when initial denominators are small, these states nonetheless all saw Hispanic growth of between 96 and 148% (Passel, Cohn, & Lopez, 2011).

Finally, we hold on to the concept of a "NLD" mostly because it has unfortunate predictive power. *Hispanic* (the term of most government datasets) appears to be a predictor in new Latino diaspora states of lesser academic success, as the next section traces.

EDUCATIONAL OUTCOMES IN THE NEW LATINO DIASPORA

Are Latinos in the new Latino diaspora subject to the equivalent obstacles and hazards as those that have hindered Latino achievement in traditional Latino locations? One way to answer that question would be to ask the families themselves whether they believe they are better off in new diaspora schools.

Wortham and Contreras (2002), for example, reported that Latino families in one rural New England community found the quality of schools to be higher than those they had previously attended in Texas border communities. Parents also found the area and the schools to be freer of dangers for their children, such as drugs and gang violence. Thus Latino families may be judging the quality of schooling their children receive more by comparison to previous educational experiences in established Latino communities or in Mexico (Zúñiga & Hamann, 2006) than by comparison to the educational experiences of other ethnic and racial groups at the same school. *Zúñiga and Hamann (2006) in their study of children encountered in Mexican schools with prior school experience in the U.S. also recorded that many students explained their move/return from the U.S. as precipitated by a desire to get away from drugs, gangs, and violence. So some return migration and some migration to the NLD seems precipitated by a similar dynamic.*

Another potential source for optimism was provided by Stamps and Bohon (2006) who found that Latinos living in "new gateway" (Suro & Singer, 2002) metropolitan areas in the U.S. tend overall to have higher educational levels than counterparts in established areas. However, they cautioned that this result may be because of in-migration to new gateway areas by more highly educated Latinos in search of economic opportunities.

In spite of these encouraging signs, large education achievement datasets such as high school graduation statistics tell a different story. Table 1.1 below allows us to see how well Latino students were doing in a number of new Latino diaspora locations in 2005-2006. The third column shows the percentage of these state's public (pre)K–12 enrollment that was Latino. Comparing column 3 to column 5, in none of the states listed was the Latino high school graduation rate close to what one would predict based on total Latino enrollment.

As Table 1.1 illustrates, none of the states in this cross-section of the new Latino diaspora have Latino high school graduation rates that come close to the proportion of their Latino enrollments, and the Deep South seems to be the weakest. This can be partially explained and predicted by the national age distribution of the Latino population. For instance, according to the April 2006 U.S. Census population estimates, the number of Hispanic 5- to 9-year-olds was 4,090,814. The population of 10- to 14-year-olds was 3,942,042 [96.4% of the 5 to 9 range] and of 15- to 19-year-olds was 3,622,784 [88.6% of the 5 to 9 range].

Table 1.1. Hispanic Enrollment and High School Graduation Rates as Percentage of Total in 2005–06

State	Hispanic Enrollment (2005–06)	Percentage of all Enrollment	Hispanic High School Graduates (2005–06)	Percentage of all HS Grads
Alabama	20,479	2.8	404	1.1
Arkansas	32,132	6.8	998	3.7
Delaware	11,100	9.2	322	4.6
Georgia	135,010	8.7	2,590	3.7
Idaho	33,599	12.8	1,260	8.0
Indiana	59,387	5.7	1,636	3.0
Iowa	28,145	5.8	999	3.0
Kansas	55,117	12.1	2,019	6.7
Nebraska	32,887	11.5	1,194	6.0
North Carolina	118,505	8.4	2,864	3.8
Oregon	85,461	15.9	2,717	8.3
Rhode Island	26,559	17.3	1,153	11.7
Virginia	91,557	7.7	3,556	4.8
Washington	139,005	13.6	4,893	8.0

Source: Data are derived from Sable and Garafono (2007).

However, the steeply pyramidal ratios of Latino graduates to total Latino enrollments in the states named here range from just 39% in Alabama (the lowest) to only 67% in Rhode Island (the highest). These ratios are more disappointing when one notes that new Latino diaspora parents tend to have higher education achievement levels than Latino parents in the traditional diaspora (National Task Force on Early Childhood Education for Hispanics, 2007) and that parent education levels are generally a strong predictor of parent involvement and student academic achievement (although working-class minority parents can and do participate effectively in their children's schooling [e.g., Dauber & Epstein, 1993]).

Moreover, Table 1.1 obscures some of the negative story because it compares how Latinos fare only to students who graduate from other groups within the same state. Students, for instance, in southeastern states with some of the lowest high school graduation rates in the country (Editorial Projects in Education, 2007), have a worse chance overall of finishing high school than counterparts in Midwestern states such as Iowa that rank high nationally in school completion. But in these low graduation states (i.e., with lower white and African American graduation rates), Latinos proportional success is not better. If anything it seems worse.

Another troubling indication from schooling in the new Latino diaspora comes from the Southern Regional Education Board (SREB) (2007), which found that between 1997 and 2006 Hispanic scores on the SAT or ACT had declined in 8 of the 14 new Latino diaspora SREB member states and that test score gaps between Hispanics and whites had widened in all 14 of those states.[2] Recently, the Tomás Rivera Policy Institute (2004) sharply criticized the educational treatment of Latinos in Georgia, North Carolina, and Arkansas. It noted, for example, that in Northwest Arkansas, "Hispanics have experienced difficulty making their way to local universities. While they now make up almost one-third of the K–12 student population in the public school system, the University of Arkansas in nearby Fayetteville has a 1 percent Latino student population" (p. 18). In aggregate, Latinos in the new Latino diaspora do not fare as well in school as their non-Latino peers.

Echoing this pessimism, state-by-state breakouts of high school dropout rates in 2008–09 (the most recent available from the National Center for Education Statistics [NCES]at the time of this writing in 2014) show that, in each state in Table 1.1, the Latino dropout rate was substantially higher than the White dropout rate, with North Carolina's 7.3% the highest and Virginia's nearly triple the rate compared to whites (5.0% vs. 1.7%) the biggest discrepancy. Yet the same dataset also showed that the three states with the highest Latino dropout rates—Arizona, Colorado, and Illinois—were all traditional rather than NLD states (NCES, 2011). So maybe moving to the NLD was a way to improve likely school outcomes from grim to merely poor.

EMERGING NEW LATINO
DIASPORA EDUCATION RESEARCH

As this review suggests, the state of research on education in the new Latino diaspora is still in its formative stages and at present we have more questions than answers. One question that remains to be explored, for example, is how the more limited political power of new diasporic Latino communities affects educational experiences and opportunities (see Bullock & Hood, 2006). As evidence that Latinos in the new Latino diaspora have less political power, consider that none of the 21 members of the 110th Congress's (2007–08) Congressional Hispanic Caucus came from non-traditional [i.e., NLD] states, *a fact that was also true of the 27 caucus members in 2013–14. Harklau and Colomer's chapter (this volume), which explores how Spanish-speaking teachers are often pulled from teaching assignments to be emergency interpreters, illuminates lack of political power in the microcosm of Georgia schools. Similarly, Herrera and Holmes (this volume) and Urrieta et al. (this volume) note Latino college students' frequent sense that they are not fully welcome on 4-year campuses in Kansas and North Carolina respectively, even when they fare well academically.*

One might hypothesize that a lack of obvious political power would manifest itself in lower educational achievement, but that does not seem to describe the new Latino diaspora in comparison to traditional settlement areas. According to the National Task Force on Early Childhood Education for Hispanics (2007) in the Northeast, Midwest, and South, both U.S.-born and immigrant Latino parents are more likely to have earned a college degree than the national average for Latinos. Also in the South and Midwest, Latino children of both immigrant parents and native-born parents are also more likely to have parents who have finished high school than the national average for Latinos (National Task Force on Early Childhood Education for Hispanics, 2007). If there is a link between accrued political power and group educational achievement the nature of that link is not yet satisfactorily depicted.

Another issue to be addressed in future research is: How does the particular lack of Latino educators in new diaspora communities matter? Meier and Stewart (1991) long ago identified a correlation between the proportion of Latino educators, administrators, and board members, on the one hand, and how Latino students fared, on the other. They did not claim that Latino children need Latino teachers to learn well (although they did not argue against there being value to this match either). Rather they claimed that employment of Latino educators was a good proxy for measuring the available upward mobility for local Latinos.

Using Meier and Stewart's (1991) lens, there is reason for pessimism. For example, four of Nebraska's five majority Latino school districts employed no Latino teachers in 2005–06 (of 402 teachers) (Nebraska Department of Education, 2006) and only 1% of Georgia's teachers and administrators were Latino in 2005–06 (Georgia Department of Education, 2006). One proposed remedy to the lack of Latino educators has been to provide paraprofessionals from the local community with training and support to earn teacher certification (see Dalla, Gupta, Lopez, & Jones, 2006) but thus far such programs have generated only a very finite supply of Latino teachers. *More common are efforts to help existing (largely White) teachers build their cultural knowledge related to Latino students' circumstances and backgrounds. In this volume Richardson Bruna and Sawyer separately describe two multiday travel-study initiatives that had this end.*

Another area that remains to be addressed more thoroughly is the role of race and racialized identities in Latino students' school experiences in the new diaspora. As we have noted throughout this chapter, Latinos are entering communities with historically very different racial dynamics; for example, the Southeast with a history of experiencing race as a Black and White dichotomy (see Gilpin & Beck, 2006), and the rural Midwest dominated by non-Hispanic White descendents of European settlers, with American Indians as the "other" population (Kandel & Cromartie, 2004).

As a result, established, historicized and racialized Chicano or Latino communities or identities may not yet exist in the new diaspora in the same way they do in the Southwest, for example (Bohon, Macpherson, & Atiles, 2005).

However, work in new Latino diaspora communities thus far already shows considerable ambivalence, paternalism (Richardson Bruna, 2007; Richardson Bruna & Vann, 2007; Richardson Bruna, Vann, & Perales Escudero, 2007), xenophobia (Rich & Miranda, 2004), and some troubling processes of racialization and subordination underway (Millard, Chapa, & McConnell, 2004). We have yet to fully reckon with how Latino students entering new diaspora communities are positioned and position themselves racially, and how such positioning might affect their socialization into particular life and career pathways in and out of school.

Raible and Irizarry (this volume) and Urrieta (this volume) with their use of the testimonio tradition offer difficult accounts by NLD Latinos of frustration at racialized structures and treatments. Adair (this volume) in turn documents white preschool teachers paternalistic skepticism of many Latino parents in Iowa and Tennessee. Gallo et al. (this volume) describe similar paternalism among some teachers in a working-class suburb of large East Coast city, and Contreras et al. (this volume) capture problematic framings among some K–12 teachers in Washington State. While interracial educational interaction may have been more improvisational and sometimes well-intended in the NLD, as both Villenas (2002) and Murillo (2002) pointed out in the original volume and as these chapters update, racism and discrimination are important, unresolved challenges in the NLD, from preschool through college.

We might also want to investigate the potential role of civic and religious organizations in Latino communities and youth adaptation and education. Such organizations have historically played a vital role in the educations of immigrant youth in new communities (Berrol, 1995). We might ask if and how such organizations are being formed and how they contribute to the educations of Latino youth in NLD communities. Arbelaez (2000), for example, provides an example of how civic life in one Omaha Latino community centers around church activities and is coordinated with parish legal, educational, health, and counseling services. Such work could also show how education and "educación" (Villenas, 2002) are interwoven to symbolic processes used by Latinos in new and perhaps tenuous diasporic communities to maintain a collective memory about another time and place or to reattach successive generations to the culture and traditions of homelands (see Brettell, 2006).

In the NLD and the traditional diaspora, a comparatively small number of schools have absorbed most of the growth in Latino enrollment (Fry, 2006). Sometimes, as in Lexington, Nebraska, Anglo enrollment declined (from 1,591 to 664 between 1989 and 2005) as Hispanic enrollment grew (in this case from 75 to 1,988) (Nebraska Department of Education, 2006) *and as funding inequalitites between nearby districts grew worse (England & Hamann, 2013)*. Gouveia and Stull (1997) reported that the influx of new families to Lexington in the late 1990s was also accompanied by a significant increase in student turnover. One particularly urgent issue is to find ways for these small town and rural schools that are accustomed to highly stable populations and strong informal social networks to adapt school-home communication and record keeping for a new student population that is more mobile and largely unconnected to existing informal networks. *However, as Bruening (this volume) points out, not all the NLD growth has concentrated in specific high-impacted communities, there are many communities where just one or a few Latino families have moved and where schools are faced with the legal requirement of serving English language learners (ELLs) (but exempt from No Child Left Behind assessment requirement that require minimum numbers in a category before performance can be fairly assessed).*

In her blog for *Education Week*, Mary Ann Zehr (2007) noted that there was little research on how immigrant students and ELLs were faring in the Great Plains and then pointed to Lourdes Gouviea's work at the University of Nebraska-Omaha's Office of Latino and Latin American Studies (OLLAS) as an important exception (as cited in Gouviea [2006] and Gouviea & Powell [2007]). Zehr seemed unaware of pioneering older work from Mark Grey in Garden City, Kansas in the early 1990s and current work by Richardson Bruna in a meatpacking town in Iowa (e.g., Richardson Bruna, 2007; Richardson Bruna, & Vann, 2007; Richardson Bruna, Vann, & Perales Escudero, 2007).

Conceding that there are exceptions to Zehr's (2007) claim, that she makes such a claim was hardly surprising. Media accounts of newcomers and schooling, precipitated in some instances by ICE raids and the recent nationwide debate about an overhaul of immigration laws, clearly are more numerous and visible than scholarly works. Moreover, the scholarly works that do exist are not necessarily easily found, not least because of the abundance of research on the four-fifths of Latino children who do not reside in the new Latino diaspora.[3] Zehr's claims are also unsurprising given the relative neglect of "homegrown" scholarship on diaspora communities. The preponderance of media attention and funding in recent years for work on the new Latino diaspora has gone to agencies and scholars from outside the affected communities, and this work may not always reflect a full understanding of the history or social contexts of new diaspora areas. We are also lacking in work that is explicitly comparative in nature (although see Stamps & Bohon, 2006). In preparing this review, for example, we encountered several studies that, while conducted in new diaspora areas, were nonetheless of limited value in elucidating how educational experiences might be similar to or different from the abundant existing research from established Latino settlement areas.

Finally, while the role of schools in producing low levels of Latino educational achievement elsewhere in the U.S. has been underscored, we have yet to explore the place of schools as potential sites for community support and advocacy for Latino families in new diaspora communities. Sink, Parkhill, Marshall, and Norwood (2005), for example, describe how a partnership was established between a community college and school district to provide literacy and academic instruction for Latino families and concurrent Spanish instruction for educators in one North Carolina community. *Gallo et al. (this volume) consider a university's mediation of teachers' well-intended but often paternalistic outreach efforts to Latino parents. More dramatically, in 2006 when six concurrent ICE raids at Swift Company meatpacking plants in Minnesota, Iowa, Nebraska, Utah, Colorado, and northern Texas led to the deportation of thousands and the division of undocumented parents from their U.S. citizen children, newspapers chronicled how schools became places of refuge for children whose home life had just been turned upside down (e.g., Hamann & Reeves, 2012; Jacobs, 2006; Lucin, 2006).*

CONCLUSION

Almost by definition, the concept of a "new" Latino diaspora will continue to change and evolve. The phenomenon presents educational researchers with a tremendous opportunity to trace the evolution of new communities as they become established and enter the second and third generations. Whether new diaspora communities thrive will depend on the evolution of U.S. immigration policy. The signs here are ominous. In 2007 an anti-immigration tide brought down the U.S. Senate's attempt to forge a bill on comprehensive immigration reform.

Although polls showed continued support for efforts at immigration reform that included a pathway to citizenship for those in the U.S. without documentation, a renewed effort to pass such laws in President Obama's second term was in limbo as of this writing in 2014. Prominent in opposition to such reform were Republican Iowa Congressman Steve King and Kansas' Secretary of State Kris Kobach. Much of the opposition to both efforts came from the South and Midwest, two regions of the country with unprecedented recent Latino immigration and in-migration. In 2008, nativism appeared ascendant, or at least powerful, and the prospects that Latino children—immigrant or fourth generation—would be viewed without the paternalism, fear, intolerance, or subordination seemed less sure than when these new patterns of migration began. *Perhaps in 2014, with an improved economy, such nativism is less widespread, but as the U.S. House of Representatives refusal to take up comprehensive immigration reform and the demagoguing (rather than assistance) that has been the loudest response to unaccompanied Central American minors coming to the U.S. border both reveal, it is still consequentially powerful.*

Yet there remains some promising and innovative educational news coming from the NLD as well. Several new Latino diaspora states have crafted "Dream Act" state laws permitting undocumented high school graduates to pay in-state tuition for college (Herrera, Morales, & Murry, 2007; NCSL, 2014) with Maryland, Oregon, and Minnesota recent NLD states on that list. Jacobson (2003) reports that a school readiness pre-K program in Tulsa, Oklahoma targeting African American and Latino children had particularly favorable effects on Latino youngsters' test scores. In Siler City, North Carolina, *Time* magazine reporter Paul Cuadros (2006) wrote an inspirational story about a state championship soccer team made up predominantly of Latino newcomers. Hamann, Wortham, and Murillo (2002) once raised the prospect that maybe, away from Florida, California, New York, Texas, Arizona, New Mexico, Illinois, New Jersey, and Colorado—with their entrenched habits of Latino undereducation—just maybe, in the NLD things would be better. So far that prospect seems too often unrealized. There are success stories, but not yet any large-scale success systems.

NOTES

1. *Marrow (2011) and Truax (2013) are two important researchers of immigrant youth aspirations for U.S. legal status—i.e., DREAMers—whose purview encompasses the New Latino Diaspora (NLD). With the child migrant crisis just becoming news as this book went to press, there is not yet a lot of scholarship on this topic. However, at least one NLD governor, Nebraska's Gov. Dave Heineman, made national news (e.g., Meckler, Reinhard, & Nicholas [2014] in the* Wall Street Journal) *for protesting purported federal secrecy about where child migrants were being sent, when, per current law, they were released to family members pending their deportation hearing. According to news accounts about 200 Central American child migrants had been sent to Nebraska by the summer of 2014 to stay with relatives pending the hearings on their unauthorized border crossing.*

2. The SREB states where the ACT is the dominant college entrance test include: Alabama, Arkansas, Kentucky, Louisiana, Mississippi, Oklahoma, Tennessee, and West Virginia. The SREB states where the SAT predominates include: Delaware, Florida, Georgia, Maryland, North Carolina, South Carolina, Texas, and Virginia. Texas and Florida are excluded from this calculation (as both are traditional Latino diaspora locations) although the White/Hispanic test score gap widened in both of those states too.

3. According to the National Task Force on Early Childhood Education for Hispanics [2007], one fifth of the 6,797,303 Hispanic 0- to 8-year-olds counted by the 2000 Census lived in the 41 states of the NLD.

REFERENCES

Arbelaez, M. S. (2000). *Good Friday in Omaha, Nebraska: A Mexican celebration.* Paper presented at the National Association of African American Studies & National Association of Hispanic and Latino Studies 2000 Literature Monograph Series. Proceedings (Culture Section), Houston, TX.

Beck, S. A. L., & Allexsaht-Snider, M. (2002). Recent language minority education policy in Georgia: Appropriation, assimilation, and Americanization. In S. Wortham, E. G. Murillo, & E. T. Hamann (Eds.), *Education in the new Latinodiaspora: Policy and the politics of identity* (pp. 37–66). Westport, CT: Ablex.

Berg, C. R. (2002). *Latino images in film: Stereotypes, subversion, & resistance.* Austin, Texas: University of Texas Press.

Berrol, S. C. (1995). *Growing up American: Immigrant children in America, then and now.* New York, NY: Twayne.

Bohon, S. A., Macpherson, H., & Atiles, J. H. (2005). Educational barriers for new Latinos in Georgia. *Journal of Latinos and Education, 41,* 43–58.

Bullock, C. S., & Hood, M. V. (2006). A mile-wide gap: The evolution of Hispanic political emergence in the deep South. *Social Science Quarterly, 87,* 1117–1135.

Brettell, C. B. (2006). Introduction: Global spaces/local places: Transnationalism, diaspora, and the meaning of home. *Identities: Global Studies in Culture and Power, 13,* 327–334. Retrieved October 31, 2008, www.csmonitor.com/2005/1004/p01s01-woam.htm/

Campbell, M. (2005, October 4). Post-Katrina easing of labor laws stirs debate: Foreign workers may form a big part of Gulf Coast reconstruction effort. *Christian Science Monitor.*

Campbell, P. R., (1996). *Population projections for states, by age, sex, race and Hispanic origin: 1995 to 2025, Report PPL-47.* Washington, DC: U.S.Bureau of the Census, Population Division.

Capps, R., Fix, M., Murray, J., Ost, J., Passel, J. S., & Herwantoro Hernandez, S. (2005). *The new demography of America's schools: Immigration and the No Child Left Behind Act.* Washington, DC: Urban Institute. Retrieved June 14, 2007, from http://www.urban.org/publications/311230.html

Cortina, R., & Gendreau (Eds.), (2003). *Immigrants and schooling: Mexicans in New York.* New York, NY: Center for Migration Studies.

Cuadros, P. (2006). *A home on the field: How one championship team inspires hope for the revival of small town America.* New York, NY: Rayo.

Dalla, R. L., Gupta, P. M., Lopez, W. E., & Jones, V. (2006). "It's a balancing act!": Exploring school/work/family interface issues among bilingual, rural Nebraska, paraprofessional educators. *Family Relations, 55,* 390–402.

Dauber, S. L., & Epstein, J. L. (1993). Parent attitudes and practices of involvement in inner-city elementary and middles schools. In N. F. Chauvkin (Ed.), *Families and schools in a pluralistic society* (pp. 53–71) Albany, NY: State University of New York Press.

Diaspora. (n.d.). In *Merriam-Webster's Collegiate Dictionary* (11th ed.). Springfield, MA: Author.

Editorial Projects in Education Research Center. Education Week. (2007). *Ready for what? Preparing students for college, careers, and life after high school.* Washington,

DC: Education Week Research Center. Retrieved July 16, 2007, from http://www.edweek.org/ew/articles/2007/06/12/40sgb.h26.html

England, W., & Hamann, E. T. (2013). Segregation, inequality, demographic change, and school consolidation (a micropolitan case). *Great Plains Research*, *23*(2), 171–185.

Fry, R. (2006). *The changing landscape of American public education: New students, New schools*. Washington, DC: Pew Hispanic Center.

Georgia Department of Education. (2006). *2005–2006 K–12 Public Schools Annual Report Card*. Atlanta, GA: Author. Retrieved June 19, 2007, from http://reportcard2006.gaosa.org/k12/persfiscal.aspx?TestType=pers&ID=ALL:ALL

Gilpin, I., & Beck, S. A. L. (2006). Voices from the margins: Black Caribbean and Mexican heritage women and educators in the rural South. *Journal of Praxis in Multicultural Education 1*, 29–44.

Gouviea, L. (2006). Nebraska's responses to immigration: Nebraska's context of reception, the role of policy and community responses. In G. Anrig & T. A. Wang (Eds.), *Immigration's new frontiers: Experiences for the emerging gateway states* (pp. 143–227). New York, NY: The New Century Press.

Gouviea, L., Carranza, M., & Cogua, J. (2005). The Great Plains Migration: Mexicanos and Latinos in Nebraska. In V. Zúñiga & R. Hernández-León (Eds.), *New destinations: Mexican immigration in the United States* (pp. 23–49). New York, NY: Russell Sage.

Gouviea, L., & Powell, M. A. (2007). *Second generation Latinos in Nebraska: A first look*. Washington, DC: Migration Policy Institute.

Gouviea, L., & Stull, D. D. (1997). *Latino immigrants, meatpacking, and rural communities: A case study of Lexington, Nebraska*. East Lansing, MI: Julian Samora Research Institute.

Grey, M. A. (1993). Applying concepts of marginality to secondary ESL programs: Challenges for practitioners and researchers. In *Proceeding of the Third National Research Symposium on Limited English Proficient Student Issues: Focus on Middle and High School Issues, Washington DC, August 1992* (pp. 831–850). Washington, DC: U.S. Department of Education, Office of Bilingual Education and Minority Language Affairs.

Grey, M. A. (2006). State and local immigration policy in Iowa. In G. Anrig & T. A. Wang (Eds.), *Immigration's new frontiers: Experiences for the emerging gateway states* (pp. 33–66). New York, NY: The New Century Press.

Hamann, E. T. (2003). *The educational welcome of Latinos in the New South*. Westport, CT: Praeger.

Hamann, E. T., & Reeves, J. (2012). ICE raids, children, media and making sense of Latino newcomers in flyover country. *Anthropology & Education Quarterly, 43*(1), 24–40. Retrieved from http://digitalcommons.unl.edu/teachlearnfacpub/127

Hamann, E. T., Wortham, S., & Murillo, E. G. (2002). Education and policy in the new Latino diaspora. In S. Wortham, E. G. Murillo, & E. T. Hamann (Eds.), *Education in the new Latino diaspora* (pp. 1–16). Westport, CT: Ablex Press.

Herrera, S., Morales, A., & Murry, K. (2007, April 10). *Navigating the tides of social and political capriciousness: Potential CLD student beneficiaries of the DREAM Act in the Midwest*. Paper presented at the American Educational Research Association annual meeting. Chicago, IL.

Herrera-Sobek, M. (1993). *Northward Bound: The Mexican immigrant experience in ballad and song*. Bloomington, IN: Indiana University Press.

Jacobs, J. (2006, Dec. 17). Mom, kids spend 3 days in agony. *Des Moines Register.* Retrieved December 21, 2006, from http://www.desmoinesregister.com/apps/pbcs.dll/article?AID=2006612170327

Jacobson, L. (2003, Oct. 29). Oklahoma Pre-K program found effective. *Education Week.* Retrieved June 30, 2007, from http://www.edweek.org/ew/articles/2003/10/29/09okla.h23.html?qs=@0+Hispanic+Latino

Kandel, W., & Cromartie, J. (2004). *New patterns of Hispanic settlement in rural America*. Washington, DC: United State Department of Agriculture. Economic Research Service.

Kearney, G. R. (2008). *More than a dream: The Cristo Rey Story*. Chicago, IL: Loyola Press.

Kochhar, R., Suro, R., & Tafoya, S. (2005). *The new Latino South: The context and consequences of rapid population growth*. Washington, DC: Pew Hispanic Center. Retrieved June 19, 2007, from http://pewhispanic.org/reports/report.php?ReportID=50

Lacey, M. (2006, November 5). Guatemala system is scrutinized as Americans rush in to adopt. *New York Times*, Section 1, pp. 1, 6.

Lovato, R. (2005, Nov. 15). Gulf Coast slaves. *Salon.com.* Retrieved June 28, 2007, from http://dir.salon.com/story/news/feature/2005/11/15/halliburton_katrina/index.html

Lucin, K. (2006, Dec. 14). Community prepares to help displaced children. *Worthington Daily Globe.* Retrieved December 17, 2006, from http://www.dglobe.com/articles/index.cfm?id=3239&section=collections

Lukose, R. (2007). Reflections from the field: The difference that diaspora makes: Thinking through the anthropology of immigrant education in the United States. *Anthropology & Education Quarterly, 38*(4), 405–418.

Marrow, H. B. (2011). *New destination dreaming: Immigration, race, and legal status in the rural American South*. Stanford, CA: Stanford University Press.

Mastro, D. E. (2003). A social identity approach to understanding the impact of television messages. *Communication Monographs, 70*(2), 98–113.

Mastro, D. E., & Behm-Morawitz, E. (2005). A social identity approach to understanding the impact of television messages. *Journalism and Mass Communication Quarterly, 82*(1), 110–130.

McConnell, E. D. (2004). Latinos in the rural Midwest: The twentieth-century historical context leading to contemporary challenges. In A. V. Millard & J. Chapa (Eds.), *Apple pie & enchiladas: Latino newcomers in the rural midwest* (pp. 26–40). Austin, TX: University of Texas Press.

Meckler, L., Reinhard, B., & Nicholas, P. (2014, July 13). Flood of child migrants spurs local backlash. *Wall Street Journal. Retrieved from http://online.wsj.com/articles/flood-of-child-migrants-spurs-local-backlash-1405294984*

Meier, K., & Stewart, J. (1991). *The politics of Hispanic education: Un paso pa'lante y dos pa'tras* [One step forward, two steps back]. Albany, NY: State University of New York Press.

Millard, A. V., Chapa, J., & McConnell, E. D. (2004). "Not racist like our parents": Anti-Latino prejudice and institutional discrimination. In A. V. Millard &

J. Chapa (Eds.), *Apple pie & enchiladas: Latino newcomers in the rural midwest* (pp. 102–124). Austin, TX: University of Texas Press.

Murillo, E., & Villenas, S. (1997). *East of Aztlán: Typologies of resistance in North Carolina communities.* Paper presented at Reclaiming Voices: Ethnographic inquiry and qualitative research in a postmodern age, Los Angeles.

National Center for Educational Statistics. (1998). *Downloadable tables from the compendium: State Comparisons of Education Statistics: 1969–70 to 1996–97.* Washington, DC: U.S. Department of Education. Retrieved January 29, 2008, from http://nces.ed.gov/pubs98/98018/#chap2a

National Center for Educational Statistics. (2007). *Public elementary and secondary school student enrollment, high school completions, and staff from the Common Core of data: School Year 2005–06: Table 2.* Washington, DC: U.S. Department of Education. Retrieved January 29, 2008, from http://nces.ed.gov/pubs2007/pesenroll06/tables.asp

National Center for Educational Statistics. (2011). *Table 6.Public high school number of dropouts and event dropout rate for grades 9–12, by race/ethnicity and state or jurisdiction: School year 2008–09.* Washington, DC: U.S. Department of Education. Retrieved August 22, 2014, from http://nces.ed.gov/pubs2011/graduates/tables/table_06.asp

National Conference of State Legislatures. (2014, June 12). Undocumented student tuition: State action. Retrieved from http://www.ncsl.org/research/education/undocumented-student-tuition-state-action.aspx

National Task Force on Early Childhood Education for Hispanics. (2007). *Para nuestros niños* [For our children]: *A demographic portrait of young Hispanic children in the United States.* Tempe, AZ: Mary Lou Fulton College of Education, Arizona State University.

Nebraska Department of Education. (2006). *2005–2006 State of the Schools Report: A Report on Nebraska Public Schools.* Lincoln, NE: Author. Retrieved January 27, 2008, from http://reportcard.nde.state.ne.us/20052006/Main/Home.aspx

Oboler, S. (1995). *Ethnic labels, Latino lives: Identity and the politics of (re)presentation in the United States.* Minneapolis, MN: University of Minnesota Press.

Passel, J. S. (2006). *The size and characteristics of the unauthorized migrant population in the U.S.* Washington, DC: Pew Hispanic Center. Retrieved June 19, 2007, from http://pewhispanic.org/reports/report.php?ReportID=61

Passel, J. S., Cohn, D., & Lopez, M. H. (2011). Hispanics account for more than half of nation's growth in last decade. Washington, DC: Pew Hispanic Center http:// Retrieved from www.pewhispanic.org/2011/03/24/hispanics-account-for-more-than-half-of-nations-growth-in-past-decade/

Pew Hispanic Center. (2003). *Pew Hispanic Center fact sheet: Hispanics in the military.* Retrieved July 30, 2007, from pewhispanic.org/files/factsheets/6.pdf

Pew Hispanic Center. (2006). *Estimates of the unauthorized migrant population for states based on the March 2005 CPS.* Washington, DC: Author. Retrieved June 19, 2007, from http://pewhispanic.org/factsheets/factsheet.php?FactsheetID=17

Portes, A., Guarnizo, L. E., & Haller, W. J. (2002). Transnational entrepreneurs: An alternative form of immigrant economic adaptation. *American Sociological Review, 67*(2), 278–298.

Ricento, T. (2000). *Ideology, politics, and language policies: Focus on English.* Philadelphia, PA: John Benjamins.

Rich, B. L., & Miranda, M. (2004). The sociopolitical dynamics of Mexican immigration in Lexington, Kentucky, 1997 to 2002: An ambivalent community responds. In V. Zúniga & R. Hernández-León (Eds.), *New destinations: Mexican immigration in the United States* (pp. 187–219). New York, NY: Russell Sage Foundation.

Richardson Bruna, K. (2007). Traveling tags: The informal literacies of Mexican newcomers in and out of the classroom. *Linguistics and Education, 18,* 232–257.

Richardson Bruna, K. R., & Vann, R. (2007). On pigs & packers: Radically contextualizing a practice of science with Mexican immigrant students. *Cultural Studies of Science Education, 2,* 19–59.

Richardson Bruna, K., Vann, R., & Perales Escudero, M. (2007). What's language got to do with it? A case study of academic language instruction in a high school "English Learner Science" classroom. *Journal of English for Academic Purposes, 6*(1), 36–54.

Sable, J., & Garofano, A. (2007). *Public elementary and secondary school student enrollment, high school completions, and staff from Common Core of data: School year 2005–06* (NCES 2007-352). U.S. Departmentof Education. Washington, DC: National Center for Education Statistics. Retrieved June 14, 2007, from http://nces.ed.gov/pubsearch/pubsinfo.asp?pubid_2007352

Sánchez, E. L. (2013, Jan. 1). *U.S. military, a growing Latino army. NBC Latino.* Retrieved from http://nbclatino.com/2013/01/01/u-s-military-a-growing-latino-army/

Schmid, C. (2003). Immigration and Asian and Hispanic minorities in the New South: An exploration of the history, attitudes, and demographic trends. *Sociological Spectrum, 23,* 129–157.

Singer, A. (2004, Feb.). *The rise of new immigrant gateways* [Living Cities Census Series]. Washington, DC: Brookings Institution: Center on Urbanand Metropolitan Policy.

Sink, D. W., Parkhill, M. A., Marshall, R., & Norwood, S. (2005). Learning together: A family-centered literacy program. *Community College Journal of Research and Practice, 29,* 583–590.

Southern Regional Education Board. (2007). *Improving SAT and ACT scores: Making progress, facing challenges.* Atlanta, GA: Author.

Stamps, K., & Bohon, S. A. (2006). Educational attainment in new and established Latino metropolitan destinations. *Social Science Quarterly, 87,* 1225–1240.

Suro, R., & Singer, A. (2002). *Latino growth in metropolitan America: Changing patterns, new locations.* Washington, DC: Brookings Institution.

Tomás Rivera Policy Institute. (2004). *The new Latino South and the challenge to public education: Strategies for educators and policymakers in emerging immigrant communities.* Los Angeles, CA: Author.

Truax, E. (2013). *Dreamers: La lucha de una generación por su sueño Americano [The struggle of a generation for the American dream].* Mexico, DF: Oceano.

U.S. Census Bureau. (2007). Table 3: Annual estimates of the population by sex, race, and hispanic or latino origin for Washington: April 1, 2000 to July 1, 2006 (SC-EST2006-03-53). Washington, DC: Author.

Villenas, S. (2002). Reinventing *educación* in new Latino communities: Pedagogies of change and continuity in North Carolina. In S. Wortham, E. G. Murillo, & E. T. Hamann (Eds), *Education in the new Latino diaspora* (pp. 17–36.) Westport, CT: Ablex Press.

Villenas, S. (2007). Diaspora and the anthropology of Latino education: Challenges, affinities, and intersections. *Anthropology & Education Quarterly, 38*(4), 419–425.

Wortham, S., & Contreras, M. (2002). Struggling towards culturally relevant pedagogy in the Latino Diaspora. *Journal of Latinos and Education, 1*(2), 133–144.

Wortham, S., Murillo, E. G., & Hamann, E. T. (Eds.). (2002). *Education in the new Latino diaspora: Policy and the politics of identity*. Westport, CT: Ablex.

Zehr, M. A. (2002, March 27). Oregon school district reaches out to new arrivals from Mexico. *Education Week*. Retrieved June 29, 2007, from http://www.edweek. org/ew/articles/2002/03/27/28hillsboro.h21.html?qs=@0+Hispanic+Latino

Zehr, M. A. (2005, May 11). Influx of new students can outpace teacher preparation: But training programs don't always find a receptive audience. *Education Week*. Retrieved June 29, 2007, from http://www.edweek.org/ew/articles/2005/05/11/36teachers.h24.html

Zehr, M. A. (2006, Nov. 8). Cristo Rey schools receive $6 million to expand network. *Education Week*. Retrieved July 30, 2007 at: http://www.edweek.org/ew/articles/2006/11/08/11briefs-2.h26.html?qs=cristo+rey

Zehr, M. A. (2007, March 19). Immigrants and ELLs on the Great Plains. *Learning the Language Blog at Education Week*. Retrieved June 28, 2007, from http://blogs.edweek.org/edweek/learning-thelanguage/2007/03/immigrants_and_ells_on_the_gre_1.html?qs=Latino

Zúñiga, V., & Hamann, E. T. (2006). Going home? Schooling in Mexico of transnational children. *CONfines de Relaciones Internacionales y Cienciapolítica, 2*(4), 41–57.

Zúñiga, V., & Hernández-León, R. (Eds.). (2005). *New destinations: Mexican immigration in the United States*. New York, NY: Russell Sage.

SECTION II

ACTORS AND IMPROVISATIONAL LOCAL PRACTICE (GRASSROOTS TO POLICY)

CHAPTER 2

DOING IT ON THEIR OWN

The Experiences of Two Latino English Language Learners in a Low-Incidence Context

Erika Bruening

INTRODUCTION

The New Latino Diaspora (NLD) refers to Latino populations in the 41 states that are not Arizona, California, Colorado, Florida, Illinois, New Jersey, New Mexico, New York, or Texas. This chapter describes one rural High Plains, NLD-area secondary school's attempt to meet the needs of its low-incidence population of Latino English language learners (ELLs). Latinos ELLs at this school comprised less than 0.2% of the total student population during this year-long study. An ethnographic case study conducted at the school revealed that the individual actions taken by school faculty and staff in trying to meet the needs of this low-incident student population illustrate the improvisational response typical of the NLD and of many schools where just one or two families enroll school-age children

Revisiting Education in the New Latino Diaspora, pp. 29–48
Copyright © 2015 by Information Age Publishing

who are English language learners (Bérubé, 2000; Hamann & Harklau, 2010; Zehr, 2001).

As noted by Deschenes, Cuban, and Tyack (2001), students who do not fit the school's expected learner profile face a "mismatch" (Deschenes et al., 2001) between the school's definition of success, and their own "social, cultural, and economic backgrounds" (p. 525). This mismatch can also occur when schooling becomes a "subtractive process" by removing Latino youths' social and cultural resources, thereby leaving them increasingly "vulnerable to academic failure" (Valenzuela, 1999, p. 3). Latino ELLs in low-incidence schools represent students who face such a mismatch. In part, the mismatch is linguistic, in that they are outside the mainstream student population in schools that are "completely geared toward teaching native English speakers" (Zehr, 2001). Indeed, rural school districts can find themselves unprepared when a handful of ELLs enroll in school (Bérubé, 2000; Zehr, 2001).

Additionally, the mismatch experienced by the Latino ELLs in this school was also present in self-reported ethnicity. According to the state department of education's annual report on school achievement, this school's student population was over 93% self-reported "white-not Hispanic," a percentage that had remained relatively stable—fluctuating within 4%, but remaining above 93%—within the last 15 years of provided data. The school's percentage of self-reported Latino students—referred to in the published data as "Hispanic"—was 2.6%, with the ELL student population at less than 0.2% within this particular school—a percentage that had steadily decreased from its previous height of just over 1% five years previous to this study. Thus, the Latino ELLs clearly did not fit this school's expected learner profile of a "white-not Hispanic" native English speaker. A clear mismatch existed between their learner profile—that of a Latino student whose primary language was not English – and the learner profiles of their fellow students—"white-not Hispanic" students for whom English was the primary language.

There was also a noted mismatch between the Latino ELLs' ethnic and linguistic backgrounds and the ethnic and linguistic backgrounds of their teachers. According to the state department of education's annual report on school achievement, 100% of the faculty at this school self-reported as "white-not Hispanic," all were native English speakers, and they had an average of 18+ years of teaching experience at this particular school. Given the school's high and stable percentage of "white-not Hispanic" students, its low and steadily decreasing population of English learners, and the teachers' average length of service at the school, it was unlikely that teachers had much experience working with Latino newcomers like the two Latino ELLs profiled in this chapter.

To meet the needs of students who do not fit the typical learner profile (Deschenes et al., 2001), Valenzuela (1999) has advocated for educators to demonstrate a commitment to Latino students' academic needs through a culture of caring. The school in this study had a separate course for English learners that used the cognitive academic language learning approach (CALLA), focusing on developing English learners' academic language through explicit content-area instruction and emphasis on learning strategies for content acquisition and language acquisition (Chamot & O'Malley, 1994). The course was designed by the school's ELL-endorsed instructor and implemented by that instructor on an as-needed basis at the discretion of the school administration. As will be clarified later, that this school had a ELL-endorsed instructor was largely serendipitous, as that endorsement was not a major reason for her hire at the school, nor was it formally relevant to her initial teaching assignment as a core content-area teacher. Though the administration was supportive in the design and implementation of this course, its self-directed nature mirrored Bérubé's (2000) assessment of rural schools' oft-used "growing their own" approach to ESL instruction, where teachers of ELLs in such situations "rely on their own wits" to design such courses (Zehr, 2001).

This chapter is relevant to educators who work in rural areas more likely to see small populations of Latino ELLs. Secondary content-area teachers who have ELLs enrolled in their courses can learn from the experiences of those mainstream teachers in a similar context. ELL teachers—those who often have a lonely place in their school—can understand ways in which policies affect program implementation, as well as relationships with classroom teachers and ELLs. Administrators at schools and districts with low-incidence Latino ELL populations can learn from the response implemented in this context.

Perhaps the most important contribution of this chapter, however, is the reminder that thousands of Latinos in the NLD live in low concentrations – two families here, four families there—and those who attend school often do so in environments that have little idea and only serendipitous expertise regarding how to most effectively respond to them. Interviews with school employees and the Latino English language learner student participants, collection of artifacts and keeping of fieldnotes taken during classroom observations provide a comprehensive perspective of one High Plains area secondary school's approach to meeting the needs of its small population of English language learners in mainstream classes.[1]

The "Minority" Minorities in a Low-Incidence School

The school in which this ethnographic study took place is one in the High Plains region. The school is the only comprehensive grade 9–12 high school in a small community of fewer than 7,000 residents. The community is primarily served by an agriculture-based economy, with several livestock operations located a few miles outside the city limits, and larger crop farms—primarily producing corn and soybeans—in the surrounding countryside. At first glance, the community may seem insular, with a busy downtown area replete with retail stores and several hometown banks, but is within reasonable commuting distance (and the metropolitan statistical area) of a larger city of 250,000 and hosts a church-affiliated small liberal arts college that offers undergraduate degrees to approximately 1,500 students. Based on that location, it is not unusual to have high school students whose parent(s) commute to work in the larger metropolitan city.

Working in the community as a semioutsider—commuting from the larger nearby metropolitan area to work—I had the opportunity to use an ethnographic perspective to analyze the ways in which the larger local community culture impacted the high school's culture. Akin to Peshkin's (1978) classic depiction of schooling in a different agricultural town (and in contrast with my experience attending school in the nearby larger city), this community appeared to be far more united in its support of the high school's extracurricular activities—particularly high school sports such as the football team, and the highly successful basketball team. It was not unusual to see parents of students doing their weekly shopping or running errands downtown, while wearing apparel with the school's logo and name on it. The retail stores donated their window space to the high school's annual class window-decorating competition during homecoming week. The local banks ran congratulatory ads on their electronic signs alerting the community to the accomplishments of the school's successful sports teams.

The school demonstrated above average performance in several key indicators. During the year in which this study was conducted, the high school's graduation rate was nearly 6% higher than the state average, as published in the state department of education's annual report on school districts. The same source showed that mobility rates were nearly 2% lower than the state average, with the state average remaining low relative to most of the nation. The town is composed of multigenerational families living in single-residence homes, complemented by mainly White newcomers who come to settle in a community with celebrated small-town virtues. One school faculty member had taught all her 35 years in the district, with many of her younger colleagues on the same trajectory.

Central to this chapter is the understanding that the district's percentage of self-reported Latino students—referred to as "Hispanic" in the published statistics—was considerably smaller (2.6% during this study) than the percentage of self-reported "white-not Hispanic" students (greater than 94% during this study). Although admittedly a small and low-incidence population, the school's Latino population had in fact doubled over the past five years, having comprised just over 1% five years before my study. Despite the increase in the school's Latino student population, the number of self-reported Latino students was still small enough that the state's published statistics for that subgroup's achievement on statewide assessments in reading, writing, science and math were masked, due to potential confidentiality concerns with fewer than 10 students in that subgroup. Therefore, a researcher, educator, or community member wishing to look at the school's level of achievement with its Latino students encountered a purposely hidden data set.

Although the school's self-reported Latino student population had increased, its population of ELLs had decreased. Indeed, during the academic year in which this study took place, the percentage of ELLs in this context was less than 0.2% of the total student population. As with the school's Latino student population, on the state reports of the school's performance on statewide assessments in reading, writing, science, and math, the achievements of the its ELL population were also masked, again due to potential confidentiality concerns with fewer than 10 students in that subgroup. Anyone wishing to examine the published statistics of the ELLs' achievement on statewide assessments was faced with an invisible data set.

Thus, according to the school's statistics as publicized by the state department of education, the Latino ELLs truly were an extremely small minority and essentially invisible when one looked for this particular subgroup's achievement statistics on statewide assessments—assessments that were designed with the goal of holding schools accountable for all students' achievement. However, based on my insider status, I knew that the ELLs during the profiled school year were in the group of fewer than 20 students who self-identified as Latino.

Due to the social commitment the community demonstrated toward the school, the low mobility rate, and the high school's superior graduation rate in comparison to the state average, there was a pervasive expectation that students received a quality education in this school system. This expectation was communicated through a variety of staff development sessions, in which data from state assessments and locally based assessments were analyzed to determine a targeted rate of annual improvement. Reports detailing students' targeted achievement levels were regularly sent home to parents, and used in the annual state of the school report published on the district's website.

Given those high expectations, how, then, did this high school meet the needs of its small, but perhaps high-needs, population of Latino ELLs? Bérubé (2000) profiles this dilemma by stating that rural schools, such as the context of this ethnographic case study, often have unqualified or inexperienced ESL teachers, and may find teacher training costs "prohibitive," due to their lack of funding from grants and federal subsidies aimed at English language learners.

For this particular school, one staff member had an ELL endorsement, but during the year of this study, her skills were in higher demand for other tasks, so she was assigned elsewhere instead of working with the school's ELLs in the aforementioned CALLA course. So, as the Latino ELLs in this school context spent the majority of their day in mainstream courses (Reeves, 2006), it was important for supplemental language support to be provided in the mainstream, monolingual English classes (Bérubé, 2000). In contrast to the implication of the school's publicly available statewide assessment data, these Latino ELLs were not invisible in their mainstream classes. Indeed, one of the school's ELLs, a Latina—who I will call Esperanza—was also enrolled in the school's resource (special education) program, and she received assistance in the form of a paraeducator's help in one of her core science courses. The other Latino ELL—referred to as "Tomás"—had regular meetings scheduled with his guidance counselor throughout the term; these meetings focused on study skills designed to help him pass his core content area courses in time for his impending high school graduation. Judging by the efforts of the guidance counselor and the paraeducator, this school was aware of its Latino ELLs' academic needs and sought to provide the students with individualized attention. However, the ways in which the individualized attention occurred were often "improvisational" and limited in nature, suggestive of the unorthodox, experimental approaches used in other NLD-area schools with low-incidence Latino and ELL student populations (Hamann & Harklau, 2010; Zehr, 2001).

In contrast to this school's limited approach toward meeting the needs of its low-incidence Latino ELLs, the schools in which mainstream teachers have been the most receptive to similar students' needs were schools in which there was a systematic commitment on the part of all educators to understanding, identifying, and targeting specific ways in which they could positively impact the education of Latino ELLs (Miramontes, Nadeau, & Commins, 1997; Reeves, 2006; Valenzuela, 1999). Relating this context to the literature, Valenzuela's (1999) and Carger's (1996, 2009) works illustrate that the culture of caring created through the actions of individual educators influences Latino students' sense of school as a place of positive experiences. This ethnographic case study reveals how the actions of individual educators—a paraeducator, a guidance counselor, and a classroom teacher—influenced Latino ELLs' experiences in a low-incidence environment.

Methodology

This ethnographic case study sought to "contextualize actions and experiences" (Rolón-Dow, 2005, p. 84) of two Latino/a students, who were officially categorized by the school as ELLs, in a low-incidence context. The study employed qualitative data gathering techniques, including field observations of two of the mainstream courses in which the students were enrolled, interviews with the student participants and educators in the observed mainstream courses, as well as collection of artifacts pertinent to the students' experiences in the observed mainstream courses. Conducted throughout the research process, data analysis included composition of analytic memos, coding scheme development via continuous study of the data, analysis of emergent themes through a research journal, and ensuring triangulation of major assertions, with data validation techniques including member checking and peer reviews (Merriam, 2009; Yin, 2009). This chapter was developed concurrent with the development of a dissertation and used overlapping data.

Tomás

Tomás was a Latino ELL who moved into the school district the summer before his eighth grade year. He was born in the U.S. to parents whose home language was Spanish. Officially, Tomás was an independent minor. Within this community, independent minors like Tomás were relatively rare; similar cases at the high school only occurred when there were students who became "graduates" of the local group home. His father had worked as a laborer in the local agricultural economy. After his father's employment was suddenly and unexpectedly terminated, Tomás's family— his father, mother, and younger sister- moved out of state at the beginning of his final semester in high school, but Tomás opted to finish high school in the district.

To accomplish that goal, he lived with a friend's family in town. The family with whom Tomás lived fit the demographic profile of the majority of community members, in that they were non-Latino, monolingual, English speakers. Tomás connected to his friend's family in terms of similar interests; several of the family members—including his friend, who had graduated from the same high school the previous year—worked at a local mechanic shop. Before his family's move out of state, Tomás and his father had spent time rebuilding old cars with members of this surrogate family.

Despite never holding a job prior to his family's departure, as an independent minor at the time of this study, Tomás worked at a local stockyard, rising at 4 A.M. each day. After completing a first hour excused class period —which he used to work extra hours at his job—Tomás came to school on a very regular basis. He spent his final semester retaking many courses from the previous 3 years, in order to make up previously failed credits so he could graduate with his classmates. He was on the school soccer team in earlier years, but he was not on the team during his senior year. When asked about Tomás's absence from the soccer team during his senior year, one of the coaches responded that he was "one of those players that should go on a diet."

During a crucial time in his high school career, Tomás did not have family connections in the form of regular contact and academic support from his biological family (De la Cruz, 2008). A senior class report—data compiled by the school's guidance center—indicated that over 80% of students in Tomás's grade planned to immediately enroll in some form of postsecondary education. While 80% of students in his class were going on college visits with their parents and siblings and evaluating college acceptance letters, Tomás was working nearly 30 hours per week to support himself financially. During interviews, Tomás did not state any particular plan for continuing his education after high school, indicating that he was in the 20% of his class that did not immediately plan to continue education after high school. Perhaps his plans resulted from a desire to reunite with his family, or from the experience of living with a friend who immediately entered the working world upon graduation from high school.

Tomás's guidance counselor—in whose office he completed make up work on a regular basis in order to graduate—asserted that after graduation, Tomás would likely "move out to [the state where his family had relocated] after high school ... do what they do ... maybe pick apples." When taken at face value, this comment from the guidance counselor may appear to embody a negative stereotype of migrant farm work; however, in the context of the guidance counselor's work with Tomás through regular meetings about his coursework, and a relationship that allowed friendly joking—the guidance counselor reported that he could "dish it out to [Tomás] just as often as [Tomás] could dish it back" to him—it is likely also indicative of Tomás's future plan to reunite with his biological family.

Through interviews with Tomás and his guidance counselor, who reported that Tomás "failed far too many classes to even think about college," it was evident that he was neither planning to, nor encouraged to consider, enrolling at a 2-year or 4-year college. Even Tomás's graduation from high school remained somewhat uncertain until 2 days prior to graduation, when he turned in his required log of community service hours—nearly all of which were completed performing small janitorial tasks around the school at the behest of his guidance counselor.

Indeed, Tomás's guidance counselor served as his only visibly consistent source of academic support from a school employee during this study. While the guidance counselor was aware of Tomás's status as an independent minor and past record of academic failure, and met with him independently to make up past academic deficiencies so that he could graduate with his class, this knowledge about his status as an independent minor was not clearly communicated to the rest of the teaching staff. This lack of a strong support network of school employees is especially troubling, given the assertions of Carger (1996, 2009) that Latino males are especially vulnerable to academic failure if they do not have such an academic support network. Furthermore, Saenz and Ponjuan (2009) assert that Latino males are "vanishing" from higher education, evidenced by Tomás not having plans to enroll in postsecondary education, nor having an academic support network that encouraged him to pursue the goal of postsecondary education.

Tomás's interactions with his history teacher, Mr. Green, reveal his rejection of "schooling" (Valenzuela, 1999), in terms of the content of the course and the way his education was presented by Mr. Green. Furthermore, interviews with Mr. Green revealed a "mismatch" (Deschenes et al., 2001) between his definition of academic success, and Tomás's level of attainment in that regard. Tomás was enrolled in Mr. Green's history class to fulfill his graduation requirements. Mr. Green was a veteran teacher at the school, having taught for over 30 years, nearly all of which were at this particular school. Mr. Green was the de facto "head" of the department and he taught four different sections of history courses. Tomás was in History I, the initial offering in the department, and the course that would fulfill his graduation requirements. He was the only senior in the course, and it was a rare initial enrollment for Tomás since it was not one of the courses he needed to retake due to past failure.

Mr. Green and Tomás had a preexisting student-teacher relationship, as Tomás had been in Mr. Green's study hall course the previous school year. Their relationship was fraught with tension. An initial interview with Mr. Green demonstrated his view of Tomás as a student who did too much "messing around" to be viewed as a "mature student," despite the fact that Tomás was mature enough to become an independent minor who financially supported himself while working toward high school graduation. This was a fact that Mr. Green did not acknowledge, possibly because he was unaware of Tomás's living situation. During my observations, Tomás was the student who received the majority of Mr. Green's attention, as illustrated in the following fieldnote excerpt:

> While drawing a soccer ball to complete an in class assignment, Tomás received tips on how to draw the ball [see Figure 2.1] . Pointing to Tomás's soccer ball drawing, Mr. Green said, "You could make this all one color." Tomás doesn't draw, but spins soccer ball around on his finger for approximately five minutes. Mr. Green provides Tomás tips on how he could continue to draw the soccer ball, saying "it could be all one color." Tomás draws a little while Mr. Green sits by him. Near the end of the class, Mr. Green passes by Tomás's place at the table once every few minutes to monitor his progress on his drawing. Tomás draws during those times.... For feedback, Mr. Green makes a comment to Tomás that "I know that you're not too lazy to do a good job."

Source: Photo by author.

Figure 2.1.   Tomas's soccer ball (drawn in History I).

Tomás's educational experience in Mr. Green's class included additional comments revealing the teacher's low expectations for his achievement in class, and a great deal of behavior management intervention from Mr. Green. Tomás was often taken out in the hallway by Mr. Green during class, instances where he received admonitions to "stop messing around" after various behavioral infractions. In one instance, he was reprimanded for singing rap songs to himself during in class work time. In another instance, he put his head down on the table, and refused to participate in the activity. At the end of the quarter, just before final grades were due, I interviewed Mr. Green about Tomás's grade in the course. Mr. Green said, "[Tomás] asked me if he got a 100 on [the final project]. He genuinely thinks he's going to get a 100. He just doesn't get it. He can think he's going to get a 100, but he never will. He just can't do the work, and he'll never be able to do the work."

Mr. Green's comments implying that Tomás was "lazy" and the direct statement that Tomás "can't do the work" and would "never be able to do the work" suggest deficit expectations for Tomás as an "at-risk" student (Flores, 2005), as he was the only Latino student in History I, the only senior, and the only independent minor in the course. There was a very noticeable "mismatch" (Deschenes et al., 2001) between Mr. Green's definition of academic success, and Tomás's level of achievement, as he did not fit the school's typical student profile of a "White" monolingual English speaker who lived with at least one biological parent—the sort of student whom Mr. Green had instructed for the vast majority of his career.

For his part, an initial interview with Tomás revealed that he "hated" the course, and he often acted out, as illustrated by the following field note excerpt.

> Given the assignment to design a collage, students were looking through magazines for pictures to add to their collage. While other students were quietly leafing through copies of *National Geographic* from the 1970s and 1980s for collage pictures, Tomás loudly asked Mr. Green if they could find pictures of women's lingerie or pictures of illegal drugs to put into their collages. Mr. Green responded indirectly to Tomás's comment by telling me, "I told [you] how bad the class was."

Mr. Green's negative feedback to Tomás—and Tomás's occasionally defiant disinterest in the course—continued throughout the study. After an assignment in which they were to write explanatory essays about particular texts read in class, I had the opportunity to view Tomás's finished product, complete with feedback from Mr. Green. Tomás used a variety of adjectives to describe his text, stating that the authors were "crazy sexy shiny" and that they were "so cool [he] wants to be just like them." Mr. Green's only feedback to Tomás was that he was "just trying to be cute with that sentence [sic]," with a grade of "D" circled at the top of the paper. When I asked if I could copy the paper, Mr. Green replied, "You can keep it. [Tomás] doesn't want it. He's just going to throw it away."

From Mr. Green's interviews, he viewed Tomás as the prototypical "uncaring student" outlined by Valenzuela (1999), and suggested deficit ideology (Flores, 2005) in the comment that Tomás "just can't do the work, and he'll never be able to do the work." From Tomás's interviews and my observations, he had a contentious relationship with Mr. Green, as evidenced by his comment from a quick interview in the hallway that the History I class "sucks," and that he "hates it." In his interactions with Mr. Green, Tomás demonstrated a rejection of "*schooling*—the content of [his] education and the way it [was] offered" to him (Valenzuela, 1999, p. 19, italics in original quote). Clearly, Tomás rejected the ways in which Mr. Green offered him the content of History I, in the form of negatively evaluative comments on his work and his behavior in class. On a final note about Tomás's experience in Mr. Green's History I course, he did receive a passing final grade. As Mr. Green explained, "Oh yeah, he passed. I think we've had enough of each other."

While Tomás's experience in History I was one marked by a contentious relationship with his teacher, he did seem to have one school employee who attempted to fulfill the role of an academic advocate. His meetings with his guidance counselor demonstrate the "improvisational" approach taken by many NLD-area schools (Hamann & Harklau, 2010). However, these meetings only took place in Tomás's senior year, when he was in danger of not graduating with his class. Thus, the approach seemed less about monitoring his academic success (Milambiling, 2002), and more about doing damage control after he had already failed so many courses as to face the possibility of not graduating with his class.

Additionally, no other school employees acknowledged Tomás's rarefied status as an independent minor. He was "doing it on his own," (as the chapter title suggests), during his senior year by providing his own financial support in the form of working at a local stockyard outside of school hours, and living away from his family support network. As a Latino male in a low-incidence school, Tomás was certainly not invisible—as Mr. Green's and the guidance counselor's attentions prove—but he did fall through the cracks in terms of academic achievement, unfortunately an all too common trend for Latino males (Gándara & Contreras, 2009; Saenz & Ponjuan, 2009). In the context of History I, Mr. Green managed Tomás in terms of his expectations for what constituted proper behavior and academic achievement. In the context of History I, Tomás rejected the way his "*schooling*" was offered by Mr. Green (Valenzuela, 1999, p. 19). Mr. Green's comment that Tomás "was not too lazy to do a good job" illuminates the "mismatch" (Deschenes et al., 2001) between his view of what constituted appropriate academic achievement (doing a "good job"), and how Tomás should be responsible for his own performance (he was "lazy," but not "too lazy" so as to be incapable of meeting Mr. Green's standards).

Esperanza

Esperanza was a Latina ELL who was born in the U.S., and who was part of the school's resource (special education) program. One of the school administrators remarked that they were unclear about who her legal guardians were, as they were having difficulty verifying that information with the people Esperanza referred to as "mom" and "dad." The administrator remarked that they had attempted to contact the legal guardians listed on Esperanza's enrollment form, but were having difficulty reaching them and communicating with them, as her guardians were native Spanish speakers. She attended school on a very regular basis—often coming when she did not feel well—and passed all of her core classes during the year of this study. However, Esperanza was not involved in any school-affiliated organizations or sports teams outside of the school day. Due to her placement in the resource program, she was served by a monolingual English-speaking "white-not Hispanic" paraeducator who described Esperanza as "slow at processing."

Esperanza's postsecondary ambitions were revealed through interviews. She dreamed of becoming a midwife, because she had a strong desire to help women who had "a lot of babies," like her older sister. While she said that she "liked" her classes in school, especially those teachers who "made [her] laugh," her interviews revealed a lack of personal connection with school employees. When asked who she felt she could talk to about her postsecondary goals of practicing midwifery, she revealed that she did not know of anyone working at the school who could help her. This finding, combined with the guidance counselor's aforementioned uncertainty about her guardianship, suggests that Esperanza was a student who lacked a well-known presence in the school beyond what was revealed through her demographic profile. Given Esperanza's goal of completing the postsecondary education necessary to become a midwife, having an academic support network of caring educators would help her achieve postsecondary success (De la Cruz, 2008).

The school aimed to serve Esperanza's ELL status through the use of a monolingual English-speaking "white-not Hispanic" paraeducator in her physical science course. As an insider within the school, I had previously established relationships with Esperanza, and with the paraeducator who was assigned to help her in physical science, hereafter referred to as Mrs. Forrester. Prior to my observations, in an interview, Mrs. Forrester explained that she felt it was truly important for Esperanza to be able to "do [the coursework] on her own." However, observations and interviews with Mrs. Forrester and Esperanza revealed a disconnect between Mrs. Forrester's stated goal for Esperanza to be an independent and autonomous learner, and the actual results of her "assistance" in terms of Esperanza's language proficiency and content-area knowledge.

In my first observation of Esperanza's work with Mrs. Forrester in physical science, I noted that Esperanza was not an active participant, but rather, served as a passive observer when the students were reviewing the results of a recent summative assessment, as illustrated in the following field note excerpt.

> The physical science teacher hands back tests with directions on how she graded it.... The teacher says, "It was a hard test, it is probably the hardest test of the year." Mrs. Forrester checks over Esperanza's test. After Mrs. Forrester checks the test, Esperanza puts head down on desk and covers head with hand. While going through the correct answers on the test, the teacher repeats, "these were hard, these were tricky." Esperanza intermittently checks as they go through test for about two minutes and then looks

distractedly at her fingernails and her collection of colored pens, occasionally glancing through test or looking at another student's test answers.

Esperanza's noted reluctance to review many of the test questions as the teacher went through the answers is likely explained by a comment from an interview I conducted with Mrs. Forrester. In answering my question about how she helps Esperanza with the multiple choice section on course assessments, Mrs. Forrester answered, "I read the quiz [or test] to her, and mark off two answers on the multiple choice section. After she's done with the quiz [or test], I check it and tell her which ones she should look at again." In responding to my request for clarification on her interaction with Esperanza during assessments in physical science, Mrs. Forrester responded that the amount of help provided to Esperanza "depends on her attitude and how she responds to the help I give her."

Esperanza confirmed this "improvisational" (Hamann & Harklau, 2010) method of assistance on her physical science assessments. In an interview with Esperanza, I asked her to explain how Mrs. Forrester assisted her with course assessments. Esperanza responded with the following answer:

> [Mrs. Forrester] reads the questions that are True/False or fill in the blank. She marks off two of the multiple-choice questions and checks them after I finish. She tells me which ones are wrong, and I fix them.

Based on the interview information from both Esperanza and Mrs. Forrester, Esperanza was assisted on tests and quizzes by having the questions read aloud to her, as well as having the number of potential multiple choice answers reduced from four to two. Finally, according to the participants' interview responses, out of those two possible multiple-choice answers, Mrs. Forrester checked her work and indicated which answers are incorrect. Therefore, with two multiple-choice options, if Mrs. Forrester indicated that Esperanza's initial answer was incorrect, she was left with only having to switch her answer to the one remaining possibility.

Mrs. Forrester's training was as a paraeducator for the special education program. Her job duties appeared to be largely based on the district's official job description for all paraeducators, including loosely defined duties such as:

> Stay busy; find something to do to help, if your student is working independently.... Allow student opportunity to participate as independently as possible ... [and] Be flexible and willing to work with any student ... [as well as] Take initiative to modify assignments or activities when necessary.

Based upon these guidelines, then, Mrs. Forrester was "finding something to do to help" Esperanza, by checking over her answers on her test. Similarly, Mrs. Forrester was taking "initiative to modify" the assessments when she felt Esperanza needed it. However, Mrs. Forrester did not have any specific training in how to work with ELLs, nor any formal education in the field of education; her only training was what was provided in the course of her employment. It is unsettling to consider Mrs. Forrester's assessment modifications in light of Pickett, Likins, and Wallace's (2003) assertion that "modifying content" is a teacher responsibility that should not be fulfilled by a paraeducator. Echevarria (2006) asserts that the use of untrained para-educators serves as only a short-term solution, and that such practices can hinder secondary ELLs academic development.

Esperanza continued to be a passive observer, instead of an active participant, in physical science, as evidenced by the following field note excerpts and interview about the events of a class period in which Esperanza and Mrs. Forrester completed a lab using beans to illustrate a particular point about population control. When asked to describe the events of the class that day, Esperanza replied, "We did a review for our quiz with the lab. It was a bean lab—I don't really know why we were doing it. We used beans and counted them. [Mrs. Forrester] helped me with it." When asked to describe how Mrs. Forrester assisted her in physical science, Esperanza explained that Mrs. Forrester "gives notes and study guides. Like if the notes are on PowerPoint, she prints them out for me so I don't have to write them down ... because it's easier to look at them instead of writing them."

Mrs. Forrester's assistance with the bean lab is evident in the following field note excerpt:

> Mrs. Forrester comes in to the classroom, and walks around not talking to the kids or to Esperanza. The students organize themselves into partners; Esperanza works with a male student. Mrs. Forrester repeats the lab directions to Esperanza as they begin working on the lab. Esperanza does a lot of the physical work during the lab (counting the beans, shaking the bag). Mrs. Forrester works with Esperanza on the lab during my entire observation, making calculations using a calculator and telling Esperanza to write down numbers on the lab sheet. Esperanza's lab partner doesn't participate much, as Esperanza and Mrs. Forrester do most of the work.

In summary, Esperanza's assignment appeared to be largely completed by Mrs. Forrester, with Esperanza filling in clerical tasks such as writing numbers. In keeping with her role as a passive observer in her physical science course, Esperanza stated that she "[didn't] really know why" they were doing the population lab, although she fulfilled her clerical tasks when Mrs. Forrester directed her to do so.

As with Tomás's experience working with the guidance counselor to keep him on track for graduation, the school again demonstrated the sort of improvisational response used by other NLD-area schools (Hamann

& Harklau, 2010) in addressing the needs of a student who does not fit the profile of the majority of "white-not Hispanic" native English speaking students. While it is recommended (Bérubé, 2000; Echevarria, 2006) that paraeducators like Mrs. Forrester—that is, those who work with ELLs —receive formal training in best practices for helping ELLs increase language proficiency and content-area knowledge, Mrs. Forrester herself had little formal training in preparation for working with Esperanza. As a paraeducator, she also had a lower professional status—and lower pay grade —than that of a classroom teacher. During my observations, no interaction was seen between Mrs. Forrester and the physical science classroom teacher. Based on a series of classroom observations, Mrs. Forrester was expected to assist Esperanza while operating essentially independently from any direction by the classroom teacher. Although Mrs. Forrester does not fit the bilingual profile of the paraeductors in Ernst-Slavit and Wenger's (2006) research, the lack of supervision and guidance she experienced in working with a Latina ELL is strikingly similar.

Additionally, there was no observed interaction between Esperanza and the physical science classroom teacher. Thus, the school employee with whom Esperanza had the most significant, regular contact was a well meaning, but largely untrained, paraeducator who had little formal knowledge of how to help Esperanza improve her language proficiency and content-area knowledge. Referring to the chapter title, gleaned from Mrs. Forrester's stated goal of having Esperanza "do [the coursework] on her own," one questions to what degree Esperanza achieved this level of competence, when it appeared that many of her assessments and lab assignments were completed by Mrs. Forrester. Observations and interviews revealed that Esperanza completed minimal writing and possessed, at best, limited content knowledge, as evidenced in her statement that she "[didn't] really know why" she was doing a particular lab. Given Esperanza's stated postsecondary goal to become a midwife, she would need a higher degree of content knowledge to pursue postsecondary education than what she was allowed to demonstrate on the assessments and lab exercises observed in this study.

CONCLUSIONS AND RECOMMENDATIONS

In exploring Tomás's and Esperanza's experiences in mainstream courses at a high school in which they were truly minority students, it was apparent that the school attempted to serve their needs in some way. In Esperanza's case, that meant her working with Mrs. Forrester, a largely untrained, monolingual, "white-not Hispanic" paraeducator. Esperanza's "*schooling*" (Valenzuela, 1999, p. 19) was an experience in which she became a passive observer who received modifications on assessments and assignments in her physical science course. Although Mrs. Forrester appeared well intentioned, with the stated goal of helping Esperanza develop the linguistic proficiency and academic competence to be an autonomous learner, her efforts appeared to engender the opposite result. By completing the majority of the observed assignments and assessments for Esperanza, Mrs. Forrester unwittingly hindered Esperanza's academic development in the course.

Like Esperanza, Tomás also received individualized attention from a school employee. Through meetings with his guidance counselor, ostensibly to help him improve his academic achievement in the courses required for graduation, Tomás experienced the sort of "improvisational approach" common in many NLD-area schools (Hamann & Harklau, 2010). The mismatch between the Latino ELLs—students who "don't fit" (Deschenes et al., 2001) the typical learner profile for this school—and the school's definition of academic success took distinct forms for both Tomás and Esperanza.

Tomás experienced the mismatch through Mr. Green's comments that placed the blame for failing to meet acceptable standards of academic achievement with Tomás himself. While it is tempting to attribute Tomás's lowered level of motivation to a single cause, such as lack of positive feedback from Mr. Green, Valdés (1996) states, "single-factor explanations of school failure among the children of first-generation Mexican immigrants are inadequate and cannot account for the complexity of the experience" (p. 29). Interviews conducted with Tomás during the course of this study did not reveal an easily identifiable cause for his lack of motivation; perhaps it was due to his isolation from his biological family; perhaps it was due to stress from working a job that required early-morning hours; perhaps it was due to the precarious status of his graduation from high school.

Esperanza experienced a mismatch through Mrs. Forrester's contradictions between the stated goal of their work together (helping Esperanza become an autonomous learner) and the end result where she became a passive observer with little mastery of content knowledge. Mrs. Forrester also appeared to assign blame for Esperanza's lack of academic achievement on the student herself (Deschenes et al., 2001), referring to her as "slow at processing," while simultaneously not allowing her to attempt independent work on any of the observed assignments. None of the school employees profiled in this chapter—the guidance counselor, the paraeducator, and the classroom teacher—shared Esperanza's and Tomás's linguistic or cultural backgrounds. In that sense, there was yet another mismatch between the Latino ELLs and the school employees who were supposed to help them achieve academic success.

In neither Esperanza's nor Tomás's case was there any indication that classroom teachers monitored the students' academic achievement. As

Milambiling (2002) outlines, there are ways in which schools can minimize this mismatch between their structure, and the students who don't fit the typical learner profile—and teachers play a key role in that effort. If the school had implemented Milambiling's recommended practices, including watchful integration of scaffolding opportunities in all courses, and monitoring students' successful academic performance, perhaps both Esperanza and Tomás would have faced less of a mismatch between their learner profiles and the school's educational expectations.

It is true that this school did not have a large Latino student population; such students only represented 2.6% of the total student population. However, according to publicly available data published by the state department of education, it is a population that more than doubled within a 5-year time period. As more Latino families continue to enroll school-age children in NLD-area schools, it is imperative that the schools—especially those with low-incidence populations of Latino ELLs—work to prevent further mismatches between their definition of academic success, and the newcomers' social, cultural, and linguistic backgrounds. As the stories of Tomás and Esperanza demonstrate, limited, "improvisational" approaches (Hamann & Harklau, 2010), even by those school employees as well-intentioned as the guidance counselor and Mrs. Forrester, certainly do not assure an academically successful experience for students who do not fit the expected learner profile (Deschenes et al., 2001).

In an age of increased school accountability, it is imperative that schools work with faculty and staff to determine best practices for meeting the needs of all students. As more Latino families continue to move into NLD areas, schools can no longer assume that students will fit a particular profile (Deschenes et al., 2001) while relying on "improvisational" approaches (Hamann & Harklau, 2010) for those few who do not (Zehr, 2001). Instead, schools must be prepared to meet the needs of individual learners by examining best practices and, as Deschenes et al. (2001) suggest, fitting the school experience to the learners' needs.

NOTE

1. All names of participants and courses have been altered to protect confidentiality.

REFERENCES

Bérubé, B. (2000). *Managing ESL programs in rural and small urban schools.* Alexandria, VA: Teachers of English to Speakers of Other Languages.

Carger, C. L. (1996). *Of borders and dreams: A Mexican-American experience of urban education*. New York, NY: Teachers College Press.

Carger, C. L. (2009). *Dreams deferred: Dropping out and struggling forward*. Charlotte, NC: Information Age.

Chamot, A. U., & O'Malley, J. M. (1994). *The Calla handbook: Implementing the cognitive academic language learning approach*. White Plains, NY: Addison Wesley Longman.

De la Cruz, Y. (2008). Who mentors Hispanic English language learners? *Journal of Hispanic Higher Education, 7*(1), 31–42.

Deschenes, S., Cuban, L., & Tyack, D. (2001). Mismatch: Historical perspectives on schools and students who don't fit them. *Teachers College Record, 103*(4), 525–547.

Echevarria, J. (2006). Helping English language learners succeed. *Principal Leadership, 6*(5) 16–21.

Ernst-Slavit, G., & Wenger, K. J. (2006). Teaching in the margins: The multifaceted work and struggles of bilingual paraeducators. *Anthropology and Education Quarterly, 37*(1), 62–82.

Flores, B. M. (2005). The intellectual presence of the deficit-view of Spanish-speaking children in the educational literature during the 20th century. In P. Pedraza & M. Rivera (Eds.), *Latino education: An agenda for community action research* (pp. 75–98). Mahwah, NJ: Lawrence Erlbaum Associates.

Gándara, P., & Contreras, F. (2009). *The Latino education crisis: The consequences of failed social policies*. Cambridge, MA: Harvard University Press.

Hamann, E. T., & Harklau, L. (2010). Education in the New Latino Diaspora. In E. Murillo (Ed.), *Handbook of Latinos and education: Theory, research and practice* (pp. 157–169). New York, NY: Routledge.

Merriam, S. B. (2009) *Qualitative research: A guide to design and implementation*. San Francisco, CA: Jossey-Bass.

Milambiling, J. (2002). Good neighbors: Mainstreaming ESL students in the rural Midwest. In E. P. Cochran (Ed.), *Mainstreaming* (pp. 21–30). Alexandria, VA: Teachers of English to Speakers of Other Languages.

Miramontes, O. B., Nadeau, A., & Commins, N.L. (1997). *Restructuring schools for linguistic diversity: Linking decision making to effective programs*. New York, NY: Teachers College Press.

Peshkin, A. (1978). *Growing up American: Schooling and the survival of community*. Chicago, IL: University of Chicago Press.

Pickett, A. L., Likins, M., & Wallace, T. (2003). *The employment & preparation of paraeduators: The state-of-the-art 2003*. National Resource Center for Paraprofessionals in Education and Realted Services, Center for Advanced Study in Education, Graduate School, City University of New York.

Reeves, J. (2006). Secondary teacher attitudes toward including English-language learners in mainstream classrooms. *Journal of Educational Research, 99*(3), 131–142.

Rolón-Dow, R. (2005). Critical care: A color(full) analysis of care narratives in the schooling experiences of Puerto Rican girls. *American Educational Research Journal, 42*(1), 77–111.

Saenz, V. B., & Ponjuan, L. (2009). The vanishing Latino male in higher education. *Journal of Hispanic Higher Education, 8*(1), 54–89.

Valdés, G. (1996). *Con respeto* [With respect]: *Bridging the distances between culturally diverse families and schools*. New York, NY: Teachers College Press.

Valenzuela, A. (1999). *Subtractive schooling: U.S.-Mexican youth and the politics of caring*. Albany, NY: State University of New York Press.

Yin, R. K. (2009). *Case study research: Design and methods* (4th ed.). Thousand Oaks, CA: Sage.

Zehr, M. A. (2001). ESL students pose a special challenge for rural schools. *Education Week, 20*(41), 6.

CHAPTER 3

LEARNING FROM THE *TESTIMONIO* OF A "SUCCESSFUL" UNDOCUMENTED LATINO STUDENT IN NORTH CAROLINA

Luis Urrieta, Jr., Lan Kolano, and Ji-Yeon O. Jo

Testimonios are a strategic, oral art of Latin American origin and subaltern memory. *Testimonios* are generally a novel-length account—a narrative with the authority to convey conditions of truth and representation by those who have historically been denied such voice (Beverly, 2000). Traditionally, the *testimonio* bears "witness" to a living "truth," a body—the life of the person giving the account, acting, in practice, in a space that continues and elicits the listener's (reader's) consciousness in knowing that abuse and violence, physical and/or symbolic, exists (Poniatowska, 1971). *Testimonios* are also about survival and *sobrevivencia* as a testament to resiliency and triumph.[1] While controversy over the veracity of *testimonios* has always existed, negative attention to Rigoberta Menchú's *testimonio* by David Stoll (1999) has

Revisiting Education in the New Latino Diaspora, pp. 49–70
Copyright © 2015 by Information Age Publishing

raised ethnocentric questions in the Western academy about *testimonio* as legitimate epistemology (Lincoln, 2000).

In this chapter, we revisit the importance of the *testimonio* as a methodological and theoretical tool in Latina/o Studies research, including in studies of the New Latino Diaspora (NLD). We present and discuss what we can learn from a "successful" Latino student's *testimonio* in North Carolina given to us in 2001. We use "successful" in quotations because by whitestream standards Roberto (pseudonym) was a successful man and a successful student.[2] Despite coming from a poor, undocumented, Mexican immigrant family and working as a child farmworker, he became an honor student in high school and subsequently graduated from one of the most prestigious universities in North Carolina. However, his apparently seamless and successful story obscures a very different and painful experience for Roberto.

While Roberto's *testimonio* will speak for itself, we offer insights about the implications of his narrative to the racialized citizenship incorporation of Latina/o immigrants in North Carolina (Villenas, 2002), as well as about the importance of *testimonio* as a research methodology and theoretical tool when working in Latina/o communities (Latina Feminist Group, 2001). Roberto's *testimonio*, which references school experiences in the late 1980s and 1990s, precedes current acrimony about 'Dream Acts' (federal or state), but it usefully anticipates and informs contemporary issues of Latina/o access to higher education. (See also Herrera and Holmes [this volume].)

TESTIMONIO

Rich in its Latin American roots, the *testimonio* is traditionally used by the narrator as a denunciation of violence—especially state violence—and as a demonstration of subaltern resistance (Warren, 1998). The power of such first-person, novel-length accounts is in their metaphor of "witnessing" and enduring violence through real life experience (Beverly, 2000; Poniatowska, 1971; Zimmerman, 1995). The urgency of the *testimonio* aims to bring immediate and emotive attention to an issue and has been called by Jara and Vidal (1986) a "*narración de urgencia*" (an urgency narrative) in an effort to raise the listener's (or reader's) consciousness about an issue. In recent years, Latina scholars have also used *testimonio* to testify to resiliency and *sobrevivencia* in face-to-face theorizing and production originating in the very private spaces of *papelitos guardados* (Latina Feminist Group, 2001). The Latina Feminist Group (2001) states that by *testimoniando* (testifying), they tell their stories using a complex genre with multiple antecedents from which to theorize and share similar experiences (Delgado Bernal, 2008).

Despite accusations about misuses of this genre (e.g., Stoll, 1999), *testimonios* have pragmatic as well as aesthetic value for studying identity (Yúdice, 1991). *Testimonio* as a decolonizing methodology (Smith, 2001) functions as a "confrontation to authority" that "interrupts" whitestream fieldwork narrative analysis and is political in nature (Lincoln, 2000). Unlike with other investigative designs, here the narrator (research participant) is not positioned in the traditional interviewer/interviewee role that relies on the interviewer as the "means" to speak to the hegemony and to denounce the injustices perceived (Beverly, 2000). With *testimonio*, the researcher is displaced by the narrator, who uses the interviewer to get her/his message across to a wider, traditionally external and un(der)aware audience. In the *testimonio*, the voice of the narrator demands to be heard by a juror. The listener (or reader) then "knows" of the injustice and becomes responsible for making her/his own ethical judgment over what is being denounced. Orality and experience are privileged in a *testimonio*.

According to Beverly (2000), part of the incorporation of this qualitative methodology into the qualitative research "tool box" in Western scholarship is due to its adoption from subaltern groups in the 1960s by middle and literate classes (Poniatowska, 1971), especially feminists, who began to use the *testimonio* as a cathartic and liberatory practice. In the 1980s, Mayan activist Rigoberta Menchú (Menchú, 1983) made this genre better known when she called global attention to the genocidal conditions in which Guatemalan Mayan communities lived. *Testimonio* has also come to have strong affinities with autobiographical writing, autoethnography, and indigenous story telling (Smith, 2001). In giving a *testimonio* the narrator is free to be emotive, persuasive, and active in denunciating perceived wrongs.

The Latina Feminist Group (2001, p. 12) aptly and strongly suggests that *testimonio* should be the primary methodology to use when studying *latinidades* because it is "a more organic way of creating and generating knowledge." *Latinidades* in this chapter means the wide range of different Latina/o identities and experiences. *Testimonio* allows the narrator the authority and power to negotiate and create self-authorship (identification) and voice by disrupting traditional, pre/scriptive, and soliciting confessional, semistructured, and especially highly structured interviews. *Testimonio* allows the narrator the epistemological location to re-center the discourse of *latinidades* in a personal, emotional, human, and experiential way. This is important because of the psychological revealing of traumatic, painful and yet resilient and *sobreviviente* Latina/o identities, outside of traditional academic discourse (Urrieta, 2003). Yúdice (1991) similarly argues that *testimonio* as a narrative genre is an important form of studying identity because it allows the narrator the agency to speak in less restricted ways; thus, revealing more deep and meaningful dimensions of identity.

Given the self-narration premise of the genre, we as researchers cannot demand that people give us *testimonios* while conducting qualitative or ethnographic research in Latina/o communities (or any other communities). When appropriate, *testimonios happen* because they are living narratives that belong to the narrator, not to the interviewer. Narrators seize the moment and the sympathetic ear of the researcher when the conditions feel right and trust is present to tell a *testimonio*. Emotion and *confianza* (trust) play an important role when *testimonios* happen. *Testimonios* are a gift of trust and alliance. We also believe, however, that researchers can play a chronologically slightly later step and role regarding to which audiences and with what framing *testimonios* are disseminated. In this chapter, we will use Roberto's *testimonio* as an undocumented student in North Carolina as an example of the many issues this form of narrative can reveal about different Latina/o identities and experiences.

THE CONTEXT:
LATINAS AND LATINOS IN NORTH CAROLINA

Economic growth has attracted migrations of Latinas and Latinos to the South during the past four decades (Fennell, 1977). Census data show that 9 of the 10 fastest growing Latina/o counties in the nation are located in the Southern states of Arkansas, Georgia, and North Carolina. In 2000 there were close to 400,000 Latinos living in North Carolina, an increase of 394% from 1990 (U.S. Census Bureau, 2000), a statistic slightly different than that presented in Chapter 1 of this volume, but representing a large increase.[3] In the 2010 U.S. Census, Latina/os numbered 800,120 and were close to 8.4% of the total population in the state. This suggests that the influx of Latinas/os has been continuous and impacting the overall demographics of the state, affecting school systems and transforming the Southern workforce in several sectors.

Studies of Latina/o communities in North Carolina show that Latina/o labor in meat/chicken processing (Kandel & Parrado, 2004), construction, and the service and agricultural sectors was welcomed by employers increasingly in the 1990s (Cravey, 1997; Villenas, 1996, 2001), but often leaves employees vulnerable to exploitation (Murillo, 2002). Although not all Latina/o immigrants to North Carolina fit the same demographic profile, the majority (65.1%) in 2000 was of Mexican heritage (North Carolina Latino Health Report, 2003). Despite the high percentage of Latinas/os of Mexican backgrounds, the 1997 Economic Census (the economic census most pertinent to the data we will present in this chapter) showed that minorities of Mexican heritage owned merely 21% of all Latina/o businesses and 2.3% of all minority businesses in the state. Overall Latinas/os owned

11.8% of all minority owned businesses and 1.3% of all businesses, even though in 2000 they accounted for 4.7% of the total population. In 2006, Latinas/os owned 1.4% of all firms in North Carolina and accounted for 6.7% of the total population.

The 1997 Economic Census showed that 73.3% of all Latina/o businesses were in construction, service, and not-further-classified "other" industries. These included personal services, business services, and special trade contractors in construction. These data showed that the bulk of the Latina/o immigrant labor force in North Carolina in the 1990s, although diverse, tended to be unskilled and of Mexican origin.

It is estimated that at least one third of this labor was in agriculture, a population often undercounted in census data. Latina/o immigrants in North Carolina, according to Villenas (2002), especially those of working class backgrounds, have to re/interpret their social realities as racialized beings (as Hispanics), as they strive for a better life in a historically racially dichotomous (Black/White) region. While initially the immigrant Latina/o population tended to consist mostly of men (Tienda & Wilson, 1992), increasingly women and children are now also part of the migration trend (Villenas & Moreno, 2001) although the Latina/o population in North Carolina remained overwhelmingly (3/5) male in 2003 (North Carolina Latino Health Report, 2003).

LATINA/O EDUCATIONAL ATTAINMENT IN NORTH CAROLINA

The increased number of Latina/o children in North Carolina schools has been cause for consternation for many whitestream educators who often have been ill-prepared to face their new student or parent clientele (Machado-Casas, 2006). Villenas (2001) found that White legislators often produced "benevolently racist" (paternalist and colonialist) policy legislation toward Latina/o immigrants, especially in education, that did not meet the needs of the new communities (a pattern repeated at more local levels [Villenas, 2002], as well). Efforts by teachers and other school personnel trying to "successfully" educate Latina/o students and certain groups of Asian immigrants often resulted in programs that were ineffective and based on preconceived stereotypes of racial groups (Rong & Preissle, 1998).

Only recently have data been gathered on Latina/o student achievement in North Carolina, but many studies (Education Watch, 2004; López, 2007; Wainer, 2004) show cause for concern. Wainer (2004) identified a "crisis in Education" and "new type of segregation" especially affecting Latina/o youth in the South. The biggest concern raised by Wainer was the alarming overall 55.5% dropout rate among Latina/o youth in North Carolina, but there are other issues that deserve attention. For example, according to 2000 census data, Latinas/os ages 5–24 made up 7% of the total population in North Carolina and only accounted for 5% of the public K–12 population. This lack of population parity, while it could possibly reflect the phenomenon of young adult males seeking work and not enrolling in schools, could also reflect the effects of, in part, high attrition rates. Pertinent to Roberto's *testimonio* as a successful undocumented student in North Carolina, of the 5% Latina/o enrollment in K–12 North Carolina schools, only 2% enrolled in AP calculus and AP English language and composition courses in 2000. Of those enrolled only 47% passed the exam with a score of 3 or higher. Moreover, only 1% of gifted and talented (GT) students were Latina/o while they accounted for 3% of those identified for special education services. Only 44.5% completed high school, the lowest completion rate of any racial group in North Carolina and lower than the Latina/o national average of 51.5%. Only 2% of students enrolled in 2-year colleges in North Carolina were Latina/o with a completion rate of 10.5%.

Undoubtedly, an important issue in immigrant-receiving states like North Carolina is that undocumented student status often limits access to higher education even when Latina/o students are academically competitive (Abrego, 2006; Flores & Chapa, 2009; Flores & Horn, 2009–2010). López (2007) found that for the college-ready Latina/o students in her ethnographic study in North Carolina, structural limitations made it almost financially impossible for them to access higher education. López's study concluded that the state of North Carolina was losing out on the valuable transnational capital undocumented students possess and recommended that the state reconsider passing legislation to allow undocumented students to pay in-state tuition. North Carolina, like other states, has refused to fully allow undocumented students to qualify for in-state tuition due to their interpretation of the 1996 Illegal Immigration Reform Immigrant Responsibility Act provisions (Oseguera, Flores, & Burciaga, 2010), although since 2009 it has allowed qualified undocumented students to pay in-state tuition at community colleges (National Conference of State Legislatures, 2014).

THE STUDY

The *testimonio* we are about to present was drawn from a larger qualitative research study carried out in North Carolina during 2001–2003, using life history interviews (Tierney, 2000; Luken & Vaughen, 1999). Through narrative analysis (Kramp, 2004) the larger study explored Asian and Latino participants' reflections about their cultural and linguistic identity and schooling experiences growing up in North Carolina during the 1980s and 1990s. Two, 1.5 generation, educationally mobile, Latino students were part of this study (Quach, O. Jo, & Urrieta, 2009). Our definition of *educationally mobile* included that they be enrolled or had graduated from a four-year college or university. Echoing Harklau, Losey, and Siegal (1999), we defined *1.5 generation* as a student who was born in another country, but who immigrated to the U.S. as a young child and had spent the majority of his/her life in the U.S.

In addition to the life history interviews, ethnographic data were gathered with the Latino participants over a period of 2 years (2001–2003). Our reflexive orientation in ethnography (Davies, 2001) pushed us to have a more intimate understanding of their life experiences, especially considering the specific context of Latina/o students in North Carolina. For that reason we conducted formal and informal observations of the participants that ranged from their working lives to the intimacy of their family contexts.

In this article we focus on one of the two Latino participants in this study—Roberto. Roberto was part of the early migration of farmworker families that came to North Carolina during the mid-1980s, and we are confident that his *testimonio* will generate questions that need to be raised in future and much needed research on Latina/o students in the NLD. During data analysis, we realized that we had recorded Roberto's *testimonio* as part of an interview conducted by Urrieta in March of 2001. This segment of the interview was evocative, lengthy, and in first person and clearly transmitted an urgent issue—the pain and struggle behind being a "successful" undocumented Latino student in North Carolina.

Roberto

By several interpretations Roberto was a "success" story, especially with regard to education. Roberto was born in the early 1970s and was the eldest of four brothers, all of whom were born in Mexico. He was raised doing farmwork, while living in a small trailer in rural North Carolina. Both of his parents were Mexican immigrants and he was of the 1.5 generation. His father had little formal schooling, and his mother had no formal schooling and did not know how to read or write. Roberto's father came to the U.S. before the rest of the family and ultimately qualified for legalization through the 1986 Immigration Reform and Control Act; however, because Roberto was over age 18 when legalization for the rest of the family was approved years later, only his younger siblings were eligible to adjust their immigration status. Roberto grew up with many household and out-of-the-home responsibilities, including translating for adults in his community as a young boy in roles akin to those documented so well by Orellana (2009).

Roberto learned English rather quickly and became an honor student in high school, taking several AP courses and counting as part of the 1% of Latina/o students identified as gifted-and-talented (GT).

Despite his undocumented legal status, Roberto attended several universities in North Carolina and Mexico, and graduated from one of the most prestigious public universities in the state. In 2001, Roberto worked as an informal educator to the Latina/o community in North Carolina, had started a radio talk show, and also helped Latinas/os in the local community and throughout the state with legal advice in general and on immigration issues in particular. By whitestream accounts Roberto's story seemed noteworthy, a solid example of upward educational mobility, perhaps for political conservatives even a testament of the "American dream." However, Roberto's story through his own interpretation was far from a happy journey to "success."

Although we did not set out to solicit *testimonios*, Roberto, gave us his. While conducting an interview with Roberto in 2001, Urrieta commented that it was amazing how, given the conditions of his upbringing in rural North Carolina and during a time when very few Mexican families lived in the area, he had been so successful. A long moment of silence followed. At first, Roberto smiled and looked down at the floor, then he looked up with piercing eyes, and Urrieta realized Roberto was upset. With a strong, quivering, and yet forceful voice he asked Urrieta smiling, "So you think I'm successful huh?" Urrieta stopped, put his pen down, and did not answer. Roberto's *testimonio* proceeded as follows, however, some parts have been shortened, indicated by ... due to space limitations. We have italicized it so it looks different from the rest of the chapter and the rest of the book.

Roberto Telling the Unpleasant

My father first came to the United States before the rest of the family. When we first arrived, we came to Florida, then North Carolina, then Texas. After a while, my father decided that we should go back to Mexico because my younger brothers were starting to mix their English and Spanish and he did not like that so he sent us back. After a couple of years though—I had just finished the sixth grade in Mexico—he went and brought us back to the U.S. again.

I remember that I never had problems learning English or in school here (in the U.S.) because my dad's threat was that if I failed anything he would take us out of school. He would take us out of school and just make us work. So, in a way, there wasn't an option. It was either you had to learn or you had to learn. My dad was that type of man, very strict.

I remember in '86, we had just gotten back to the U.S. So I knew a little English because 3 years before we had been here already, but I had forgotten it. I remember though, that in Mexico this one time a group of (White) American tourists went to an academic competition that my school had attended. It was a state competition.

I was representing my school in social studies and politics. I remember they asked me, "What's your name?" I didn't understand. I remember afterwards when I was already back here and I had figured things out a bit more, what they had asked me. At that time though I didn't understand what they said. It was like I didn't know English anymore and I had completely forgotten it.

My grammar in Spanish was very good, but when I returned to Mexico in 1983 around mid-year, my grammar was very bad. But, by the time I finished sixth grade, I was one of the best students. I represented the school in literature. I was good at diagramming sentences. I kicked ass. In prose, I was good at presenting cases of prose and another thing I did was debate. So I knew language well in Spanish so the transitions to English were not big problems for me.

What was hard about growing up here was the physical labor out in the fields and I hated it! That's one of the big things that stand out between growing up here in North Carolina and growing up in Mexico. I hated being asked by my teachers what I had done for the summer because all I did for the summer, every summer was work in the fields. It was cucumber, watermelon, cantaloupe, or tomato picking, rain or shine, from May through June, and picking tobacco rain or shine from June through early September, 7 days a week, for 12 to 15 hours per day. Teachers assume that everyone goes to summer camps and hangs out during the summer. What stupidity! In Mexico I would NOT have had to work as much! (angry)

In Mexico I was one of the best in my studies, I wouldn't have struggled as much to prove my abilities. Here I constantly had to prove that I was smart, that I knew things. Teachers here assumed that because we didn't speak English that meant that we didn't know anything. How wrong they were!

Here I never felt comfortable with the culture. In Mexico I was one of the popular guys and here I could never establish myself with the culture of my age group. I was always an outsider, an oddity. That's something that, in my opinion stands out, you know because I really didn't date much. I didn't date because, one, my father didn't allow that and two, because I wasn't very popular. I mean I wasn't popular ... I was popular, but as a novelty ... as someone people were not used to seeing. People stared, they sure did, but not for good reasons!

My brother Martin was popular because he understood the culture and he integrated himself well, even Pedro (youngest brother), who is a bit shy understood the culture well and was able to integrate himself well into it, me for example, never, never. That is what stands out the most. I would have been a lot more social if I would have been in Mexico. Here I was usually pretty lonely, out in the fields, without any neighbors close by, nada *[nothing],* nada *[nothing]....*

Here it wasn't until I went to the university that I started to develop my social skills and even had a social life. But my dad also didn't allow that, he wanted ... he thought we were going to get into problems because we were men. He thought we might get a girl pregnant or get into fights or something like that. He was real militant, but I think he was just scared we would get into trouble and he wouldn't be able to help us.

I remember that I wanted to play sports ... I wanted to play soccer. When I was in Mexico I used to be a pretty good player.... Here my father never had time off from his job or he would get home too tired to take us to play. He never wanted to take me to try outs; he never wanted to take us. I hated that because I knew that the only way that I could integrate myself well into the culture was, especially in high school was through sports. In Mexico I had that. I mean I was in sixth grade, and I wasn't a great player or anything or a great athlete, but I knew that was my entry or way into the culture here.

I also remember a couple of times people invited me to their parties, but my father ... first, he wanted me to work on weekends and, two, he didn't let us. He didn't believe in staying over. That's what stands out. That's what I feel. That's why when I read ... I don't know if you've read one of Daniel Ortega's poems. He was the president of Nicaragua, I think. Well when he was a prisoner as a young man, what he most hated about the government was that they had robbed him of his youth. When I read that poem, I made a very strong connection with it. I feel like me growing up here robbed me of my youth. I had too many responsibilities as a child. I was a kid and I was expected to act like a grownup always, every day, all of the time!

I understand my parents worked twelve to fifteen hours per day, but it was hard on me because I had to be the mom and dad for my brothers. I was in charge of cooking, homework, laundry, diapers, everything until my parents got home. If anything went wrong it was my responsibility as the oldest son. I never had time to be a child myself and I'm sure they hated having to work so much.

In school, because of our high math skills, my younger brother and I were placed into advanced math classes by the tenth grade. I have to thank an African American teacher for that. She challenged us to prove that we knew the material. I'm not sure if she didn't believe that we knew it, but by the time I graduated I was taking four Advanced Placement classes and two honor's classes. My father's original family plan was for us to go to school until the tenth grade. See to him that was way more education than he ever dreamed of, so he thought that would make us very educated people. He wanted us to open up a family-run auto-mechanic shop and that way all of our economic hardships would be solved. But, I knew I was smart and I wanted to attend the North Carolina School of Math and Science, but my dad's boss wouldn't let him take the evenings off to attend the parent meetings. That made me very angry because I know I would've done well there, but I couldn't go.

Growing up in rural North Carolina was a very White/Black experience, which only made me re-affirm my Mexican identity, my Mexican nationalism. I knew that I was Mexican and I only became much more proud of that. Schooling was very Black and White though, for example, in school I remember they had a White student president, a Black student president, White vice-president.... Everything they had was White and Black. They even had a Black prom and a White prom and, as a Mexican, I wasn't invited to either one.

I remember Ms. Jefferson, a tall beautiful, young African American administrator. I remember her because she encouraged me to run for student office. She was so beautiful that I felt astounded by her and people around me kept encouraging me to run for office too, so I accepted. I remember that I … you know we were joking amongst the raza *(other Mexicans) it was Ricardo, Cuco, and myself. That was all the* raza *there were at the school, and there was a girl who was a* pocha *(U.S.-born Mexican) and the friends I used to work with … the nerds I guess. They challenged me to ask a question. I remember that I sat down and there was a session when we could ask whatever we wanted to ask, so I raised my hand. I asked, "I know there's a White officer and a Black officer for all the positions, so where do Mexicans fall in if I run for office?" I remember that the whole assembly was laughing and laughing. They thought that was very funny. I said, "I'm not Black and I'm not White, so where do I fit in?"*

Mr. Butler one of the school's White administrators said, "Well, we'll let you choose." There was a White cheerleader, Mary, and she was nominated for historian. Her and I, we didn't get along. She got along with everyone because she was a cheerleader, but only the White people. I remember I was nominated for historian also along with her. So Mr. Butler asked me if I wanted to be historian for the bolillos *(Whites) or the Blacks. Everyone continued laughing, so I don't know what got into me and I said, "Since I'm in-between, I'll represent both." Then there was a long moment of silence. A lot of the teachers kept looking at each other too. Then Mr. Butler responded, "We can do that because you're not White or Black. If you win, you will be historian for both and if anyone else wins we will continue having two."*

So I remember that the Black guy running for historian withdrew. I think Ms. Jefferson asked him to, but I'm not sure, but Mary didn't back off. I remember a lot of people campaigned for me, but mostly the Black students. Ms. Jefferson helped out a lot. I'm not sure, but I think they just wanted to see if I would lose (slight grin) It was fun … you know it wasn't serious. I remember I won by a landslide and we embarrassed Mary. From then on, they started having only one student representative for each office.

When I graduated from high school, I graduated with honors and eventually I was admitted into several colleges and universities. But because I didn't have my papeles *(legal immigration status) I was not eligible for financial aid. I was devastated and kept thinking of a way to do this. It was my dream to go to college. I attended Eastern Carolina University until they notified me they wanted my legal residency papers immediately. I was so upset. I really was angry because instead of college being a fun experience there were roadblocks at every turn.*

I eventually became so disappointed that I decided to return to Mexico for some time. In Mexico I attended the Mexican National Autonomous University and was living well by Mexican standards, but I realized that there are very little opportunities in Mexico and I was taking a fellow Mexican's chance for a better life. Plus my whole family was in the U.S., so I didn't have any strong connections with Mexico anymore. So I decided to return to North Carolina. Here I knew that if I finished my degree I would not be taking another fellow Mexican's chance, but a White person's opportunity and somehow that would give me satisfaction.

I hate to say this, but I have a lot of resentment towards bolillos *[Whites]. I feel like I hate them sometimes. I remember every time they made fun of me, every White teacher who laughed when I said I wanted to go to college, every White financial aid counselor who asked me for my social security number with stabbing eyes, every White bouncer who didn't let me enter bars because I didn't have an ID. I remember too many things and I have a lot of anger inside of me. It hurts me inside and it comes out as anger. It hurts me inside.*

I was eventually admitted to the University of North Carolina without any financial assistance. I ended up working my way to pay tuition and manage a family life. You see I was married by then. But I finished and got my degree. I was always stressed about money. I had two or three jobs at once and I slept very little. I was always so tired and I couldn't believe some bolillos *just spent their time partying and going to classes while they attend college!*

It was hard to grow up in North Carolina and "make it here" [signs quotations with his fingers]. That's why I hate it when someone tells me you were lucky! Or you were successful! If I could, I would take them and choke them until they stopped breathing! What does my success translate to? What was the price of my success? Do you know? Do you have any idea?

I'm sure even in a place like California or Texas I would have been successful, but under these conditions, here in North Carolina, to be "successful" (laughs), it's unimaginable! I grew up in a depressing atmosphere because I didn't have anyone to socialize with. In a way, I feel that we (the family) are a failure, not a success, because somewhere else I would have had more success, you know? A different type of success, you know? I had dreams in Mexico, here I have anger and resentment. By being here in North Carolina, as a child, I feel I sacrificed one of the most valuable things one has in life, and that's life itself. And now, it's too late; I can never get it back! No one, no one can give me back my innocence, no one can give me back my youth!

DISCUSSION

There are many themes that emerge from this testimonio, but perhaps the two that stand out the most are that of Roberto's sense of being robbed of his youth and of sacrificing life itself. Roberto's testimonio bears witness to his lived experience in a brown body that is a *sobreviviente* in a contradictory, both hostile and welcoming (Gitlin, Buendía, Crosland, & Doumbia, 2003), environment for Latinas/os like North Carolina. The contradiction lies, as Murillo (2002, p. 228) wrote in the previous *Education in the New Latino Diaspora* volume in that, "The labor is welcomed, but not the entire human being." Roberto's body and his words bear witness to immigrants' struggle for economic and psychological *sobrevivencia* and also educational "success," not necessarily because of the system, but despite the "roadblocks" in the system, especially those roadblocks to access higher education as an undocumented student.

In previous work (González, Plata, García, Torres, & Urrieta, 2003) we expressed the need to understand Latina/o immigrant children's identities through *testimonios*. Undocumented immigrant children often do not make the decision to come to the United States; as argued in *Plyler v. Doe* (1982), adults in their lives make the decision based on economic hardships, and often it is the children who are first thrust into the American whitestream in institutions like schools. In this way, undocumented Latina/o immigrant children are at the forefront and in some of the most vulnerable positions to experience both overt and "benevolent" racism, prejudice, and discrimination.[4]

Most teachers' whitestream assumptions about what children do during summer vacation, and especially about the abilities or perceived deficits of Latina/o immigrant students, ring through in Roberto's *testimonio*. Roberto expressed that he constantly had to prove that he was smart, because it was not an expectation teachers had of people like him. The schooling system in many ways placed roadblocks for Roberto, including institutional, cultural, and social discrimination, coupled with what *he felt* were shortsighted, economically myopic laws that deny in-state tuition for higher education to undocumented students.

While immigrant families struggle to make ends meet, is it fair for children to work physically as hard as Roberto did, regardless of who they are, and why and how they came to the United States? Who hires Latina/o children to work in this way? Why are some Americans fine with children picking their crops, or busing their tables, or washing their dirty dishes behind the walls of fancy restaurants?

Moreover, the issue of child labor is of global concern. It is estimated that there are 186 million child laborers worldwide (Basu & Tzannatos, 2003), while in the U.S. the Child Labor Coalition (2007) estimated that there were approximately 500,000 child farmworkers alone in 2007. Although legislation has been repeatedly introduced to protect child laborers in the U.S.—the version current at the time of this writing was called the Children's Act for Responsible Employment—no new child protections have actually been enacted since the Fair Labor Standards Act of 1938.

Latino Racial Incorporation and Educational Access

Roberto's *testimonio* corroborates with prior studies of Latinas/os in North Carolina that raise concern over the unequal racial incorporation Latinas/os experienced in the NLD (Wortham, Murillo, & Hamann, 2002; Villenas, 2007). Racial stereotypes and expectations and unequal access to economic resources have influenced this difference in incorporation into the traditionally Black/White racial dynamic of the South. Although there is an element of racial ambiguity illustrated when Roberto is allowed by Mr. Butler to choose if he wants to represent the White or Black students [see also Beck and Allexsaht-Snider (2002) for a similar example of a female Latina student in Georgia], it was known to Roberto that Mexicans fell outside the realm of Whiteness. In another interview Roberto said, "we [Hispanics] were definitely not White and that was made clear to us." And yet some African American teachers like Ms. Jefferson, we speculate, saw in Latinas/os, like Roberto, the possibility to disrupt the segregationist order of *de facto* race relations in school contexts where often African American communities lost more than they gained with integration (Hughes, 2006).

Roberto, because of his darker skin complexion and ethnic background, was in some ways more closely associated with African Americans, while some of our Asian American students in the larger study, at times had more leeway in most closely associating with Whites [see Quach, O. Jo, & Urrieta, (2009)]. Our data therefore suggest that African American teachers, like Ms. Jefferson, were the most helpful socially and academically to Latina/o students, like Roberto. In this system of racial incorporation, Latinas/os, like Roberto, came to occupy a lower racial classification than that of Whites, but yet rather nebulous when it came to African Americans, although it was clear that Whites like Mr. Butler knew that Mexicans were also not Black. However, it was not just simply a skin-shade phenotype match that allowed some African American educators and students like Roberto to be supportive of each other, but also the less-gradient oriented fact that both groups were not White and from groups that both were historically, whether locally or on a broader national scale, discriminated against, that also led to their affinity.

The racial ambiguity of Latina/os in North Carolina did not always, however, result in supportive minority-minority relations. Roberto commented that on other occasions, the racial ambiguity of Latina/os caused, in his experience, a strain in minority-minority, especially Black-Brown relations, where fear of displacement as a minority occurred. Such strain is unfortunately also common and sometimes results in violence, often framed as a "problem," without addressing the role that White supremacy and White privilege play in such race relations. Heeding Murillo's (2002) call to also focus attention on Whites in these contexts, we now turn our attention to whitestream conceptions of citizenship.

Whitestream Citizenship and Undocumented Latina/o Students

The equation of Whiteness with citizenship in U.S. society operates not only to reify existing White supremacist power dynamics but also to afford Whites the luxury of substituting their cultural and racial identity for full citizenship (Ladson-Billings, 2004). This equating of full citizenship status and Whiteness denies these rights to those excluded from, to various degrees, Whiteness (Urrieta & Reidel, 2008). This conflation of Whiteness and citizenship makes it difficult for members of the White group to recognize the ways in which their cultural and racial identities are often interchangeable with their citizen identities and full legal rights (Williams, 1991), including the right to a quality education and financial need-based assistance. Given the nebulous and often unequal ways in which legal residency and conditional citizenship is granted to people (Olivas, 2004), important questions arise about how and why undocumented Latina/o students continue to be excluded from higher education via a denial of their long-term presence/attendance in U.S. schools, or, like Roberto, are only begrudgingly included with extra obstacles put in their way and an expectation that they should be grateful for exceptions made on their behalf.

Some legislators and other lobbyists continue to advocate for the approval of a federal DREAM Act (Development Relief and Education for Alien Minors) as a sound educational policy and economic investment measure to support higher education for undocumented students like Roberto. However, we believe staunch conservative opposition to fully support and approve the DREAM Act is related to who these legislators' consider to be "fit" for full, or even partial citizenship. Undocumented students' uninspected entry to the U.S. at an age when they were not able to, or allowed to make their own decisions, like Roberto, is only one small piece of a larger whitestream citizenship puzzle.

López (2007), for example, highlights that the undocumented students in her North Carolina study were in many ways, the "All-American" ideal student. López's high school students, similar to Roberto, certainly disrupted the whitestream's notions of Latina/o students' supposed cultural deficits; yet, their long-time residence and cultural citizenship in North Carolina was denied for in-state tuition purposes, while relegating them to non-citizen status. Vanderbilt professor Stella Flores's (2010) quantitative research on state Dream Acts overwhelmingly shows that in-state resident tuition significantly affects the college decisions and increases the college enrollments of students who are likely to be undocumented, as with Roberto and the "ideal students" in Lopez's study. Overall, Flores's extensive data show that state Dream Acts have significant income and other economic and social benefits for all people (Flores, 2010).

CONCLUSION: TESTIMONIO AND LATINA/O STUDIES RESEARCH

The importance of *testimonio* in working with Latina/o communities, especially new, less-established, immigrant Latina/o communities in the New Latino Diaspora, cannot be emphasized enough. While it is unpleasant and uncomfortable to hear of the hardships and the violence that is often endured by Latina/o immigrants in new contexts, it is important to realize that these realities exist and that they too are part of the many *latinidades* that we, as researchers, need to understand. In this case, Latina/o immigrants' *testimonios*, like Roberto's, provide a tool to "talk back" to the hegemony of xenophobia, racism, and exclusion being waged against new communities of Latina/o displaced economic refugees (Anzaldúa, 1987). Roberto talked back to Urrieta's assumptions of his success, to give testimony of the costs of his educational attainment and his *sobrevivencia* under harrowing conditions. Although striking, we learned a lot about Roberto's will, his identity, and his strength. We also learned of the importance of *testimonio* in Latina/o Studies research—the genre, how to identify a *testimonio*, and the use of *testimonios* as gifts of trust when working in Latina/o communities.

We learned that not all people give *testimonios*, and that because *testimonios* are a gift they cannot be demanded from people, or obtained by following prescripted interview protocols in qualitative research. *Testimonios* are *given* because of a sense of trust and alliance that should be determined by and under the control of the narrator, not the interviewer. As such, researchers working with Latina/o communities should be trained to understand and be able to recognize when a research participant is giving a *testimonio* and is not merely "rambling" or "straying from" the focus of an interview, especially because *testimonios* may not follow a linear narrative style. Understanding and being exposed to *testimonios* is imperative for rich insight this narrative genre can contribute to Latina/o Studies research. However, because we understand that not all people give *testimonies*, we encourage Latina/o Studies scholars to explore important and necessary ways to build trusting and long-term relationships with their participants.

In order to further develop the use of *testimonio* as a qualitative tool for working with Latina/o communities we suggest that, first, researchers explore the use of *Composed Testimonios*. A *composed testimonio* is a novel-length account written in first person that addresses an urgent matter, but is not necessarily given by the narrator all at one time. We believe that data from a series of conversations or interviews with one participant can be used to put together a *composed testimonio* over time. By drawing relevant narrative from multiple interviews a specific issue can be addressed as a *composed testimonio*, put together by the researcher, but always in consultation and collaboration with the testifying research participant. We cannot emphasize this enough. Richard Rodriguez's (1982) *Hunger of Memory* and John Phillip Santos's (1999) *Places Left Unfinished at the Time of Creation* might fit in this category, from a more self-authored, scholarly perspective.

Second, we believe there are also possibilities for producing *collective testimonios*, or one in which the researcher can draw from multiple research participants' interview data, or multiple *testimonios*, when available. A *collective testimonio* is one that incorporates the voices of several participants, who may or may not know each other, into a novel-length account centered on certain issues or themes that may or may not be written in first person under a fictive name to protect the participants. Focus group interviews would be especially conducive for producing *collective testimonio*; however, representative interview data from several research participants over prolonged periods of time may also be used. Again, collaboration and respectful and honest consultation between researcher and participants is of utmost importance. Elena Poniatowska (1971) offers a compelling and moving collective *testimonio* of the events surrounding the murders of protesting university faculty and students in Plaza Tlatelolco in Mexico City by the Mexican military in 1968. Most recently, Chicana, Latina feminists Alarcón, Cruz, Guardia Jackson, Prieto, and Rodríguez-Arroyo (2011) offer a *collective testimonio* of their schooling experiences as Chicanas, Latinas in a White, patriarchal, and heterosexist U.S. society.

Denzin and Lincoln (2000) state that qualitative research is about tensions, contradictions, and hesitations, and the use of *testimonio* is a clear example of these. In the context of the NLD, as in other contexts involving Latinas/os, *testimonios* matter because they reveal insights from a domain that would otherwise be overlooked. The complexity of Roberto's life in achieving "success" would have been less complete, had he not given us his *testimonio*. Both traditional qualitative and quantitative research tend to prefer detached and omniscient voices in which we usually hear filtered versions of the lived experience of research participants (Urrieta, 2003). *Testimonio* removes or at least reduces the gap between the reader and the subject of inquiry; thus, we hear Roberto be angry, elegiac, perhaps even contradictory, as he tries to make sense of his experience, the messages society shares both with and about him, and his sense of whom he should be. That voice should not be denied by either whitestream hegemony nor by the regular tenets of qualitative research.

NOTES

1. Trinidad Galván (2005, p. 11) defines *sobrevivencia* as a type of survival and resiliency that goes beyond mere economic survival and that includes cherished everyday interactions and measures.
2. We use the term *whitestream* as opposed to *mainstream* in an effort to de-center Whiteness as dominant (Urrieta, 2009). Sandy Grande (2000) first referred to "whitestream" as the cultural capital of Whites in almost every facet of U.S. society. Whitestream, according to Claude Denis (1997), is a term that plays on the feminist notion of "malestream." Denis defines *whitestream* as the idea that while (Canadian) society is not completely White in sociodemographic

terms, it remains principally and fundamentally structured on the basis of the Anglo-European White experience. We suggest that the same holds true in the United States.

3. North Carolina is reflective of the changing demographic trends occurring throughout the U.S. South. Between 1990 and 2000, North Carolina experienced the fastest immigrant population growth of any state in the nation (Wainer, 2004).

4. Villenas (2002, p. 31) refers to "benevolent racism" as those programs and policies espoused by well-intended public service and care providers toward Latina/o families in the New Latino Diaspora, but that are based on deficit and assimilationist frameworks that sought to "help" Latino families in their "plight." Villenas advocates that policy should be made *with* the New Latino Diaspora, rather than for it.

REFERENCES

Abrego, L. J. (2006). "I can't go to college because I don't have papers": Incorporation patterns of Latino undocumented youth. *Latino Studies, 4,* 212–231.

Alarcón, W., Cruz, C., Guardia Jackson, L., Prieto, L., & Rodríguez-Arroyo, S. (2011). Compartiendo nuestras historias: Five *testimonios* of schooling and survival. *Journal of Latinos and Education, 10*(4), 369–381.

Anzaldúa, G. (1987). *Borderlands/la frontera: The new mestiza.* San Francisco, CA: Aunt Lute Books.

Basu, K., & Tzannatos, Z. (2003). The global child labor problem: What do we know and what can we do? *The World Bank Economic Review, 17*(2), 147–173.

Beck, S. A. L., & Allexsaht-Snider, M. (2002). Recent language minority education policy in Georgia: Appropriation, assimilation, and Americanization. In S. Wortham, E. Murillo, Jr., & E. T. Hamann (Eds.), *Education in the new Latino diaspora, policy and the politics of identity* (pp. 37–66). Westport, CT. Ablex.

Beverly, J. (2000). Testimonio, subalternity, and narrative authority. In N. K. Denzin & Y. S. Lincoln (Eds.), *Handbook of qualitative research* (pp. 555–565) Thousand Oaks, CA: Sage

Child Labor Coalition. (2007, June 12,). *CARE Act Would Protect 500,000 Child Farmworkers* (Press Release).

Cravey, A. J. (1997). The changing South: Latino labor and poultry production in rural North Carolina. *Southern Geographer, 37*(2), 295–300.

Davies, C. A. (2001). *Reflexive ethnography, a guide to researching selves and others.* London, England: Routledge.

Delgado Bernal, D. (2008). La trenza de identidades: Weaving together my personal, professional, and communal identities. In K. González & R. Padilla (Eds.), *Doing the public good: Latina/o scholars engage civic participation* (pp. 135–148). Sterling, VA: Stylus.

Denis, J. C. (1997). *We are not you: First nations and Canadian modernity.* Peterborough, Ontario, Canada: Broadview Press, Collection Terra Incognita.

Denzin, N., & Lincoln, Y. (2000). *Handbook of qualitative research* (2nd ed.). Thousand Oaks, CA: Sage

Education Watch North Carolina. (2004). *Key education facts and figures.* Education Trust.

Fennell, V. (1977). International Atlanta and intergroup relations. *Urban Anthropology, 6*(4), 345–354.

Flores, S. M. (2010). State dream acts: The effect of in-state resident tuition policies and undocumented Latino students. *Review of Higher Education, 33*(2), 239–283.

Flores, S. M., & Chapa, J. (2009). Latino immigrant access to higher education in a bipolar context of reception. *Journal of Hispanic Higher Education, 10*(4), 317–330.

Flores, S., & Horn, C. L. (2009–2010). College persistence among undocumented students at a selective public university: A quantitative case study analysis. *Journal of College Student Retention: Research, Theory, and Practice, 11*(1), 57–76.

Gitlin, A., Buendía, E., Crosland, K., & Doumbia, F. (2003). The production of margin and center: Welcoming-unwelcoming of immigrant students. *American Educational Research Journal, 40*(1), 91–122.

González, M. S., Plata, O., García, E., Torres, M., & Urrieta, L. Jr. (2003). Testimonios de inmigrantes: Students educating future teachers. *Journal of Latinos and Education, 2*(4), 233–243.

Grande, S. M. A. (2000). American Indian geographies of identity and power: At the crossroads of Indígena and mestizaje. *Harvard Educational Review, 70*(4), 467–498.

Harklau, L., Losey, K. M, & Siegal, M. (Eds.). (1999). *Generation 1.5 meets college composition: Issues in the teaching of writing to U.S. educated learners of ESL.* Mahwah, NJ: Lawrence Erlbaum.

Hughes, S. (2006). *Black hands in the biscuits, not in the classrooms: Unveiling hope in the struggle for Brown's promise.* New York, NY: Peter Lang

Jara, R., & Vidal, H. (1986). *Testimonio y literatura.* Minneapolis, MN: University of Minnesota Institute for the Study of Ideologies and Literatures.

Kandel, W., & Parrado, E. (2004). Hispanics in the American South and the transformation of the poultry industry. In D. Arreola (Ed.), *Hispanic spaces, Latino places: Community and cultural diversity in contemporary America* (pp. 255–276). Austin: University of Texas Press.

Kramp, M. K. (2004). Exploring life and experience through narrative inquiry. In K. deMarrais & S. D. Lapan (Eds.), *Foundations for research: Methods of inquiry in education and the social sciences* (pp. 103–121). Mahwah, NJ: Lawrence Erlbaum Associates.

Ladson-Billings, G. (2004). Culture versus citizenship: The challenge of racialized citizenship in the United States. In J. Banks (Ed.) *Diversity and citizenship education: Global perspectives* (pp. 99–126). San Francisco, CA: John Wiley.

Latina Feminist Group. (2001). *Telling to live: Latina feminist testimonios.* Durham, NC: Duke University Press.

Lincoln, Y. (2000). Narrative authority vs. perjured testimony: Courage, vulnerability and truth. *Qualitative Studies in Education, 13*(2), 131–138.

López, J. (2007). *We asked for workers and they sent us people: a critical race theory and Latino critical theory ethnography exploring college-ready undocumented high school immigrants in North Carolina* (Unpublished dissertation). University of North Carolina, Chapel Hill.

Luken, P. C., & Vaughan, S. (1999). Life history and the critique of American sociological practice. *Sociological Inquiry, 69*(3), 404–425.

Machado-Casas, M. (2006). *Narrating education of new indigenous/Latino transnational communities in the south: Migration, life, and its effects on schooling* (Unpublished dissertation). University of North Carolina, Chapel Hill.

Menchú, R. (1983). *Me llamo Rigoberta Menchú y asi me nació la conciencia* [My name is Rigoberta Menchú and that's how my awareness was born] (E. Burgos-Debray, Editor). Barcelona, Spain: Argos Vergara.

Murillo, E. (2002). How does it feel to be a problem? Disciplining the transnational subject in the American south. In S. Wortham, E. Murillo, & E. Hamann, (Eds.), *Education in the new Latino diaspora: Policy and the politics of identity* (pp. 215–240). Westport, CT: Ablex.

National Conference of State Legislatures. (2014, June 12). *Undocumented student tuition: State action.* Retrieved from http://www.ncsl.org/research/education/undocumented-student-tuition-state-action.aspx

North Carolina Latino Health 2003 Report. (2003). Retrieved from http://www.nciom.org/projects/latino/latinopub/C2.pdf

Olivas, M. (2004). IRIRA, The DREAM Act, and undocumented college student residency. *Journal of College and University Law, 30*, 435–464.

Orellana, M. F. (2009). *Translating childhoods: Immigrant youth, language, and culture.* New Brunswick, NJ: Rutgers University Press.

Oseguera, L., Flores, S., M., & Burciaga, E. (2010). Documenting implementation realities: Undocumented immigrant students in California and North Carolina. *Journal of College Admission, 206*, 37–43.

Pyler v. Doe, 457 U.S. 202 (1982).

Poniatowska, E. (1971). *La noche de Tlatelolco: Testimonio de la historia oral* [The night of Tlatelolco: Oral history testimonies]. Mexico, D.F.: Biblioteca ERA.

Quach, L., O. Jo, J., & Urrieta, L., Jr. (2009). Understanding the racialized identities of Asian students in predominantly white schools. In R. Kubota & A. Lin (Eds.), *Race, culture, and identities in second language acquisition: Exloring critically engaged practice.* New York, NY: Routledge.

Rodriguez, R. (1982). *Hunger of memory.* Boston, MA: David Godine.

Rong, X. L., & Preissle, J. (1998). *Educating immigrant students.* Thousand Oaks, CA: Corwin Press.

Santos, J. P. (1999). *Places left unfinished at the time of creation.* New York, NY: Viking Books.

Smith, L. T. (2001). *Decolonizing methodologies: Research and indigenous peoples.* London, England: University of Otago Press.

Stoll, D. (1999). *Rigoberta Menchú and the story of all poor Guatemalans.* Boulder, CO: Westview Press.

Tienda, M., & Wilson, F. D. (1992). Migration and the earnings of Hispanic men. *American Sociological Review, 57*(5), 661–678.

Tierney, W. G. (2000). Life history and the postmodern challenge. In N. Denzin & Y. Lincoln (Eds.), *Handbook of qualitative research* (2nd ed., pp. 537–553). Thousand Oaks, CA: Sage.

Trinidad R. G. (2005). Transnational communities en la lucha: Campesinas and grassroots organizations "globalizing from below." *Journal of Latinos and Education, 4*(1), 3–20.

Urrieta, L., Jr. (2003). Las identidades también lloran/identities also cry: Exploring the human side of indigenous Latina/o identities. *Educational Studies, 34*(2), 148–168.

Urrieta, L., Jr. (2009). *Working from within: Chicana and Chicano activist educators in whitestream schools.* Tucson, AR: University of Arizona Press

Urrieta, L. Jr., & Reidel, M. (2008). Citizenship normalizing and white pre-service social studies teachers. *Social Justice: A Journal of Crime, Conflict, and World Order, 34*(2), 91-108.

U.S. Census Bureau. (1990). Census: General demographic characteristics. Retrieved from www.census.gov

U.S. Census Bureau. (1997). Economic census: Minority-and women-owned businesses in North Carolina. Retrieved fro http://www.census.gove/epcd/mwb97/nc?NC.html

U.S. Census Bureau. (2000). Census: General demographic characteristics. Retrieved from www.census.gov

U.S. Census Bureau. (2010). Census: North Carolina–Fact Sheet–American Fact-Finder. Retrieved from www.census.gov

Villenas, S. (1996). The colonizer/colonized Chicana ethnographer: Identity, marginalization, and co-optation in the field. *Harvard Educational Review, 66*(4), 711–731.

Villenas, S. (2001). Latina mothers and small-town racisms: Creating narratives of dignity and moral education in North Carolina. *Anthropology and Education Quarterly, 32*(1), 3–28.

Villenas, S. (2002). Reinventing educación in new Latino communities: Pedagogies of change and continuity in North Carolina. In S. Wortham, E. Murillo, & E. Hamann (Eds.), *Education in the new Latino diaspora: Policy and the politics of identity* (pp. 17–35). Westport, CT: Ablex.

Villenas, S. (2007). Diaspora and the anthropology of Latino education. *Anthropology and Education Quarterly, 38*(4), 419–435.

Villenas, S., & Moreno, M. (2001). To valerse por si misma between race, capitalism, and patriarchy: Latina mother-daughter pedagogies in North Carolina. *Qualitative Studies in Education, 14*(5), 671–687.

Wainer, A. (2004). *The new Latino south and the challenge to public education: Strategies for educators and policymakers in emerging immigrant communities.* Los Angeles, CA: Tomás Rivera Policy Institute, University of Southern California.

Warren, K. (1998). *Indigenous movements and their critics: Pan-Mayan activism in Guatemala.* Princeton, NJ: Princeton University Press.

Williams, P. (1991). *The alchemy of race and rights.* Cambridge, MA: Harvard University Press.

Wortham, S., Murillo, E. G., Jr., & Hamann, E. T. (Eds.). (2002). *Education in the new Latino diaspora, policy and the politics of identity.* Westport, CT. Ablex.

Yúdice, G. (1991). Testimonio and postmodernism. *Latin American Perspectives*, *18*(3), 15–31.

Zimmerman, M. (1995). *Literature and resistance in Guatemala: Textual modes and cultural politics from El Señor Presidente to Rigoberta Menchú*. Athens, OH: Ohio University Center for Intercultural Studies.

CHAPTER 4

RACIALIZATION AND THE IDEOLOGY OF *CONTAINMENT* IN THE EDUCATION OF LATINA/O YOUTH

John Raible and Jason Irizarry

Sitting there in the school office, I couldn't even hear what they were saying. While the principal yelled at me, I played the fight over and over again in my head: The White kid started it. He threw yogurt at me. I went to get a teacher. But the teacher didn't even listen to my side of the story. She just blew me off. I felt like I had to do something. So I approached the kid, he stepped to me, and I punched him in the face. I mean; it was self-defense. Finally, the principal stopped yelling and said, "Get your things; it is time to go." I saw him pointing to the police officer who came to pick me up and take me in.

This *testimonio* from Ramiro, one of our student participants at Rana High School (see Urrieta, Kolano, & O. Jo [this volume] for more about the logic and process of *testimonios*), illustrates the profound disconnect between schooling and the frustration and marginalization experienced by numerous young people as a result of their positioning by adults as deviant, dangerous criminals (Meiners, 2007; Tilton, 2010). Predictably, the other student in Ramiro's anecdote was not sent to the principal's office; only

Revisiting Education in the New Latino Diaspora, pp. 71–91
Copyright © 2015 by Information Age Publishing

the youth of color was disciplined in this event. In the minds of too many school authorities, Black and Brown youths, like Ramiro, are often labeled as troublemakers and outcasts. This leads some schools to collude problematically with law enforcement by criminalizing what in less punitive times would have been understood as misguided youthful behavior (Raible & Irizarry, 2010). As we became more aware of his story, we were concerned that Ramiro (and others like him) would become just another statistic—an incarcerated youth of color rather than the successful, college-bound high school student we knew him to be.

Many urban youth frequently must interact with police officers and other gatekeepers around and within school grounds, passing through security checkpoints and metal detectors in order to get to their classrooms. Understandably, students who are treated in this way as part of their schooling often internalize implicit lessons about criminality, race- and class-based profiling, and perceptions of the locus of danger in the minds of the adults who teach and supervise them.

In recent years, investigations of the links between schooling and the rising rates of youth incarceration in the United States have exposed what has come to be called the school-to-prison pipeline (Lewis & Vazquez-Solorzano, 2006; Meiners, 2007; Raible & Irizarry, 2010; Wald & Losen, 2003). Punitive "get-tough" laws that addressed youth violence in the closing decades of the 20th century led to harsher sentencing policies that have had a disproportionate impact on poor urban youth of color (Cammarota & Fine, 2008). For example, the rise of so-called zero tolerance policies in schools parallels the rise in rates of both school exclusion and youth incarceration.

Youth of color in particular are targeted for various measures of *containment*, or the curtailment of their freedom and mobility, that often takes different forms. This chapter addresses the ideological discourse of containment and calls attention to the role and responsibility of educators, particularly those that work with youth who are part of the New Latino/a Diaspora. Our aim is to motivate teachers and social justice activists to better understand—and then work with youth to interrupt—the school-to-prison pipeline and the related dynamic of containment that effectively curtails the educational aspirations of working class urban students, particularly those who are Brown and Black, and who are increasingly deemed dangerous, undesirable, and disposable.

Exposing the School-to-Prison Pipeline

Our interest in urban youths and their involvement with discipline as a system of social control (both in and outside of school) has led us, as educational researchers, to examine our personal participation in the school-to-prison pipeline. Alarmingly, an overwhelming majority of the Latina/o students we have worked with have found themselves, at various times, detained or incarcerated within the penal system. Other students have reported to us the surprising number of their friends and family members who have served time behind bars. These individuals are not necessarily "bad kids," and getting to know them as multifaceted persons caused us to wonder about the menacing clouds of the prison-industrial complex (Davis, 1999) gathering over the urban poor communities with which we have interacted over the years. The insights we have gained into our students' lived realities further led us to question our own complicity as teachers, as well as the role of schooling itself, in perpetuating what strikes us as eerily predictable patterns of discipline and punishment aimed at controlling the behavior—and containing the aspirations—of urban youth. Far from fulfilling the youthful dreams for better futures, we have sought to understand the ways in which schools often work at cross purposes for students from marginalized backgrounds.

By way of clarification, we use the term *minoritized* to suggest that while Black and Brown students may share status as members of historical numeric minority groups, in many cases they constitute the majority of the student body within the schools they attend. Research has documented that numerous urban school districts are more segregated now than during the heyday of the Civil Rights movement, leaving many youngsters in our nation's cities to attend predominately Brown and Black schools (Orfield & Lee, 2005; Saporito, 2007). Moreover, in more and more communities, students of color can hardly be said to constitute "minorities" when their community populations are overwhelmingly Black and Brown. *Minoritized* captures (better than "minority") the ongoing political and social status that racializes Black and Brown individuals in predictable, frequently stereotyped, ways.

Following a similar definitional logic, we use "Brown" to denote collectively individuals of Latina/o descent. Recognizing that race as a social construct renders almost meaningless any facile categorizations of diverse people of mixed Indigenous/Native, African, and European ancestry as a discernible "race" (e.g., as "Hispanic or "White"), we have struggled with how to accurately and adequately refer to students and communities known variously as "Hispanic" and "Latina/Latino." For us, "Brown" captures the politically charged, racialized, and hybrid identities, characterized by sociohistorical phenomena that include race mixing (*mestizaje*), colonization, transnational migration, assimilation, and deculturalization. "Brown" further signifies a common origin from some combination of three distinct *raíces* or roots, (namely Indigenous/Native American, African, and European). Yet "Brown" as a marker for community and identity also involves more contemporary patterns pertaining to socioeconomic class, transnational status, performances of linguistic identities, and is tempered by gender and other identities. Every term that attempts to label and describe a diverse group of people has its limitations. "Hispanic," for us, overemphasizes linkages to colonial Spain while negating equal value to (or obscuring) African, indigenous, or other cultural linkages that are an integral part of identity for many Latinas/os. In our usage, "Brown" reflects the broader character of a Latina/Latino racialized identity in a highly race-conscious society that continues to reward and punish largely along the lines of skin color, even as we recognize that the intersectionality of systems of oppression based on other identity characteristics (such as gender, sexual orientation, and socioeconomic class) is operationalized simultaneously.

Given recent escalating tensions around immigration issues (and the concurrent surge of anti-immigrant legislation across the United States in both traditional and New Latino Diaspora states, most notably in Arizona, Nebraska, and Alabama), we have become particularly alarmed at the ways discipline and heightened surveillance play out in schools purportedly serving youth in the New Latino/a Diaspora. As members of the largest minoritized group in the demographically changing United States, Latina/ Latino or Brown youngsters currently face challenges in childhood and adolescence that threaten a pessimistic fate. Since today's youth represent our nation's future, and if that future is, in fact, becoming Browner demographically with each passing year, we believe strongly that schools must secure far better opportunities for students from all backgrounds, especially those in emerging Brown communities who, after all, will comprise the numeric majority in numerous cities and states in the not-too-distant future.

Focus of Inquiry

Drawing from data collected as part of a 2-year ethnographic study of a group of high school students embedded in a fairly recently emerged Latino/a Diaspora community in New England, this chapter discusses the discourses of containment, specifically as they target our Brown youth participants. The seven students who took part in the project were high school seniors by the time the study concluded:

- Alberto (Mexican American, age 18)
- Carmen (Puerto Rican, age 18)
- Jasmine (Puerto Rican, age 18)
- Natasha (Mexican American, age 18)
- Ramiro (Puerto Rican, age 19)

- Taína (Puerto Rican, age 18)
- Tamara (Puerto Rican & White, age 18)

Our chapter draws from students' experiences and *testimonios* to document the youths' interactions with various containment discourses and their relationship to the school-to-prison pipeline. In the spirit of Murillo (2002), we aim to call attention to the links between the pervasive nature of policies and practices aimed at containing Latinas/Latinos as a group with current events such as fear-driven national discussions of immigration and the growing presence of the prison system in the lives of Brown families. Of particular interest to us as teachers and teacher educators are those certain school practices involving the hypersurveillance of urban minoritized students. We explore how, when left unacknowledged by educators, inattention to containment discourses that directly affect Brown youth may contribute to students feeling distant from and uncared for by their teachers, which has been shown to be a critical influence on the school trajectories of many Latina/Latino students (Flores-Gonzalez, 2002; Valenzuela, 1999). We raise questions about the effects on Brown youth when teachers and administrators uncritically accept popular culture representations of issues pertinent to Latinas/Latinos, take up systematic surveillance, and participate in containment measures as part of their professional identities and responsibilities. Finally, we underscore the need for educators to critically analyze and interrupt the discourses of containment by rejecting the school-to-prison pipeline as the template for the education of minoritized youth. We call on fellow educators to stand steadfastly in solidarity with minoritized students and the communities in which they reside, and to strive for schooling that will help them achieve, rather than curtail, their youthful aspirations.

METHODS

Using critical race theory (CRT) in education (Ladson-Billings & Tate, 1995) and Latino/a CRT, otherwise known as LatCrit (Sleeter & Bernal, 2004) as analytic tools, our study highlights the racialized aspects of discourses of containment as well as the ways in which race and ethnicity interact with other identity markers to target Latinas/Latinos for discrimination. To that end, we employ the methodology of *counterstories* (Solórzano & Yosso, 2002; Yosso, 2005) or compelling narratives emerging from communities of color that challenge majoritarian discourses to foreground the voices of participants. In doing so, we critically examine the internalization (by teachers and students alike) of popular discourses of containment, and speak back to and challenge these oversimplified and problematic narratives that have become entrenched in the national imagination. We also draw upon *testimonios* (Delgado Bernal, 1998; Urrieta et al. [this volume]) as an innovative methodology that documents subaltern voices and perspectives embodied by the Brown youth student participants in our study.-

The seven student participants were part of a multiyear YPAR (Youth Participatory Action Research) project led by one of the authors (Jason Irizarry) in an urban high school in New England with a burgeoning population that is representative of the settlement patterns that characterize the New Latino/a Diaspora. While these high school students were recruited randomly, it so happened that 100% of the participants have had an immediate family member arrested and/or incarcerated. Based on the youths' perspectives—shared in focus groups, one-on-one interviews, and in students' journals—we developed *testimonios* that reflected the students' collective experiences. The collection of *testimonios* is a qualitative methodology emerging from the field of Latin American studies and gaining traction within LatCrit scholarship. *Testimonios* honor and affirm sources of knowledge that are often overlooked or delegitimized within academic research (Delgado Bernal, 1998; Urrieta et al. [this volume]) and "seek to disrupt the apartheid of knowledge in academia, moving toward educational research guided by racial and social justice for Communities of Color" (Pérez Huber, 2009, p. 640). We include *testimonios* as a form of counterstorytelling to document the voices of our Brown students as they confront the influence of the school-to-prison pipeline in their everyday lives. Crafted and narrated by the authors for a primarily academic audience, the *testimonios* nonetheless accurately reflect the voices and perspectives of the student participants. *Testimonios* were triangulated through review by the students, who assured us that, while perhaps not expressed in the exact language of youth, the *testimonios* nevertheless represent their lived experiences.

Theoretical Framework: LatCrit and Critical Race Theory

The discussions from which the *testimonios* emerged took place in a high school class led by Dr. Irizarry geared specifically for Brown high school juniors and seniors. As we witnessed a pattern of students confronting and naming racism as an influential factor that affects all aspects of their lives (including schooling), it became clear that we needed an analytical framework that spoke directly to race and racism while allowing for consideration of other interlocking systems of oppression, including sexism, heterosexism, linguicism, ageism, and classism. As a result, because of the ways we have observed and interacted with various groups of Brown high school students as they were being racialized both in and out of school, our research draws theoretically on both CRT and LatCrit. Our decision to adopt LatCrit as an analytic tool was influenced, in part, by the analysis of Christine Sleeter and Dolores Delgado Bernal (2004), who argued that multicultural education could be sharpened in three significant ways. First, they maintained that a focus on race and racism furthered the important anti-racist goals of critical multiculturalism, while forwarding an analysis of the intersections of racism with other forms of domination. They argued further that CRT could challenge hegemonic epistemologies and ideologies (e.g., notions of meritocracy, objectivity, and neutrality), pointing out the benefits of counterstorytelling as both a pedagogical practice and tool that could be useful in educational research (p. 245).

Our understanding of LatCrit traces its growth from CRT to address issues that were often previously excluded in CRT. LatCrit extends the scope of CRT to address how variables other than race, (including gender, class, immigration status, language, accent, ethnicity, and culture) intersect to shape the experiences of racialized peoples (Delgado & Stefancic, 1993; Yosso, 2006). LatCrit challenges the standard Black/White binary that tends to limit considerations of race and racism to the power relations between African Americans and European Americans, thereby creating more discursive space for Latinas/Latinos, who as a group typically span racial categories, as well as for individuals who may identify as multiracial or multiethnic. Such an expansion is crucial to understanding the complexity of the context enveloping Brown youth in schools today, while taking into account other intersections with culture and ethnicity.

We have been influenced by the work of scholars Daniel Solórzano and Dolores Delgado Bernal (2001) who forwarded five themes that underpin a LatCrit framework in education. Their work has pushed CRT toward a more specific focus on Brown contexts. These themes include: (a) the centrality of race and racism and intersectionality with other forms of subordination; (b) the challenge to dominant ideologies; (c) the commitment to social justice; (d) the centrality of experiential knowledge; and (e) the interdisciplinary perspective (pp. 312–315). These five tenets shaped all aspects of our study from data collection through analysis.

FINDINGS

Welcome to America: Legacies of Colonization and Imperialism

All that stuff on TV bothers me, about how immigrants are messing this country up. Everything you hear is about how we are bad people. But we work hard and just want a chance at the American Dream. My family came here from Mexico, true. But don't get it twisted: this country took over half of Mexico, now they act like we are foul because WE come here. I want what any kid wants, to go to college, make something of myself, get a good job to support my family. But we don't have the DREAM Act, so I have to pay out-of-state tuition, which is like three times the in-state rate. Even though I have lived here since I was 7 years old, I still don't have the same chances as everyone else. This makes it hard for all Latinos, regardless of their immigration status. So it is hard enough to graduate high school and go to college. Now because of my status—I don't have official papers—I don't have the chance to go to college. I just want a chance to contribute to this society. But it is clear to me that they really don't want me here. (Alberto)

Our perspective on containment as an ideology is informed by the history of intercultural contact during the expansion of the United States as a nation. Historians have has pointed out the significant use of nationalism to build unity during the first century and a half of the White nation-building project:

> American nationalism—our modern sense of ourselves as a national community—as well as American imperialism, marked a newly narrowed and deepened opposition between Americans and non-Americans, manifest especially in the Spanish-American War. The defeat of the last independent Indian nations as well as the official closing of the frontier with the 1890 census gave this rising nationalism a contiguous and continental geography. (Hale, 1999, p. 6)

Hale (1999) connects nationalism with nation building and imperialism, which we argue has significant implications for the containment of Brown youth, both today and historically. The annexation of much of Mexico after the Mexican-American War, the colonization of Puerto Rico after the Spanish-American War, and the containment of conquered Native tribes and nations under the newly implemented system of Indian reservations all speak to the historic strategic movement of peoples and the restructuring of boundaries in the service of American nation-building.

The legacy of colonization and imperialism has enduring effects on schooling, as well as on race relations. In 21st century U.S. popular culture, public representations of containment—the literal removal from society of young individuals who are first branded as criminals and then labeled and restrained as dangerous deviants—have become a source of both profit, as suggested by the economic success and viability of the prison industrial complex (Bowie, 2012), and even as entertainment, as evidenced by the rash of "reality" television programs and other dramas focused on walled-off social spaces. These media images of containment for the young include prisons, drug rehabilitation facilities, juvenile detention centers, and Homeland Security deportation centers. The media's current infatuation with televising the suffering of detained pariahs reflects society's acceptance of an increasingly punitive and incarceration-oriented culture, which, as predicted by Michel Foucault (Foucault & Droit, 1975), is indicative of the extent to which the panoptic model of surveillance and social regulation has invaded the national consciousness.

Running parallel to a steady diet of containment narratives that televise the punishment of "immoral outsiders" is a political discourse that has been fixated on the hot button issue of illegal immigration (Catalano, 2011), especially from the United States's immediate neighbor to the south, as a national problem of great urgency that is said to overwhelm local communities and schools. With the most tangible, visible solution offered being the construction of a hundreds of miles-long wall or fence along the U.S.-Mexico border along with the round-up and deportation of so-called illegals and their children (often without regard for the children's legal citizenship status), the national conversation has turned to *how*, not *whether*, to hold back the burgeoning Brown, Spanish-speaking masses that are "invading" the United States (Santa Ana, 2002).

"They Always Be Hawkin' Us:" Teachers Agents of Surveillance

The parallels between schools and prisons as institutions of control and behavior management are not lost on students. Whether they wind up suspended in school or out, Brown students describe feeling watched and excluded from school spaces that they perceive are reserved for Whites:

> *Teachers here always be hawking [watching] us. They like want you to mess up, so they can catch you out there and throw you into In-School Suspension. As soon as I walk into class, the teachers be looking for a reason to throw me out. They always think the White kids are doing good, but they be scheming. No matter how much I try, they always be on me. It's like... they just don't want Latinos here. (Alberto)*

In our previous work (Raible & Irizarry, 2010), we addressed ways in which teachers are encouraged, often in the name of accountability, to become agents of surveillance and behavior management. We also explored the potential for schools to become sites of youth resistance to heightened surveillance and the possibilities of a counter-narrative to the "expectation of incarceration" (Meiners, 2007) for youth that have been effectively written off as problem children. For example, Pedro Noguera (2008) describes how, in more and more urban schools, police officers, security guards, and administrators have taken on the role of managing and enforcing school discipline, while in most cases teachers actually initiate the discipline process by making referrals. Noguera points out how teachers, therefore, exert tremendous influence in determining which students receive discipline and for what reasons, thereby actually initiating many youth on the school-to-prison trajectory.

When students like Alberto feel watched and unwelcome, their negative perceptions are rooted in reality. For example, in her study of Chicago school reform policy and its effects on the regulation of urban youth, Pauline Lipman (2003) argued that reforms in that city "concretely and symbolically 'crack down' on African American and Latino youth who are seen as largely superfluous ... and dangerous in the racialized social landscape of the city" (p. 82). Lipman drew parallels between school accountability measures aimed at corralling minoritized youth, relating these to other efforts implemented throughout the city that were intended to make Chicago more attractive to tourists and high-paid managers, technical workers, and business services at the core of the city's economy (p. 83). Lipman's research helps connect the dots between social engineering schemes, racialization, and the experience of schooling in the minds of minoritized youths.

Thus far, we have advanced an admittedly somber argument to suggest that officially sanctioned surveillance of the young, including that carried out in the name of education, increasingly leads to containment, figuratively and literally. In our view, the physical and symbolic containment of Brown youth is related to the historic attempts to regulate or manage diversity (and to keep communities of color oppressed).

Educational research has indicated the ways in which ostensible efforts towards addressing the educational problems among various immigrant minority groups has, in fact, resulted in the maintenance of the political and economic subordination of the very communities educators claim to help (Spring, 2004). Building on this literature that documents the uses of schooling to manage youth populations viewed by ruling elites as threatening, troublesome, and undesirable, the experience of our student participants demonstrated how the discourse of containment marks contemporary Latina/Latino youths as hyper-racialized beings. Given such dynamics extant in today's society, students become acutely aware of the containment measures implemented to curtail their freedom of movement.

Research has documented the seemingly paradoxical finding that for many immigrant youths, their length of residence in the United States correlates with declining health, attitudinal, and educational outcomes (Portes & Rumbaut, 2006; Suárez-Orozco & Suárez-Orozco, 2001). For example, in their multimethod study of immigrant youths, Steinberg et al. (1996) concluded that "becoming Americanized is detrimental to youngsters' achievement, and terrible for their overall mental health" (pp. 97–98). A more recent study suggests that first-generation immigrants, those most recently arrived in the United States, tend to outperform their second- and third-generation schoolmates on measures of academic success and achievement (Hu-DeHart et al., 2008). While one might reasonably expect that living in the United States for a longer duration would result in future generations having increased access to social institutions, greater proficiency in standard English, and increased acculturation that could result in academic success, the converse is actually true, at least for non-White populations. This "immigrant paradox" suggests that the longer (generationally speaking) that immigrants remain in the United States, the worse their children and grandchildren perform in schools. The findings of these important studies find resonance in the lived experience of our Brown student participants.

> *My grandmother was born here. We have been here a long-time, but we still don't do good in school. English is my main language. I don't even speak Spanish ... the main language for a lot of my friends is English, but you don't see us on the honor roll and stuff. That's all White kids. (Carmen)*

Many Latina/Latino students are keenly aware of the ongoing controversy over immigration, exemplified perhaps most graphically by the recently erected fence between the United States and Mexico. Many young people took part in protests against the controversial Arizona law that ostensibly targets so-called illegal aliens and in advocacy efforts aimed at supporting the Dream Act. Brown students and families in the Southwestern United States in particular must anticipate being targeted by self-appointed vigilante groups as well as federal Immigration and Customs Enforcement (ICE) agents that patrol the border between the two nations, whether the families are documented, undocumented, or U.S. citizens. These efforts to forcibly target suspected "illegals" are not confined to *la frontera* (the border regions), but are visible in communities across the spectrum of the New Latino/a Diaspora, even those that are geographically distant from the long-standing Brown communities throughout the Southwest.

For example, in 2007, New Haven, Connecticut was the first city in the country to approve the establishment of resident identification cards, which would require individuals, regardless of citizenship or immigration status, to possess identification necessary to access services such as creating a bank account or securing a library card. Within 48 hours of the passage of the new law, federal ICE agents conducted raids across the community, arresting almost three dozen suspected "illegals." During the deportation hearings for several of those arrested, improprieties were brought to light that demonstrate the far-reaching grasp of efforts to intimidate and control Brown communities:

> [The immigrants] said in affidavits that agents barged into both homes after residents had opened their doors only a little.... Witnesses alleged in court

documents that parents were arrested in front of their frightened children, agents refused to identify themselves and told people in the homes to shut up. (Chris, 2009)

Reflecting on the ICE raids in New Haven, which incidentally is not far from the community in which our youth participants reside, one undocumented student offered the following observation:

> *Those raids made me feel like more petrified. I always live with that fear that they might come take me, my mother or father or somebody in my family. Then what? What can I do? That's why I gotta stay on the low sometimes. I was thinking about applying for college, but I gotta put a social security [number] in the boxes. What if they start asking me questions and stuff? You know if they did it in New Haven they can do it here. (Alberto)*

The progeny of undocumented immigrants are particularly vulnerable to the threats posed by containment, finding themselves enmeshed in debates over social benefits such as in-state tuition at institutions of higher education, access to health care, and even citizenship for the U.S.-born children of so-called "illegals." Such debates discursively rope in the hopes and dreams of hundreds and thousands of young people and can be said to represent the symbolic containment of Latina/Latino youth—and arguably the very future of the Diaspora.

For growing numbers of students, particularly those attending schools in urban areas that are personally involved with the penal system (whether because they have family members who are incarcerated or because they themselves are caught up in the bureaucracy of juvenile justice), containment plays out in practical experience through incarceration and other out-of-home custody placements. Ramiro shared a poignant story that relates the outcome of his arrest for the school fight described at the chapter opening. His *testimonio* speaks to the separation of children and parents, and the emotional toll that can take on Latina/o families:

> *I had to do three weeks in the work camp. When I saw my mother's face, that was hard. I wanted to cry. I work all the time to help her. But now I couldn't work ... and plus she had to see me like that. (Ramiro)*

The separation of children from their parents is one of the more poignant manifestations of the containment discourse that we have witnessed.

BUSCANDO AMERICA: "IS THIS WHY WE CAME HERE?"

Immigrant youth naturally become attuned to the prejudices and fears of the dominant host society. This may be particularly true for students of Mexican and Puerto Rican descent, the two largest ethnic groups within the Latino/a Diaspora. As members of colonized and racialized groups, students of Mexican and Puerto Rican origin inherit a legacy of collective treatment that is rooted in each sending entity's historical relationship to the United States, including the legacies of the slave trade and genocide against Native populations. In practical terms, this legacy plays out in the relationship between families and schools, and can be felt in the tensions between today's students and teachers.

Schools are often perceived as hostile to the aspirations of Latina/Latino families and communities. For example, educational research has demonstrated that many Latina/o students are acutely aware of their teachers' low expectations and furthermore, feel unchallenged by their school experiences (Carger, 1996; Romo & Falbo, 1996; Valdés, 1996). Other studies have shown that immigrant youth of color adapt quickly to the caste-like racialization model that persists in the United States (Bailey, 2001; Stepick, 1992; Waters, 1999). The findings from their Harvard Longitudinal Immigrant Adaptation Study (2001) revealed to researchers Carola Suárez-Orozco and Marcelo Suárez-Orozco that racism and anti-immigrant hostilities were recurring themes among immigrant youth. According to these researchers, such youth are highly aware that "many in the dominant culture do not like them or welcome them" (p. 98). This attitude was borne out among our students at Rana High School:

> *My family came here for a better life for us. But it is like they don't want us here. Because I don't have [citizenship] papers, it is like I am a criminal. I want to go to college but we don't have the Dream Act here [in my state]. I have to worry about* La Migra, *I have a hard time finding jobs, and I can't really go to college. I ask myself: Is this why we came here? (Natasha)*

Immigrant youth and other students of color typically attend schools that are more racially segregated today than they were 30 years ago (E. García, 2005). In addition, less money is spent on urban Latina/Latino students than on students in wealthier suburban schools (Nieto, 2004). In their lived experience, increasing numbers of Brown youth daily cross clearly delineated borders as they move between home, school, and work. Not only must they navigate symbolic boundaries erected through cultural and linguistic differences, but they inevitably find themselves being treated as "a foreigner, an alien, or an intruder" (E. García, 2005, p. 499).

Immigrant youth who entered U.S schools with positive aspirations often find their hopes diminished the longer they stay. Many urban students confront a "climate of insurmountable obstacles, cultural hostility, identity threats, and psychological disparagement" (Suárez-Orozco, Suárez-Orozco, & Doucet, 2004, p. 430). As students navigate the borders between home, neighborhood, and school, they are undoubtedly cognizant of the ways that their daily border crossings take place in a political climate in which institutions and practices that affect their lives, such as immigration, incarceration, and education itself, have become highly publicized and politicized.

CONCLUSION

I don't know what the big deal is. Isn't the United States a nation of immigrants? Then why are they hating on us so much? In Social Studies they talk all that.... Isn't this the supposed "land of opportunity" [making air quotes with her hands]? Hmm, I just want to get a good education and a good job and help my family, just like them. (Natasha)

In recent years, education has continued to garner substantial attention in public forums and policy debates, stretching from the federal government to local communities across the United States of America. Central to most of these conversations is concern over academic outcomes, as researchers, policymakers, and politicians alike have referenced the so-called "achievement" gap (we prefer *opportunity* gap [Carter & Welner, 2013; Ladson-Billings, 2000]) that exists between students of color and White students, between more affluent students and students from lower socioeconomic strata, and between native English-speakers and those who are learning English as an additional language. Because of their status as the largest and fastest growing group of minoritized students and their particularly sobering educational indicators, Brown students have increasingly become recipients of remedies intended to improve public education, with educators often locating the problem of underachievement squarely on the shoulders of youth, their families, and communities without any acknowledgement or understanding of the sociopolitical and sociocultural contexts in which efforts to educate youth—and Brown youth specifically—unfold (Irizarry & Raible, 2009; Stein, 2004). That is to say, the education of minoritized groups has never been a politically neutral undertaking (DuBois, 1903/2007). Schooling for minoritized communities historically reflects the ideologies and political needs of the dominant society (Spring, 2004).

Our analysis of the current ideology that we refer to as *containment* took as its starting point the premise that any relevant discussion about the education of Latinas/Latinos must take into account the increasingly polarized and racialized debate about the presence and very place of Brown people in contemporary U.S. society. Drawing on the experiences of students we know and teach, we advanced the metaphor of *containment* to explicate the ways in which education can be seen to serve the needs of powerful elites and self-appointed social engineers, rather than Brown students in pursuit of their own personal and collective aspirations.

As education researchers, our abiding interest is in understanding the sociopolitical context in which schooling occurs. We concur with one of the leading architects of multicultural education, Sonia Nieto, who has argued consistently that educators must develop a clear understanding of the sociopolitical context in which education takes place (Nieto & Bode, 2012). More specifically, our current research investigates the socialization processes affecting Brown students, particularly the children of recent immigrants who find themselves adjusting to life in the United States while being racialized in particular ways. We further concur with Banks and Banks (2007, p. 318), who asserted that the manner in which minoritized students are received by schools is directly related to the manner in which immigrants are treated by society. Banks and Banks stressed the importance, therefore, for educators to consider the ways in which immigrant populations are viewed and, as Nieto insists, to understand the sociopolitical realities in which their education takes place.

In our view, the emerging anti-Latina/Latino immigrant backlash circulating throughout the first decade of the 21st century represents the boiling over of deep-seated, historical antagonism between the colonizers and the colonized (Memmi, 1965), for example, unfinished contests over definitions of citizenship and national identity, that is, over who gets to be counted as an American. Moreover, the current political climate reflects growing majoritarian anxieties around recent shifts in the dynamics of U.S. race relations that culminated most visibly with the election of Barack Obama as the nation's first President who is a person of color. The backlash—summed up in the vitriolic political slogan *"We want our country back!"*—specifically targets visible immigrants, particularly those who are raced as Brown, and creates a climate that students and their families may perceive as hostile to their educational aspirations, if not their actual freedom of movement. We argue that such aspirations are effectively curtailed under an ideology of *containment,* which we link to the educational arm of a broader punitive "push-back" against Black and Brown advances in recent years.

Rather than emerging as a new-fangled, 21st century dynamic, containment historically has been a driving force in the nation's treatment of minoritized students as the nation's leaders and social reformers have responded to demographic diversity (see Joel Spring's [2004] illuminating history of the uses of schooling to suppress various racial groups in the United States). While containment may have worked effectively as a White supremacist strategy for managing diversity in the past, we call for today's educators to resist such outmoded and problematic approaches to meeting the needs of an increasingly diverse society by embracing an explicitly anti-racist approach that advances a more egalitarian and critical multicultural education that is more relevant to (and respectful towards) students and teachers in the 21st century (Pollock, 2008).

Teachers today should bear in mind that the sociopolitical context in which the education of Brown youth occurs is rooted in a protracted history of cultural clashes that have flared up periodically, beginning with the historic contest between European colonizers of the Americas. The conflicts between England, France, Spain and other European powers—not to mention the original indigenous inhabitants, who were overwhelmed by imported diseases, fire power, and heinous genocidal acts—underwrites the history of the present-day culture wars. In a real sense, current debates over the place of Brown people in U.S. society, reflected in controversies surrounding immigration reform, bilingual education, and English-only initiatives, represent the continuation of unresolved political conflicts about social and economic control of colonized territory. It is too simplistic to accept the majoritarian romanticized story of the "nation of immigrants," as if the nation's history is merely a pleasant commingling of diverse cultures, all of which arrived with open hearts and minds and a generosity of spirit, ostensibly to pursue religious freedom and economic security for their families. As a subaltern perspective of history reminds us, large parts of what is now the United States belonged to various nations for decades, if not centuries. The story of Brown people in America is not simply a tale of recent newcomers. It is a deeper and more complex story of intercultural conflict and conquest, of virtual winners and losers. In some communities, the conflicts rage on, if only on an emotional or ideological level. Families continue to struggle with issues of ethnic pride and identity, in which language issues and racial discrimination continue to weigh significantly. In this way, today's schools become the battleground for unfinished contests from the past.

To reiterate, the point of this chapter is simple and blunt: Containment has historically been a tool for the suppression and management of "undesirable" populations that have stood in the way of U.S. progress in the project of White nation-building. Containment is now manifest in New Latino Diaspora locales like it long has been elsewhere, even though it can be understood that containment often works at cross-purposes of today's educators, especially those who view education as a key to positive integration into the U.S. social order and greater access to the American Dream. Rather than the ideology of containment dissipating through some benevolent march of progress, our research shows how it continues to influence the larger social order with schooling a key venue for its operation. Indeed, containment takes on new twists and eerie manifestations that impact the educational achievement and life chances of the fastest growing minority group in the country.

Unfortunately, we do not think it is mere hyperbole to view the amalgamation of various measures of containment as an orchestrated response to what has come to be known as the "browning" of America, a phenomenon feared by some dominant elites as "the Hispanic challenge" (e.g., Huntington, 2004). Any discussion of educational failure and achievement among Brown youth that ignores the dynamics of containment is doomed to present an incomplete and ineffectual picture. It is our intention to shine a spotlight on the ways containment operates, from our students' perspective, to illustrate how it is often used against a growing youthful Brown population that is deemed potentially criminal and seen as threatening, undesirable, and needing restraint and tighter social control.

The question remains for educators to answer, both personally and collectively: *To what end do we educate the documented and undocumented Brown children who sit before us in new Latino/a Diaspora classrooms?* It is clear from listening to our student participants that discourses of containment weigh heavily on their minds and in their everyday realities. Involvement with the penal system is perhaps the most visible manifestation of containment as it plays out in our students' lives, but even those not formally chastised acknowledge both fears and skepticism of being contained and their faith that the system is for them is undermined. Narratives of containment in the media (even referencing events that physically occur on the other side of the country), such as debates over the DREAM Act, the border fence, Arizona's "papers please" law, vigilante justice, and ICE raids, all reinforce the feeling among Brown youth that they are unwelcome and unwanted. For educators to be effective with such populations, ignoring these realities and perceptions runs the risk of further alienating teachers from their students and making school irrelevant.

An explicit attention to anti-racism by incorporating student concerns into the curriculum is one way to address these issues. When teachers sensitively bring up topics that pertain directly to students' own lives and families, trust is engendered and stronger bonds of solidarity may be forged. As teachers exhibit a willingness to learn from students about the previously hidden aspects of their lives, the purpose of education and schooling can be reworked, with a clear agenda to interrupt the forces of domination and oppression that would render students mute and passive. But for this to happen, teachers must open their eyes and start paying attention to the shifting winds of popular opinion and specifically, to the rising tide of anti-immigrant sentiment among large sectors of the population. Teachers have the power to work to make sure that the education they offer speaks directly to the needs, concerns, and aspirations of students and their families. It is our hope that by working together, consciously and intentionally, that a more hopeful discourse that encourages, rather than contains, the ambitions of Brown youth may emerge.

We reject the template for racialization based largely on the historic treatment of African Americans and its current application to the burgeoning Latino/a Diaspora that would position Brown people as the "new Blacks."

As educators, we cannot stand by passively while schooling becomes an arm of the prison-industrial complex that is being used literally to contain and control increasingly diverse and potentially rebellious urban youth populations. The strength and prosperity of the nation's Browner future requires teachers to stand in solidarity with urban minoritized students and to steadfastly interrupt school-to-prison pipeline dynamics that criminalize far too many youth and squander their educational careers.

In conclusion, we have argued for a connection between the counter-stories and *testimonios* presented here and an emerging racist ideology of containment, particularly targeting Brown and other minoritized youth, combined with more generalized adult surveillance of youthful bodies and behavior in schools. We have pointed out the ways in which containment symbolizes the apparently preferred strategy promulgated by dominant social forces in response to the demographic "browning" of the United States. For newcomers in the New Latino/a Diaspora, the racialization they experience upon entering the hyper-racialized U.S. sociopolitical context runs the risk of potentially teaching youth their "proper place" at the bottom of the social hierarchy, effectively rewriting the American Dream narrative with a far from happy ending. The future we work to materialize through education must offer a brighter destination than simply life behind bars or in the threatening shadows of pending deportation.

REFERENCES

Bailey, B. H. (2001). Dominican-American ethnic/racial identities and United States social categories. *International Migration Review, 35*(3), 677–708.

Banks, J. A., & Banks, C. A. (2007). *Multicultural education: Issues and perspectives* (6th ed.) New York, NY: Wiley & Sons.

Bowie, N. (2012). *Profit driven prison industrial complex: The economics of incarceration in the US.* Montreal: Global Research. Retrieved from http://www.globalresearch.ca/profit-driven-prison-industrial-complex-the-economics-of-incarceration-in-the-usa/29109

Cammarota, J., & Fine, M. (2008). *Revolutionizing education: Youth participatory action research in motion.* New York, NY: Routledge.

Carger, C. L. (1996). *Of borders and dreams: A Mexican-American experience of urban education.* New York, NY: Teachers College Press.

Carter, P., & Welner, K. G. (Eds.). (2013). *Closing the opportunity gap: What America must do to give every child an even chance.* New York, NY: Oxford University Press.

Catalano, T. (2011). Xeno-racism and discursive construction of "us" vs. "them": Cosa Nostra, Wall Street, and immigrants. Unpublished doctoral dissertation, University of Arizona.

Chris, T. (2009). ICE Agents Conduct Illegal Raids in New Haven. Retrieved January 25, 2011, from Talk Left website at http://www.talkleft.com/story/2009/6/9/1435/57438 on

Davis, A. (1999). "Prison Industrial Complex" (compact disc recording). Alternative Tentacle. Original Release Date: December 14, 1999.

Delgado Bernal, D. (1998). Using a Chicana feminist epistemology in educational research. *Harvard Educational Review, 68,* 555–582.

Delgado, R., & Stefancic, J. (1993). Critical race theory: An annotated bibliography. *Virginia Law Review, 79,* 461–516.

DuBois, W. E. B., (2007). *Souls of black folks.* New York, NY: Oxford. (Original work published 1903)

Flores-González, N. (2002). *School kids/Street kids: Identity development in Latino students.* New York, NY: Teachers College Press.

Foucault, M., & Droit, R. P. (1975). Michel Foucault On the Role of Prisons. Interview by Roger-Pol Droit. Retrieved February 7, 2008, from http://www.nytimes.com/books/00/12/17/specials/foucault-prisons.html

García, E. (2005). *Teaching and learning in two languages: Bilingualism and schooling in the United States.* New York, NY: Teacher's College Press.

Hale, G. E. (1999). *Making Whiteness: The culture of segregation in the South, 1890–1940.* New York, NY: Vintage.

Hu-Dehart, E., Garcia, M., Garcia Coll, C., Itzigsohn, J., Orr, M., Affigne, T., & Elorza, J., (2008). *Rhode Island Latinos: Debunking myths & uncovering truths. Evidence from the New England Latino survey.* Providence, RI: Brown University, Center for the Study of Race and Ethnicity in America.

Huntington, S. (2004, March–April). The Hispanic challenge. *Foreign Policy, 141,* 30–45.

Irizarry, J. G., & Raible, J. (2009). As cultures collide: Unpacking the sociopolitical context surrounding English language learners. In H. R. Milner (Ed.), *Empowering teachers for equity and diversity: Progressive perspectives on research, theory, and practice* (pp. 95–115). New York, NY: Palgrave.

Ladson-Billings, G., & Tate, B. (1995). Toward a critical race theory of education. *Teachers College Record, 97,* 47–67.

Ladson-Billings, G. (2000) Racialized discourses and ethnic epistemologies. In N. K. Denzin & Y. S. Lincoln (Eds.), *Handbook of qualitative research* (2nd ed., pp. 257–278), Thousand Oaks, CA: Sage,

Lewis, T., & Vazquez-Solórzano, E. (2006). Unraveling the heart of the school-to-prison pipeline. In C. A. Rosatto, R. L. Allen, & M. Pruyn (Eds). *Reinventing critical pedagogy: Widening the circle of anti-oppression education* (pp. 63–78). Lanham, MD: Rowman & Littlefield.

Lipman, P. (2003). Cracking down: Chicago school policy and the regulation of black and Latino youth. In K. Saltman & D. Gabbard (Eds.), *Education as enforcement: The militarization and corporatization of schools* (pp. 81–101). New York, NY: Routledge Falmer.

Memmi, A. (1965). *The colonizer and the colonized.* Boston, MA: Beacon.

Meiners, E. (2007). *Right to be hostile: Schools, prisons, and the making of public enemies.* New York, NY: Routledge.

Murillo, E. G., Jr. (2002). How does it feel to be a problem? "Disciplining" the transnational subject in the New South. In S. Wortham, E. G. Murillo, & E. T. Hamann (Eds.), *Education in the New Latino Diaspora: Policy and the politics of identity* (pp. 215–240). Westport, CT: Ablex.

Nieto, S. (2004). *Affirming diversity: The sociopolitical context of multicultural education* (4th ed.). Boston, MA: Pearson Education.

Nieto, S., & Bode, P. (2012). *Affirming diversity: The sociopolitical context of multicultural education* (6th ed.). Boston, MA: Pearson Education.

Noguera, P. (2008). *The trouble with black boys and other reflections on race, equity, and the future of public education.* New York, NY: Wiley & Sons.

Orfield. G., & Lee, C. (2005). *Why Segregation Matters: Poverty and Educational Inequality.* University of California Los Angeles: Civil Rights Project/Proyecto Derechos Civiles. Retrieved October 10, 2012, from http://civilrightsproject.ucla.edu/research/k-12-education/integration-and-diversity/why-segregation-matters-poverty-and-educational-inequality/orfield-why-segregation-matters-2005.pdf

Pérez Huber, L. (2009). Challenging racist nativist framing: Acknowledging the community cultural wealth of undocumented Chicana college students to reframe the immigration debate. *Harvard Educational Review, 79*(4), 704–730.

Pollock, M. (Ed.). (2008). *Everyday antiracism: Getting real about race in school.* New York, NY: The New Press.

Portes, A.. & Rumbaut, R. G. (2006). *Immigrant America: A portrait* (3rd ed.) Berkeley, CA: University of California Press.

Raible, J., & Irizarry, J. (2010). Redirecting the teacher's gaze: Youth surveillance, teacher education, and the school-to-prison pipeline. *Teaching and Teacher Education, 26,* 1196–1203.

Romo, H., & Falbo, T. (1996). *Latino high school graduation: Defying the odds.* Austin, TX: University of Texas Press.

Santa Ana, O. (2002). *Brown tide rising: Metaphors of Latinos in contemporary American public discourse.* Austin, TX: University of Texas Press.

Saporito, S. (2007). Mapping educational inequality: Concentrations of poverty among poor and minority students in public schools. *Social Forces, 85*(3), 1227–1253.

Sleeter, C. E., & Bernal, D. D. (2004). Critical pedagogy, critical race theory, and antiracist education. In J. A. Banks & C. A. M. Banks (Eds.), *Handbook of research on multicultural education* (pp. 240–258). San Francisco, CA: Jossey-Bass.

Steinberg, L. D., Brown, B. B., & Dornbusch, S. M. (1996). *Beyond the classroom: Why school reform has failed and what parents need to do.* New York, NY: Simon & Schuster.

Solórzano, D. G., & Delgado Bernal, D. (2001). Examining transformational resistance through a critical race and LatCrit theory framework: Chicana and Chicano students in an urban context. *Urban Education, 3,* 308–342.

Solórzano, D. G., & Yosso, T. (2002). A critical race counterstory of race, racism and affirmative action, *Equity and Excellence in Education, 35*(2), 155–168.

Spring, J. (2004). *Deculturalization and the struggle for equality: A brief history of the education of dominated cultures in the United States.* New York, NY: McGraw-Hill.

Stein, S. (2004). *The culture of education policy.* New York, NY: Teachers College Press.

Stepick, A. (1992). The refugees nobody wants: Haitians in Miami. In G. J. Grenier & A. Stepick (Eds.), *Miami Now!* (pp. 57–82). Gainesville, FL: University of Florida Press.

Suárez-Orozco, C., & Suárez-Orozco, M. (2001). *Children of immigration.* Cambridge, MA: Harvard University Press.

Suárez-Orozco, C., Suárez-Orozco, M., & Doucet, F. (2004). The academic engagement and achievement of Latino youth. In J. Banks (Ed.), *The Handbook of Research on Multicultural Education* (pp. 420–437). San Francisco, CA: Jossey-Bass.

Tilton, J. (2010). *Dangerous or endangered? Race and the politics of youth in urban America.* New York, NY: New York University Press.

Valdés, G. (1996). *Con respeto: Bridging the distances between culturally diverse families and schools.* New York, NY: Columbia University, Teachers College Press.

Wald, J., & Losen, D. (Eds.). (2003, Fall). Deconstructing the school-to-prison pipeline. *New Directions in Youth Development: Theory, Practice, Research, 99.*

Waters, M. C. (1999). Sociology and the study of immigration. *American Behavioral Scientist, 42,* 1264–1267.

Yosso, T. J. (2005). Whose culture has capital? A critical race theory discussion of community cultural wealth. *Race Ethnicity and Education, 8*(1), 69–91.

Yosso, T. J. (2006). *Critical race counterstories along the Chicana/Chicano educational pipeline.* New York, NY: Routledge

CHAPTER 5

MIGRANTES INDÍGENAS PURÉPECHAS

Educación Bilingüe México-Estados Unidos[1]

Casimiro Leco Tomás

International migration between Mexico and the United States has a long and dynamic history, which has had different stages, as migration routes have changed throughout the years. Initially, the major states receiving immigration from Mexico were California, Arizona, and Texas. More recently, new routes have brought immigrants to states in the center and southeast of the United States (as identified by Wortham, Murillo, & Hamann, [2002]). This newer migration is identified as the "New Latino Diaspora" (NLD).

North Carolina is among the states receiving the new wave of Latino immigration (Murillo, 2002; Urrieta, Kolano, & O. Jo, [this volume]), Villenas, 2002). The important number of Latinos present in North Carolina makes it an interesting research site for this study. Considerable numbers of Purépechas, an indigenous group from Mexico, have migrated to parts of North Carolina, concentrating in the Appalachian Mountains.

In this chapter we focus on the education of the migrant Indian community of Purépecha, from the Mexican state of Michoacán, in regards of the state of North Carolina. We aim to analyze the ways in which education has affected the members of this community, their participation in a broader society, and their standing in a transnational context. For this study, "Indian" is defined as the people living in rural areas, speaking one of the 56, still-extant, Mexican, indigenous languages, exhibiting their own set of customs and national identity, although the focus is on just on the Purépecha.

One of the relevant elements of the Purépecha culture is its ethnic identity, which is particular not only on its folklore, but also on its structure, social organization, and understanding of the world. At various times, this identity has been questioned and challenged by the Mexican political system through its institutions. These Mexican institutions' exclusion and subordination of the Purépecha has resulted in resistance from the members of that community to various education policies from their government. Instead, the Purépecha have sought an education that is bilingual, highlights the worth of their culture, makes a case for their legitimate rights, and respects autochthonous culture and the preservation of their ethnic identity.

Even though Mexico has become a predominantly urban country in terms of where its population lives, a disproportionately high percentage of Mexican immigrants come from rural environments. The areas in which Mexico's Indian population lives often feature dire living and working conditions. From the total migrant population, 40% are Indians entering the American labor market. They get employed in activities related to farming, services, and construction. About 70% of these labor immigrants lack legal documentation (López, 2003).

According to figures from Secretaría del Migrante de Michoacán (SMM, 2011), there were 16 million Mexicans living in the United States at the beginning of the second decade of the 21st century; 3½ million were from *Michoacán* and 120 thousand were indigenous Purépechas. Among the latter, around 20% were school-age children.

The migratory route of Purépechas is a relatively new and has taken them to the southeast of the United States, although many of these families also have longstanding migration roots in the state of California. The formation of Purépecha communities that encompass U.S. geographies responds to particular historic, intergenerational, gender, and educational considerations. In the Southeast, the Purépechas have formed "transnational Indian communities" that trigger questions about little explored dimensions of the NLD.

The Purépecha communities express their traditions and customs in these environments as part of the ethnic identity that characterizes them in specific locations such as Bells, Tennessee; Foley, Alabama; Cobden, Illinois; Saint Louis, Missouri; Cornelia, Georgia; and Burneville and Oxford, in North Carolina. There are additional places, such as Reynolds, Oregon; Reading, Pennsylvania; and Battle Creek, Michigan, that are not included in this study but in which there are also Purépechas. The Purépechas are understood as a typical Mexican population by mainstream Americans, but that understanding is incomplete.

Upon their arrival in the United States, Purépechas coming from Mexico face issues in areas such as language and the education of their children. Children and parents encounter an education model different from the one in their rural sending communities, even more so if the schools they attended in Mexico were bilingual and they received transitional bilingual education in both Purépecha and Spanish (with Spanish understood as the second language). When such students arrive in the United States any native language support is only from Spanish to English. Although Mexico does have education programs that support Indian languages, these programs are insufficient to cover the education needs of all the Indian groups (Leco Thomas, 2009). In any event, the challenges of learning English and learning in English are significant for the Purépecha, and viewing Spanish language support as a nod to home culture can be complicated and misleading.

When the student becomes part of transnational migration, s/he encounters an environment that demands her/him to learn English. However, the language that prevails among Purépechas—even those in the United States—is Purépecha. Spanish is often their weaker and less-used second language. This scenario portrays the importance of finding bilingual programs in the United States that facilitate overcoming linguistic barriers and aspiring to a better quality of life for Purépechas. Some Purépecha migrant communities, such as Cherantzicurini and Quinceo (referencing their Michoacán sending communities) that have gone to Reynolds, Oregon, have had access to strong English as second language (ESL) programs that have obtained auspicious results. Unfortunately, not all the U.S. states in which Purépechas live have these programs (Marquez, 2010).

In order to facilitate the analysis, this chapter is divided in five sections: (1) *Indian migration from Michoacan in the United States*, in which this migration is set in context of contemporary international migration; (2) *Purépechas in the United States*, in which we look at the presence of *Purépacha* migrants "on the other side"; (3) *Education of migrant Purépechas*, in which we take a look at the stages of the education process for these migrant Indian communities; (4) *Purépechas in U.S. schools*, in which we try to represent the schooling experiences of the Purépechas in the United States; (5) *Binational migrant education: Mexico-United States*, which analyzes how education policies in Mexico address migrant communities in general and Purépecha Indians in particular due to their particular vulnerabilities.

Indian Migration From Michoacán In The United States

Mexican migration into the United States has a long historic tradition, which has been studied from different disciplines and approaches, focusing on specific aspects that have made emphasis on social and geographic issues, social networks, financial transfers, and education. Our interest is on the latter.

Mexico is an interesting country, with vast historic, cultural, geographic, and linguistic wealth. There are over 56 distinct Indian groups (Instituto Nacional de Estadística, Geografía e Informática, 2010). The social groups living in rural areas are Indians, *mestizos* (mix of White and Indian) and ranchero associations (Barragán, 1997). Of the 16 million Mexican migrants living in the United States (SMM, 2011), 85% came from semi-urban and rural municipalities (Herrera, 2011). The Indian population participating in the migration flow from Mexico to the United States is heterogeneous. Two of the groups with the best organization and largest representation in the U.S. are the Mixtecos and the Zapotecos from Oaxaca (Escárcega & Varese, 2004; Fox & Rivera, 2004; Rivera, 1999a, 1999b, 2000; Santos   Rufino, 2004). These groups are followed by the Náhuatl from Puebla, who are concentrated in the New York area, along with many *mestizo* Poblanos (Smith, 2004, 2006). Another Indian group is the *Purépechas* from *Michoacán*, who have settled mostly in the Southeast of the United States (Anderson, 2004, 1999; Leco Thomas, 2009; Martínez, 2001), although several communities' presence in Oregon and Illinois has already been noted.

The indigenous population in the state of Michoacán is composed of four ethnicities, which inhabit four geographic regions: the Mazahuas and the Otomíes in west, the Náhuatl on the coast, and the Purépechas in the center-north, with Purépechas the most numerous (Índice de Desarrollo Humano-Michoacán [IDHM], 2008). The Purépecha región is divided in four subregions: The Eleven Villages' glen, the Zacapu's marsh, the Lake Patzcuaro basin, and the Sierra Purépecha. The characteristics of Purépecha migration vary according to the local history, social networks, and routes of each subregion. Nowadays, there are communities that feature national migration patterns only, other communities combine national and international flows, and others migrate almost only internationally. This study focuses primarily on the Sierra Purépecha region since it hosts the highest concentrations of Purépecha population, the most Purépecha language speakers, and a high percentage of international migrants in the United States (Leco Thomas, 2009).

The main activities in the Purépecha region are seasonal agriculture, forestry, craft manufacturing, bricklaying, livestock, "street vending," and self-employment. Families alternate two or three of these activities in order to balance their budgets, although thousands of families rely 100% on the financial remittances from relatives in the United States (López, 1999, 2000, 2003). High rates of unemployment, poverty, illiteracy, health issues, and lack of housing are prevalent in this region, as are high migration rates to the United States. Drug-trade related violence has also landed Michoacán in international news (e.g., Zabludovsky, 2012). All of these are causes of dropping out of school. The situation of the schooling system in Michoacán is so contentious and controversial that nowadays one can find "phantom" schools in which there are no students present but only a list with student names in order to justify the salary of the teacher and by this means keep alive disputes of power among rival teacher union factions. These "phantom" schools are found in towns such as Gómez Farías (López & Gómez, 2003), Patamban, Urapicho, Nurio, Cochudo, and Cherán (Leco Thomas, 2009). This list is not exhaustive; these inconsistencies are widespread across the state.

Although school dropout rates are heightened due to migration to the United States and education is far from cutting-edge (IDHM, 2008), the government has a long, if intermittent, tradition of caring about bilingual and Indian education (Sáenz, 1936). The Purépecha region has been an implementation site for pedagogic experimentation projects such as the Carapan in 1932 and Tarasco in 1939, which introduced Purépecha-speaking indigenous students to the Spanish language (Maldonado & Leco Thomas, 2008). Nowadays, the Ministry of Education (Secretaría de Educación Pública, [SEP]), via the corresponding offices of SEE (Subsecretaría de Educación, [SEE]) in Michoacán and the Office of Indigenous Bilingual Education (Departamento de Educación Indígena Bilingüe), attends to the educational needs of the Indian groups. The main goal of this effort is to provide education to the Indian communities, teach their mother tongue, and rescue their culture. For this purpose, teachers are prepared in a special program offered by the Escuela Normal Indígena de Michoacán (Leco Thomas & Tehandón, 2008).

Education and migration are closely related in the region we are studying. Some school dropouts have been due to emigration, but it is also tied to the circular flow of children between schools in Mexico and the United States. Additionally, many youth show just moderate enthusiasm for schooling, since the established course of action in the local culture is to "travel north."

The dire situation of the job market has been another cause of emigration in this region. Low salaries, bans on various forms of forestry activities, the low profits on farming, the lack of markets to sell their crafts, and, above all, the way in which the social networks have strengthened around migration are enduring features of the local environment.[2] The perceptions of schooling as too lengthy and its benefits (if any) as too delayed are related to economic, cultural, and educative considerations.

In the Purépecha community, "traveling north" is often perceived as a sign of manhood in similar ways as getting married. It is a means to take on family responsibilities, such as childbearing, to get a job to pay to build a house, to take religious leadership positions in the community, and to continue with the family tradition of migration (Leco Thomas, 2009). The emigration of Purépechas to the North includes men, women, elders, children, and whole families with little distinction of social status, education level, religious or political affiliations and documentation status (Leco Thomas, 2003).

Purépechas in the United States

It was since 1990 when scholars started to note that indigenous people were also part of the international migratory flow and that they were entering the United States in increasing numbers. Since then, their presence in the United States has acquired growing importance (SMM, 2011) in the literature about Mexican international migration (Leco Thomas, 2011) as their migration became more organized by families and even entire communities.

However, the origins of Purépecha migration can be traced back to the Mexican Revolution (1910) and its aftermath (the 1920s). At that time, there were only sporadic cases of migration. It was not until "Programa Bracero" (1942–1964), which focused on recruiting agricultural workers from specific regions of Mexico, that migrant numbers grew considerably (Cardoso, 2010). Once this program ended, American policymakers expected migration to stop, but Purépechas continued traveling to the United States.

Purépecha out-migration from rural Michoacán increasingly combined both national and international patterns. While some emigrated from their communities to Mexico's cities, others ventured to the United States. In 1986, the U.S. Immigration Reform and Control Act (IRCA) allowed many the opportunity to regularize their migratory status. Those who could benefit from this law then brought their relatives to the United States (who began a process to regularize their status too). The emigration boom in the Purépecha region went on from approximately from 1990 to the mid-2000s. However, the economic crisis in the United States and related anti-immigrant laws have slowed flows since 2008 (Leco Thomas, 2009).

The routes of the Purépecha migration in the United States can be examined by the states they have chosen as destinations: (1) the first states in which migrants settled in were California, Texas, and New Mexico. These states are considered historic or traditional by the literature on migration (Hamann & Harklau, 2010). But many of those who have lived for decades in these states have moved in the last few years to the Southeast and they have been joined by more Purépecha migrants directly from México. Hence new regions have been configured as destinations for Mexican migration (Durand, 2004). (2) This includes states such as Kentucky, Tennessee, Illinois, Missouri, Louisiana, Alabama, Mississippi, Oklahoma, Florida, Georgia, North Carolina, and South Carolina (Anderson, 1999). A majority of migrants in these states are considered "the new migrants", since this may be their first trip into the United States. (3) A third group of "new states" attractive to Purépechas includes Oregon, Wisconsin, Ohio, New York, Nevada, and Washington; and finally (4) Alaska and Canada are sites where migrants go for seasonal jobs and under contract (Leco Thomas & Hernández, 2011).

Purépechas have been employed in the United States in farming, services, and factories. An important portion is concentrated in pine plantation and logging, tobacco, tomatoes, cucumbers, potatoes, sweet potatoes, peaches, apples, and citrus. Other migrants have found employment in restaurants as dishwashers and cleaning staff, plus gardening, fabric mills, food production, and road and building construction (Leco Thomas, 2009).

A majority of Purépechas come from rural agricultural environments and have settled in rural areas in the U.S. Southeast. Their identification with their destination areas includes geographic reasons and due to considerations related to culture and social networks with Purépechas from other communities. The Purépecha community has added, if modestly, to the growth of Latino population in this region of the United States. A majority of the newcomer Latinos were males (63%) and young, with an average age of 27. More than a half of them were born in other countries (57%), did not complete high school (62%), and do not speak English (57%) (Ikeda, 2005).

There is still little research on the "New South" of the United States and the presence of Latinos in these areas (Hamann, 2003; Henken, 2006; see also Allexsaht-Snider, 2002; George, 2006; Hamann, 2002; Murillo, 2002; Villenas, 2002; and Zúñiga et al., 2002 from the original *Education in the New Latino Diaspora* book; and Adair, this volume; also see López, 2006; George, 2006; Harklau & Colomer, this volume; Lynn, this volume; and Urrieta et al., this volume). Writing more holistically about Mexican diaspora populations in new U.S. locations, Robert Smith (2004, p. 88) wrote:

> [T]here can be another 300,000 Mexicans living on the outskirts of the city, in New Jersey, Connecticut, and the suburbs of New York. The agricultural industries of the East Coast—from the fields of mushrooms in Pennsylvania, the chicken processing plants of the Delmarva Peninsula, the tomato harvest near the Canadian border, the peach cutting in Athens, Georgia—now rather depends on Mexican labor.

Census experts estimate that in the near future Latino populations will form the largest minority on the East Coast.

The state of North Carolina makes for an interesting site for this study. This state has attracted an important number of Latinos—Purépechas from Michoacán among them–who have found relatively favorable life and work conditions for them to prosper. North Carolina has strong historic connections with the African American community and has gone through civil rights struggles for African Americans, Appalachian Whites, Latinos, and American Indians. These groups now engage in constant disputes over territory, the labor market, and recreational spaces. Although anti-immigrant laws have tightened in North Carolina, the Purépechas continue in their effort to thrive there (Leco Thomas, 2009).

It is precisely in this context that Purépechas have formed a "transnational community" according to Glick-Schiller who defines "transnational space" as:

> the construction of a social space that connects places geographically discontinuous located in more than one nation-state by trans-migrants who live their lives in fragmented ways. In other words, trans-migrants have interests, acquire responsibilities, make decisions, and keep connections of varied nature that transcend national frontiers. (Glick Schiller, Basch, & Szanton Blanc, 1992)

In these "new destinations" (Zúñiga & Hernández-León, 2005), in the mountains of North Carolina (e.g., Burnsville, Spruce Pine, Newland, Boone), the Purépechas have been recreating traditions, customs, and their ethnic identity through civic, religious, and cultural representations.[3] In this environment, which shares the cooler highlands weather of their native Michoacán, they learn local ways to work the fields and exploit the forest. This is also a "redistribution" site for "new migrants," who are brought from Mexico to their "new homes" by the "coyotes," who charge U.S.$3,500 for each trafficked person.

The cost of living in this region is much lower than other U.S. locales. When we mention Purépechas living in these areas, we often refer to whole families. However, we do not have accurate information on how many they are because there are no figures in either Michoacan's Migrant Registry or the National Institute of Migration in Mexico or the United States' census.

However, we know about their presence by social networks, financial remittances, and transnational links (Anderson, 2004).

In these new locations, some migrants have accessed work permits, drivers licenses, insurance, and identifications, even though many are undocumented. Correspondingly, many migrants take on piecework or are employed through seasonal contracts and they are in constant fear of being detained by immigration enforcement. It is quite a novel experience for those just arriving from Mexico, but those who have lived in the U.S. for a while are more familiar with it.

The idea of clustering together in one place is protective, but also supports socializing, sympathizing, and sharing their culture with other members of the ethnic group. The so-called "mountains" are famous and familiar among the Purépecha community. They have become an imagined part of the community even for those Purépechas who live in Mexico and who have never traveled outside their communities, let alone to the 'mountains' of North Carolina. These Purépecha are able to create meaning from the discourse that they hear from their migrant relatives around the celebrated and boasted about "El Norte."

Transnational communities are generated among sites situated in distinct geographic areas (i.e., one community with multiple locations). As elaborated by Guerra (1998), these are places that, in spite of geographic distance, remain intrinsically related and connected with country, family, and everything that happens in the native town via phone, computer, and written communication.

Education of Migrant Purépechas

In order to understand the education of Purépecha migrants in the United States, it is necessary to review the history of migration, as well as considerations of gender, generational relations, and education level of the migrant population. I obtained such information from fieldwork in several places with people native to the region. This work reviewed the following five periods: The first stage included migrants who began their adventure during the Mexican Revolution (1910–20), the postrevolution, or during "Cardenismo" (1928–1940) when Michoacán's own Lázaro Cardenas dominated Mexican national politics. The formal education level of these migrants was almost nil, having completed the second grade at the most. The second stage (1943–1964) includes those who participated in the "Bracero" Program. Although they were still few, those fortunate ones who attended school typically made it only to about fourth grade. The third stage begins at the end of the "Bracero" Program and goes on until before

IRCA. These migrants usually had completed their primary education and often had begun their secondary education (i.e., *secundaria*, grades 7–9).

The last two stages correspond to migrants with higher education achievement. The fourth began after IRCA and extends until present. Since then, the education level has grown progressively among migrants; almost all read and write; almost all have completed *secundaria* (which has been mandatory in Mexico since 1992), and many have at least some years of *preparatoria* (high school). Finally, the last stage corresponds to the small percentage of Purépecha migrants who attended college or even earned a degree in Mexico but still decided to emigrate. I call this sector "qualified human capital."

As seen, changes in education of migrant Purépechas has been slow and in correspondence with the larger economic, social, and cultural conditions. Presently, the education of migrants acquires a new level of complexity due to a new migrant sector. At the end of the 1990s, people with university degrees, who did not find employment opportunities in their places of origin increasingly found an outlet for that conundrum in emigration to the United States.

This human capital, upon arrival to the United States, encounters difficulties to realize its professional and academic potential because of language barriers, legal status, cultural misunderstandings, and lack of information about how to access professional opportunities. They are unaware of how the American education system works, how binational programs operate, and what government agencies and educational organizations can best provide them with advice on how to navigate the system to validate their foreign credentials.

This flow of 'human capital' represents an important loss for Mexico, since the investment on the education of these professionals goes out from the country with them. This is a consequence of a political system that has been unable to keep up with the expectations of the college graduates and young professionals. Emigration and school dropout rates have direct consequences for Mexico. The education provided to each individual has a cost that sees little return in the local economy if that educated person then leaves (Cruz, 2011). Although the migration of youth may well be inherently related to social networks for family reunion, there are also cultural considerations that need to be taken into account. The idea of migration to the United States as an opportunity to accumulate faster symbolic and representative capital is well established among members of Indian communities.

Gender roles are strongly defined in Michoacán's Purépecha region. Indian women truncate their career aspirations at the moment they marry a "migrant" and a few months after they are taken to the United States. This is coherent with local rituals in which the wife is to obey the decisions of her husband because it is part of the custom (Jacinto, 1988). This is a long-standing mindset that is well established in the Indian community, albeit subject to change like gender norms all over the world (e.g., Villenas, 2002).

Although the Purépecha region has options for youths to continue their education, many of them prefer not to do so and they head instead to the United States. Local environmental factors such as "gossip culture" and the effect of social networks test the resilience of the individuals. Initially, one of the goals of the Michoacán state government in order to counter the migratory exodus was—in collaboration with local authorities and education leadership—to create more seats in more higher-level schools. Participating institutions include the Instituto Tecnológico Superior Purépecha, Escuela Normal Indígena de Michoacán, Universidad Indígena Intercultural de Michoacán y Universidad Pedagógica Nacional (Leco Thomas & Tehandón, 2008). Although an assortment of higher education institutions have been prepared to provide bilingual education, emigration continues.

In her study of divided families, Dreby (2010) recounts that dozens of parents from Oaxaca, who live in the United States, are interested in encouraging their children in Mexico to study. A similar phenomenon occurs in the Purépecha region; parents in the U.S. whose children are being raised in Mexico by grandparents or other relatives are more and more interested in making their children study. This interest could be explained as a compensatory measure to their own migration; as a way to reduce the likelihood that their children will have to leave their country. At a young age, children from these divided families take on social responsibilities, such as attending community assemblies, conducting fundraisers for local festivities, caring for property and protecting the honor of the family. Of course many of these same youths are just waiting to complete the obligatory education, to becoming legal-age adults, and then to leave to the United States.

Other youth from divided families do not go to school, or, if they do, it is irregularly. They feel a lack of affection, love, and motivation from their away-from-home parents. They are vulnerable to dropping out, emotional volatility, alcoholism, drug addiction, gangs, disturbing the social order, and marrying at very young ages (López, 2003).

When a young married couple from the Purépecha region makes the decision to emigrate, they normally do so without legal documentation. Being underage, they find it difficult to get a job; the American education system requires them to be in school and they even have to hide their married status otherwise they would face legal punishment. Early youth weddings are common in Indian communities. Within their communities, the wedded couple is free to act upon their roles as spouses and even parents. This behavior is not penalized, but instead is consistent with the custom from an early age to teach boys and girls different household and job-related activities as preparation for when they decide to get married. However, in the United States, marital roles may change and the young couple has to abide by the laws that mandate them to attend school.

Purépechas in U.S. Schools

The Purépecha community established in the 'mountains' (of North Carolina) has an important presence in local schools. Unfortunately many of the children have limited language skills not only in English but also in Purépecha and Spanish. Children find themselves struggling to overcome proficiency issues in both home and school languages, and schools struggle to communicate with students and parents because they lack Purépecha-speaking interpreters. This contributes to some Purépecha parents feeling uncomfortable attending school meetings, and these same parents often find it difficult to orient and support their children with their homework as the children advance grades in school.

In spite of these challenges, since 1990 it is becoming slowly more common to hear in Purépecha towns of Mexico of children of these emigrants graduating from a university in the United States. For the Purépecha community, college graduation from a Mexican university represents a great achievement not only for the individual but also for the community. These individuals are even highly regarded by their peers because their achievement brings prestige and safety to themselves and their families, as well as the possibility to access better conditions of work and living. However, parents prefer their children to graduate from a U.S. university, so this is even more highly regarded. However, college education is still quite difficult to access and graduation is a rare achievement.

Many Purépecha youth truncate their studies because of their undocu-mented status, the high costs of college tuition, and/or the cumbersome college admission processes. Like many Mexican communities in the U.S., many Purépecha are aware of the proposed DREAM Act that would allow those who migrated to the U.S. as children to attend college as part of a pathway toward residency (Pérez, 2012). However, they are also aware that as of this writing (in 2014) that is still unrealized. The lack of access to college has pervaded into the culture of these communities. In interviews with migrants some have explained:

> No, that's not for us; it is too difficult to attend college. It requires too much money, loans from the bank, and many years of work just to pay back. It is better to get a job and make money right away so one can buy whatever one wants, such as a car, and build a house in the town. Moreover, I have

many little siblings after me and one has to help the parents. (Migrant in Burnsville, N.C., 2006)

That excerpt shares just a few of the reasons this interviewee had for not pursuing higher education. Additional explanations related to not having financial means to pay for courses, the limited education attainment level of their parents, and the ways these influence goals about their children's education. Youth, when they come of age, are expected to get a job to help their family. They are expected to get married and start a family of their own. In this cultural scenario, it seems more logical to work instead of investing years in a university degree. Smith (2004, p. 101) acknowledges that messages can be contradictory:

[Youth] are overwhelmed—even insecure—in a school where they don't speak English. Moreover, they see the dire economic situation of their family and they know their parents started working when they were adolescents. Then the pressure they feel for giving up school and beginning to work is too strong, and at the same time perhaps they feel that if they give up they would be betraying the dream of their parents who are eager to have their children succeed in school.

From a different angle, the education of Purépecha migrant women in the United States is different than the one found in their towns in Mexico. As documented by Wortham (2002) on his investigation of Mexican immigrants in a rural community in the northeastern United States, women were more likely to continue studying and graduate from high school and head to college. In North Carolina, gender differences were not as rigid as in the traditional Purépecha communities.

In the United States, female students show a significant advantage over male school-age youth. They perform better academically, advancing to higher grades and becoming more likely to graduate from college. Gender is a relevant consideration in school achievement. Purépecha girls may be more likely to complete their homework because their activities after class are supervised more closely and/or because they have to spend more time at home in order to help looking after their siblings while adults are away working.

Although the idea that children are better off preparing themselves for studying in a university in the United States is well established among Purépecha parents and caregivers, it is also true that these adults believe that once their young find their way in the American system, they will not want to go back to Mexico anymore. They believe that as young Purépechas learn a new style of living from that one of their parents and community, they would also find it more difficult to insert themselves in the Mexican labor market. These youth might distance themselves from their families and marry outside of their community. So worried parents have cause to articulate the "myth of return" (Cortina, 2004, p. 66; Espinoza, 1998) which refers to the fact that, for the first years after migrating to the United States, both parents and children keep the attachment to their language and local customs and they keep alive the hope of returning to their land as soon as possible. For this reason, parents raise their children in the United States with the same norms and cultural beliefs current in Mexico

Consistent with "the myth of return," some Purépecha families decide to send their children back to be schooled in Mexico even if they have been born in the United States. Sometimes this choice is explained by the intention of preventing their children from learning bad habits from the Anglo-Saxon culture. The presence of these youth in Mexico can also be a familial strategy to help to take care of the grandparents, the house, and/or the family's responsibilities to their home community. These youth, then, become representatives of the family and take on political and religious responsibilities on behalf of absent adults. But the stay, even temporary, of these children in Mexico can be a significant step backward for their education. If these children come back to the United States, they have to readapt to the environment, catch up in English, and navigate various curricular discontinuities. Worse, although these children often need special programs to allow them to achieve age-level proficiency, the English language support programs and specialized teachers are concentrated in elementary education. In turn, the English language infrastructure that does exist in secondary schools has to meet the challenge that academic language use in these higher grades is more advanced. Meanwhile, these secondary students routinely change classrooms and teachers five or more times per day (because of the specialization of the teachers).

On this topic, one Purépecha parent told us about his fears and concerns about the future of his child:

> My son Adriel was born there in *El Norte*. He is fifteen years old. When he attended school there [in the U.S.], he spoke English well, but since we spent the last eight years here [in Mexico] he has forgotten already. We would like to return, but we don't have documentation and there is no way to send him by himself although I wish there was so he could learn English and be there with my in-laws. He doesn't want to leave us, … but I anticipate that he is going to suffer a lot when he decides he wants to go and goes to school there when he is more grown up. (Parent in Cherán, Michoacán, 2007)

In contrast with the experiences of migrant parents living in the United States and sending their children to their hometowns in Mexico, Mr. Ariel was concerned about the reverse situation, that the destiny of his son born in the United States but enrolled in Mexico would face problems should he return to American schools in the future.

The Purépecha migrant community of North Carolina allows us to realize how complicated it can be for parents and teachers to make informed decisions about the education of their young. The experience of Purépecha parents with the American education system begins when they need to find a school for their children to attend. They quickly find that they need to find interpreters, since they don't know how to communicate in English in order to complete the paperwork. Through these mediators (who may know little or nothing about the Purépecha language or particular ways), the parents then learn about the problems of social, cultural, economic, psychological, and pedagogic nature that need to be overcome. Sometimes they learn about racism and discrimination against the undocumented Mexicans and Indians. Even then,

> The school system in the United States presses on the students to integrate socially and culturally in the American "ways of living" and forces them to deny their national identity and language. Therefore, those born in Mexico are frequently left out from of both curricular and extracurricular activities in public schools. The cultural environment of most schools does not encourage the vindication of cultural identity or the custom of using the mother tongue. (Cortina, 2004, p. 66)

Binational Migrant Education: Mexico-United States

The children of migrants who travel from one place to another have learned to move on both sides of the border, to experience geographies simultaneously or first one space and then another, to compare schools and curriculum plans, pedagogies, educational environments, and assessments, to study the history of each country, and, alas, to assimilate racism which often subordinates them.

The expectations of immigrant students in American schools are expressed in different ways. To this end,

> Newcomer students who do not speak English are classified, separated, and provided with inadequate materials and inconsistently trained teachers, and [they] are denied access to basic subjects content. Despite feeling more Americanized, they remain separated and poorly served due to their race and their native language. (Cortina, 2004, p. 69)

Fortunately programs have been created that support this vulnerable sector of society, that try to educate parents, teachers, and students that the children of migrants have certain rights and responsibilities so that they can send their children to school during their stay in Mexico. The children who cross the border have the opportunity to join one of the schools participating in the Programa Binacional de Educación Migrante (PROBEM) in Mexico (Estudio Binacional, 1999; Leco Thomas, 2006). Michoacán's educational system, based on a memorandum of understanding signed in August 1990 by the U.S. Department of Education and the Secretariat of Public Education (SEP) of Mexico, offers the possibility to register the children of migrants in some entry-level school either primary or secondary.

The Binational Program of Migrant Education (PROBEM) was born in the state of Michoacán with the idea of supporting families that continually move between Mexico and the United States. There are two main purposes of this program: (1) to ensure the continuity of the educational processes of students who move between the two countries, providing support to integrate schooling even within a school-year, also providing advice and course credit during the winter holiday period, and (2) to strengthen social and educational relations between Mexico and the United States through the exchange of academic and cultural experiences with teachers and students from both countries (Jara, 2007, p. 179). In Michoacán there were approximately 5,000 binational children and about 2,000 Purépecha children facing this situation as of 2010 and their stories were similar (Leco Thomas & Hernández, 2011). However, PROBEM was working more and harder in states like California than in the new destinations of Latinos like North Carolina.

CONCLUSIONS

The social phenomenon of international migration between Mexico and the United States is an interesting field for analysis. Although it has been approached from different perspectives, there are still areas where it has not been studied in depth. One essential example of where further research is needed is the case of education of the Indian migrant population in a global context. Explanations of the education achievement of this population have to do with the migration waves, with the socioeconomic and cultural conditions in which they live, and with the educational profile of parents and caregiver. The inadequate education of adults limits their ability to support the participation of children in school, diminishes their interest on attending school meetings in both Mexico and the United States, and affects their perceptions of study as means to ensure prosperity.

The vision about education of migrant children has been gradually evolving in Mexico, where now it is now largely understood as desirable that children attend school. However, some factors still affect Purépecha students negatively, such as having to share the school year between Mexico and the U.S. schools as part of binational migration patterns. Students face different approaches to pedagogy, content, and curricula and have to deal with additional problems such as inability to understand English, feelings of neglect, and even discrimination by the teacher in the classroom. Above all these problems, Purépecha students have to deal with racism in both U.S. and Mexican contexts.

Although migrants are increasingly interested in having their children study, some parents prefer to send their child back to Mexico despite being born in the United States. They do so in order to minimize the costs and care of their grandparents and sometimes to avoid perceived temptations and hazards in the United States. Parents following this strategy anticipate that once their children grow up, they can come back to continue studying in the United States. But this trajectory brings a host of problems for the student, such as substantial school disparities between the two countries, not being on grade level according to their age, and difficulties in adapting and integrating to school life. Children who come to the U.S. for the first time from Mexico face similar issues as those who return as adolescents. Conversely, the children of migrants who remain in Michoacán show a clear disregard for further study, showing negative attitudes and disobeying the rules, reaffirming their interest in migrating to the U.S., and continuing the family tradition of the social network.

In Mexico, the most difficult period to overcome for youth is when they are in middle and high school, due to issues of age, culture, and their socioeconomic condition. Those who manage to succeed during this stage can access top-level schools to get a degree. However, once they graduate in Mexico, limited job prospects restrict where they can grow professionally. Only a small share manages to find a job with career prospects. Others find migration to be the solution to their pressing tribulations.

Many migrants arrived to the United States, including Indians of Michoacán, needing services such as education. It would be important for the U.S. school system to recognize the growing population of Mexican and Mexican-American students and to try to understand their situation (Urrieta, 2010). A course of action to consider would be to create and promote more bilingual programs for the migrant community in order to better serve this sector, which remains vulnerable.

A quick look at the education of children of Purépecha migrants in the mountains of North Carolina reveals that there are no adequate programs for these students to acquire English as a second language. They attend a variety of schools. Teachers and authorities are already aware of this situation. Parents and students are interested on the possibility of Mexican teachers who can support them. However, PROBEM has not arrived there yet (Villalva, 2006; Zúñiga, 2006).

The analysis above has exposed the situation of the Purépecha Indian migrant community from Michoacán, Mexico. The scenario described has many similarities with those in which other increasingly binational Mexican Indian groups live, although under particular conditions and in different geographical areas of Mexico and the United States. Of course it takes a lot of effort and resources to conduct research, design plans, and implement programs around education of migrants. It is imperative that these efforts increase in order to implement public policies that strengthen and care for this migrant society sector in Mexico and in the United States.

NOTES

1. This chapter was originally written in Spanish. In recognition of that fact we have left the chapter title in that language. In translation, the title would be: "Indigenous Purépecha Migrants: U.S./Mexico Bilingual Education."
2. The importance of the role that networks play in the maintenance of migration in most migrant communities is well known, especially in support and solidarity for new migrants (Durand, 1994). Once the migration process begins, the social ties between communities of origin and of destination grows and expands to form real networks of relationships, which ultimately reduce the risks and costs (economic and psychological) associated with undocumented migration (Cortina, 2004).
3. In Burnsville, NC, they celebrate their patron saint St. Francis of Assisi, practice the "korpus" or barter, establish marriage alliances in the Purépecha fashion, dress in Purépecha style for special events, dance to Pirekuas and Bajio beats and sounds, dance the "danza de los viejitos" (dance of the elders) in contests within the Purépecha community, prepare traditional foods, and practice traditional medical skills all as a way to concurrently socialize and display/assert their ethnic identity.

REFERENCES

Anderson, W. D. (1999). Familias tarascas en el sur de Illinois: la reafirmación de la identidad étnica. In G. Mummert (Ed.) *Fronteras Fragmentadas*, (pp. 145–166). México: El Colegio de Michoacán, A.C./CIDEM.

Anderson, W. D. (2004). Púrepecha migration into the U.S. Rural Midwest: History and current trends. In J. Fox & G. Rivera Salgado (Ed.), *Indigenous Mexican migrants in the United States* (pp. 355–384). La Jolla, CA: Center U.S. Mexican Studies and Center for Comparative Immigration Studies (UCSD).

Barabas, A. M. (2001). Traspasando fronteras: los migrantes indígenas de México en Estados Unidos. *Cuadernos del sur,* 7(16), 97–110.

Barragán L. E. (1997). *Con un pie en el estribo. Formación y deslizamientos de las sociedades rancheras en la construcción del México moderno.* México: El Colegio de Michoacán/Red Neruda.

Beck, S., & Allexsaht-Snider, M. (2002). Recent language minority education policy in Georgia: Appropriation, assimilation, and Americanization. In S.

Wortham, E. Murillo, & E. T. Hamann (Eds.), *Education in the new Latino diaspora: Policy and the politics of identity* (pp. 37–66). Westport, CT: Ablex.

Cardoso M., G. (2010). *El Programa Bracero en el municipio de Uruapan y su impacto socioeconómico 1942–1964.* Unpublished thesis UMSNH, Morelia, Mich., México.

Cortina, R. (Ed.). (2004). Factores transnacionales y el desempeño escolar de los inmigrantes mexicanos. In *Poblanos en Nueva York. Migración rural, educación y bienestar* (pp. 57–74). Puebla, Puebla: Universidad Iberoamericana Puebla.

Cruz B., E. C. (2011). *La diáspora calificada y el desarrollo basado en el conocimiento: region centro occidente de México.* Unpublished doctoral dissertation, ININEE-UMSNH, Morelia, Mich. México.

Dreby, J. (2010). *Divided by borders: Mexican migrant and their children.* Berkeley, CA: University of California Press.

Durand, J. (1994). *Más allá de la línea. Patrones migratorios entre México y Estados Unidos.* México: Consejo Nacional para la Cultura y las Artes.

Durand, J. (2004). *Nuevas regiones y destinos de la migración mexicana.* Texto inédito, facilitado por el autor, Guadalajara, Jalisco, Universidad de Guadalajara.

Escárcega, S., & Stefano V. (Eds.). (2004). *La ruta mixteca.* México: Universidad Nacional Autónoma de México.

Espinoza, V. M. (1998). *El dilema del retorno. Migración, género y pertenencia en un contexto trasnacional.* México: El Colegio de Michoacán/El Colegio de Jalisco.

Estudio Binacional. (1999). *Revisión de la bibliografía escrita por autores mexicanos sobre las características demográficas y económicas de los migrantes mexicanos a Estados Unidos,* 14.

Fox, J., & Rivera S. G. (2004). *Indigenous Mexican migrants in the United States.* La Jolla, CA: Center U.S. Mexican Studies and Center for Comparative Immigration Studies

George, C. (2006). *Transitioning through life with grace: From Mexico to the American South and from elementary to middle school.* Paper presented at the Latin American Studies Association, XXVI International Congress, San Juan, Puerto Rico.

Glick Schiller, N., Basch, L. G., & Szanton Blanc, C. (1992). *Towards a transnational perspective on migration: Race, class ethnicity and nationalism reconsidered.* New York, NY: The New York Academy of Sciences.

Guerra, J. (1998). *Close to home: Oral and literature practices in a transnational Mexicano community.* New York, NY: Teachers College Press.

Hamann, E. T., (2002). ¿Un paso adelante? The politics of bilingual education, Latino student accommodation, and school district management in southern Appalachia. In S. Wortham, E. G. Murillo, & E. T. Hamann (Eds.), *Education in the New Latino Diaspora: Policy and the politics of identity* (pp. 67–97). Westport, CT: Ablex.

Hamann, E. T. (2003). *Educational welcome of Latinos in the New South.* Westport, CT: Preager.

Hamann, E. T., & Harklau, L. (2010). Education in the New Latino Diaspora. In E. G. Murillo (Ed.), *Handbook of Latinos and education* (pp. 157–169). New York, NY: Routledge.

Henken, T. (2006). Undocumented in Dixie: Mexican-Indian Inmigration in Rural, "New South" Alabama, en *CIMEXUS. Revista de Investigaciones México-Estados Unidos*, Vol.1, No.1, México: ININEE/UMSNH/Centro de Investigaciones México-Estados Unidos, Julio-diciembre, pp. 141, 146 y 149

Herrera T., H. A. (2011). *Evaluación del desempeño municipal. Propuesta metodológica para los municipios semi-urbanos del estado de Michoacán*. México: INAP.

Ikeda, N. (2005). Hispanos crecen a todo galope en el sur. *Qué Pasa: Noticias con Acento Latino, 11*(38), 1, 4.

Índice de Desarrollo Humano-Michoacán. (2008). Morelia, Mich.: Instituto de Investigaciones Económicas y Empresariales/Universidad Michoacana de San Nicolás de Hidalgo/Gobierno del Estado de Michoacán.

Jacinto, Z. A. (1988). El costumbre en Cherán. In *Mitología y modernización* (pp. 112-154). México: El Colegio de Michoacán/Gobierno del Estado de Michoacán.

Jara, C. L. (2007). Programa Binacional de Educación Migrante. In *Jorhéguarinhi*, (pp. 162, 181–185). Zamora, MI: Universidad Pedagógica Nacional/Unidad.

Kochhar, R., Suro, R., & Tafoya, S. (2005). *The New Latino South: The context consequences of rapid population growth*. Washington, DC: Pew Hispanic Center and Pew Research Center Project.

Leco Thomas, C. (2003). La migración temporal con visas H2-A en un pueblo de la Sierra Purhépecha. In G. López Castro (Ed.) *Diáspora Michoacana*, (pp. 307-335). México: El Colegio de Michoacán/Gobierno del Estado de Michoacán.

Leco Thomas, C. (2006). Educación Binacional. Purhépechas en escuelas bilingües México-Estados Unidos. *CIMEXUS Revista de Investigación México-EU* (Vol.1). México: Instituto de Investigaciones Económicas y Empresariales de la Universidad Michoacana de San Nicolás de Hidalgo.

Leco Thomas, C. (2009). *Migración Indígena a Estados Unidos. Purhépechas en Burnsville Norte Carolina*. México: Universidad Michoacana de San Nicolás de Hidalgo/Instituto de Investigaciones Económicas y Empresariales/Centro de Investigaciones México Estados–Estados Unidos/Coordinación de la Investigación Científica/Secretaría del Migrante Michoacán/Facultad de Historia, 350 pp.

Leco, Thomas, C., & Hernández, V. J. (2011). El programa de la contratación: Michoacanos en Estados Unidos, Alaska y Canadá. In J. C. L. Navarro Chávez & C. Leco T. (Eds.), *Migración Internacional. Movilidad Poblacional en el Mundo*. México: UMSNH.

Leco, Thomas, C., & Tehandón Chapina, J. G. (2008). *La Escuela Normal Indígena de Michoacán. Historia, Pedagogía e Identidad Étnica*, México: Universidad Michoacana de San Nicolás de Hidalgo/Instituto de Investigaciones Económicas y Empresariales/Escuela Normal Indígena de Michoacán.

López, C. G. (1999). La educación en la experiencia migratoria de niños migrantes. In G. Mummert (Ed.) *Fronteras Fragmentadas*, (pp. 359-374). México: El Colegio de Michoacán.

López, C. G. (2000). Richard y sus amigos, sociometría de las relaciones en la escuela: Michoacán y Chicago. *Relaciones. Estudios de Historia y Sociedad* de El Colegio de Michoacán, *21*(83), 119–138.

López, C. G. (Ed.). (2003). *Diáspora michoacana*. México: El Colegio de Michoacán/ Gobierno del Estado de Michoacán.

López, C. G., & Gómez, L. D. (2003). Los niños como actores sociales en la migración. In G. López Castro (Ed.), *Diáspora michoacana* (pp. 147–164). México: El Colegio de Michoacán/Gobierno del Estado de Michoacán.

López, J. (2006). *Disconnect and Southern drawl: Latino experiences in a rural elementary school in the new South.* Paper presented at the Latin American Studies Association, XXVI International Congress, San Juan, Puerto Rico.

Maldonado G., A,, & Leco T., C. (2008). *Una educación para el cambio social: la experiencia del cardenismo en Michoacán, 1928–1940.* México: Universidad Michoacana de San Nicolas de Hidalgo.

Marquez, J. (2010). *Informe técnico sobre la situación de los niños purépechas en Reynolds, Oregón.* Unpublished.

Martínez, R. (2001). *Crossing over: A Mexican family on the migrant trail.* New York, NY: Metropolitan Books/Henry Holt and Company.

Murillo, E. (2002). How does it feel to be a *problem?* "Disciplining" the transnational subject in the American south. In S. Wortham, E. Murillo, & E. Hamann (Eds.), *Education in the new Latino diaspora* (pp. 215–240). Westport CT: Ablex Press.

Pérez, W. (2012). *American by heart: Undocumented Latino students and the promise of higher education.* New York, NY: Teachers College Press.

Rivera, S. G. (1999a). Mixtec activism in Oaxacalifornia: Transborder grassroots political strategies. *American Behavioral Scientist, 42*(9), 1439–1458.

Rivera, S. G. (1999b). Binational organization of Mexican Migrants in the United States. *Social Justice, 26*(3), 27–38.

Rivera, S. G. (2000). La reorientación de la migración del México rural y la participación política de indígenas migrantes en México y los Estados Unidos, In N. Clan, P. Castillo, A. Álvarez, & F. Manchón (Eds.), *Las Nuevas Fronteras del Siglo XXI* (pp. 372–396). México: La Jornada Ediciones/UNAM/UAM/ Chicano Latino Research Center, University of California, Santa Cruz.

Sáenz, M. (1936). *Carapan. Bosquejo de una experiencia.* Lima, Perú: Librería e Imprenta Gil.

Santos Rufino, D. (2004). La experiencia del Frente Indígena oaxaqueño Binacional: crisis interna y retos futuros. In J. Fox & G. Rivera Salgado (Eds.), *Indígenas mexicanos migrantes en los Estados Unidos.* México: Universidad de California Santa Cruz/Universidad Autónoma de Zacatecas/Miguel Ángel Porrúa.

Secretaría del Migrante en Michoacán. (2011). *Informe anual.* Morelia, Michoacán, SMM.

Smith, R. C. (2004). Imaginando los futuros educativos de los mexicanos en Nueva York. In *Poblanos en Nueva York. Migración rural, educación y bienestar* (pp. 87–112). Puebla, México: Universidad Iberoamericana Puebla.

Smith, R. C. (2006). *Mexican New York. Transnational lives of new immigrants.* New York, United States of America: University of California Press.

Urrieta, L. (2010). *Working from Within: Chicana and Chicano Activist Educators in Whitestream Schools.* Tucson, AZ: University of Arizona Press.

Villalva, K. (2006). *Navigating a new linguistic landscape: Latinos in North Carolina classrooms.* Paper presented at the Latin American Studies Association, XXVI International Congress, San Juan, Puerto Rico.

Villenas, S. (2002). Reinventing *educación* in New Latino Communities: Pedagogies of change and continuity in North Carolina. In S. Wortham, E. G. Murillo, & E. Hamann (Eds.), *Education in the New Latino Diaspora* (pp. 17–36). Westport, CT: Ablex Press.

Wortham, S. (2002). Gender and school success in the new Latino diaspora. In S. Wortham, E. G. Murillo, & E. Hamann (Eds.), *Education in the New Latino Diaspora* (pp. 117–141). Westport, CT: Ablex.

Wortham, S., Murillo, E. G., & Hamann, E. T. (Eds.). (2002). *Education in the New Latino Diaspora: Policy and the politics of identity.* Westport, CT: Ablex.

Zabludovsky, K. (2012, August 3). Reclaiming the forests and the right to feel safe. *New York Times*, p. A4.

Zúñiga, K. (2006). *Latino/a Parental involvement and student achievement in Rural North Carolina.* Paper presented at the Latin American Studies Association, XXVI International Congress, San Juan, Puerto Rico.

Zúñiga, V., & Hernández-León R. (Eds.). (2005). *New destinations: Mexican immigrants in the United States.* New York, NY: Russell Sage Foundation.

Zúñiga, V., Hernández-León, R., Shadduck, J., & Villarreal, M. O. (2002). The new paths of Mexican immigrants in the United States: Challenges for education and the role of Mexican universities. In S. Wortham, E. G. Murillo, & E. T. Hamann (Eds.), *Education in the New Latino Diaspora: Policy and the politics of identity* (pp. 99–116). Westport, CT: Ablex.

CHAPTER 6

A CULTURAL POLITICAL ECONOMY OF PUBLIC SCHOOLING IN RURAL SOUTH GEORGIA

The Push/Pull Dynamics of Immigrant Labor

C. Allen Lynn

> Migration between countries occurs if and when it "resolves" social and especially class contradictions inside both of them. One set of contradictions pushes people out of a country just as another set of contradictions in other countries pulls them in. Finally, while migration "resolves" some social contradictions, it likewise engenders or aggravates others. (Wolff, 2006, p. 1)

The experiences of Latino immigrants in nontraditional receiving communities are becoming much better documented phenomena than when Education in the New Latino Diaspora (Wortham, Murillo, & Hamann, 2002) was first published. However, with the passage of time and the growing familiarity with the situation come new developments

Revisiting Education in the New Latino Diaspora, pp. 115–131
Copyright © 2015 by Information Age Publishing

and a shifting of circumstances that further complicate matters. Recent developments in the southeast region of Georgia are a good example. Until the 1980s this section of the country was almost exclusively biracial (i.e., White and African American) and had been so for generations. There were some Latino migrant workers then who held the distinction of being the immigrant group in the area, but few had settled there. Since then, local farmers and businesses have maintained their desire for cheap labor, and demographics have been in flux, with the eventual switch in status from migrants to settlers just the first of a chain of unforeseen consequences, particularly in the area schools.

Writing about Chinese immigrants in Mississippi, Loewen (1971) asserted, "A biracial system of etiquette has no provision for a third race" (p. 73). Updating his question and applying it to a particular Georgia town, perhaps we should ask whether a previously biracial system, then a triracial one, can make provision for a fourth race?

Since the turn of the century, the small towns of Statesboro and Claxton, Georgia (located in Bulloch and Evans counties respectively) have experienced an influx of dozens of Korean immigrant families who arrived in order to work at a local poultry processing plant. Silent in this chapter are the voices of the Latino poultry workers, farm hands, students and teachers that have lived in these communities for years. However, as Murillo (2002) suggested, in order to better understand education, policy, and the politics of identity in the Latino Diaspora we sometimes need to partially shift the focus away from Latinos themselves. Following Murillo's recommendation, this chapter focuses on the experiences of new Korean immigrants in a region only recently settled by Latinos. Troubling the community's response to the Koreans' arrival reveals much about the perception of immigrants in the United States (including a complex taxonomy of which types of newcomers are and are not welcome) and, more importantly, what does and does not happen when they arrive.

The arrival of Korean immigrants to this community brings to light an issue that has traditionally been the focus of urban education researchers: Who gets access to the best education in a given locale? By analyzing the cultural, political, and economic factors involved, I show how the events in this setting highlight the difficulty Latinos (the third racial group to come to Claxton) have faced in obtaining adequate education in this community. The analysis reiterates that, even in rural settings, "poorly performing" schools tend to serve the most impoverished populations in the United States and are located in the most disadvantaged areas (Roscigno, Tomaskovic-Devey, & Crowley, 2006). Equally, the arrival of Korean immigrants at Claxton Poultry adds depth to the New Latino Diaspora (NLD) storyline. Latinos began arriving in southeast Georgia in large numbers beginning in the late 1990s. Anti-immigrant legislation and the threat of enforcement caused industries such as poultry to reassess the sources tapped for labor. Hiring Korean immigrants who are "legal" served two purposes for the industry. It minimized the threat of U.S. Immigration and Customs Enforcement (ICE) raids (and the overnight loss of a large portion of the workforce). It also introduced a new threat to existing employees. A "model minority" used as a new labor force served as an incentive to white, African American, and Latino workers alike to submit to the terms of plant-production regimes or face the prospect of being driven out of a job (Griffith, 1995). Essentially, this chapter is a cautionary tale about how the growth of Latino immigrant communities in nontraditional receiving locales can be met with backlash, closing doors for some while presenting opportunity for others. It also points to a dynamic, little explored in the other chapters, of how ICE enforcement under George W. Bush and Barack Obama's presidencies, has in several communities led to a demand for non-Latino immigrant labor because Korean, Karen, Somali, Sudanese, and other groups are presumed to be less likely to be working without legal documentation.

THEORETICAL FRAME AND RESEARCHER ORIENTATION

What follows is a chronological narrative of the events as I interpret them through a cultural political economy approach. Marx' main focus was on the social reproduction of exploitation. Taking this a step further, more recent theorists have applied his theories specifically to education. Althusser (1971), building on Marx, stated that schools act as a tool for reproducing the conditions needed to perpetuate the skills and rules for establishing order—that is, "a reproduction of the submission to the ruling ideology for the workers and a reproduction of the ability to manipulate the ruling ideology correctly for the agents of exploitation and repression" (p. 133). What is interesting in the case at hand is the fact that those involved are immigrants (both "legal" and "illegal") competing to make gains in the very system that influenced their decisions to emigrate in the first place. Compelled to leave their countries of origin in search of better economic opportunities, both Latino and Korean newcomers found themselves still competing for scarce economic resources, but in a different setting. Marxist theorist Slavoj Zizek (2009) put it this way:

> What makes capital exceptional is its unique combination of the values of freedom and equality and the facts of exploitation and domination: the gist of Marx's analysis is that the legal-ideological matrix of freedom-equality is not a mere "mask" concealing exploitation-domination, but the very form in which the latter is exercised. (p. 125, emphasis in original)

Encouraged to come work and then given little in return, immigrants are often welcomed and unwelcomed at the same time (Gitlin, Buendia, Crosland, & Doumbia, 2003). This chapter explains why schools and the public sector in Claxton were what Bowles and Gintis (2002) referred to as "the loci of conflicts stemming from the contradictory rules of the marketplace, the democratic polity, and the patriarchal family" (p. 2). The participants in this case, all welcomed for the cheap labor they provided, fit into niches prearranged by historical trends and modern conventions. Troubling their situation revealed much about the inequities of such conventions and the possible direction of future trends.

Before delving deeper into the chapter, a bit of disclosure is warranted. To say that I am a complete insider in the community described would be both true and false. I grew up one hour away from Claxton in Vidalia, home of the famed Vidalia Sweet Onion. While production of that sweet onion variety started back in the 1930s (and President Carter offered them as White House gifts during his presidency in the 1970s), it was not until the 1990s that the brand was trademarked and marketing took off in earnest. With the marketing came demand—consumer demand that led to labor demand: enter the Mexican migrant worker. The region saw a marked change in racial demographics as a result. During my senior year at Vidalia High School in 1989, we had exactly one Latino student. By 2011, Latinos made up 20.5% of the total K–12 population in Toombs County (Douglas, 2010) and, correspondingly, Vidalia Sweet Onions had become a multi-million dollar industry.

My life changed just as radically. I have lived mostly outside of Georgia since graduation from high school. A stint in the Air Force, service with the Peace Corps in Honduras, teaching in New York City, as well as 2 years of teaching in Brazil, provided experiences that forever altered my worldview. Also, my wife is from Korea, a country that I have visited for extended stays twice thus far. As you will see these details matter; I held a unique position juxtaposed between most of the groups noted in this chapter. And while I saw these events through the lens of an Anglo, heterosexual, male researcher with working-class roots, my lens had many filters. The description is colored accordingly.

ETHNOGRAPHIC BACKGROUND

Irrespective of research that suggests immigrants actually boost the overall U.S. economy (e.g., Nadadur, 2009), at the local level newcomers were seen as a threat to low-skilled working class adults and a drain on the local infrastructure and services (Fennelly & Federico, 2008). In line with Griffith's 1995 assessment of immigrant labor in Georgia's poultry industry, in 2011 some residents in the small-town of Claxton held extremely restrictionist views of immigration, yet their town was also the home of industries most consistently employing immigrant labor. The anti-immigrant politics that dominated the state and local governments in Georgia (e.g., HB 87, the "Illegal Immigration Reform and Enforcement Act of 2011" which was signed into law by Governor Nathan Deal) were not linked to capitalism or the interests of capital. On the contrary, the free circulation of labor was in the interests of big capital. Zizek (2009) argued that essentially, it is the local businesses who were inherently multiculturalists and tolerant. I add a caveat: The poultry processing plant's welcome of Latinos was only partial. As the subsequent hiring of the Korean immigrants showed (which is further detailed momentarily), an alternative source of cheap immigrant labor was welcomed because it was expedient.

Best (2010) noted that when considering politics, "it is more fruitful to take seriously the network of relations between particular ideas and the daily practices and desires to which those ideas give expression and shape" (locations 904-15). Since Georgia's Latino population began to grow, the anti-immigrant policies and enforcement in Georgia have both reflected and amplified public anxiety over multiculturalism (Beck & Alexsaht-Snider, 2002). Georgia was one of the 31 states that passed a nonbinding English-only law (http://www.us-english.org/). Passage of the Security and Immigration Compliance Act in April of 2006 also put Georgia at the helm of a growing number of states implementing heightened restrictions against informal immigration. The act ordered state agencies to cooperate with federal immigration enforcement programs. A direct result of such enforcement opened the door for the arrival of Koreans in Claxton.

In September of 2006, a raid by U.S. Immigration and Customs Enforcement (ICE) at the Crider Poultry processing plant in Stillmore left that plant without two-thirds of its work force. Laotian Hmong refuges living in Minnesota were recruited to fill a number of the vacancies. And as Baptist pastor Ariel Rodriguez subsequently related, "The employers around here are still afraid of hiring Hispanics. They're afraid that immigration agents are coming, the workers are going to disappear, and they'll have to pay fines" (Ludden, 2007).

It appeared that Claxton Poultry was well aware of the risks at Crider Poultry and started to develop a solution to their labor demands long before suffering a similar fate. Such tactics are not uncommon in an industry that sometimes sees a workforce turnover rate as high as 100% in a year (Human Rights Watch, 2004). I will discuss the arrangement with Korean workers below. First, however, I would like to comment on the nature of race relations and labor in Georgia and the sort of environment the Korean workers entered.

New South, Old Hierarchy

The complexity of class relations in southeast Georgia has its roots in the culture of racism that emerged as slavery was dismantled: "Though certain humans could no longer be seen as chattels, they could be placed into a social hierarchy that legitimized the call for those at the bottom to provide the manual labor for those at the top" (Kayatekin, 2001, p. 228). This was the case for African Americans, as well as poorer Whites, in Bulloch and Evans Counties until well after desegregation. In the 1980s Latino immigrants started to arrive in the area to harvest the heavily marketed Vidalia Sweet Onions and there was another shift in the hierarchy of labor. Because of the low socioeconomic status of the Latinos who came to the area to work in agriculture and poultry processing, Latino was synonymous with "Mexican" in this region and that term was often said in a derogatory way. As Fennelly and Frederico (2008) pointed out, the arrival of immigrants to rural communities such as Statesboro and Claxton often occurred in concert with the loss of small farms, expansion of large-scale farming, and the "Walmartization" of the area. It was therefore not surprising that anyone perceived as a threat to wages and a sign of the changing times would be treated negatively.

Enter into this mix Korean immigrants. As of May 2011, Claxton Poultry had hired 153 Koreans. The overwhelming majority of the Koreans interviewed for this chapter came from middle-class backgrounds. Their motivations for leaving South Korea, a country seemingly on the rise, were multifaceted. Korea suffered an economic crisis in the late 1990s that left the country reeling. The Korean economists took a neoliberal stance that pleased the International Monetary Fund (IMF) and investment banks, but created greater uncertainty for most middle-class Koreans undermining confidence and diminishing opportunities (Chang, 2008).[1] However, the Koreans did not leave their homeland strictly because their prospects were seen as limited. The decision to emigrate was a combination of economic hardships, on the one hand, and perceived better opportunities, on the other. Work in Claxton offered the promise of good schooling for their children and permanent residency in the United States. Equally, Georgia was one of the 10 states with the largest Korean immigrant populations. An estimated 52,500 Korean Americans resided in the state in 2010, facilitating the move for most of the new residents (http://www.2010census. gov/2010census/). While many arrived with no ties in the rural community, the round trip drive to Atlanta for a visit to Korean supermarkets and businesses could be done in one day.

In the remaining sections, I outline how Koreans came to work at Claxton Poultry. The nature of the arrangement itself says much about the deferential treatment of the Koreans versus Latinos. However, the lengths to which businesses would go in order to avoid confrontations with regulators while maintaining a cheap labor force also says much about the plight of Latinos living within the confines of new immigration laws. Stories such as this one could be harbingers for other Latino populations in similar settings.

Kukjei and Claxton Poultry Make a Deal

Although U.S. regulations forbade employers to require a worker to stay in a job for a fixed time as a stipulation for obtaining permanent residency, an article in the *Claxton Enterprise* suggested that this was the case at Claxton Poultry. The Koreans working for Claxton Poultry paid thousands of dollars to an immigration broker, Kukjei Immigration Development Corporation (KIDC), which took care of the visa paperwork and acted as a go between for the plant and the Koreans. An article in the *Claxton Enterprise* explained:

> Once the immigrants arrive in the United States and begin work at Claxton Poultry, they will receive permanent residency visas. However, if they do not fulfill their 1-year obligation to work at the plant, the immigrants would not be considered permanent residents and would not be able to receive U.S. citizenship. (Cunningham, 2005, 1A)

When interviewed by the *Statesboro Herald* about their newfound situation, immigrants referred to their position as a "sensitive situation" (Hallman, 2005, 1A). In Maryland, Purdue Chicken used a similar program during the 1990s. Purdue (a much larger employer) eventually ended the practice after a series of articles in the *Washington Post* revealed the spurious nature of the program (Pae, 1999). A conversation with a manager at Claxton Poultry suggested that, as of January 2011, the program in Claxton was still actively seeking workers from Korea under the same arrangement with KIDC.

Neither the newspaper articles nor the employee at Claxton Poultry elaborated upon the exact figure paid to KIDC nor the nature of that arrangement. However, interviews with numerous Korean workers revealed that some of them paid up to $20,000 for the opportunity to work at Claxton Poultry with the caveat that the deposit would be reimbursed at the end of the one-year work period. The offer was advertised in some of Korea's major newspapers. Meetings with KIDC in Seoul vaguely outlined the nature of the work, while also promising a safe rural setting and high-performing schools for the workers' children. The majority of the workers, with very few exceptions, cashed in on their deposit after one year of work for Claxton Poultry and moved away from Bulloch County. While "the pipeline" remained open, the workers arrived and left on a rotating basis.

The legal status of the Korean workers at Claxton Poultry raised an interesting issue. "Undocumented" workers have few legal rights. Oftentimes, they are treated as invisible in the community. The employer does not want to admit that they are there. Neither does the worker want to raise awareness of their presence in fear of being fired or deported (Chavez, 2012). However, Koreans with legal status fit into a different niche. Because they were here "legally," and also perceived by many as a "model minority" (Lee, 2006), they were not feared as an outside threat; instead they were fully normalized and "drowned in the indistinct crowd of citizens" becoming invisible as well (Zizek, 2009, p. 119). The local newspapers in Statesboro and Claxton portrayed the Koreans as middle-class and arriving with money, in contrast to the restrictionist view of Latino immigrants (whether they are documented or not). A newly arrived Korean worker described it this way, "The overall education level of Koreans is high, with most having at least a bachelor's degree.... Koreans want to work hard, follow laws and be a positive part of the community.... We want to invest our money here." (Hallman, 2005, 3A). This was truly a win/win for Claxton Poultry. They got their cheap labor and at the same time did not have to worry about U.S. Immigration and Customs Enforcement like their counterparts at Crider Poultry. Moreover, they did not suffer much backlash from the local community and the steady turnover of workers meant that rather than organize for better wages or working conditions they often just moved on.

There were additional factors that possibly influenced Claxton Poultry's choice of Korean workers and their subsequent acceptance by the local community. In 2006, Kia Motors held the groundbreaking ceremony for their manufacturing plant in West Point, Georgia (about a 4-hour drive from Claxton). It was the first of its kind in the United States. Researchers at Georgia Tech estimate that Kia would generate an annual economic gain of $4 billion a year (Schwarz, 2010). My point here is that recent events such as the opening of the Kia plant in west Georgia and the ICE raid in nearby Stillmore left a certain impression on local residents, one that painted Koreans as "good" immigrants and Latinos as "bad." In the "cultural circuit" where local residents draw upon the information at hand in order to make meaning (Hall, 1997), immigrant groups were often perceived in a certain way without being given the benefit of the doubt (Chavez, 2008). The Korean workers and their entire families were offered permanent residency whereas Latino migrant workers were never afforded that option.

However, it would be imprudent to suggest that the Korean immigrants were welcomed without comment. An interview with a former administrator for Bulloch County schools revealed the feelings of some local residents during the period when Koreans first started to arrive. The local newspaper had recently run an article describing the arrival of the Korean workers. Jill (pseudonym) recounted an incident in a restaurant where a number of men questioned her about the costs of educating the new Koreans. They asked Jill, "Ya'll going to pay for their education with our tax dollars?" (personal communication, May 27, 2011). The owner of the restaurant told the men to leave her alone and the issue was dropped. However, Claxton Poultry did receive a threatening letter from the headquarters of the Ku Klux Klan in Ellijay, GA, a few weeks after the *Claxton Enterprise* newspaper article ran. The overarching message of the letter was that Claxton Poultry was stealing jobs from working-class white people by hiring Koreans. As of this writing, there was no public record that Korean workers had suffered any physical abuse. However, incidents like the restaurant confrontation tend to indicate that although there was little overt outcry over the arrival of the Korean workers, it was not unnoticed by local residents.

Claxton Poultry—The 3-Ds (Dirty, Dangerous, and Demanding)

Claxton, GA's, only real claim to fame is the somewhat comical label of "Fruit Cake Capital of the World." Two other somewhat less risible options for employment are one of the state's largest apiaries and the local poultry processing plant. However, the town remains a sleepy backwater. Only one event in the town's history could be considered noteworthy in the annals of history. In 1984 a meteorite fell in Claxton and struck a mailbox. The mailbox was subsequently sold for $83,000 because of its unique status of having been struck by a meteorite (http://www.meteorlab.com), surely a windfall for someone in such a cash-strapped community.

While the apiary was one of the largest in the state, it only employed 5–9 workers at any given time and had annual sales of less than $500,000 in 2006 (http://www.manta.com). Conversely, at the time of this writing, Claxton Poultry had over 1,600 employees and was a multimillion-dollar operation. While, on the surface, the plant appeared to be a great addition to the local economy when founded in 1949, the success of the business hinged upon a steady supply of cheap labor that was difficult to maintain. Georgia poultry plants, like much of the United States, began to rely on a mostly Latino workforce beginning in the 1990s (Griffith, 1995). In the second half of the aughts, however, Georgia became a 'leader' in restrictive immigration policies (Sabia, 2010). Incidents such as the aforementioned Crider Poultry plant raid in 2006 as well as the ongoing battle between immigration officials and Vidalia Onion growers (Rojas, 2011) were not unknown to employers of immigrants, both documented and undocumented. Although Latino workers were a majority in many meat and poultry plants around the country (Human Rights Watch, 2004), the industry also had a record of shifting hiring practices in accordance with local conditions. The employment patterns of Claxton Poultry mirrored that of the poultry industry as a whole, reflecting targeted recruitment as well as the recent changes in the character and enforcement of immigration laws in Georgia (Griffith, Broadway, & Stull, 1995).

The long-term nature of Claxton Poultry's quest for an alternative source of cheap labor and the lengths to which they were willing to go in order to obtain one was revealed to me in the interview with Jill. She shared with me that Claxton Poultry approached the school almost a year before the first Korean workers arrived and inquired about the feasibility of Bulloch County schools accommodating 80 and possibly up to 300 new families.[2] The school was happy with the idea of a "model minority" group coming to the district. As Jill stated, "We just knew that education was very important to Koreans.... Math-wise I saw it as a plus for our school system because the kids had a lot of ability" (personal communication, May 27, 2011). She went on to explain that the teachers voiced no complaints about the large influx of Korean students. The biggest hurdle appeared to be money for the extra classrooms needed. Jill contacted the local state representative, explained the situation, and "lo and behold, we got $250,000 of revenue immediately" (personal communication, May 27, 2011). It appears that the state representative was a supporter of local business, or at least a well-established local business with an apparently foolproof source of cheap labor.

Essentially, the KIDC, Claxton Poultry, and Bulloch County schools' deal arrangement included a number of compromises: KIDC assured the Korean recruits that their children would be able to attend good schools, Claxton Poultry facilitated funding for the schools, and Bulloch County gained what they perceived to be a boost in test scores. All of this however hinged upon an agreement by the Korean workers to devote one year of their lives to a job that had the highest rate of injury and illness in the manufacturing sector (Human Rights Watch, 2004).

Intriguingly, Jill told me she was not made aware of the fact that the length of the agreement between KIDC and the Korean workers was one year. After the 1-year period for the first families ended, the Korean families started to leave. She and the other administrators did not understand why, but thought that the families may have felt uncomfortable in the community. I explained the nature of the 1-year contract and she was surprised. An elementary school English to speakers of other languages (ESOL) teacher explained that teachers were similarly surprised. Once the initial contact with the school was made to solidify the arrangement, the plant made no other effort to follow up.

The balance of this chapter will focus on the differences in the two communities in question at the time of the arrival of the Korean immigrants. Claxton, on the one hand, was a much smaller and poorer community, while Statesboro was the larger, more prosperous neighbor. While observing some of the most glaring differences between the two communities, it is important to keep in mind that the Korean workers not only made a conscientious decision to chose one school district over the other, that possibility was made available through maneuvers by Claxton Poultry, Bulloch County schools, and the state of Georgia.

The Communities

In December of 1864, on their march to the sea, troops led by General William T. Sherman stopped in Statesboro. A union officer asked a saloon proprietor for directions to Statesboro. The man replied, "You [sic] standing in the middle of town." The soldiers destroyed the courthouse—a crude log structure that doubled as a barn when court was not in session—and continued on their way to Savannah (http://www.georgiaencyclopedia.org). In the subsequent 147 years, "The Boro" grew into a bustling college town with an estimated population of 27,158 in 2011 (http://www.census.gov). Agriculture and Georgia Southern University, the largest university in the southern half of the state, drove the local economy. Until the early 1990s, this section of the country was an almost exclusively White and African American. However, the growth of large-scale agriculture made the area part of the NLD. Latino migrant workers arriving then held the distinction of being *the* immigrant group in the area. The growth of Georgia Southern University from an agriculture and mechanical school to a doctoral/research university also diversified the population.

The premeditated decision of the Korean workers' to live in Bulloch County and send their children to that school district (instead of Evan County Schools) says much about who gets access to better schools in this area of the United States. Comparing a few facts about the neighboring school districts will illuminate some of the stark contrasts between the two. First, the population of Bulloch County is much larger than that of Evans County, at 67,761 residents versus 11,646, respectively. The history of the two counties reflects the economic divisions that have long been present in the region. Bulloch County was created in 1776 and named after one of Georgia's first governors, Archibald Bulloch, whose great-great grandson was President Theodore Roosevelt (http://www.bullochcounty.net). Evans County was not established until 1914, and its main claims to fame were the aforementioned fruitcakes and mailbox meteorite incident. The respective county seats further displayed the stark differences between the neighboring counties. Claxton had a population of 2,276 and Statesboro had much larger population of 27,158.

Table 6.1 shows some interesting facts about Bulloch versus Evans County with regard to median household income. While the information available does not include Korean households (the data are from the 2000 census, prior to their arrival), it does give a feel for the situation the Koreans entered. The disparity in income for Hispanics (the term used by the U.S. Census Bureau) living in the adjoining counties is telling when compared with the educational outcomes for the same group. The breakdown for median household income for Blacks and Whites was virtually the same. However, Hispanics in Bulloch County made more than the median income, while those in Evans County made more than a third less. Equally, 41.7% of Hispanics were below the poverty level in Bulloch County during the same period while that figure was 54.6% in Evans County.

Table 6.1. Economics—Median Household Income by Race and Hispanic Origin: 1999–2008

	Bulloch	Evans
Total	$29,499	$25,447
White	$34,994	$30,668
Black	$18,941	$17,555
Hispanic	$31,458	$16,164

Source: *The Georgia County Guide* (Douglas, 2010).

Education

The amount of money spent on schooling in the respective school districts calls further attention to the differences in affluence. Bulloch County's total expenditures on K–12 education in 2007–2008 were $2,171 per capita, while Evans County spent only $1,560 per capita in the same time period, thus reflecting the poorer local tax base.[3] This is not surprising considering the historical differences of wealth between the two counties. What the schools were able to offer says much about how that difference in wealth was maintained. Bulloch County had an Advanced Placement program and their students scored higher on both the Scholastic Assessment Test (SAT) and the American College Testing (ACT). Sixty-nine percent of their graduates had college preparatory diplomas in the 2007-2008 school year (Douglas, 2010). Claxton High School was a Needs Improvement School Year 2. The school had failed to make adequate yearly progress (AYP) in English/language arts and/or mathematics for the third year in a row

(http:www/evans.k12ga.us). Only 63.5% of their graduates had college preparatory diplomas during the same time period.

There is another telling statistic here. Table 6.2 shows the breakdown
of the student population by race. Evans County had become a majority-
minority school district by the time the Korean workers arrived.

**Table 6.2. K–12 Enrollment—Percentage of Total by
Race/Ethnicity, 2007–2008**

	Bulloch	Evans
Total	10,174	1,854
White	36.5	41.9
Black	56.8	40.6
Hispanic	3.2	14.9
Asian	1.0	0.7

Source: The Georgia County Guide (Douglas, 2010).

Additionally, 1.2 % of the students in Bulloch County were labeled
English language learners (ELL) while Evans County had 7.9% of its
students in this category. A more troubling statistic was the number of economically disadvantaged (ED) students. Bulloch County Schools had 52.8%
ED students in the 2007–2008 school year while more than three fourths
(75.6%) of Evans County Schools' students were in this category (Douglas,
2010). Bulloch County Schools catered to a more affluent student body
and offered an education that afforded more options for social mobility
after graduation, while Evans County students came from more modest
backgrounds and attended struggling schools with less success and fewer
resources. Given this, it should be no surprise that Korean families who
held education in such high regard settled en masse in Bulloch County
even though they were drawn to the area by employment in Claxton.

CONCLUSIONS

When contemplating the best way to deliver a rich description of the circumstances of the participants in this short chapter, I felt torn about how
to best represent the situation. There were multiple factors at play, most of
which were out of the control of those involved. As Ribera-Fumaz (2009)
points out, "Social processes are co-constructed by cultural, political, and
economic processes" (p. 457). One cannot be considered without acknowl-

edgment of the role of the others. I was therefore attracted to a theoretical lens that included all three of these elements. The approach to cultural political economy used here is a critical framework, informed by Marxist political economy, Foucault's concept of power/knowledge, and critical race theory (Dumas & Anyon, 2006).

In this vein, there are a few comments that I would like to make about this situation that bring it back to the juxtaposition of traditional Latino diaspora versus NLD locales. The question that begs to be asked about this situation is: Why not just offer permanent residency to the undocumented poultry workers already in place? Although politicians have debated the amnesty issue heatedly for years (and the U.S. Senate even passed a bill that would have allowed this, but that had dim prospects in the U.S. House of Representatives as of this writing), this simple action would solve many of the problems facing employers in this region of the United States.

That solution aside, there is another troubling question: Why was the $250,000 made available to Bulloch County never offered to Evans County, a school district in more dire circumstances? As the continually dismal graduation rates for Latinos in Evans County evidenced, this population was "not so much invisible or unseen as *under-seen* or *mis-seen*; they do not count for nothing so much as for very little" (Hallward, 2008, p. 104, italics added). As Foucault's (1980) concept of power suggests, Latino immigrant families were not excluded from participating in education. Yet, their continual underperformance and the public schools' inability (or ineffectual efforts) to alter educational outcomes for Latino students modulate the conditions necessary for maintaining the status quo. The situation is strikingly similar to the inequities of schooling in Korea, only the nationalities of the actors have changed.

Foucault (1980) pointed out, "the historical *raison d'être* of political power and the principle of its concrete forms and actual functioning, is located in the economy" (p. 89). The state of Georgia supplied the $250,000 to Bulloch County because it sweetened the deal needed to attract the Korean workers. Their acceptance of the arrangement allowed a multi-million dollar business to continue with its profitable labor practices. At the same time, both lawmakers and Claxton Poultry were able to avoid any conflict related to immigration laws, thus largely sidestepping the issue. Commenting on local opportunity and institutional resources/investments, Roscigno, Tomaskovic-Devey, and Crowley (2006) state:

> Families and schools, as distinct although often overlapping institutional spheres, are embedded within and shaped by places—places that vary significantly in opportunity and, consequently, resources. Here we are recognizing both *the spatial patterning of opportunity and the ways in which local opportunity permeates or mitigates inequality through more familiar and proximate institutional (i.e., family and school) channels.* (p. 2124, emphasis in original)

While the Latino parents of Evans County were certain to want to same outcomes for their children as the parents of the Korean students in Bulloch
County, achievement outcomes were sure to remain at a level below that of
their more affluent neighbors so long as the current structural impediments
remained in place, so long as transnationally mobile aspiring Koreans were
given a different welcome than their Mexican and Central American peers.

NOTES

1. Mexico suffered the same sort of economic problems as a result of the 1982
   debt crisis and the 1994 peso devaluation (followed by the passage of NAFTA
   and the *Ejercito Zapatista Liberacion Nacional* [EZLN] uprising), forcing many
   Mexicans to look for alternatives outside of Mexico (Hogenboom, 1998).
2. Statistics for the Bulloch County 2011–2012 school year indicated 191 Asian
   students enrolled (The specific number of Korean students within this demographic was not available).
3. Note, these figures refer only to the local contribution to schooling, not the
   total per student expenditure, which also included state and federal monies.

REFERENCES

Althusser, L. (1971). *Lenin and philosophy and other essays* (Ben Brewster, Trans.) . New
    York, NY: Monthly Review Press.
Beck, S., & Allexsaht-Snider, M. (2002). Recent language minority education
    policy in Georgia: Appropriation, assimilation, and Americanization. In S.
    Wortham, E. Murillo, & E. Hamann (Eds.), *Education in the new Latino dias-
    pora: Policy and the politics of identity* (pp. 37–66). Westport, CT: Ablex.
Best, J. (Ed.). (2010). *Cultural political economy.* New York, NY: Taylor & Francis
    e-Library.
Bowles, S., & Gintis, H. (2002). Schooling in capitalist America revisited. *Sociology
    of Education, 75,* 1–18.
Chang, H. (2008) *Kicking away the ladder.* London, England: Anthem Press.
Chavez, L. R. (2008). *The Latino threat: Constructing immigrants, citizens, and the nation.*
    Stanford, CA: Stanford University Press.
Chavez, L. R. (2012). *Shadowed lives: Undocumented immigrants in American society* (3rd
    ed.). Stamford, CT: Cengage Learning
Cunningham, C. (2005, February 10). The Koreans are coming! *The Claxton Enter-
    prise,* p. 1A.
Douglas, C. (Ed.). (2010). *The Georgia county guide.* Athens, GA: The University of
    Georgia Press.
Dumas, M., & Anyon, J. (2006). Toward a critical approach to education policy
    implementation: Implications for the battle(field). In M. Honig (Ed.), *New
    directions in education policy implementation: Confronting complexity* (pp. 149–
    168). Albany, NY: State University of New York Press.

Fennelly, K., & Federico, C. (2008). Rural residence as a determinant of attitudes toward US immigration policy. *International Migration, 46*(1), 151–190.

Foucault, M. (1980) *Power/Knowledge: Selected interviews and other writings 1972–1977.* New York, NY: Pantheon.

Gitlin, A., Buendia, E., Crosland, K., & Doumbia, F. (2003). The production of margin and center: Welcoming-unwelcoming of immigrant students. *American Educational Research Association, 40*(1), 91–122.

Griffith, D. (1995). Hay trabajo: Poultry processing, rural industrialization, and the Latinazation of low-wage labor. In D. Stull, M. Broadway, & D. Griffith (Eds.), *Any way you cut it: Meat processing and small-town America* (pp. 129–152). Lawrence, KS: University of Kansas Press.

Griffith, D., Broadway, M., & Stull, D. (1995). Introduction: Making meat. In D. Stull, M. Broadway, & D. Griffith (Eds.), *Any way you cut it: Meat processing and small-town America* (pp. 1–15). Lawrence, KS: University of Kansas Press.

Hall, S. (1996). Gramsci's relevance for the study of race and ethnicity. In D. Morley & K. Chen (Eds.), *Stuart Hall* (pp. 411–440). New York, NY: Routledge.

Hallman, J. (2005, April 2). Korean immigrants begin learning English. *Statesboro Herald,* p. 1A.

Hallward, P. (2008). Order and event. *New Left Review, 53,* 97–126.

Hogenboom, B. (1998). *Mexico and the NAFTA environment debate: The transnational politics of economic integration.* Utrecht, The Netherlands: International Books.

Human Rights Watch. (2004). *Blood, sweat, and fear: Workers' rights in U.S. meat and poultry plants.* Washington, DC: Author.

Kayatekin, S. (2001). Sharecropping and feudal class processes in the postbellum Mississippi delta. In J. Gibson-Graham, S. Resnick, & R. Wolff (Ed.), *Re/ presenting vlass: Essays in postmodern Marxism* (pp. 227-246). Durham, NC & London, England: Duke University Press: .

Lee, S. (2006). Additional complexities: Social class, ethnicity, generation, and gender in Asian American student experiences. *Race Ethnicity and Education, 9*(1), 17–28.

Loewen, J. (1971). *Mississippi Chinese.* Cambridge, MA: Harvard University Press.

Ludden, J. (2007). Hmong fill jobs left empty by immigration raid. Retrieved from http://www.npr.org/templates/story.php?storyID=10461104

Murillo, E. (2002). How does it feel to be a problem?: "Disciplining" the transnational subject in the American south. In S. Wortham, E. Murillo, & E. Hamann (Eds.), *Education in the new Latino diaspora: Policy and the politics of identity* (pp. 215–240). Westport, CT: Ablex.

Nadadur, R. (2009). Illegal immigration: A positive economic contribution to the United States. *Journal of Ethnic and Migration Studies, 35*(6), 1037–1052.

Pae, P. (1999, December 1). Chicken plant jobs open U.S. doors for Koreans. *The Washington Post.* p. A1.

Ribera-Fumaz, R. (2009). From urban political economy to cultural political economy: Rethinking culture and economy in and beyond the urban. *Progress in Human Geography, 33*(4), 447–465.

Rojas, L. (2011). *Economics vs. enforcement: The long-running Vidalia onion saga.* Retrieved from http://www.multiamerican.scpr.org/2011/05/economics-vs-enforcement-the-long-running-vidalia-onion-saga/

Roscigno, V., Tomaskovic-Devey, D., & Crowley, M. (2006). Education and the inequalities of place. *Social Forces, 84*(4), 2121–2145.

Sabia, D. (2010). The anti-immigrant fervor in Georgia: Return of the nativist or just politics as usual? *Politics & Policy, 38*(1), 53–80.

Schwarz, M. (2010, March 25). Kia breathes life into old Georgia textile mill town. *USA Today.* Retrieved from http://usatoday.com

Wolff, R. (2006). *Immigration and class.* Retrieved from http://www.rdwolff.com/

Wortham, S., Murillo, E., & Hamann (Eds.). (2002). *Education in the new Latino diaspora: Policy and the politics of identity.* Westport, CT: Ablex.

Zizek, S. (2009). *First as tragedy, then as farce.* London, England: Verso.

CHAPTER 7

THE SECRET MINORITY OF
THE NEW LATINO/A DIASPORA

Stephanie Flores-Koulish

A Latina baby arrives on our shores, having been whisked away from her motherland, her mother. That baby grows up surrounded by people who do not look like her. That child does not learn the language of her people. She grows up and wonders about her motherland, her mother. She longs for the day when others surrounding her have brown skin and dark hair, like her own, a day that will never come. She wishes she did not stick out. She wishes people would stop asking her where she is from. She wishes her people would accept her as one of their own. She does not really know where she is from. She does not *conoce* Colombia. Yet, she desperately wishes she did know her motherland, her mother, herself. She wants to know about what makes Colombia unique among other Latin American nations. What types of foods would she have eaten had she stayed? What types of holidays would she have celebrated? What does the national anthem sound like? What do its lyrics mean? Why has there been so much civil war strife in her country? Why is there little to no positive representation of her country in U.S. media? She is a Latina, living in diaspora, longing for a reconnection with her motherland, her mother. However, unlike other Latinos in the New Latino Diaspora (NLD), she cannot turn to any community of other Latinos like herself, at least not very easily. Schools

Revisiting Education in the New Latino Diaspora, pp. 133–151

provide her little to no solace when it comes to educating her about her own ethnicity, her language. She is an island of one in a sea of others who seem very much unlike herself. At other times, she is the ultimate chameleon, fitting in within a variety of communities. I am that Colombiana, living in diaspora, an adopted Latina, raised in suburban Maryland by a family that was Irish/English, German, and Mexican-American. No longer must we remain silent, a shameful secret among our brethren, for we have a unique perspective that lends a distinctive eye on our collective condition.

Edmund Hamann and Linda Harklau (2010) explain that *new Latino diaspora* is a term describing the migration of Latino/as to regions in the U.S. where they have not typically lived, thus outside of Florida, California, Texas, and six other states. Further, they originally presumed that Latino children were growing up in Latino families, yet they acknowledged with transracial adoption, this is often not the case. This chapter then, acknowledges the inclusion of Latino/a adoptees as part of the larger NLD.

Adopted Latino/as, both domestic and international, complicate the question of what constitutes the NLD (Hamann & Harklau, 2010). Like other transnational adoptees, Latino/a adoptees complicate and blur notions of cultural group membership given their status within multiple categories (Miller-Loessi & Kilic, 2001). In other words, Latino/a adoptees look like others within the NLD in that we are Latinos/as living in locales not traditional to Latino/as, yet in many ways we are different: We are assumed to have cultural knowledge that we might lack. Our siblings, who are obviously part of our family might not affiliate with or be seen as part of our same identity groupings, and so on. By complicating cultural group membership, scholars might pause the next time they attempt to create rigid borders around who counts as Latino/a and who does not (Ferdman & Gallegos, 2001). Additionally, those who are unaware of the diversity within the Latino/a community would certainly broaden their perspectives upon considering adopted Latino/as.

Latino/a adoptees in transracial or transcultural families are a unique population that is frequently overlooked in "multicultural" literature, yet there are a myriad of diversity and identity challenges for this group that are sorely needing to be met through new research, research that could provide a foundation for updated policies and practices. As a transcultural adoptee myself, I intend to provide my voice as a member of this group with the hopes of acknowledging and thus honoring our unique circumstances. However, though no one case can accurately capture the countless diversity among Latino/a adoptees, providing a first person perspective, certainly conveys weight.

In conceptualizing this sociocultural phenomenon, I will use sociocultural lenses to show how Latino/a adoptees, hereafter "LADs" (a purposeful pseudo-blend abbreviation conveying the first two letters from the word "adoptee" following the "L" in Latino/a), are both a legitimate part of the NLD and, simultaneously, outside of it. More specifically, I will describe the uniqueness of LADs, as well as their intersection with the New Latino/a Diaspora (NLD). They are two conjoined communities, and herein, I will show that their lived experiences concurrently overlap and exist in separate spheres, a paradoxical existence.

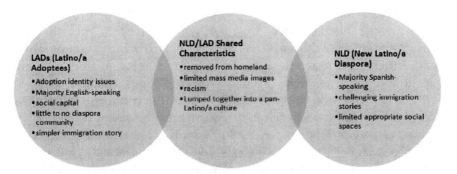

Figure 7.1. Similarities and differences between LADs and the NLD.

Figure 7.1 highlights the elements that LADs share with those in the NLD as well as what is distinct. I will describe each more fully later in the chapter. I begin with a brief description of LADs. Then, to provide important context, I briefly discuss the complicated epistemology of identity for adopted people. From there, I will report on theory and research related to transracial and transcultural adoption. Thus, I will make the case that Latino/a adoptees raised in transcultural homes make up a unique group that deserves distinctive consideration when discussing the new Latino/a Diaspora for their shared and different experiences. Finally, I will conclude with suggestions for what we learn as a result of considering LADs within the New Latino/a Diaspora, and where we might move from here. Throughout, I will enter the story autobiographically, since this story is my own in many ways, yet even after it is published, it will always be a work in progress.

Living the Ultimate Diaspora Existence: The Latino/a Adoptee

Migration occurs in a myriad of ways with family members seeking opportunities not found in their home nation a dominant contemporary image. Yet there is another global migration trend, albeit small, which is exempt from the typical immigration criticism: the adoption of children from abroad. According to a U.S. Department of State (n.d.) website, in 2008 more Guatemalan children were adopted into the U.S. than from any other country. The tenth most frequent sending country to the U.S. for adoption during that year was Colombia. Adoption domestically or from abroad is often hailed as a humanitarian mission, to save poor children from their impoverished, unwanted environments so that they can be raised in loving middle class households (or with Madonna or Angelina Jolie), a good colonial liberal argument. Or adoptees are precious gifts, providing comfort to otherwise childless families desiring to parent. These perspectives, while viewed as noble by some, often emanate from everyone but the adoptees themselves (Trenka, Oparah, & Shin, 2006).

What happens once a brown child realizes the confusion of being so different from her parents? From her classmates? From her community *in situ* and of origin (Friedlander, 1999)? Adoptees are storied as targets of miraculous and/or charitable intervention (Hamann, 2002), and so how dare they disturb the dominant narratives? Yet how can they quietly exist between the margins? Clearly, the picture is incomplete without their story, and herein that story is my story, or at least my story is one version of that story.

As this volume attests, new Latino communities simultaneously succeed and suffer due to their pioneering. They can succeed given the opportunities they have to create positive first-hand contacts with majority communities. At the same time, however, they might suffer in their isolation from a larger Latino/a community and the social infrastructure that exists as a result. LADs have that same familiar challenge, but with two important complications. That is, LADs are not only strangers in a strange land, but strangers within our own homes, our own families. In transcultural households we may be the only member of our family from the nondominant culture. Moreover, at least when we start in the NLD, we are still children.

Below is a stanza from Lorna Dee Cervantes' poem (Refugee Ship) that describes the sense of alienation one might feel after looking at their reflection in the mirror (Camacho-Gingerich, Branco-Rodriguez, Pitteri, & Javier, 2007).

> I feel I am a captive
> Aboard the refugee ship.
> The ship that will never dock.
> El barco que nunca atraca. (Cervantes, 1981)

Later in the poem, Cervantes, not an adoptee, even uses the phrase "orphaned" to describe her relationship to her Spanish name, a nod to the tight connections between language or mother tongue and identity, yet another fierce separation.

I am the protagonist in this poem, metaphorically. The visage in the mirror, my presentation to others, is Latina, and with that image come expectations and assumptions about who I am (Andujo, 1988). As a LAD, though, what I have felt inside is often distanced from my facade, like the drifting ship Cervantes describes. At the same time, I have come close enough to my "dock" to get a vague sense of what it looks like. From what I have uncovered, my Colombian birthmother was among the first in the new wave of immigrants to this country following the 1965 Immigration Act, also the year of my conception. I've been told that she came alone to work for the diplomatic corps as a domestic in Washington DC according to the adoption agency's nonidentifying records. My father too was a Colombian living in Washington DC. That is about the extent of my knowledge of these two people who created me. Colombian, however, is what I am. But, growing up as a child, living in the diasporic suburbs of Washington DC, I did not have too many opportunities to know what that meant.

I grew up in a mixed race, White and Black, working class to poor, community in the 1970s. Nowhere did I hear Spanish being spoken except for an occasional word by my Mexican American father. In that environment, it was difficult for me to begin the journey of self-discovery that philosopher and fellow adoptee, Kimberly Leighton (2005) theorizes on in her work. More specifically, Val Middletown, Kieran Coleman, and Chance Lewis' book chapter in *White Teachers/Diverse Classrooms* (2006) refers specifically to transracial adoptees in the following quote:

> We see African American youth raised in predominately White settings as "at risk" as they experience isolation, identity issues, categorization, and a lack of community and family connectedness. We see these experiences occurring in African American families and in White families with adopted children of color. (p. 168)

I vividly recall other girls in school obsessively playing with my hair. And often I was asked, "Where are you from?" "Are you Indian?" "Are you Chinese?" I was exotic in this Black and White working class community. I tried to avoid offering much as an answer, for I was never sure myself who I was. I had no Latin American role models, aside from Charo on TV, and no peers, aside from the new neighbors from El Salvador in the early 1980s. Living in diaspora, thus, created, for me, a sense of unease and unawareness. My family's lower social class also worked to thwart opportunities for travel and exposure to differences beyond the Black and White that surrounded us.

A recently released study reported that transracially and/or transculturally adopted children have a type of "double consciousness" (Du Bois, 1903). As with Du Bois (1903), there is an awareness that the world presumes you fit into a certain category, but you are aware that that category seems incomplete and elusive. More particularly, there is a disconnect with two distinct cultures or ethnicities, their biological and their adopted (Evan B. Donaldson Adoption Institute, 2009; Friedlander, 1999). This makes the task all that more difficult in terms of integrating the adopted identity with their racial and/or ethnic selves, or the selves they present to others.

According to Sally Haslanger (2005), racial identity is like a map. It is not entirely cognitive, but at times "somatic" (p. 283) or, unconscious. Racial identity is also dependent upon surroundings, which for transracial adoptees can get more complicated. Whether LADs live around and interact with other Latinos is clearly not entirely under our own control. So, while adoptees might try to take on a different identity—that of their adoptive families, for example—the bid to be seen as part of such a group may not be entirely successful (Becker, 1990). Adoptees are, at least, always possessors of the identity that others see. Thus, there is precariousness to their very being, which can easily be jolted by added stress from others' insensitivities (Andujo, 1988). Thus, my own attempts at becoming solid in my identity (as a brown skinned White person) were thwarted by others surrounding me who thought they knew who I was.

In their study titled "Beyond Culture Camp: Promoting Healthy Identity Formation in Adoption" (2009), the Donaldson Institute provides research on insensitivities occurring to transracially/transculturally adopted children across ethnic and racial lines. For example, they found that 39% of adult adoptees adopted from Korea to the U.S. reported experiencing racial discrimination as children from their teachers. The anti-immigration wave of the early 21st century is marked by a heightened period of racism against Latino/as in particular. And, as Estela Andujo (1988) found, "once (sic) adoptees are beyond the confines of their immediate families, they will experience the same interactive threats all minorities experience in society" (p. 4). There have been multiple incidents where I have experienced microaggressions, have been taken less seriously, and so forth, despite the educational ranks to which I have risen. The impact of these interactions and experiences on children, especially when doled out by teachers, can have devastating effects both in school and beyond. Specifically, related to learning environments, adoptees can experience "stereotype threat" (Steele & Aronson, 1995), or the internalization of a belief system of one's capabilities, which impacts academic performance. In the case of LADs, their threat becomes impacted by and similar to the threats experienced by the NLD. My own identity confusion and estrangement perhaps contributed greatly to my own K–12 challenges to the point of obtaining a paltry high school academic record and low SAT scores, which combined with no family financial support, leaving me with little to no choices for higher education, and so I chose to join the Air Force in lieu of college after high school. I was in search of finding the "exotic" community to which I belonged in the wider world.

ADOPTED CONTEXT: IDENTITY AND EPISTEMOLOGY

As a result of litigious secrecy (i.e., closed adoption records), the origins of my own existence remain out of my permissible grasp. What I could have been as a Colombian-descent child of Colombian parents remains at the level of the imaginary (Honig, 2005). As an adopted person with only vague genealogical awareness, I have mainly had my environment at my disposal to carve out my identity, my sense of who I would become, who I can still become. I have known that I was adopted from my earliest memories. My adopted parents told me that "I was special" because they chose me, while other families "got stuck" with their children. But what lay dormant beneath this fairytale was that they were able to choose me, because someone else, my biological mother, rejected me.

I was recently reminded of how difficult it is to fathom mother/child separation and loss. I remember reacting viscerally (as an adult and now mother) when I learned of a 2 year-old girl who was found at a nearby gas station just off a major East Coast highway in a bathroom, crying for her mother who was nowhere to be found. In a second example, after the massive 2010 earthquake in Haiti, I found myself absorbed by the intense focus turned toward the children there, those orphaned by the disaster, and even those who were already orphaned, who became further displaced because of the destruction of their orphanages. U.S. church aide workers were arrested for allegedly "saving" some of these orphans by transporting them over the border to an orphanage in the Dominican Republic. Rescuing orphaned children, a virtuous action for some, like for these church aide workers, does not make up for the heartrending realities of mother/child separation. It is impossible then to deny that parental rejection or loss lies at the heart of our deepest existential sensitivities. What happens for those of us then who live with this fundamental loss?

A few writers have forayed into this territory. Nancy Verrier (1993) wrote a groundbreaking book called *The Primal Wound* in which she theorized that in fact, adoptees do suffer a tremendous loss through the process of adoption. She wrote,

> The child actually experienced being left alone by the biological mother and being handed over to strangers. That he may have been only a few days

or a few minutes old makes no difference. He shared a 40-week experience with a person with whom he probably bonded in utero, a person to whom he is biologically, genetically, historically, and perhaps even more importantly, psychologically, emotionally, and spiritually connected. (p. 10)

The late B. J. Lifton (2009) also described elements left out of the popular discourse on adoption: "the pain, the feeling of emptiness, of being outsiders" (p. 7). This state of being perennial outsiders corresponds with diaspora concepts in the way that those living in diaspora long for a homeland. In the case of adoptees the motherland is, literally, the mother. For LADs, the challenge multiplies when we consider the commonalities with the NLD.

Philosopher Kimberly Leighton's (2005) thesis is that being adopted is an identity unto itself. This view is appealing because she sees this identity not in terms of a deficit for all that is not known, but instead as a possibility for all that can be. She writes that adoption "has been a way to make sense of the tensions produced by being both at once the product of one's environment and someone whose meaning always exceeds that environment" (p. 147). This possibility is not a fantasy of sorts, but rather it suggests that there is a self of one's existence that is always unknown, thus always possible. This is not the way that most people, including some adoptees, view identity. As I stated earlier, there is a deep-seated fear of the unknown associated with adoption for its disconnect between mother and child. Leighton describes an encounter she had with a group of adoptive parents she spoke to about her own search for her birth family that resulted in her finding her birthmother. She sensed that they desired to hear that she came to know an objective reality about herself that had previously been a missing piece of her identity. She describes having disappointed the adoptive parents because, for her, it was her encounter with her birth mother that led her to believe that there would be no way for her ever to have a firm grasp of her identity. Thus, the more she found out, the more she knew she would never know a true identity. No amount of knowledge of one's biological roots can provide static answers of one's identity. It is therefore, up to us to just be "all that we can be," even if this is admittedly a trite, well-worn phrase that some might even question as an impossibility.

Be all you can be is an inadequate phrase without the solid ground that comes from knowing and/or being a full-fledged member of one's culture and ethnicity. Tobias Hubinette (2004), a Korean adoptee raised in Sweden, describes adoptee identity as a place within the post-colonial descriptor, "the third space." He cites Homi Bhabha's work on this concept and describes it "as the space where culture has no unity, purity or fixity, and where primordial notions of race and nation have been replaced by a floating and hybrid existence" (p. 9). Yet, while one's pursuit for a hybrid existence seems plausible and preferable for LADs, it is important to make our presence known to other Latino/as, so that they can reach out in an embrace as cultural brothers and sisters. On the other hand, we need to show the dominant culture as well that, although we were adopted into their culture and as a result, we might have access to a certain type of social capital, we will always carry with us our façade, which dictates certain expectations from the larger society. Anti-racist activism was certainly not something I experienced within my own family and community; however, it is a crucial component for LADs and their cultural brethren living together in diaspora.

LADs AS DIFFERENT FROM OTHERS IN THE NLD

According to the National Center for Education Statistics (Kewal-Ramani, Gilbertson, Fox, & Provasnik, 2007) report *Status and Trends in the Education of Racial and Ethnic Minorities*, "In 2005, 6.9 million Hispanic elementary and secondary students spoke a language other than English at home" (p. 64). More recently, the Pew Hispanic Research Center (2009) released a report called *Between Two Worlds: How Young Latinos Come of Age in America* that found 79% of the second-generation claim to have a command of Spanish compared with 38% of third-generation youth. While attrition in language acquisition occurs over generations of immigrants, for LADs, given their transcultural circumstances, Spanish language acquisition is dependent upon other factors, such as schooling opportunities.

Given the transcultural rearing of many LADs, we are most likely living in households in which Spanish is not our first language, and more likely, we do not know the language at all. In my own circumstances, for example, our community was entirely English speaking, and though my Chicano father grew up speaking Spanish, he would only speak to me with a periodic word or phrase on occasion. Yet, language can be such a defining characteristic of one's cultural identity. Herein lies one of the deepest separations that can occur between LADs and other Latino/as: the lack of a shared language, or, more precisely, the lack of a shared first language, the language most often used to express intimate thoughts.

For LADs, a native or near-native command of English brings greater access to the dominant culture. Yet, ironically, with the ease of access can come a wider gulf between LADs and other Latino/as struggling to learn English and suffering from the ensuing racism of English-only movements. Each is helpless when language separates them. While LADs without Spanish may yearn for missed connections, Spanish-speaking Latino/as may look upon the LADs with suspicion for not speaking their supposed mother tongue.

In fact, I have experienced this very isolation and rejection from Spanish-speaking Latinos, and it is painful to my marrow because, as much as I have tried to learn Spanish, the intense internalized psychological expectations of knowing inside that my Spanish will never be what it is assumed to be, or what it should have been, have impaired my learning. In other words, my façade dictates to others that I have a firm grasp of the language, and because of that, I have found it troubling to even try, for fear of negative judgments about the quality of my language abilities.

There is also an irony when it comes to the different ways each group is perceived. Robert Koulish, in his book *Immigration and American Democracy* (2010), claims that the public discourse on immigration has moved to an extreme racist and xenophobic sentiment such that strong-arm immigration policies can be easily justified. He writes that simply using the term "illegal alien" dehumanizes and criminalizes personhood rather than activity. Perhaps this also explains the rise in hate crimes against Latino/as (Mock, 2007). For example, there was recently a high profile story in Shenandoah, PA where the federal government charged local police officers with evidence tampering in the case of a fatal beating of a Mexican man at the hands of two young White men (Smith, 2009), one of a plethora of emerging hate-based crimes.

Clearly, dominant society's perceptions of Latino/as in the early 21st century hover in and around the negative. Yet for LADs, the perception can be quite the antithesis, as Hubinette (2004) describes in his work when he discusses the view that international adoption of children stems from "colonial desires" of the *other* reflecting "global racial hierarchies" (p. 5). David Eng (2003) describes "the transnational adoptee as complicating the borders between exploitation and privilege" (p. 6), and a transforming of "object" (orphan) to "subject" (adoptee) that is "worthy of investment— economic protection (capital accumulation), political rights (citizenship), and social recognition (family)" (p. 7). So, while some Latino/as experience discrimination in the 21st century for their perceived disruptions and economic costs, LADs are desirable, perceived as having the potential to fulfill an adoptive family's deep desire for wholeness, whether as humanitarians, to fulfill parental/familial desires, or for some other reasons. Hubinette writes, "assimilation becomes the ideal as the adoptee is stripped of name, language, religion and culture, only retaining a fetishised non-white body, while the bonds to the biological family and the country of origin are cut off" (p. 6). By default, LADs act as good will ambassadors counteracting the negative perceptions of their NLD brethren, but without the stigma stemming from the differences in cultural immersion. The positive ambassador role is not of the LADs' choosing; thus, it can become a burden of weight and responsibility.

The unique access LADs have to the dominant culture comes as a result of the families that raise and socialize us. So in NLD communities, LADs will most likely be separated from our Latino/a peers in schools as soon as the schools read the names and see the parents. We are not placed in segregated ESL classes (Valdés, 2001), and thus, we are as different from some Latino peers as we are in our adoptive families. And in many circumstances, we are the only NLD within our communities. Also, LADs's families often possess the cultural capital to advocate for their children in ways that might not occur for other newcomers. Thus, LADs can be accepted as U.S. dominant culture insiders, but again, ironically, while this empowers us personally, it also separates us further from our biological origins.

Gina Samuels and Fariyal Ross-Sheriff (2008) suggest that this challenging status of inside/outsiders is best thought about through the lenses of intersectionality. Specifically, it is important to acknowledge shifting notions of oppression and privilege to understand "what is valued in one context may not be valued in another. What is oppressed in one context may be elevated in another.... We must begin to theorize privileges and oppressions not as fixed statuses but as fluid and dynamic" (p. 8). This perspective can also help to complicate nations of diaspora.

A defining characteristic of diaspora comes from the new community building that can occur while living "in exile" (Butler, 2001). In other words, Jews, African Americans, and other cultures come together as a result of their shared diasporic conditions, or longing and remembrance of a bygone homeland. In the NLD, cultural bonding no doubt forms quickly albeit in smaller communities as a matter of survival and success. For Latino/as, however, it becomes complicated given the fact that U.S. society lumps together individuals from an array of ethnic cultures into one pan-Latino culture (Oboler, 1995).

In other words, a shared NLD is also somewhat complicated given that national ethnic ties outweigh a sense of collective ethnicity (Pew Hispanic Research Center, 2009). Outside of the formal confines of the U.S. Census, fewer than 22% of Latino/as, regardless of their generational status, self-identify as "Hispanic" or Latino/a. Surprisingly, only half of the third-generation Latino/as self-identify as "Americans" with a third of second-generation identifying as such. Seventy two percent of first-generation Latino/as self-identify with their country of origin, while 41% of second-generation Latino/as do this, and a high number, 32%, of third-generation Latino/as self-identify with their families' home countries. Additionally, the researchers found that about two thirds of this age group felt that there were more intragroup differences than similarities among Latino/as living in the United States, yet this same percentage expressed intragroup compatibility. And so, if it is this complicated for immigrant Latinos from many different nations, what is it like for LADs who may or may not know firmly their country of origin, especially those Latino/as adopted domestically? Or, how is it that LADs obtain specific national cultural understanding as opposed to generic pan-ethnic awareness? With whom do we commune in diaspora?

Latino/a and other transnational adoptees, in their circumstantial isolation from the rest of the Diaspora community, may share some of the same longings, but they are not intrinsically part of a larger, intergenerational network of shared ethnic solidarity. There are, however, attempts at creating an adoptee diaspora.

Adoptees from Korea have actualized this element of diaspora and formed their own community, moving beyond the collective Western label of adopted Asians or Asian immigrants. Hubinette (2004) describes how Korean adoptees in Europe started a group in 1986 that later united with Korean adoptee groups in other parts of world. Hubinette explains that 150,000 Korean children were dispersed around the Western world between 1953 and 2001. Additionally, he explains that the Korean government has attempted officially to embrace Korean adoptees as members of the larger Korean diaspora, but for adoptees, that definition did not correspond with traditional notions of diaspora given adoptees' lack of language and myth of homeland, as well as, intermarriage. So given their differences from other diasporic Koreans, they formed a third space that has led to online and real time networking, conferences, and other social events and opportunities.

With the advent of the Internet, there are more possibilities for connecting LADs together pan-ethnically as well as within ethnic national groups. There is a Colombian-adoptee Yahoo group, and through that group, small subgroups have gathered socially in regions as dispersed as Minnesota and New York City. Pro-Busqueda is a human rights organization that attempts to reunite families from war-torn El Salvador, whether adopted or otherwise. Patrick McDermott's (2006) chapter in *Outsiders Within* on being an El Salvadoran adoptee describes the nuances of his particular exodus to the U.S. from a country at war and intimates a collective of other adoptees from El Salvador. And as the Guatemalan adoptees continue to come of age and create a collective community, there will be even more opportunities for specific Latino ethnic national collaboration. I did not meet another LAD until I was an adult.

Generally, LADs's opportunities are minimized due to their dispersion; however, the Internet does hold promise for bringing together a third space for Colombian, El Salvadoran, Chilean, Guatemalan, and so forth, adoptees around the world. There they can finally find a community with which to share what it is like being of a particular Latin American origin within a Western adopted family, and knowing little of one's homeland. These online (and otherwise) opportunities to form LAD communities are indeed much more rare than it would be for most immigrant Latinos of the NLD to find each other in nonvirtual community.

Yet another difference between international LADs and other Latino/a immigrants comes from the differences in their migration stories. Whereas many Latino/a immigrants may have struggled through bureaucracy to arrive in the US, or perhaps they entered illegally, most LADs, especially those born after 1983, received automatic citizenship under the Child Citizenship Act (CCA) of 2000 upon the completion of their adoption. Very few LADs have stories of being a stowaway with their parents to reach the United States (though some have uncovered stories of their being products of the black market [McDermott, 2006]). Quite the contrary as middle-class White Americans swoop down like storks and fly home with a brown skinned, automatic U.S. citizen. Therein lies a tremendous difference between LADs and other Latino/a adoptees: a vast gulf between our actual immigration stories, devoid of the obvious struggles and tribulations that make up many immigration stories. Of Chinese adoptees, Karen Miller-Loessi and Zeynep Kilic (2001) write, "Perhaps there is some understandable envy here at the ease of transit for these little girls, compared to the hardship and suffering of so may first-generation immigrants" (p. 251). This vast difference could even create animosity, leading to further rejection of LADs from their blood brethren. And so, while there could be a legitimate case made for LADs to be exiled from the NLD, there are also many ways that we are inevitably united, namely, for the fact that we are both living away from our ethnic roots.

LADs AS LEGITIMATE IN THE NEW LATINO/A DIASPORA

Just as we can acknowledge the chasm separating two Latino/as, LAD and "traditional" immigrant, so too must we imagine that in fact there can be many similarities with the New Latino/a Diaspora. Primarily, there may be complicated legal issues for each group (Camacho-Gingerich et al., 2007). As one example, some LADs (those born before 1983) have faced possible deportation due to neglect on the part of their adoptive families who never filed for full citizenship for their children (Archibald, 2011). In fact, there is even a nonprofit corporation, Ethica (ethicanet.org) that has as part of its mission to aid those adoptees who require assistance in obtaining their due citizenship. Some are not so lucky, however. In a recent newspaper article (Shin, 2011) describing the impending deportation of a Korean adoptee found guilty numerous times for theft, they reported that ICE (U.S. Immigration and Custom Enforcement) had deported a "large number" of adoptees in recent years. It is one thing to imagine undocumented Latino/as in Arizona being shipped back to the Mexican side of the border by our border patrol where they have social and cultural capital to rebuild their lives within the existing community. However, imagine an adult LAD with little to no command of Spanish and no known contacts in Mexico among this crowd?

This image is one way to imagine why transnational adoptees are in diaspora, some even consider us as members of a "victim diaspora" (Hubinette, 2004; Miller-Loessi & Kilic, 2001). Harkening back to Robin Cohen (2003), Miller-Loessi and Kilica (2001) and Hubinette (2004) describe this subset of diaspora communities as one that is associated with homeland trauma, which led to displacement (like Armenian, Jewish, African, Irish, and Palestinian diasporas). In the case of LADs, the trauma comes from the separation, not only from one's motherland, but also, literally, one's mother. While this might paint a differential between LADs and other Latino/a immigrants, one can also easily find parallels among these childhood populations. As I have explained earlier, deep distress can result from international adoption. In describing adopted Chinese girls, Miller-Loessi and Kilic write, "They are the innocent victims of circumstance" (p. 250), a claim that can easily tie together all transnational adoptees with Latino/a children whose parents force them to cross the U.S. border illegally. Undocumented Latino/a children who are brought across our borders by their relatives may suffer trauma during the transit process, or even as a result of being removed from known environs (Suárez-Orozco, Yoshikawa, Teranishi, & Suárez-Orozco, 2011). For example, there are numerous stories of "coyotes," or smugglers, who for a fee, assist border crossers, a corrupt free-market opportunity (U.S. Immigration Support, n.d.). Similarly, Guatemalan adoptions have been halted due to corruption and violation of the Hague Adoption Convention and Intercountry Adoption Act of 2000 (U.S. Department of Homeland Security, 2008). And so, there are clearly parallels among young Latino/a immigrants, whether adopted or not, sharing victim diaspora status.

Tying together LADs with other Latino/a immigrants in the NLD further, as I described above, are the limited to dangerous media representations of Latino/as, which ironically have the potential to impact LADs, particularly when we are not within the protective bubble of our White adoptive families (Andujo, 1988). Our façade is what others view, and thereby expectations are hoist upon us. Judgments and assumptions are made. What results then has the potential to complicate our lives, putting us in solidarity with our nonadopted Latino/a brethren. Additionally, however, a consideration of the impact of Latino/a racism on LADs can complicate the anti-Latino/a sentiments at large. Ellen Herman (2008) writes:

> Debates about immigration and national security, border enforcement, and terrorism that have raged since September 11, 2001, may seem distant from

transnational family making. They are not. They link global orders to personal life, outline a geopolitics of kinship, and expose the great hopes and terrible disappointments that Americans associate with negotiating the difference between "them" and "us." (p. 6)

In other words, adoptive (White) families eagerly open their doors to LADs, while others in the wider society might shut their doors (or at least make assumptions) upon encountering them. What makes the difference?

A removal from one's homeland, one's motherland, one's culture, can clearly have devastating effects on Latino/a immigrant children, whether they enter the country illegally or not. In the case of LADs, the disconnect is a loss that differs existentially given the separation between mother and child, motherland and child. David Eng (2010) describes this profound loss using Freudian lenses to describe a filmmaker/Korean adoptee's autobiographical portrayal within the film *First Person Plural*. In an analysis of the filmmaker's self-representation, he writes, "Racial melancholia thus describes a psychic condition by which vexed identification and affiliations with lost objects, places, and ideals (of Asianness) as well as Whiteness, remain estranged and unresolved" (p. 116). He shows how Asian immigrants and transnational adoptees share racial melancholia, only differing in the ways that it is experienced (or tossed aside) intersubjectively and intergenerationally (as in the case of Asian immigrants) versus intrasubjectively (for Asian adoptees), resulting in a loss of emotional agency for the Asian adoptee given her lack of psychic connections.

LADs, THE NEW LATINO/A DIASPORA, AND FORWARD MOVEMENT

Nitza Hidalgo (2005) claims that there is a "collective experience of oppression, familism [and] shared values, core values in the service of resistance" for Latino/as (p. 377). Further, Hidalgo also explains that when Latino/as become aware of their collective histories in relation to race, class, gender, and so forth, from various perspectives, we learn about how oppression has shaped our very existence. This realization leads Latino/as to take responsibility to help make systemic changes for enhanced equity in the form of collective resistance to hegemony and engagement in social movements.

Much of this collective engagement centers on bettering the family unit, thus the concept of "familism." Hidalgo (2005) quotes William Vega (1995, p. 7) to define *familism* as "strong emotional and value commitments to family life." Family life here extends beyond the nuclear family outward. I argue that this awareness can impact LADs in similar ways, for as I wrote earlier, we share much of the same discrimination that other Latino/as experience, and as well, our very existence can be viewed in terms of social (in)justice. Therefore, much justification exists for Latino/a immigrants to seek out and embrace LADs, especially given the potential for the LADs to assist our Latino brethren using their nurtured social capital.

Researchers too should take heed to acknowledge this complicated identity status, to consider new ways of thinking about identity aside from a developmental approach. Developmental lenses are pragmatic and useful in many circumstances, namely Amanda Baden and Robbie Jean Stewart's (2000) framework for transracial adoptees. Yet the fractured and precarious nature of transcultural adoptees should also lead one to seek out more fluid, postmodern perspectives on identity as well (Eng, 2010). Additionally, there has been a recent surge in research related to Korean, Chinese (girls), and Vietnamese adoptees. However, there has been very little mention of the particular plight of LADs and more specifically, the nuances of adoptees from the particular Latino ethnic national groups. It would serve the world of scholarship to pursue this work in more detail.

CONCLUSION

As members of the NLD, Latino/a adoptees' status as outside/insiders provides us with unique lenses through which to view our own situations, but perhaps more importantly, we are empowered in ways that could lend a unique type of support and solidarity in the struggle against oppression, especially on behalf of Latino children. We frequently suffer similar discrimination, yet we also have a status bestowed with social capital given our insider knowledge and experiences of the dominant culture. We feel as though we are on an island of one in a sea of others who seem very much unlike ourselves. The blandness of the suburbs, in my case, further drained from me the confidence to discover who I was, without succumbing to the exoticism that others pegged on me. At other times, we are the ultimate chameleons, fitting in within a variety of communities. We LADs are living in the NLD; therefore, there is the potential to enter into a symbiotic relationship with Colombian, El Salvadoran, Mexican, and so forth, scholars in our shared pursuits of equity on behalf of peoples of color. There is much that our experiences can lend to the process, but only in solidarity can we become stronger. *Viva la Raza!*

REFERENCES

Andujo, E. (1988). Ethnic identity of transethnically adopted Hispanic adolescents. *Social Work, 33*(6), 531–535.
Archibald, M. (2010). Judge orders woman adopted as baby deported to Mexico. Retrieved March 27th, 2012 from *The Tacoma News Tribune* http://www.

thenewstribune.com/2010/12/10/1459364/judge-orders-woman-deported-to.
html

Baden, A., & Steward, R. J. (2007). The cultural-racial identity model: A theoretical framework for studying transracial adoptees. In R. A. Javier, A. Baden, F. A. Biafora, & A. Camacho-Gingerich (Eds.), *Handbook of adoption: Implications for researchers, practitioners, and families* (pp. 90–112). Thousand Oaks: Sage.

Becker, A. (1990). The role of the school in the maintenance and change of ethnic group affiliation. *Human Organization, 49*(1), 48–55.

Butler, K. D. (2001). Defining diaspora, refining a discourse. *Diaspora: A Journal of Transnational Studies, 10*(2), 189–219.

Camacho-Gingerich, A., Branco-Rodriguez, S., Pitteri, R. E., & Javier, R. (2007). International adoption of Latin American children: Psychological adjustment, cultural and legal issues. In R. A. Javier (Ed.), *Handbook of adoption: Implications for researchers, practitioners, and families* (pp. 149–159). Thousand Oaks, CA: Sage.

Cervantes, L. D. (1981). Refugee Ship. *Emplumada.* Pittsburgh, PA: University of Pittsburgh Press.

Cohen, R. (2003). *Global diasporas: An introduction.* Seattle, WA: University of Washington Press.

Du Bois, W. E. B. (1903). *The souls of black folks.* Chicago, IL: A. C. McClurg.

Eng, D. L. (2010). *The feeling of kinship: Queer liberalism and the racialization of intimacy.* Durham, NC: Duke University Press.

Evan B. Donaldson Adoption Institute. (2009, November). *Beyond culture camp: Promoting Healthy Identity Formation in Adoption.* Retrieved November 27, 2009 from http://www.adoptioninstitute.org/research/2009_11_culture_camp.php

Ferdman, B., & Gallegos, P. (2001). Racial identity development and Latinos in the United States. In C. Wijeyesinghe & B. Jackson (Eds.), *New perspectives on racial identity development: A theoretical and practical anthology* (pp. 32–36). New York, NY: New York University Press.

Friedlander, M. L. (1999). Ethnic identity development of internationally adopted children and adolescents: Implications for family therapists. *Journal of Marital and Family Therapy, 25*(1), 43–60.

Hamann, E. (2002). ¿Un paso adelante? The politics of bilingual education, Latino student accommodation, and school district management in Southern Appalachia. In S. Wortham, E. Murillo Jr., & E. Hamann (Eds.), *Education in the new Latino diaspora: Policy and the politics of identity* (pp. 67–98). Westport, CT: Ablex.

Hamann, E., & Harklau, L. (2010). Education in the New Latino Diaspora. In E. Murillo (Ed.), *Handbook of Latinos and Education* (pp. 157–169). New York, NY: Routledge.

Haslanger, S. A. (2005). You mixed? Racial identity without racial biology. In S. A. Haslanger & C. Witt (Eds.), *Adoption matters: Philosophical and feminist essays* (pp. 265–290). Ithaca, NY: Cornell University Press.

Herman, E. (2008). *Kinship by design: A history of adoption in the modern United States.* Chicago, IL: University of Chicago Press.

Hidalgo, N. (2005). Latino/a families' epistemology. In P. Pedraza & M. Rivera (Eds.), *Latino education: An agenda for community action research A volume of the national Latino/a education research and policy project* (pp. 375–402). Mahwah, NJ: Lawrence Erlbaum Associates.

Honig, E. A. (2005). Phantom lives, narratives of possibility. In T. A. Volkman (Ed.), *Cultures of transnational adoption* (pp. 213–222). Durham, NC: Duke University Press.

Hubinette, T. (2004). *Demographic information and Korean adoption history: Guide to Korea for overseas adopted Koreans.* Seoul, South Korea: Overseas Koreans Foundation.

Kewal-Ramani, A., Gilbertson, L., Fox, M., & Provasnik, S. (2007). Status and Trends in the Education of Racial and Ethnic Minorities (NCES 2007-039). National Center for Education Statistics, Institute of Education Sciences, U.S. Department of Education. Washington, DC.

Koulish, R. E. (2010). *Immigration and American democracy: Subverting the rule of law.* Milton Park, Abingdon, Oxon. New York, NY: Routledge.

Leighton, K. (2005). Being adopted and being a philosopher: Exploring identity and the "desire to know" differently. In S. A. Haslanger & C. Witt (Eds.), *Adoption matters: Philosophical and feminist essays* (pp. 146–170). Ithaca, NY: Cornell University Press.

Lifton, B. J. (2009). *Lost & found: The adoption experience* (3rd ed.). Ann Arbor, MI: University of Michigan Press.

McDermott, P. (2006). Disappeared children and the adoptee as immigrant. In J. J. Trenka, J. C. Oparah, & S. Y. Shin (Eds.), *Outsiders within: Writing on transracial adoption* (pp. 105–116). Cambridge, MS: South End Press.

Middletown, V., Coleman, K., & Lewis, C. (2006). Black/African american families: Coming of age in predominantly white communities. In J. Landsman, & C. W. Lewis (Eds.), *White teachers, diverse classrooms: A guide to building inclusive schools, promoting high expectations, and eliminating racism* (pp. 162–184). Sterling, VA: Stylus.

Miller-Loessi, K., & Kilic, Z. (2001). A unique diaspora? the case of adopted girls from the people's republic of china. *Diaspora: A Journal of Transnational Studies, 10*(2), 243.

Mock, B. (Winter 2007). Immigration backlash: Hate crimes against Latinos flourish. *Intelligence Report*, 128. Retrieved March 3, 2010, from http://www.splcenter.org/get-informed/intelligence-report/browse-all-issues/2007/winter/immigration-backlash

Oboler, S. (1995). *Ethnic labels, Latino lives: Identity and the politics of (re)presentation in the United States.* Minneapolis, MN: University of Minnesota Press.

Pew Hispanic Research Center. (2009, December 11). *Between two worlds: How young Latinos come of age in America.* Retrieved January 5, 2010, from http://pewhispanic.org/reports/report.php?ReportID=117

Samuels, G. M., & Ross-Sheriff, F. (2008). Identity, oppression, and power: Feminisms and intersectionality theory. *Affilia: Journal of Women and Social Work, 23*(5), 5–9.

Shin, S. W. (2011). Korean woman, adopted as infant, facing deportation in Arizona. Retrieved from http://newamericamedia.org/2011/01/korean-woman-adopted-as-infant-facing-deportation-in-arizona.php

Smith, R. (2009, December 17). Pennsylvania cops accused of hate crime cover-up. Retrieved February 12, 2010, from http://www.npr.org/templates/story/story. php?storyId=121576402HYPERLINK "http://www.npr.org/templates/story/ story.php?storyId=121576402&ps=rs"&HYPERLINK "http://www.npr.org/ templates/story/story.php?storyId=121576402&ps=rs"ps=rs

Steele, C. M., & Aronson, J. (1995). Stereotype threat and the intellectual test performance of African Americans. *Journal of Personality and Social Psychology, 69*(5), 797–811.

Suárez-Orozco, C., Yoshikawa, H., Teranishi, R., & Suárez-Orozco, M. (2011). Growing up in the shadows: The developmental implications of unauthorized status. *Harvard Educational Review, 81*(3), 438–472.

Trenka, J. J., Oparah, J. C., & Shin, S. Y. (Eds.). (2006). *Outsiders Within: Writing on transracial adoption.* Boston, MA: South End Press.

U.S. Department of Homeland Security. (2008). USCIS announces changes to Guatemalan adoptions. Retrieved February 14, 2011, from http://www.uscis. gov/portal/site/uscis/menuitem.5af9bb95919f35e66f614176543f6d1a/?vgnex toid=2ec1959a5ea09110VgnVCM1000004718190aRCRD&vgnextchannel= 1958b0aaa86fa010VgnVCM10000045f3d6a1RCRD

U.S. Department of State. (n.d.). Intercountry adoption: Statistics, adoptions by year. Retrieved March 3, 2012, from http://adoption.state.gov/about_us/ statistics.php.

U.S. Immigration Support. (n.d.). Illegal immigration from Mexico. Retrieved February 14, 2011, from http://www.usimmigrationsupport.org/illegal-immigration-from-mexico.html

Valdés, G. (2001). *Learning and not learning English: Latino students in American schools.* New York, NY: Teachers College Press.

Verrier, N. N. (1993). *The primal wound: Understanding the adopted child.* Baltimore, MD: Gateway Press.

CHAPTER 8

DEFINED BY LANGUAGE

The Role of Foreign Language Departments in Latino Education in Southeastern New Diaspora Communities

Linda Harklau and Soria Colomer

Reflecting language ideologies at both the regional and national levels, language policy in Georgia schools has generally taken a strong English-only orientation (e.g., Beck & Allexsaht-Snider, 2002). Nevertheless, schools still deal daily with the reality of students and families who are bilingual or who can communicate only in Spanish. This chapter shows how some schools draw upon the only existing bilingual resources they may have—Spanish language education programs—to work with these new students. We synthesize across two studies in north Georgia schools, one chronicling what happens when schools use existing Spanish-language classes for a new Latino heritage speaker population, and the other describing the experiences of Spanish teachers who suddenly find themselves playing unofficial roles as translators, interpreters, counselors, or parent liaisons.

Revisiting Education in the New Latino Diaspora, pp. 153–170
Copyright © 2015 by Information Age Publishing
All rights of reproduction in any form reserved.

Although our sample from these two studies is relatively small, the ubiquity of repurposing within those schools leads us to believe that repurposed Spanish teachers and Spanish classes figure prominently into new Latino diaspora schools' strategies for dealing with Spanish-speaking students and families. Nevertheless, we also find that these efforts remain makeshift. They are half-measures that both students and teachers view as inadequate and inappropriate. Why, then, do they persist? We argue that schools' improvisational responses to students' home language backgrounds reflect in part a chronic lack of resources and bilingual school personnel. However, we also argue that they are indicative of an effort to minimize and contain change to one small part of the school and curriculum.

BACKGROUND

A defining characteristic of new Latino diaspora communities has been a lack of experience and expertise in working with immigrant families (Hamann, Wortham, & Murillo, 2002; Hamann & Harklau, 2010). Piedmont Appalachia offers several cases in point. The Piedmont had little history of in-migration until quite recently and was characterized by a highly stable, predominantly White and poor population (Kochhar, Suro, & Tafoya, 2005). However, beginning in the late 1980s, Latino immigrants were recruited to the area to work in poultry processing, carpet mills, and other industries. Between 1990–2000, driven by a thriving Sunbelt economy, the population in north Georgia grew 15–25% overall, while the Latino population grew by over 700% (Kochhar et al., 2005). It is not only the rapidity of the Latino population increase that has made the Southeast unique, but also that the newcomers have been predominantly foreign-born (Hamann, 2003; Kochhar et al., 2005). The Latino newcomers have also been a relatively homogeneous group, with the vast majority of Mexican heritage (U.S. Census Bureau, 2009). Also, while some new Latino communities have been numerous and concentrated enough to form majorities in their schools (e.g., Dalton City Schools and Gainesville City Schools), in many other schools, despite rapid growth, Latinos/as have remained a distinct minority (Georgia Department of Education, 2009). In Georgia, few schools outside of metro Atlanta had any history of working with linguistic minority students before the late 1980s, and the sort of statewide guidelines and regulations for immigrants and language issues that have long been in place in California or New York were missing or unenforced. Although demographics have changed since then, educators in many parts of the state have remained relatively uninformed about the rights of linguistic minority students. Southeastern public schools have often been characterized by high rates of low-income students and have been notoriously underfunded (Aud et al., 2011), leaving little room in their budgets for specialized educational services for language minority students.

New immigrant settlement areas like Georgia are also unlike traditional immigrant-receiving areas in their school language policy history. Bilingual education once flourished in states like California, Texas, or Florida before the backlash commencing in the 1980s, and it has left a lasting legacy of home language resources for educating children and communicating with families (e.g., Crawford, 1992). On the other hand, states like Georgia have virtually no history of incorporating students' home languages into the schools (but see Hamann [2003] for an exception). Reflecting recent language ideologies at both the regional (e.g., Beck & Allexsaht-Snider, 2002) and national (e.g., Ricento, 2005) levels, language policy in Georgia schools has tended therefore to take a strong "problem" orientation, seeing students' Spanish-English bilingualism as only a deficit in English. State educational policy has tended to equate immigrant education not with incorporating newcomers' home languages and cultures into the school, but rather with providing intensive English instruction that will supposedly hasten their integration with other students.

Of course, even if English-only schooling has been the implicit policy of most Georgia schools, in practice educators still communicate daily with students and families who are Spanish bilinguals or who have low levels of English proficiency. Lacking in personnel and linguistic resources designated to communicate with immigrant families, schools have needed to draw on whatever bilingual resources are at hand. There has been a fair amount of work on the myriad official and unofficial roles taken by English to speakers of other languages (ESOL) teachers (e.g., Clemente & Collison, 2000), paraprofessionals, and Spanish-speaking students (Morales & Hanson, 2005; Orellana, 2001; Tse, 1995) in translation and school-family communication. However, we have virtually no information on what happens to some of the only established Spanish bilingual resources that are likely to be at the disposal of most schools in diaspora communities: Spanish classes and Spanish teachers.

What happens when Spanish programs that have traditionally served an English monolingual academic elite are suddenly repurposed to serve a mixed audience that includes heritage speakers with vastly different instructional strengths and needs? What happens to Spanish teachers who are unofficially cast as impromptu or *dual role* (Colomer, 2010; Messias, McDowell, & Estrada 2009; Moreno, Otero-Sabogal, & Newman, 2007, p. 331) translators, interpreters, and school representatives? These questions are addressed here.

METHODS

The analysis presented here is based on two complementary studies that we have already drawn on for publication (Colomer & Harklau, 2010; Harklau, 2010). Harklau's (2010) analysis is based on longitudinal case studies of two Latino/a students who were part of a larger study and who were enrolled in advanced Spanish as a foreign language classrooms in rural Georgia high schools. One was a Mexican American student from a rural Mexican background who was educated completely in the United States, and the other was a Salvadoran refugee from an urban middle-class background who was educated in San Salvador through seventh grade before coming to Georgia.

In turn, Colomer (Colomer & Harklau, 2010) conducted extended interviews with 26 current or former Spanish teachers working in north Georgia schools. Most taught at the high-school level, although the sample also included three middle school teachers and one elementary school teacher. A school district foreign language coordinator was also included to gain additional perspective.

The primary source of data for both studies was interviews. Harklau (2010) conducted 20 to 90-minute open-ended interviews with case study students at 3 to 4 week intervals over the 5½ years of the study. Colomer and Harklau (2010) used a semistructured interview protocol in hour-long interviews with each educator. All interviews in both studies were transcribed and subjected to an inductive and recursive process of analytic memo writing and coding (Kvale & Brinkman, 2009). The underlying assumption in interview-based studies such as these is that, "[D]iscourse, rather than other kinds of human activities or behavior, is ... the best available window into cultural understandings and the way that these are negotiated by individuals" (Quinn, 2005, p. 3). Qualitative interview studies aim to uncover the often tacit, taken-for-granted assumptions that individuals share with others in their sociocultural worlds and that they draw upon when interacting with others.

SPANISH CLASSROOMS IN THE NEW LATINO DIASPORA

In recent years there has been an increasing scholarly and pedagogical focus on the teaching of heritage languages, particularly Spanish (e.g., Brinton & Kagan, 2007; Roca & Colombi, 2003; Valdés, Fishman, Chávez, & Pérez, 2006). However, the bulk of this work has focused on areas where there are large, multigenerational, Spanish-speaking communities. Classes specifically for heritage language speakers of Spanish remain relatively rare in the new diaspora communities in our studies. Rather, heritage speakers are integrated into instruction that has traditionally served a clientele of academically elite, predominantly White, monolingual speakers of English. Both studies found that it is commonplace to put Spanish-speaking immigrants in such classes because of an assumption that Spanish classes will be comfortable environments for them. Harklau's (2010) research, however, did not bear out this assumption. She found three main problematic areas for immigrant Latino/a youth in traditional Spanish classes. First, she found a conflictual relationship between the standard Iberian variety of Spanish favored in Spanish-as-a-foreign-language classrooms and curricula, and the varieties of Spanish actually used by Spanish-speaking immigrant students (Valdés, Gonzáles, García, & Márquez, 2003).

For example, even though Roberto was an educated, native speaker of standard Salvadoran Spanish, in his Spanish advanced placement (AP) course, he was expected to develop a command of Penninsular grammar points such as the use of *vosotros*, a form which, he pointed out, "We [Salvadorans] don't use it," because it was "more specially in Spain and stuff like—they use it." Hamann (2003) notes a similar phenomenon devaluing of the Spanish of Mexican teachers whose credentials were not recognized in Georgia and who were forced to work as paraprofessionals in the Dalton City Schools in the 1990s at the same time Georgia accorded full credential privileges to teachers visiting in an exchange program with Spain.

Izzie, coming from a modest rural Mexican community, spoke a variety of Spanish considered nonstandard. Also, like many heritage speakers raised in an English-dominant society (Montrul, 2004), she had gaps in Spanish academic and literacy skills. Her Spanish teachers seemed to be at a loss when dealing with Izzie's dialect and even stigmatized it the classroom. She reported, for example, that her Spanish 3 teacher "didn't like the way we talked." Izzie reported that her teacher had told Latinos/as in her class that instead, "We have to speak 'international Spanish' ... she's like 'That's how you say the word where you're from, but in international Spanish, you say it this way.'"

International Spanish is not a neutral term; rather, it reflects a prescriptive view of language promulgated by Spanish language academies (e.g., Instituto Cervantes, 2004). Izzie had the impression that her Spanish 3 teacher only asked her and other heritage language speakers about their dialect in order to judge it as incorrect. She observed that, "Sometimes she'll ask us, you know, like, 'How do you say things?' and she's like, 'No, that's not the way you say it.'" and "mostly she asks *us* and then she tells *us* that it's wrong!" Perhaps the worst case was when teachers actually ignored and silenced the native speakers of Spanish in their classes. Izzie reported that her Spanish 2 teacher "don't call on us very much. Spanish people? He don't call us, just Americans." To Izzie, then, *international Spanish* was a way of telling her and other bilinguals in her class that "Spanish is not really theirs, but instead belongs to some other group of speakers who get to decide the rules about what is appropriate" (Leeman, 2005).

At the same time, at home, Izzie's family explicitly rejected "international Spanish" as a betrayal of their heritage. Izzie reported that, "I told my mom about the way she speaks and the way we speak. She's like, 'She's just making y'all dumber!'" Her mother complained that Izzie would be unable to communicate with family in Mexico and explicitly encouraged Izzie to retain her dialect, explaining that "She doesn't want me to not know my language, where I come from and everything. She says, 'You shouldn't lose that, cause that's something you should be proud.'"

Students were not only assailed for their dialect features by teachers in Spanish classes, but even by fellow Latino/a bilingual peers, who could likewise re-voice and re-instantiate ideologies of standard Spanish and make language proficiency an index of one's authenticity as "Hispanic." Roberto, for example, often adopted a slightly mocking tone in describing the Spanish literacy of Mexican-American peers in his Spanish 3 class. He laughed when describing one classmate's lack of proficiency, "I guess she was born in [sic] here.... But she can't read that—in Spanish," adding patronizingly, "but she tries, she tries." In his Spanish 4 class, however, the tables were turned and Roberto became insecure about his own command of Spanish when a new, highly educated student from Mexico joined the class. In all, then, these makeshift hybrid Spanish classes were not necessarily the safe or comfortable places educators might assume them to be and in fact could be a threatening social arena where Latino immigrants found their language proficiency and even legitimacy as "Hispanic" questioned.

A second way that traditional Spanish classrooms failed immigrant Latinos in these new diaspora schools was by presenting their home cultures in essentialized ways, as the object of what has been termed "cultural tourism" (Kubota, 2004). High culture was privileged in these classrooms, and the teacher's and text's presentation of culture was treated as more authoritative than the students'. A substantial component of both Izzie's and Roberto's Spanish classes was the study of Hispanophone artists and art, Spanish literature, plays, and poetry. The students regarded this content unenthusiastically and at times as alienating. Roberto, for example, described one play, *La Mariposa Blanca*, as "kind of freaky." When Izzie tried to make a class project on an artist more personally relevant by including information on his life and times, her teacher insisted she limit herself to a discussion of his art. Conversely, Izzie reported that her teacher expressly tried to prevent informal Spanish talk from entering the classroom, recalling that her teacher "would always say that we gossip and everything, and we shouldn't be doing that. So, she didn't like us speaking Spanish."

The curriculum also instilled feelings of vulnerability and uncertainty in Izzie and Roberto about their authenticity as representatives of their own home language and cultures. For example, Roberto's Spanish 3 class used a text on the histories of Spanish-speaking countries. In October, he commented, "We already did a history from Mexico, so we are doing history from Guatemala." In November they moved on to Cuba and Puerto Rico. Likewise, Roberto's Spanish 4 class used a text on legends from various Spanish-speaking countries. At one point he observed that "it's from my place. We're doing El Salvador. " "Doing" Mexico, or Guatemala, or El Salvador conjures up a list of countries to check off ("this week El Salvador, next week Costa Rica...") on a crowded tour schedule. While this "kaleidoscope approach" (Herman, 2007) at least challenges the notion that "real" Spanish is only associated with Spain; at the same time, its superficial focus on cultural artifacts such as art, historical figures, legends, festivals, and customs tends to essentialize and reduce Hispanic cultures to something static rather than presenting them as diverse, constantly shifting, and connected with the everyday lives of real people. Kubota (2004) also noted a tendency for textbook publishers to self-censor and skirt sociopolitically sensitive issues that might be politically contentious.

While the weaknesses of the cultural tourism approach may have gone unnoticed by these classes' traditional clientele of U.S.-born White middle class monolinguals, immigrants found it disquieting. For example, when the cultural tourist lens was focused on his own home country, Roberto did not recognize the portrayal. He uneasily reported that "in Spanish, there's, like, some pages about El Salvador, so—but I don't know some of the people in there. Like, a famous poet, I didn't know he was famous." When another text discussed the *cipitio*, Roberto was disturbed that "they got it a different way, in the textbook. It's not the same." Roberto's teacher, to her credit, encouraged him to tell her "if something's wrong with the book, I have to tell her. Like something's not real." Yet the collective weight of teacher and textbook authority seemed to lend greater legitimacy to their version than Roberto could muster for his, and only served to accentuate his own uncertainties of his grasp of Salvadoran culture. When I asked, "You're the expert, aren't you? " he ruefully laughed and replied, "No, not really! Not really!"

Izzie likewise found her grasp of Mexican culture being questioned in Spanish class. She complained that her teacher was, "always talking about Hispanic culture, and what they believe in. And *we*—we, the Hispanics, we get mad sometimes. When she's speaking about our culture and everything. Because she tells it different than what we know." While instruction on high culture in Spanish-speaking societies might be a worthy goal, the problem for immigrants in these classes was the tendency for the school's and the text's rendition or interpretation of culture to be presented or interpreted as authoritative and unanswerable. It thus posed another threat to students' sense of themselves as authentic representatives of their heritage countries and cultures. Even more problematic here was Izzie's sense that everyday conversational uses of Spanish were actually proscribed in the classroom.

A final way that Spanish classes failed Latino/a immigrants in these new diaspora communities was in reinforcing and perpetuating social hierarchies in the broader school. Advanced Spanish classes in these communities brought together two disparate social groups: (a) Spanish classes' traditional clientele; namely, privileged, White, academically successful students; and (b) Latino/a immigrants who in these communities tended to come from lower than average socioeconomic backgrounds, had poorer than average academic achievement, and were often subject to racism and xenophobia at school and in the community. Both Roberto and Izzie perceived a social chasm between themselves and their friends who they identified as "Hispanic," and the category of "Americans" or "Whites," which they saw as synonymous. Schools tend to reinforce social hierarchies and systems of privilege in the broader community and society (Foley, 1990; Stanton-Salazar, 2001; Suárez-Orozco & Todorova, 2003; Valenzuela, 1999). Izzie perceived that "White kids" were privileged at her school and became angry when a Latina friend was reprimanded by the school for wearing a skirt that was too short at the same time that cheerleaders were wearing much shorter skirts. Mixed Spanish class peer relations in these new Latino diaspora communities served to reflect and perhaps even accentuate social divides. Students related stories of a double standard where White students were able to use cell phones in class or talk to friends while Latino/a students displaying the same behavior were accused of misbehavior. Izzie reported that she was accused of cheating when she translated quiz directions from English into Spanish for a Latina friend. She had challenged her teacher, "why are you helping American people translate to English if you don't want me to translate to Spanish?"

The "mainstream" assumption in both these new Latino diaspora communities was that Spanish classes would be a comfortable and even affirming place for Latino/a adolescents. Nevertheless, the schools' improvisational response of putting Latino/a heritage speakers into existing Spanish classrooms without changing curricula or instructional practices instead served to reinforce Spanish-speaking students' alienation and marginalization at their schools. In spite of Roberto's academic advantages in Spanish, he refused to take the AP test and quietly withdrew from his Spanish classes, becoming a mediocre student. Izzie took a more resistant stance. After serious arguments with her Spanish 2 teacher, he "just told me to sit down and shut up." Likewise, in Spanish 3, Izzie and her teacher quickly came to loggerheads, and in class she said that she "just try to ignore her. I won't say anything." Likewise, she reported that her teacher "just ignores me. That's what she does."

Tragically, Spanish-as-a-foreign-language instruction at these schools actually distanced students from their own linguistic and cultural heritage and accentuated their struggles to define themselves affirmatively and academically. Ironically, the Spanish teachers Roberto, Izzie, and other Latino students encountered were themselves somewhat marginalized in the practices of these predominantly White monolingual communities. We turn next to teachers' perspectives and experiences.

SPANISH TEACHERS IN DIASPORA COMMUNITIES

Underscoring how recently and suddenly the immigrant population in their schools had appeared, many of the north Georgia Spanish teachers Colomer interviewed could still recall when the first native Spanish speakers arrived in their school or district. Several teachers had initially been the *only* Spanish-English bilingual educator not only in their own school, but sometimes in their entire district (Colomer, 2010; Colomer & Harklau, 2010.

Perhaps unsurprisingly, then, these Spanish teachers soon found themselves inundated by translating and interpreting requests, often regarding content well outside their areas of academic expertise. The sheer number and diversity of these requests was remarkable. While they came most often from other subject-area teachers, teachers also frequently found themselves translating for everyone from the principal to the counselors to the school secretary to the school nurse to the cafeteria manager. Besides school personnel, requests to translate also came from students, parents, local merchants, hospitals, and police. Spanish teachers reported translating everything from school records to newsletters to homework assignments to illicit student notes. They were often asked to make phone calls to students' homes or pulled out of class to interpret at parent-teacher meetings, IEP meetings (for special education), disciplinary meetings, or to explain bus routes and other school procedures to parents.

One major problem with this informal, ad hoc solution to new diaspora schools' inability to communicate with Spanish immigrant students and families is that Spanish teachers are not trained as translators/interpreters and often lack the requisite level of language proficiency (and socialization to the professional norms of counseling, special education, etc.). While professional translators of written texts or interpreters in aural/oral communication require a level of proficiency in the Superior range of the ACTFL proficiency standards and court interpreters an Advanced-High proficiency, K–12 Spanish teacher certification in the United States generally requires proficiency only in the Advanced-Low range (Swender, 2003). In particular, while professional translators and interpreters are expected to have a basic knowledge of dialect variation and registers in a wide variety of technical fields (Ward, 1992), Spanish teachers work in a more circumscribed target language environment of standard Spanish linguistics and literature. Moreover, with most of their students they can revert to English if a particular point is proving difficult to convey. Not so with interpreting/translating.

Spanish teachers in Piedmont new diaspora communities noted their limitations in terms of listening comprehension on the telephone, understanding and using unfamiliar dialects, and the automaticity needed to interpret at a rapid conversational pace. Others noted their lack of specific technical vocabulary and terms that were needed to interpret, for example, at meetings relating to special needs children or to ask parents about immunization documents. As one teacher commented, "I don't necessarily know all the technical language for that at all, and I find myself describing it in different ways and I just pray and hope that they understand what I'm talking about." Many teachers said that they prefaced interpreting tasks by telling parents and administrators that "I'm really not a translator. Excuse me, I'm not sure if I'm going to get all the words right." Nonetheless, and perhaps most worrisome, teachers noted that any mistranslations they made were likely to go undetected. One commented, for example, "The administrator is not gonna know, really, because the administrator can't speak Spanish."

Even if they felt competent to provide verbatim translations of such terms, teachers pointed out that Latino parents unfamiliar with the U.S. educational system might not fully understand translated school communication without extra explanation. As one teacher of Puerto Rican descent pointed out, "You can't really translate 'Graduation Test' ... because it's different in our countries than it is here." One educator noted that the parents of Latino students recommended for the "Student Support Program" were typically told only that,

> Esto es para ayudarle al niño" [This is to help the child]. That's it.... The parents were under the impression that it was a good program because the kid would get special attention, but they didn't understand that the underlying assumption was that the kid was having some sort of learning difficulties.

An emerging body of literature on other unofficial translators such as children of immigrants and paraprofessionals echoes these teachers' concerns and confirms that translation and interpretation involve more than simple linguistic competence (Morales & Hanson, 2005; Orellana, 2001, 2009; Tse, 1995; Valdés, 2003).

Besides translating and interpreting, Spanish teachers were often asked to expand their roles in other ways in new Latino diaspora communities. There can be a significant tension between the position of institutional agent and spokesperson and the role of parental spokesperson and advocate (e.g., Martinez-Cosio & Iannacone, 2007, p. 350). Some of the roles that Spanish teachers took on as liaisons with the Spanish-speaking immigrant community were a natural extension of world language educators' traditional roles. For example, many sponsored Spanish or international clubs that encouraged

Latino membership. They also used their conversance with linguistic and cultural diversity to help other educators understand cultural differences. One Spanish teacher, for example, was asked by another teacher to explain, "Why do they [Latino students] get so close and why do they get so close to me when they want to talk?... Is that cultural?"

Other roles were more multifaceted and onerous. For example, Spanish teachers' expected roles as homeroom teachers were also expanded when they became the default homeroom teacher to all Spanish-speaking students at their schools. As a result, teachers often reported especially large and demanding homeroom advising groups. Moreover, they found that they became *de facto* school counselors for many of these students. One, for example, said that she not only helped her advisees choose classes and checked up on their academic progress, but also "if a girl is upset, you know, she might come to me because she cannot express exactly how she feels to a counselor." Another recounted how one of her students had approached her in tears, confiding that she was being physically abused by her husband.

As in Harklau's (2010) study, teachers reported that schools assumed that Spanish classrooms would be a "comfort zone" or "home away from home" for Spanish-speaking students. Many Spanish teachers tried to take this responsibility to heart. In particular, one of the few teachers who taught a Spanish class specifically for heritage language speakers embraced this role, saying that "Necesitan una persona que hable su idioma y entienda su cultura así no tienen que molestar la maestra. Les digo que tengo que cambiar mi título a pastora. [They need a person who speaks their language and who will understand their culture so they don't have to bother the teacher. I tell them that I have to change my title to preacher.]"

While ESOL (English for Speakers of Other Languages) teachers often take on similar multifaceted roles in the education of Latino students in established immigrant-receiving areas (e.g., Trickett et al., 2011), Colomer (2010) found that many ESOL teachers were only part-time or itinerant teachers in these new immigrant communities. In addition, several teachers reported that administrators routinely undercounted English learners at their schools in order to avoid incurring the additional expense of hiring an ESOL teacher. They sometimes also hired ESOL teachers who did not speak Spanish and thus could not communicate with the majority of parents of English learners at their schools. As a result, even in schools with ESOL teachers, Spanish teachers reported that they were often "deputized" to teach English learners and communicate with their families.

Even further afield from their instructional training and official job duties, Spanish teachers often reported that they became *de facto* counselors and administrators. For example, one teacher was called from her classroom to call the mother of a student who had been caught skipping school at the park with friends, one of whom had marijuana. While making the call, moreover, the Spanish teacher realized that, "She's got a shirt on with a lot of [Spanish] profanity that nobody had picked up on." Another time, she was asked by counselors to call a parent about a potentially suicidal child.

Not only educators, but also students and families called on Spanish educators to intercede on their behalf with a counselor or another teacher. This might include, for example, asking for an extra credit assignment or ensuring the placement of students in classes with "empathetic" teachers. Some teachers reported hand-scheduling Latino students for classes and meeting with counselors and other educators to argue for higher track placement. Spanish speaking families, with few cultural "insiders" in the communities where they found themselves, even asked Spanish teachers to help them with non-school matters such as applying for citizenship, buying a house, getting a job, or going to the doctor.

Spanish teachers reported that impromptu requests to translate or to do other liaison work often came from many directions, and that the requestors might not be aware of the work that teachers were already doing for others at the school. As one observed,

> If that was the only phone call that I was making, I wouldn't have a problem, but other people are asking me to tell the parents that their child is failing or that their child is constantly coming late and ... I always felt like maybe I should tell somebody that this has really become a problem.

The extra workload was also made more burdensome by the fact that requests were often made without advance warning, leaving Spanish teachers without planned time with their classes or to prepare for instruction. As one described it,

> I was never scheduled or never supposed to translate. It was just a matter of ... "the liaison is off on other business so you need to come step in, we'll cover your class...." Someone would come find me and it was like, Yoink! Pull me out.

Teachers reported that students and even some parents complained to them about the disruptions caused to their Spanish classes by their translating and other tasks. While some districts had translators on call, as one Spanish teacher noted, going "through the district procedure of getting an interpreter ... can take quite a while to do." Unfortunately, this meant that Spanish teachers were most likely to be called on in unexpected and urgent situations, such as student fights or medical emergencies.

Seemingly simple or routine requests and assignments for the Spanish teacher often had a hidden additional workload attached to them. For example, one request to interpret for a single educator at a meeting ultimately meant interpreting for everyone present. Likewise, homeroom teachers of Spanish-speaking students often became default translators for school events such as orientation and Parents' Night. In some instances teachers were asked to take on translation and liaison tasks that were not even at their school. One teacher reported that the primary school in his district sent memos to middle and high school Spanish teachers summoning them to interpret at parent conferences without compensation. Another teacher was taken out of her class by the police to translate at the scene of a car wreck.

In a handful of cases Spanish teachers reported that supervisors had intervened on their behalf when the workload had grown out of control. One district foreign language coordinator had asked educators from throughout the district to document the time they were spending on translation and other tasks. Another Spanish teacher reported that her department head stood up on behalf of foreign language teachers who were doing an exceptional amount of translation at the school. One teacher reported advocating for herself, writing a letter to her principal asking her to explain to teachers that "I'm not, like, their on-call translator." However, in another instance, a teacher reported that her principal volunteered her time to translate for parent-teacher conferences at another school even though she herself had already declined.

However they may have felt about the work, Spanish teachers often perceived that they could not refuse requests coming from superiors. As one observed, "When a principal or ... your supervisor tells you to do something, you should pretty much do it." Others agreed to tasks because they did not want to disappoint colleagues or be seen as difficult. Some said, "I'm a nice person" or, more starkly, "I'm a sucker." Teachers sometimes felt that their extra efforts were underappreciated and taken for granted. For example, one reported that when she had complained to her principal about extra work, the principal had just replied, "Well, that comes with the job." Moreover, as one Spanish teacher observed with frustration, "there is really nothing that's standardized or anything" in terms of guidelines for performing these jobs at her school, and "it just felt all so under the table-ish, that it wasn't official."

Teachers reported that not only were they taking on impromptu, make-shift roles for which they were poorly prepared and little compensated, but that the constant interruptions also had an adverse impact on their formal jobs in Spanish classrooms. The use of Spanish teachers for these multifaceted roles may have seemed cost-free to administrators and other educators, but it did not come without a price, diminishing the quality of classroom instruction. Ironically, in the small rural communities these teachers worked in, they were not only putting in extra work but also risking their own social capital at the school on behalf of the newcomers, and their efforts could be met with hostility. For example, one teacher reported that one counselor "almost told me to shut up. He said, 'I think you defend the Latinos too much.'"

Even more dubious than asking Spanish teachers to serve all these diverse roles, teachers reported that they were seldom given any training or even directions on how to handle sensitive legal and ethical matters. As one teacher described it, "Somebody throws you in a room and says, 'Call this parent and say blah-blah-blah.'" Even Spanish teachers who enjoyed the work noted their discomfort with being positioned as the Spanish-speaking voice of institutional authority. They were particularly uncomfortable entering circumstances of which they had little prior knowledge. As one teacher recalled, "They would just e-mail and say, you know, 'Could you translate this conference after school?' It was just always awkward because I didn't know the kid. I didn't teach any of these kids." Another teacher contended, "I'm kind of representing the school, right? I need to know more than what I know." Spanish teachers expressed distress about times when they felt that families were receiving partial or incorrect information. As one put it, "There are so many things that would be potential lawsuits with anybody else, but, because we're dealing with a sector of the population that doesn't really know how the system works, they can get away with a lot without anybody saying, 'Wait a minute!'"

IMPLICATIONS AND CONCLUSION

From these studies, we believe that Spanish language programs and Spanish educators play a far larger and more contentious role in new Latino diaspora schools' adaptation to Latino immigrants than has previously been reported. However, we think it is important to point out that the uses of Spanish classes and Spanish teachers in these communities are largely improvisational. They are not principled or planned choices but rather the result of a lack of monetary and personnel resources, and perhaps equally a lack of institutional will. Our studies showed that while neither teachers nor students found these improvisational practices ideal, they worked just well enough from the schools' perspective to allow them to carry on as usual without having to make more fundamental changes or to find more appropriate solutions to working with Spanish-speaking students and families.

In what ways might Spanish language programs be appropriate and useful resources for Spanish speaking students in new Latino diaspora communities? For one thing, while the foreign language program's traditional constituency may not have seen a problem with the old status quo of Spanish classes aimed at elite monolinguals, it was poorly suited to building on the knowledge and capacities of the schools' new Latino populations. While previous work has tended to assume the possibility of instruction aimed specifically at HL speakers, it is unlikely that high schools in small rural new diaspora communities can provide such instruction, for budgetary as well as ideological reasons. Instead we need to think more about what Spanish instruction needs to look like if it is going to accommodate "the new mainstream" (Enright, 2011), where multilingual, multicultural, and transnational students are a significant and growing presence. Herman (2007), for example, suggested that instruction focus on how the arts and literature were not just dead on the page but rather had arisen out of particular constellations of social, historical, economic, and political conditions and were linked to the concrete personal experiences, perhaps experiences that overlapped with that of students such as Izzie and Roberto and their families. This might include relating Spanish class content more explicitly to issues such as social class disparities, urban migration and environmental degradation, regional and ethnic tensions, forms of government and political turmoil, as well as course content and constructs from other academic subjects such as economics and history.

This chapter also makes it apparent that Spanish educators were being asked to take on tasks for which they were unqualified and unprepared. At times, these requests were even coercive. Moreover, the very fact that this work was unofficial (i.e., it was not part of the Spanish teacher's job description) paradoxically made it easier to overlook the extra time and effort that it cost Spanish teachers. Even for the willing, taking on sociopolitical work of this nature can be a perilous undertaking in rural southeastern areas where small town allegiances and politics may hold sway and teacher unions and tenure may be weak. No matter how much they do, they seem to often be plagued by feelings of guilt that they do not do enough, when in fact the fault more often seems to be in schools and administrators who have resorted to stopgap measures rather than providing more substantively for the needs of their new immigrant student population.

Temporarily setting aside the right and wrong of these practices, more systematic inquiry is needed into the competence of Spanish teachers to engage in this work. Research is needed to gauge the level and types of Spanish language proficiency that are necessary to be an effective school-based language broker in contexts outside the Spanish classroom, and to serve as the basis of language policy and legal and ethical guidelines for translation/interpretation in schools.

Accommodations for new immigrant students and families cannot fall completely to Spanish educators. Schoolwide efforts are needed to overcome the stigmatization of not only Spanish but also Spanish speakers in these communities, where newcomers have yet to be integrated into local social networks or leadership, and where they have had little presence or representation at their children's schools (Miramontes, Nadeau,

& Commins, 2011). Perhaps because many Latino students come from working-class, rural Mexican backgrounds, they are lagging behind White students on a range of educational indicators, including high school graduation rates and scores on state and national achievement tests. If there is a "problem" here, it is not a language problem per se but rather a broader problem with an achievement gap that is strongly associated with race, ethnicity, and class.

Efforts to gain resources for multilingual Latino students and their families must therefore be a schoolwide commitment, bolstered by school administrators, state departments of education, and university faculty. This study also underscores the need for schools to take proactive steps to establish open lines of communication with new immigrant communities. Many teachers interviewed by Colomer pointed out that if their school had communicated effectively with Spanish-speaking immigrant parents about its expectations and rules in the first place, many of the emergencies they encountered would not have existed. This takes administrative leadership and visibility and not just a bit of the Spanish teacher's time.

REFERENCES

Aud, S., Hussar, W., Kena, G., Bianco, K., Frohlich, L., Kemp, J., & Tahan, K. (2011). The Condition of Education 2011. Washington, DC: U.S. Department of Education, National Center for Education Statistics.

Beck, S. A. L., & Allexsaht-Snider, M. (2002). Recent language minority education policy in Georgia: Appropriation, assimilation, and Americanization. In S. Wortham, E. G. Murillo & E. T. Hamann (Eds.), *Education in the new Latino diaspora: Policy and the politics of identity* (pp. 37–66). Westport, CT: Ablex.

Brinton, D., & Kagan, O. (Eds.). (2007). *Heritage language education: A new field emerging*. New York, NY: Routledge.

Clemente, R., & Collison, B. B. (2000). The relationships among counselors, ESL teachers, and students. *Professional School Counseling, 3*(5), 339–349.

Colomer, S. (2010). Dual role interpreters: Spanish teachers in new Latino communities. *Hispania, 93*(3), 490–503. doi:10.1353/hpn.2010.0018

Colomer, S. E., & Harklau, L. (2010). Spanish teachers as impromptu translators and liaisons in new Latino communities. *Foreign Language Annals, 42*, 658–672.

Crawford, J. (1992). *Hold your tongue: Bilingualism and the politics of English only*. Reading, MA: Addison-Wesley.

Enright, K. A. (2011). Language and literacy for a new mainstream. *American Educational Research Journal, 48*(1), 80–118.

Foley, D. E. (1990). *Learning capitalist culture: Deep in the heart of Tejas*. Philadelphia, PA: University of Pennsylvania Press.

Georgia Department of Education. (2009). School Reports. 2009-2010. Retrieved November 22, 2011, from http://www.doe.k12.ga.us/ReportingFW.aspx?P

ageReq=211&StateId=ALL&PID=61&PTID=67&CTID=215&T=0 &FY=2010

Hamann, E. T. (2003). *The educational welcome of Latinos in the new South*. Westport, CT: Praeger.

Hamann, E. T., & Harklau, L. (2010). Education in the New Latino Diaspora. In E. G. Murillo (Ed.), *Handbook of Latinos and Education* (pp. 157–169). New York, NY: Routledge.

Hamann, E. T., Wortham, S., & Murillo, E. G. (2002). Education and policy in the New Latino Diaspora. In S. Wortham, E. G. Murillo, & E. T. Hamann (Eds.), *Education in the New Latino Diaspora: Policy and the politics of identity* (pp. 1–16). Westport, CT: Ablex.

Harklau, L. (2010). High school Spanish in the New Latino Diaspora. *Critical Inquiry in Language Studies, 6,* 211–242.

Herman, D. M. (2007). It's a small world after all: From stereotypes to invented worlds in secondary school Spanish textbooks. *Critical Inquiry in Language Studies, 4*(2-3), 117–150.

Instituto Cervantes. (2004). III Congreso Internacional de la lengua española (Third International Congress of the Spanish Language). Retrieved June 12, 2008, from http://www.congresosdelalengua.es/rosario/ponencias/default.htm

Kochhar, R., Suro, R., & Tafoya, S. (2005). *The new Latino South: The context and consequences of rapid population growth*. Washington, DC: Pew Hispanic Center.

Kubota, R. (2004). Critical multiculturalism and second language education. In B. Norton & K. Toohey (Eds.), *Critical pedagogies and language learning* (pp. 30–52). New York, NY: Cambridge University Press.

Kvale, S., & Brinkman, S. (2009). *InterViews: Learning the craft of qualitative research interviewing*. Los Angeles, CA: Sage.

Leeman, J. (2005). Engaging critical pedagogy: Spanish for native speakers. *Foreign Language Annals, 38*(1), 35–45.

Martinez-Cosio, M., & Iannacone, R. M. (2007). The tenuous role of institutional agents: Parent liaisons as cultural brokers. *Education and Urban Society, 39,* 349–369.

Messias, D., McDowell, L., & Estrada, R. D. (2009). Language interpreting as social justice work: Perspectives of formal and informal healthcare interpreters. *Advances in Nursing Science, 32,* 128–143.

Miramontes, O. B., Nadeau, A., & Commins, N. L. (2011). *Restructuring schools for linguistic diversity: Linking decision making to effective programs* (2nd ed.). New York, NY: Teachers College Press.

Montrul, S. (2004). Convergent outcomes in L2 acquisition and L1 loss. In M. S. Schmid, B. Kopke, M. Keijzer & L. Weilemar (Eds.), *First language attrition: Interdisciplinary perspectives on methodological issues* (pp. 259–279). Philadelphia, PA: John Benjamins.

Morales, A., & Hanson, W. E. (2005). Language brokering: An integrative review of the literature. *Hispanic Journal of Behaviorial Sciences, 27,* 471–503.

Moreno, M., Otero-Sabogal, R., & Newman, J. (2007). Assessing dual role staff-interpreter linguistic competency in an integrated healthcare system. *Journal of General Internal Medicine, 22,* 331–335.

Orellana, M. F. (2001). The work kids do: Mexican and Central American immigrant children's contributions to households and schools in California. *Harvard Educational Review, 71*(3), 366–389.

Orellana, M. F. (2009). *Translating childhoods: The cultural roots of standards reform in American education.* New Brunswick, NJ: Rutgers University Press.

Quinn, N. (2005). Introduction. In N. Quinn (Ed.), *Finding culture in talk: A collection of methods* (1st ed., pp. 1–34). New York, NY: Palgrave Macmillan.

Ricento, T. (2005). Problems with the 'language-as-resource' discourse in the promotion of heritage languages in the U.S.A. *Journal of Sociolinguistics, 9*(3), 348–368.

Roca, A., & Colombi, M. C. (2003). *Mi lengua: Spanish as a heritage language in the United States, research and practice.* Washington, DC: Georgetown University Press.

Stanton-Salazar, R. D. (2001). *Manufacturing hope and despair: The school and kin support networks of U.S.-Mexican youth.* New York, NY: Teachers College Press.

Suárez-Orozco, C., & Todorova, I. L. B. (Eds.). (2003). *Understanding the social worlds of immigrant youth. New directions for youth development, no. 100.* San Francisco, CA: Jossey-Bass.

Swender, E. (2003). Oral proficiency testing in the real world: Answers to frequently asked questions. *Foreign Language Annals, 36*, 520–526.

Trickett, E. J., Rukhotskiy, E., Jeong, A., Genkova, A., Oberoi, A., Weinstein, T., & Delgado, Y. (2011). "The kids are terrific: It's the job that's tough": The ELL teacher role in an urban context. *Teaching and Teacher Education, 30*, 1–10. doi:10.1016/j.tate.2011.10.005

Tse, L. (1995). Language brokering among Latino adolescensts: Prevalence, attitudes, and school performance. *Hispanic Journal of Behaviorial Sciences, 17*, 180–193.

U.S. Census Bureau. (2009). State & County QuickFacts. DP-1 General Population and Housing Characteristics. Retrieved September 29, 2009, from http://factfinder.census.gov

Valdés, G. (2003). *Expanding definitions of giftedness: The case of young interpreters from immigrant communities.* Mahwah, NJ: Lawrence Erlbaum.

Valdés, G., Fishman, J. A., Chávez, R., & Pérez, W. (2006). *Developing minority language resources: The case of Spanish in California* (1st ed.). Buffalo, NY: Multilingual Matters.

Valdés, G., Gonzáles, S. V., García, D. L., & Márquez, P. (2003). Language ideology: The case of Spanish in departments of foreign languages. *Anthropology & Education Quarterly, 34*, 3–26.

Valenzuela, A. (1999). *Subtractive schooling: U.S.-Mexican youth and the politics of caring.* Albany, NY: State University of New York Press.

Ward, M. J. (1992). Translation and interpretation: What teachers should know. *The French Review, 65*, 578–588.

CHAPTER 9

HETEROGENEITY IN THE NEW LATINO DIASPORA

Stanton Wortham and Catherine Rhodes

When our volume *Education in the New Latino Diaspora* (Wortham, Murillo, & Hamann, 2002) was published more than a decade ago, it described a rapidly changing social reality in parts of the United States that had not traditionally been home to Latinos. Over the prior decade large numbers of Latinos had been settling in the South, the Midwest and the Northeast, transforming the demographics of many communities. These newcomers brought energy, talent, and aspirations, but they also presented symbolic and practical challenges to host communities. Symbolically, longstanding residents struggled to make sense of the newcomers, as they had no famil-iar models of identity that fit Latinos. These new destinations lacked "the virulence of anti-immigrant sentiments and historical baggage of intense interethnic and interracial conflicts found in older destinations" (Gouveia Carranza, & Cogua, 2005, p. 45), but they also lacked community leaders and service providers with knowledge about Latino cultures. Practically, service institutions like schools had few Spanish-speaking adults and strug-gled to serve newcomers who often spoke limited English.

In the decade-plus since our earlier volume appeared, New Latino Dias-pora (NLD) communities have continued to change rapidly. As described in the various chapters of this new volume, the Latino population has contin-

Revisiting Education in the New Latino Diaspora, pp. 171–181
Copyright © 2015 by Information Age Publishing
All rights of reproduction in any form reserved.

ued to increase dramatically in many places across the South, the Midwest, the Northwest, and the Northeast. Many suburban and some urban communities have become new destinations for Latino migrants, while most of the largely rural towns reviewed in our earlier volume have continued to receive Latino newcomers. Especially after the economic shock in 2008, the rate of Latino immigration to the U.S. has slowed or stopped, but many Latino migrants have settled and begun families, and they now have children who were born in the U.S. or came here as young children. For the first time since 1970–1980, between 2000 and 2010 the Mexican American population grew faster as a result of U.S. births (7.2 million) than because of new immigrant arrivals (4.2 million) (Pew Hispanic Center, 2011). These U.S.-born children were entering the U.S. school system in kindergarten, and thus their needs and challenges differ from the older Mexican-origin children who were relatively more numerous a decade ago. Whereas in 2002 the prototypical NLD resident was a bachelor or someone living with only a relative or two, in 2012 the prototypical resident in many communities was living in an intact nuclear family with young children. Immigration rates may have declined, but millions of Latinos who arrived in NLD communities over the past two decades remain there. The chapters in this new volume describe the rapid changes, challenges and opportunities that these Latino migrants and their host communities continue to experience.

In this commentary on the seven preceding chapters we discuss the heterogeneity across NLD communities. As described in Hamann and Harklau's introduction to this volume, migrants often have different experiences in NLD settings than in areas of traditional Latino settlement—because of the lack of entrenched stereotypes and the rapidly changing social and economic situations—and it is worth examining commonalities across NLD towns. NLD communities are subject to some similar forces. But they are also diverging. Some have become very welcoming to Latino migrants, while others have erected legal and symbolic barriers. Some integrate migrants into important institutions and value their humanity, while others treat them like expendable labor (a theme Murillo [2002] emphasized in the original *Education in the New Latino Diaspora* volume). Some communities house other ethnic groups who can be either sympathetic to migrants or serve as foils used to denigrate Latinos. (Sudanese, Somali, and Burmese refugees have become increasingly common portions of the workforce in rural meatpacking communities, positions that a decade ago were almost exclusively Latino [Jordan, 2008].) These and other divergent features of NLD communities mean that researchers must attend closely to the distinct situations in various communities if we hope to understand the opportunities, challenges and trajectories of Latino residents in areas of nontraditional settlement.

Heterogeneity

At least two kinds of heterogeneity lead to divergent experiences for Latino migrants in NLD communities. First, heterogeneous resources and constraints contribute to the stance taken by host residents and to the challenges and opportunities faced by migrants. Towns vary in the presence of local Latino leadership, local economic circumstances, geographic location, local demographic and migrant histories, local educational circumstances, local social service infrastructures, and the availability of housing, among other potential factors. Even towns very close to each other, and demographically similar to one another, can vary along key dimensions and thus offer different experiences, challenges, and opportunities (Hamann, Eckerson, & Gray, 2012).

Second, both individual migrants and whole communities are changing over historical time (Massey & Sánchez, 2010). The initial Latino migrants arrived in different communities at different times, and rapid increases in population have also happened at different historical moments. In general, over the past decade, NLD communities have seen reductions in the proportion of single adults and growth in numbers living as unified young families, but different communities have made this transition at different times. Whether a community has followed the typical trajectory and where it is in that trajectory varies.

Within a NLD community individual experiences also differ. Individuals come to a town at different points in their migration trajectories, with some coming directly from Mexico (or increasingly Central America) while others have lived for years in other U.S. communities. Individuals migrate at different stages in their ontogenetic development, and their experiences vary dramatically if they arrive as a child, an adolescent, or an adult. The individual migrant's trajectory also intersects with the town's trajectory, and it can make a difference if a child arrives during the early stages of ethnic community formation or a much later stage. It also matters how an individual's trajectory intersects with more widely circulating national discourses about migrant populations (Hamann, 2003; Santa Ana, 2002). For example, someone coming of age as an adolescent during the unsuccessful mobilization at the end of the Bush presidency for comprehensive immigration reform may be drawn toward activism in a way younger sibling negotiating the xenophobic backlash a few years later (epitomized by Alabama's anti-immigrant HB 56, passed in 2011) would not.

It would be a mistake to adopt universal models that identify one or two factors and try to predict migrant experiences. Both variability across communities and the historical trajectories of communities and individuals mean that social scientists must consider more complex configurations of influences and pathways to understand any focal phenomenon with respect to migrant experiences (like the prognosis for an individual migrant student or the climate of a given town). In the rest of this commentary we illustrate this point with respect, first, to research we have been doing in one NLD town over several years and then with reference to the seven preceding chapters in this volume.

One New Latino Diaspora Town

We have been doing research in one mid-Atlantic NLD community for almost a decade, studying not just the schools but also local churches, newspapers, police, policymakers, businesses, health care, other service providers, and individual families (Mortimer, Wortham, & Allard, 2010; Wortham, Allard, Lee, & Mortimer, 2011; Wortham, Mortimer & Allard, 2009; Wortham, Mortimer, & Allard, 2011; Wortham & Rhodes, 2012). We provide a brief overview of this work here, to illustrate how heterogeneous factors come together to shape challenges and opportunities for Latino migrants in one town. Marshall (a pseudonym) is a suburb in a large metropolitan area that has only recently become home to many Mexican migrants. Marshall has about 35,000 residents. Of these, 100 were Mexican in 1990, increasing to 2,000 in 2000 and 8,000 in 2010 (U.S. Census Bureau, 2011). So Marshall's Latino population has grown from 3% to 28% in this 20-year period, with Mexicans composing the largest proportion. Other groups include African Americans, a small Asian American population, and Anglo residents, some of whom were foreign-born immigrants or the children of immigrants, primarily from Ireland and Italy.

The town's African American population began with some arrivals at the end of the 19th century, but most Black residents or their ancestors arrived in the decades after World War II. After Marshall's founding by English and German settlers two centuries ago, Irish immigrants arrived in the 19th century, followed by two waves of Italian immigrants in the 20th century. Smaller groups of Puerto Rican, South Asian, and Caribbean newcomers settled in Marshall in the 1970s, although most have since moved on. The population changed significantly between 1990 and 2010—from 70% White, 25% African American and 3% Latino, to 32% White, 35% African American, and 28% Latino (78% of these Latinos were Mexican). Latinos comprised 28% of the school district population in 2012, and almost 50% of kindergarten enrollment. Residents of Marshall, both new and longstanding, have described it as a somewhat more welcoming place than many NLD communities. Marshall schools have provided language resources for parents and students, churches have welcomed migrants and provided services in Spanish, and even the police department has offered rudimentary Spanish lessons to its officers. While responses to Latino migrants vary across the town, many longstanding residents see the newcomers as assets to the community and compare them with earlier Italian immigrants who are seen as hardworking, family-oriented people.

We argue that a number of factors influence the relatively welcoming reception new Latino migrants receive in Marshall. Given limited space, we will discuss three: the town's distinct local character, which involves a unique immigration history; the historical stage in the town's experience with more widely-circulating patterns of immigration; and the town's internal variability with respect to individual migrants' historical dates of arrival how these intersect with the town's historical stage of immigration and the ages at which migrants arrive.

Marshall's Italian and Italian American community arrived in two relatively large waves over the past century. The Italian community began early in the 20th century, but a substantial number of Italian immigrants arrived in the decade or two after World War II. Some of this latter group are still more comfortable speaking Italian than English. This is important, because Italian-origin residents feel some affinities with Mexican migrants and respond to them more positively than do other "Anglo" residents with more distant immigrant histories (we put "Anglo" in quotes because we have learned not to refer to Italian Americans as Anglos—after being lectured more than once on how Latin was a language spoken in Italy and so, if anyone is "Latino," then it's Italians).

Both Whites and Mexicans have compared Mexican newcomers to the Italians and other immigrant groups who were seen as assets to the community. In this respect, Mexican migrant residents were seen as model minorities: hard working, uncomplaining people whose work and faith are rejuvenating the town as they pursue the American Dream (Wortham, Mortimer, & Allard, 2009). With some exceptions, Italian Americans (and some Irish Americans) have often been more sympathetic to Mexican migrants than have other residents, explaining that they remember their own immigrant roots, also belong to the Catholic church, and/or because Mexicans have a similar language and similar emphasis on family. Thus, one distinctive aspect of Marshall is its immigrant history—specifically the continuing presence of Italians—and this makes the town somewhat more sympathetic to Mexican migrants than some other NLD communities.

Another distinctive aspect of Marshall involves an atypical early phase of Mexican immigration, beginning in the 1970s. Martha (a pseudonym) arrived in Marshall over 30 years ago from Mexico. She met her American husband, the son of Italian immigrants, when he was a tourist in Mexico. He brought Martha to live with him in Marshall, and she was the only Mexican in town at that time. Martha experienced extreme isolation in Marshall, and her uncle suggested that her husband invite some of her sisters to keep her company. Over the years, Martha and her husband helped a number of her siblings and cousins immigrate to Marshall. Initially, the transition was difficult, as Martha and her family members found themselves having to perform menial labor, such as housekeeping and restaurant kitchen work, which were unfamiliar roles for members of a college-educated, middle-class Mexican family. But eventually Martha's extended family and Mexican acquaintances settled in Marshall, created businesses, and raised families.

Throughout this time, Martha's family played a central role in the Mexican migrant community in Marshall, as family members maintained close ties to more recently-arrived Mexican migrants, even as economic success and some degree of assimilation pulled Martha's family toward a more established, mainstream, American lifestyle. Martha and her relatives became cultural brokers in Marshall. As a certified elementary school teacher, she has provided valuable direction for newly arrived Spanish-speaking migrant parents and their children. Earlier, she and her husband also provided shelter, contacts, and other forms of social capital to other migrants. The role of cultural broker has now been adopted by her siblings and acquaintances, who connect newer Mexican migrants with employment information, cultural events, and housing. Martha and her family played a key role in how Marshall's Latino migrant community grew from its earliest stage to a larger NLD community, showing how networks of support can play a crucial role in helping migrants overcome challenges and seize opportunities.

Because of Martha and her family (six of her siblings moved in and around Marshall), the early stages of this Mexican migrant community were somewhat different from those of other towns like Marshall. First of all, many of the *solteros* ("single men") and fragmented families who arrived in the early years of Latino migration to Marshall were connected to Martha herself. These extended family and friendship networks were an important resource for newcomers. Second, Martha and some of her siblings served, and continue to serve, as bilingual, middle-class brokers who help local institutions serve Mexican migrants more effectively. In addition to Martha's work with the school system (where she translates regularly for the Superintendent and others), her brother has been centrally involved in the Latino business association that works with town officials, and her sister has served on the board of local social service agencies.

A third factor influencing Marshall's reception of new Latino migrants is the town's internal variability with respect to individual migrants' historical dates of arrival. For example, the contingent fact that many Mexican migrants began settling with their families in Marshall and having children there is important. Other towns that experienced earlier or later surges of Mexican schoolchildren are at different points in their development of a bilingual population in the schools, children whose educational prospects differ from those of their siblings who entered American schools at older ages or who went directly to work. As Mexican families have settled across the United States, most have focused on their children's futures and emphasized education. But it is much more difficult for a monolingual Spanish-speaking migrant child who arrives at age 12 to catch up and navigate the American school system than it is for his 6-year-old sibling. Marshall has enrolled a large group of younger, English-Spanish bilingual Mexican-origin children, creating a substantial presence in Marshall elementary schools and an increasing one in secondary schools. This makes it easier for the schools to serve Mexican-origin children and has changed educators' stereotypes about what these children can accomplish academically.

Much of this transition was made possible, at least in part, by the early establishment of a small Mexican community nucleus in Marshall. While Marshall's explosive Latino community growth happened only in 21st Century, the Latinos who made up less than 3% of the population before it began to grow were instrumental in its establishment. So Marshall's transition from *solteros* to families has been mediated by the presence of a longstanding, more economically secure group of middle-class Mexican business owners and professionals, with Martha at its core. This has made Marshall somewhat distinctive and a more hospitable place for newcomers.

Individuals within a NLD town like Marshall vary widely. They arrived in the town at different points in the development of the migrant community, and they arrived at different points in their lifespans. They came into families that were more or less intact and they connected to work and school differently. When a migrant arrived in Marshall makes a large difference to his or her migrant experience. Early arrivals had easier access to Martha and her family, and they were not part of a more overwhelming group of Spanish speakers needing services from the schools and social service agencies. Later arrivals have had an easier time speaking only Spanish in their daily lives, because of the many Mexican businesses and the larger, Spanish-speaking Latino community.

Being born in the U.S. confers citizenship, which makes a large difference. But arriving in early childhood is also an advantage, as it allows a migrant to attend elementary school in the U.S. and master English. Arriving as an adolescent is much more difficult, because secondary school demands a faster pace and content standards which are difficult to meet while also learning English. Migrants who arrive at different historical moments in the process of the development of an NLD community will have different resources available to them. The broader community of longstanding residents will also be at different stages in their familiarity with and their acceptance or rejection of the new migrants. All of these factors shape how a given Latino individual negotiates and advances within Marshall.

Revisiting Education in the New Latino Diaspora

Making sense of any Latino migrant's trajectory, or of the character of any NLD town, then, requires attention to heterogeneous characteristics, resources and historically emergent processes. Marshall offers somewhat more opportunities and somewhat fewer challenges than many similar towns, although it is not an ideal environment for Latino migrants. The seven chapters preceding this one also illustrate the heterogeneity of migrant experiences, challenges and opportunities in NLD towns across the country.

The chapter by Bruening describes a town with a lower concentration of Latino residents than many other NLD communities. This town may be earlier in the process of Latino migration than most others, or it may be following an alternative trajectory. In her analysis Bruening shows how the low numbers of Latino migrant students in the town change those students' experiences in school. First, the district has only one teacher with English Language Learner (ELL) credentials, and she is given other duties during the year of Bruening's study. As with other NLD towns, the limited staff expertise and limited knowledge about how to serve Latino migrant students reduce the quality of services. The very low concentration of ELLs in this town makes the situation even worse, however. Second, the small numbers mean that educators can muddle through with individualized services for students, without having to design more systematic and purposeful approaches. This town is not the only one to offer weak services for Latino migrant students, but it shows how a low percentage of Latino students makes those students' challenges and opportunities different than in many NLD towns with larger Latino populations.

Harklau and Colomer describe towns with much higher percentages of Latino migrant students. But they also describe how school districts muddle through, trying to provide required services to Latino students while minimizing the change in procedures required for doing so. They show, for instance, how the district "repurposes" Spanish-as-a-foreign-language teachers to serve as translators and liaisons. They also describe the sad, ironic outcome of placing Latino students in Spanish-as-a-foreign-language classes—an initiative which had the goal of making them feel competent and included—but where the result was instead alienation and marginalization when Latino students' dialects and specific cultural knowledge were devalued in favor of Iberian or academic Spanish. Another distinctive feature of these districts was the hostile political climate: one which provided limited resources to schools in general, and very limited resources for ELLs, alongside a strong commitment to English Only policies. Some other NLD towns have similar attitudes and constraints, but education in northern Georgia seems particularly influenced by them.

Lynn describes interesting interethnic dynamics in a NLD town that has recruited Koreans to work alongside Latinos in poultry processing plants. Many NLD towns face the complexity of placing migrant Latinos in an ethnic landscape that includes blacks and whites. But Lynn's case shows the complications of adding another salient ethnic group. The Koreans serve several functions for the town: as reliable workers with documents, they will not be deported and leave employers without labor; their presence is a tacit warning to Latinos that they should work hard and not complain; and they help to favorably position the local schools, which welcome Korean children at least in part because they tend to do well on standardized tests. This situation compares intriguingly with what we observed in Marshall, where Mexican migrants were considered by many longstanding residents to be the model minority, which they contrasted with Blacks (Wortham, Mortimer, & Allard, 2009).

Raible and Irizarry describe a site in which Latino migrants are considered deviant, even dangerous and threatening. They show how school discipline procedures and an emphasis on "containment" racialize Latino students and constrict their opportunities. Their research takes place in a different type of setting, an urban area in the Northeast that has a sizable Puerto Rican community. Puerto Ricans have a different history of migration to the United States than do more recent Latino migrants, with a longer timescale of presence in the U.S. and access to legal status, but they nonetheless often receive more antagonistic treatment from longstanding populations. The mixing of Mexican and Puerto Rican residents in this community makes it distinctive and seems to encourage the surveillance and racialization that both groups encounter in school.

The chapter by Urrieta and his colleagues also shows that some Mexican origin students in more typical NLD towns experience virulent racism in American schools. Drawing on a *testimonio* ("testimony") from one young man, they both demonstrate the importance of this genre as a methodological innovation for research in the NLD and give a vivid example of one person's sometimes typical and sometimes distinctive experiences as a migrant.

Leco Tomas describes another type of heterogeneity: the fact that some NLD migrants have indigenous backgrounds in Mexico. He shows how the history of subordination and marginalization in Mexico leads Purépechas in the U.S. to advocate for linguistic and cultural rights, and how they emphasize informal education within the family as a supplement to schooling. He also describes how these Purépecha communities are transnational, with young people moving back and forth to Mexico, and how this allows them to maintain some indigenous traditions in dance, food, medicine, and so forth.

Finally, Flores-Koulish offers still another dimension of individual variation in the NLD: the experiences of Latino children adopted by non-Latino parents in areas of nontraditional settlement. This is a small group, but their situations are distinct from more typical NLD residents who live with their birth families. She provides a detailed and moving description of how Latino transracial adoptees' life experiences are similar in some respects to other members of the NLD—in their relative isolation and unfamiliarity—but different in others—in native language and lack of a Latino community.

Taken together, these chapters introduce several dimensions of variation in the New Latino Diaspora and illustrate many ways in which individuals and towns have distinctive experiences, opportunities, and challenges. They provide an important complement to the more overtly policy implementation-oriented chapters of the other half of the book. As others have noted (e.g., Hamann & Rosen, 2011), policy reduces individuals to roles (e.g., student, teacher, employee) and places to types of places (e.g., Marshall becomes just a town, Marshall High School becomes just a high school). That is predictable and not always lamentable, but it is reductive and objectifying; these seven chapters resist such reduction and remind us that schooling, coming of age, and the formation of community are all not synonymous, ahistoric processes. Ethnographic work like that included here is crucial, because we cannot fall back on generic accounts of immigrant experiences even for a distinctive population like Mexican migrants in the NLD. Instead, we must attend to several dimensions of variation and identify those that are relevant to explaining heterogeneous migrant trajectories in any given town or individual case.

REFERENCES

Gouveia, L., Carranza, M., & Cogua, J. (2005). The Great Plains Migration. In V. Zúñiga & R. Hernández-León (Eds.), *New destinations* (pp. 23–49). New York, NY: Russell Sage Foundation.

Hamann, E. T. (2003). *The educational welcome of Latinos in the New South.* Westport, CT: Praeger.

Hamann, E. T., Eckerson, J. M., & Gray, T. (2012, November). *Xenophobia, disquiet, or welcome? Community sense-making and related educational environments in the New Latino Diaspora.* Unpublished paper presented at the American Anthropological Association annual meeting, San Francisco, CA.

Hamann, E. T., & Rosen, L. (2011). What makes the anthropology of educational policy implementation "anthropological"? In B. Levinson & M. Pollock

(Eds.), *Companion to the anthropology of education* (pp. 461–477). New York, NY: Wiley Blackwell.

Jordan, M. (2008, June 6). Burmese refugees bail out meatpacker JBS Swift. *Rocky Mountain News*. Retrieved from http://m.rockymountainnews.com/news/2008/ jun/06/burmese-refugees-bail-out-meatpacker-jbs-swift/

Massey, D., & Sánchez, M. (2010). *Brokered boundaries: Creating immigrant identity in anti-immigrant times*. New York, NY: Russell Sage Foundation.

Mortimer, K., Wortham, S., & Allard E. (2010). Helping immigrants identify as "university-bound students": Unexpected difficulties in teaching the hidden curriculum. *Revista de Educación, 353*, 107–128.

Murillo, E. G. (2002). How does it feel to be a *problem*? "Disciplining" the transnational subject in the New South. In S. Wortham, E. G. Murillo, & E. T. Hamann (Eds.), *Education in the new Latino diaspora* (pp. 215–240). Westport, CT: Ablex.

Pew Hispanic Center. (2011). *The Mexican-American boom: Births overtake immigration*. Washington, DC: Author. Retrieved December 10, 2012, from http:// pewhispanic.org/files/reports/144.pdf

Santa Ana, O. (2002). *Brown tide rising: Metaphors of Latinos in contemporary American public discourse*. Austin, TX: University of Texas Press.

U.S. Census Bureau. (2011). *American fact finder:* U.S. Census 1990, Tables P001, P006, P008 and P009 (Summary Table File 1); U.S. Census 2000, Tables P1 and P8 (Summary File 1); U.S. Census 2010, Table P2, Hispanic or Latino and Not by Race. Retrieved December 10, 2012, from http://factfinder2. census.gov/

Wortham, S., Mortimer, K., & Allard, E. (2009). Mexicans as model minorities in the New Latino Diaspora. *Anthropology & Education Quarterly, 40*, 388–404.

Wortham, S., Mortimer, K., & Allard, E. (2011). Homies in the New Latino Diaspora. *Language & Communication, 31*, 191–202.

Wortham, S., Allard, E., Lee, K., & Mortimer, K. (2011). Racialization in payday mugging narratives. *Journal of Linguistic Anthropology, 21*, E56–E75.

Wortham, S., & Rhodes, C. (2012). The production of relevant scales: Social identification of migrants during rapid demographic change in one American town. *Applied Linguistics Review, 3*, 75–99.

Wortham, S., Murillo, E. Jr., & Hamann, E. (Eds.). (2002). *Education in the New Latino Diaspora*. Westport, CT: Ablex.

SECTION III

EXISTING INFRASTRUCTURE RESPONDS

CHAPTER 10

TEACHER PERCEPTIONS, PRACTICES, AND EXPECTATIONS CONVEYED TO LATINO STUDENTS AND FAMILIES IN WASHINGTON STATE

**Frances Contreras, Tom Stritikus,
Kathryn Torres, and Karen O'Reilly Diaz**

INTRODUCTION

Latino students in Washington State represent the largest segment of students of color within the K–12 population. And with this unprecedented growth in the state (see Hamann & Harklau (this volume), schools have not kept pace with the demands of educating this population equitably. Between 1986 and 2007, the non-Latino White student population in Washington's K–12 public schools grew by only 6 percent, compared to 372% growth for Latinos. This growth reflected changes in both rural areas in the eastern part of the state and urban districts along the Puget Sound cor-

Revisiting Education in the New Latino Diaspora, pp. 185–205
Copyright © 2015 by Information Age Publishing

ridor. Throughout eastern Washington's rural communities, for example, Latinos have a long history of settlement (Gamboa, 1999) and are often the majority rather than the minority (Hamann & Harklau, 2010), often exceeding 75% of district student populations. In western Washington, commonly known for the urban and suburban school districts, the growth of the Latino population in some school districts has outpaced statewide growth rates by several hundred-percentage points. In 2007, there were 43 school districts statewide with 1,000 or more Latino students, 23 of which were located in western Washington.

At the same time, the state has made very little progress towards diversifying the teacher workforce. In 2008 for example, 93% of Washington's public school teaching population was White. Not only is there a literature that documents how Latino students do better in districts with more Latino educators (e.g., Meier & Stewart [1991]), our data will also show that a cultural and linguistic disconnect exists between Latino students and the schools that they attend, in our case in the state of Washington.

While Latino students are distinct for being part of the fastest growing K–12 public school population nationwide, they are distinct, too, in that they consistently rank at the bottom or near the bottom on state assessments and other indicators of academic achievement, particularly the ELL (English Language Learners) student population. Examining test scores, however, does not tell us much about why Latino students continue to struggle in school more than any other population in Washington's K–12 schools. Moreover, examining low test scores ignores the robust, multifaceted literature that shows that Latino students can do as well or better in school as any other population (e.g., Gándara & Contreras [2009], Lucas, Henze, & Donato [1990]).

Our study team undertook a mixed-method study to critically examine issues facing Latino students in Washington State at the beginning of the second decade of the 21st century. The study had three primary goals. The first, in an overt recreation at a state scale of the core question of *Education in the New Latino Diaspora* (Wortham, Murillo, & Hamann, 2002), was to compare patterns of achievement in regions of the state that have historically had a large Latino population (the eastern rural region) with those whose demographic shift is more typical of new destination cities (the urban Puget Sound region). Our second goal was to better understand Latino parents' and students' perceptions of schooling in different regions. And our third goal was to examine the role that teachers play in responding to the Latino Diaspora and changing context of schools. Specifically, we addressed the following research questions in the statewide study:

1. Do Latino students possess the same opportunities to learn as their peers in both areas that have historically had a Latino community and those that have not?

2. What are the perceptions of parents and students with respect to their experience with U.S. schooling?
3. How do teachers in multiple district contexts (urban, urban ring, rural) define their role in educating Latino students given the current shifting demographics in the state?

Teachers play a crucial role in fostering or stifling Latino student aspirations, preparation, and achievement through the expectations they establish and communicate to their Latino students in their classrooms (Contreras et al., 2008). They send signals about a student's ability and college aptitude and selectively encourage or inhibit the transition to college through a multitude of practices and efforts that occur within the classroom and through their interaction with Latino parents.

Like many previous studies from elsewhere, findings from this study document a persistent achievement gap in Washington State between Latino students and their non-Latino White peers. This was found across multiple assessments and indicators of academic achievement used in Washington State. In 2007–2008 for example, Latino students statewide did not meet the federal government's adequate yearly progress (AYP) requirements in reading or math at any grade level—elementary, middle school or secondary. A central argument of this chapter is that poor achievement is in part the result of insufficient opportunities to learn for Latino students. While we focus on teacher survey and interview responses, teachers are but one aspect of the school context and their actions (and inactions) by no means fully explain the persistent gaps in achievement and college transition. Still, we have isolated these data from teachers because there is great potential for influencing Latino achievement by focusing on professional development for the teacher workforce and developing a base of culturally responsive and bilingual teachers. In turn, it follows that such professional development has a starting point, and we hope this chapter helps depict what the starting point was as of 2011.

THEORETICAL FRAMEWORK FOR THE STUDY

This chapter draws upon several bodies of literature from the fields of education, sociology, history, and public policy that explore the various factors that contribute to student success in school. Research from these fields highlights that it is insufficient to consider test scores as the sole measure of the achievement gap. Doing so may lead policymakers and educators to label students as "underachievers." While there are students who do not perform well on exams or in school, we feel that state leaders have not looked deep enough to find out whether this is a result of individual effort, opportunities to learn within the educational system, or some combination of such factors. In particular, we see a lack of attention on state leaders' part to what teachers do and do not do, do and do not believe, and how the teacher preparation apparatus in Washington plays a role in these dynamics.

Scholars have argued that several factors contribute to the educational experiences and achievement patterns of underrepresented students (Gándara & Contreras, 2009). The theoretical framework presented here (Figure 10.1) provides insight into this complicated issue. It takes into account individual background characteristics (Coleman, 1988; Tienda & Mitchell, 2006a, 2006b; Valdés, 1996; Valencia, 2002; Valenzuela, 1999), community and school resources, and the nature of the school culture with regards to college aspirations—all factors that have been theorized to contribute to students' experience in school and improved academic achievement (García, 2001; McDonough, 1994; Valenzuela, 1999).

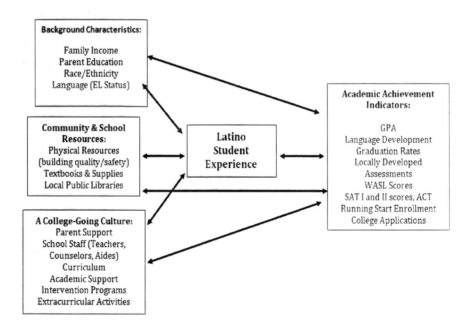

Source: Contreras et al. (2008). Understanding Opportunities to Learn for Latino Students in Washington State. Report Prepared for the Washington State Legislature and Commission on Hispanic Affairs.

Figure 10.1. Theoretical framework for Latino student achievement and creating opportunities to learn.

It is well documented in the literature that Spanish-speakers struggle academically, generally doing poorer in school and exhibiting higher dropout rates than children from other immigrant groups (Goldenberg, 1996; Suárez-Orozco, Suárez-Orozco, & Todorova, 2008). For them, background characteristics may provide some explanation, as families from Mexico and Central America generally come from lower socioeconomic and educational backgrounds than other immigrant groups. In the U.S., they are considered racial and ethnic minorities with low status relative to their non-Latino White peers, and this may lead to the internalization of negative self-image (Suárez-Orozco & Suárez-Orozco, 2001).

However, an analysis of Latino underachievement in schools must also take into account the community and school resources available to students (Portes & Rumbaut, 2006) and the amount of cultural support their schools provide for academic success and pathways to college. Latinos who are English learners are especially likely to be disadvantaged by the schools they attend, which may be financially under resourced, without adequate materials or teachers trained to meet their needs (Gándara, Maxwell-Jolly, & Driscoll, 2005). In this study, we analyzed the integration of all of these factors to begin to understand the influence they have on Latino student achievement beyond individual explanations and test scores.

RESEARCH METHODS

The research team employed a mixed-method approach, using both quantitative tools and qualitative approaches to answer the research questions for this study. The findings from the study draw from a two-pronged data collection strategy. This chapter reports on the results from survey data, field notes, focus groups, and interviews in eight representative school districts ($n = 14$ schools) throughout the state of Washington.

Primary Data Collection

Parents, teachers, and students from eight school districts were surveyed from October 8, 2008 to November 21, 2008. Students were surveyed to better understand various elements of the schooling process, including their perceptions of school, college aspirations, course taking patterns, and interactions with teachers and their parents ($n = 468$). Focus groups were also conducted in the high school and middle schools when possible ($n = 9$) to allow students to expand on the themes presented in the survey. This chapter primarily focuses on the teacher survey and interview data.

Teacher Sample and Characteristics

A total of 253 teachers participated in the survey, the majority of whom were female (55.4%) and White (83.4%). All of the teachers in the schools that we studied were surveyed. Only 8.3% ($n = 21$) of the teachers in the sample were Mexican American or Latino. There was also limited teacher diversity with respect to Asian American ($n = 5$), American Indian ($n = 6$), or African American ($n = 1$) teachers in the sample. Very few teachers in the schools we visited were bilingual in Spanish. Of the teachers who responded that they were fluent in another language, only 13.8% of teachers in the school districts participating in this study spoke another language, and only 8.7% of the teaching population of the district sample spoke Spanish. We also interviewed teachers from middle and high school math classes ($n = 29$). At the elementary school level for example, Latino teachers are just over 3% and at the high school level, Latino teachers represent a mere 2% of the teacher workforce. The limited teacher diversity (Figure 10.2) perhaps serves as one explanation for limited cultural and linguistic awareness between Latino students, families and teachers and school staff.

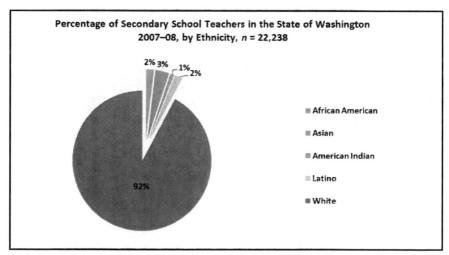

Source: Retrieved http://www.k12.wa.us/DataAdmin/pubdocs/personnel/ StaffEthnicREPORT07-08%20.pdf

Figure 10.2.   Limited teacher diversity.

We utilize select statistical approaches to evaluate the extent to which teacher responses are disproportional, and draw conclusions about the statistical significance of the contextual differences in teacher curricular work, their role in disseminating college information to students, their interactions with Latino parents and their opinions of Latino student college-ready preparation and aspirations. These approaches include chi-square, Fisher's exact test, and Fisher-Freeman-Halton exact test (Cytel Inc., 2005). These statistical approaches are applied to our teacher survey data in this chapter. Specifically, these methods indicate the probability that the differences between teacher responses in rural, urban ring, and urban schools and our survey questions could only occur by chance when there is no true difference in the population, with an error level typically set at .05. Our criteria for selecting our 8 school districts and 14 schools for this study included variables such as free and reduced lunch data, ethnic diversity, academic achievement, and geographical diversity (urban, rural, urban ring) to ensure a representative sample of districts with a healthy sample of Latino and non-Latino students. Descriptive statistics are also reported to illustrate context (e.g., student test scores) or the overall trends in teacher responses to our research questions.

THE ROLE OF TEACHERS IN EDUCATING LATINO STUDENTS

Although teachers in different districts and schools generally implement similar policies and practices to support student learning, teachers themselves often varied in their responses to what impacts their work, as well as their perceptions and interactions with and about Latino students and their parents. In this chapter, we examine how teachers in Washington State differed in their responses by urban, urban ring, and rural district context. To illuminate the nature of teacher work in this context, we integrate illustrative quotes from teachers to begin to unpack the within-and-across-district responses to teacher factors that specifically impact Latino and ELL student outcomes.

Testing and Accountability

The WASL scores for Latinos compared to their White and Asian American peers over a 10-year period illustrated consistently lower levels of achievement in reading, writing, and math. In this study we focus on math achievement levels because math is considered to be the gatekeeper for college preparation among students, and gaps in math achievement begin very early in the education pipeline, ultimately limiting later postsecondary options and aspirations for Latino and underrepresented students (Swail, Cabrera, & Lee, 2004; Chavez, 2004; Contreras, 2005; Gándara & Contreras, 2009). Further, in all of the years assessed for AYP, with the exception of 2003, Latino students did not meet the proficiency standards in Math. The gap in students meeting the WASL standard in math in 1997/98 between Latinos and Whites was 24% and in 2007–2008 the gap between Latino students and Whites was 29.4%. At the seventh grade level, the gap in the percentage of students meeting the WASL standard was 17.3% between Latinos and Whites, and in 2008, this gap was 29.7%. For 10th graders, the picture of lower achievement continues, with the gap in 1997/98 between Latinos and White students meeting the 10th grade math WASL standard was 26.5% and in 2008, the gap was 29.5%. While Latino and all students have reported gains over the past 10 years, there remains a considerable achievement gap, particularly in the subject of math.

Consistent with the current No Child Left Behind policy expectations for teachers, almost all teachers (99.2%) reported that meeting WASL standards was either a "very high priority" or a "priority" at their school. However within rural schools (Table 10.1), teachers (74.7%) were more likely to report that meeting WASL standards is a "very high priority" at their school than teachers within urban (49.3%) and urban ring (49.4%) schools (Fisher-Freeman-Halton test = 16.74, $p < .0001$). This suggests that accountability concerns are especially salient for rural teachers, which could potentially impact the curricular focus for students in these schools such as teaching to the test.

Table 10.1. Cross-Tabulation of School Type and Priority of Meeting WASL Standards

Priority of Meeting WASL Standards	School Type			χ^2	Φ
	Urban	Urban Ring	Rural		
Very High Priority	49.3%	49.4%	74.7%	16.16**	.25
	(35)	(41)	(71)		
Priority	49.3%	49.4%	25.3%		
	(35)	(41)	(24)		
Low Priority	1.2%	1.2%	0%		
	(1)	(1)	(0)		

Note. ** = $p \leq .01$. Group frequencies appear in parentheses below row percentages. N = 249.

The role of teachers has expanded and intensified during the era of accountability with teachers asked to "relate to their students differently, enact pedagogies that are often at odds with their vision of best practice, and experience high levels of stress" (Valli & Buese, 2007, p. 520). Often, in large schools, the school counselor is overburdened with student case-loads making the classroom teacher a potentially sole access point for college information for many Latino students (Contreras et al., 2008). However as the policy climate of the district becomes more high-stakes, the scope and intensification of teacher roles could potentially have unintended conse-quences for implementing these expanded responsibilities (Valli & Buese, 2007). In the case of Washington State, the policy climate has clearly influ-enced pedagogical approaches in the classroom.

Teachers discussed the pressure they felt to raise their schools' math scores and how this has led them to teach to the test. As a result, many rural schools have adopted school-wide initiatives such as "advisory period" to prepare students for the test. These advisories in many schools are class periods designed to practice WASL questions and engage in test taking strategies. A male high school math teacher from a rural high school explained for example, how he used past WASL exams with students to practice multiple question formats. Another female middle school math teacher from a rural school described how the high stakes testing climate influenced her teaching: "I'm teaching to the WASL and the standards, which I think is OK. [But] then I can't really branch out and do any fun activities that provide additional supports, because I have to cover so much in a year."

Another high school teacher from an urban ring school district describes how there is no other option within their school if they are going to make progress towards meeting AYP. This teacher also placed a degree of blame on Latinos and students with special needs as preventing their school from meeting their goals:

> I don't know what else we can do, because I'm the math department head also. So I feel kind of responsible for the whole department, but to the school itself we haven't, other than public shame, for not meeting AYP in all of the areas. And usually with us, it's either the Hispanic students or special educa-tion that have kept us from meeting it.

While the pressure to improve student performance was described among teachers from all district types, the accountability climate played a central role in influencing the teaching and pedagogical approaches of teachers from rural school districts. These findings suggest a collec-tive approach to teach to the WASL has emerged within these districts (that have some of the lowest WASL passing rates) as the answer to raising achievement, as narrowly defined by standardized test scores. While the name of the WASL exam was changed in 2010 to the Measure of Student Progress (MSP), these data suggest that the high stakes climate in Washington is likely to remain across all district contexts, and directly influence teaching practice.

Teacher Expectations for Latino Students

Over 65% of the teachers we surveyed believed that 25% or less of their Latino students would attend a 4-year college in the future. There was also district variation in teacher responses. Teachers from urban school districts were most likely to report that less than 25% of their Latino students would attend college. Teachers were more likely to consider non-Latino students in their classrooms as "college bound" or more likely to be "college ready." Lower expectations for Latino students were not only found through our survey results, but were consistently raised by teachers during the individual interviews.

With these low expectations of their 8th graders or 10th grade Latino students, it is difficult to know how these beliefs translate into practice in the classroom (Contreras, 2011). Teachers also believed that their Latino students were not prepared for college, with 30.6% of teachers responding that 25% or less are prepared attend college. Researchers have found that nonminority teachers often possess lower expectations for their Latino and underrepresented students, which influences their efforts to assist struggling minority students or provide them with the necessary academic support to raise achievement (Contreras, 2011; Contreras et al., 2008; Delpit, 1995, 2001; Hale-Benson, 1986; Haycock, 1998; Ladson Billings, 1995; Nieto, 1996; Rousseau & Tate, 2003; Tatum, 1999).

When we further asked teachers to assess their students and to give us a sense of how many Latino students expressed a desire to attend college, teachers in urban school districts were more likely to report how less than 25% of their students have expressed aspirations to attend college (Table 10.2), with over 41% of teachers reporting that less than a quarter of their Latino students *wanted* to attend college. In addition, these data do not match with the student survey data, where well over 73% of Latino students aspired to earn an associate's degree or higher (Contreras et al., 2008; Contreras, 2011). These data suggest a staggering lack of communication between urban Latino students and their teachers about the realities of Latino student aspirations for college and beyond.

Table 10.2.   Cross-Tabulation of School Type and Teacher Opinion About Expressed Latino Student College Aspirations

Perceptions of Latino College Aspirations	School Type			χ^2	Φ
	Urban	Urban Ring	Rural		
Less than 25%	41.3%	32.1%	26.1%	21.54**	.30
	(26)	(26)	(23)		
25%	22.2%	21.0%	5.7%		
	(14)	(17)	(8)		
Half-50%	20.6%	33.3%	38.6%		
	(13)	(27)	(6)		
75%	12.7%	11.1%	25.0%		
	(8)	(9)	(22)		
Over 90%	3.2%	2.5%	4.5%		
	(2)	(2)	(4)		

Note. ** = $p \leq .01$. *Group frequencies appear in parentheses below row percentages. N=232.*

Many teachers expressed how their Latino students "don't visualize themselves as a success." This was a common sentiment across district contexts in the interview data. One teacher from a rural middle school further categorized her Latino students as "unmotivated" and not seeing the "bigger picture."

> Unmotivated [Latino] students sometimes don't see the bigger picture. They haven't had any role models or any family members that have gone to universities or colleges.... They don't see themselves down the road. They just see today tomorrow or next week. They don't see a year from now or two years from now.

Another theme that emerged from the teacher data across all districts was the strong belief that Latino students did not possess role models in their home environment or community. And in rural schools, teachers further conveyed that poverty played a strong role in limiting student awareness and knowledge of their options. A teacher from a rural high school commented on the role that poverty plays in college knowledge:

> Probably the biggest challenge I think we have with these students is their poverty level, and things that they just don't know. They've never experienced certain things that you would experience a bigger town or bigger city.

These findings are consistent with the literature on aspirations and college awareness as being related to peer networks and relationships to adults that serve as role models (Gándara, 1995; Stanton-Salazar & Spina, 2003). They suggest the need for greater student exposure to efforts within the school but perhaps also out of the classroom to raise student exposure to role models, and college information. One program frequently discussed by teachers was the GEAR Up program in their school that selected students to engage in a range of college preparedness programs. Such efforts offer a viable mechanism for supporting schools in raising aspirations, achievement and providing greater support to Latino students (Gándara & Bial, 2001; Gándara & Contreras, 2009).

The Transmission of College Knowledge and Information

Since the role of teachers has intensified during this era of high stakes accountability, teachers increasingly rely on peer support networks for strategies to better engage their students and transmit information about a host of issues, including college awareness and information. Interacting with colleagues in a school setting could potentially assist teachers to better understand the requirements and demands of their expanded role. Such efforts often leads to sharing pedagogical approaches, collaboration, and a way for teachers to get feedback on their own practices in a supportive and engaged setting. Over half of the teachers (53.3%) responded that they collaborated with other teachers and school counselors to explore college or post-high-school options for students (Contreras et al., 2008). Teachers within urban schools were more likely to report that they collaborated with staff to support student higher education aspirations only a few times a year (39.7%), while teachers within urban ring and rural schools responses were more spread out across the spectrum of survey options (Table 10.3) (X^2[8, $N = 243 = 19.14$], $p < .05$). Our interview data were relatively limited with respect to understanding the ways in which teachers collaborated within their schools and district to raise college awareness among their students. A high school teacher from an urban ring school described how strategies were emerging within her school:

**Table 10.3.   Cross-Tabulation of School Type and
Frequency of Collaboration With Other Teachers and
School Counselors in Efforts to Support Students to
Prepare for College or Post-High School Options**

Frequency of Collaboration With Other Staff	School Type			χ^2	Φ
	Urban	Urban Ring	Rural		
Once or more a week	16.2%	28.7%	34.7%	19.14*	.28
	(11)	(23)	(33)		
Once or twice a month	23.5%	21.3%	31.6%		
	(16)	(17)	(30)		
A few times a year	39.7%	32.5%	28.4%		
	(27)	(26)	(27)		
Once a year	7.4%	10.0%	1.1%		
	(5)	(8)	(1)		
Never	13.2%	7.5%	4.2%		
	(9)	(6)	(4)		

Note. * = $p \leq .05$. Group frequencies appear in parentheses below row percentages. $N = 243$.

We're coming up with some good strategies and ideas and, by sharing as an entire, you know, group, we are coming up with ideas to try. So I think it's good that we aren't just hiding in our little holes and trying to do things on our own. That really represents sharing out.

A high school teacher from an urban ring district further discussed district efforts to raise college awareness because his school did not offer college nights.

Our district along with a couple other districts just had a whole college fair that was held at the event center, and students went during the day and then it was also open in the evening. I don't know, I doubt if there were translators there.

While this teacher in particular went on to acknowledge the benefits of such efforts, he also raised the issue of translators for Latino parents, which were not always offered within his school or district.

Indeed, the lack of translation services provided for parents was one of the central concerns raised in our statewide study and addressed in our recommendations to the state legislature. Teachers often discussed the limitations that a language barrier presented for them in communicating with parents, but very few discussed how they actively worked within the school to better engage their Latino parents (Contreras et al., 2008).

In fact, most teachers reported that their school offered a Spanish translator or a bilingual aide at school related events either "always" or "most" of the time for parents that do not speak English. A chi-square test of independence indicates a significant association between school type and how often schools offered Spanish translation services to Latino parents, $X^2(8, N = 228) = 20.31, p < .001$. We found that rural school (Table 10.4), teachers (68.2%) were more likely to report that their school always offers Spanish translation services to their Latino parents than teachers within urban (46.2%) or urban ring (41%) schools.

Table 10.4. Cross-Tabulation of School Type and Frequency of Spanish Translator or Bilingual Aid Available for School Events

School Accommodates for Latino Parents	School Type			χ^2	Φ
	Urban	Urban Ring	Rural		
Always	46.2%	41.0%	68.2%	20.31***	.30
	(30)	(34)	(60)		
Most of the time	36.9%	39.8%	23.9%		
	(24)	(33)	(21)		
Sometimes	12.3%	15.7%	5.7%		
	(8)	(13)	(5)		
Rarely	1.5%	3.6%	2.3%		
	(1)	(3)	(2)		
Never	3.1%	0%	0%		
	(2)	(0)	(0)		

Note. *** = $p \leq .001$. Group frequencies appear in parentheses below row percentages. N = 228.

While many teachers reported that schools offered translations services, teachers often discussed the limitations that a language barrier presented for them in communicating with parents, as the next section documents, but very few discussed how they actively worked within the school to better engage their Latino parents (Contreras et al., 2008).

Teacher Interaction With Latino Parents

Whether in Washington or elsewhere, Latino parents can often feel unwelcomed or misunderstood navigating their child's school context. When participating in activities designed to increase parental involvement (such as PTA or parent-teacher conferences), Latino parents regularly feel confused or frustrated about the school structures, expectations for parents, and the inability to communicate key information through lack of translation services (Contreras et al., 2008; Gándara & Contreras, 2009; Hill & Torres, 2010). When asked about the nature of their interaction with Latino parents, responses differed by district context with 44.1% of teachers in rural schools interacting with Latino parents at least once a month compared to teachers in urban ring (24.6%) and urban (18.5%) schools, $X^2(10, N = 224) = 36.87, p < .001$.

The competencies and insights that Latino parents can bring to the classroom about Latino student learning is often underutilized by both Latino parents (Yan & Lin, 2005) and teachers (Jones, 2003; Rodríguez & López, 2003) due to either Latino parents' deference towards teacher professionalism and expertise and/or teacher' misconceptions about Latino parents' lack of concern or knowledge about their child's education. According to our statewide study, teachers within urban schools (35.1%) were more likely to report seeking input from Latino parents about their experiences and/or their achievement in school only "once an academic year," while teachers within rural schools (38.8%) were more likely to report seeking input "once every 4–6 months," $X^2(10, N = 211) = 25.30, p < .05$.

Interaction with parents can also be through school-initiated parental involvement activities. As seen in Table 10.5, teachers in rural schools (71.2%) relied more heavily on student parent conferences to communicate with Latino parents than did teachers in urban ring (59.5%) and urban (26.9%) schools, while teachers within urban schools were more likely to report higher percentages of parent interaction through parent nights (30.8%) and discipline issues (13.5%) than their urban ring and rural peers, $X^2(10, N = 148) = 27.04, p < .05$.

Latino parents in our study expressed a lack of full knowledge of the U.S. education system and difficulty engaging school staff and teachers to better advocate for their child. This was true in both urban and rural district contexts where educational attainment levels remain very low, despite generational status, which is consistent with studies on Latino generational

Table 10.5.   Cross-Tabulation of School Type and Nature of Teacher Interaction With Latino Student Parents

Type of Contact With Latino Parents	School Type			χ^2	ϕ
	Urban	Urban Ring	Rural		
Student Parent Conference	26.9%	59.5%	71.2%	27.04*	.43
	(14)	(22)	(42)		
Discipline Issue	13.5%	5.4%	6.8%		
	(7)	(2)	(4)		
Parent Night	30.8%	18.9%	6.8%		
	(16)	(7)	(4)		
After School Program	3.8%	2.7%	3.4%		
	(2)	(1)	(2)		
Community Organization	0%	0%	1.7%		
	(0)	(0)	(1)		

Note. * = $p \leq .05$. *Group frequencies appear in parentheses below row percentages.* $N = 148$.

progress (Telles & Martinez, 2009). In turn, these structural and linguistic barriers inhibited Latino parent involvement. The efforts to schedule parent interaction around parents' schedules varied by district context, $X^2(8, N = 228) = 45.47$, $p < .001$. Teachers within rural schools (53.8%) were more likely than urban (21.7%) and urban ring (22.1%) teachers to report always making an effort to schedule parent nights and conferences at convenient times for Latino parents (Table 10.6).

Scheduling parent interaction around parent schedules (e.g., weekends, later in evening) is critical given the long hours that Latino parents work, particularly immigrant or first-generation Latino parents (Delgado-Gaitan, 1991, 2001; Sosa, 1997). The lack of Latino parent involvement has often been misinterpreted by teachers as a lack of interest in their child's school, but the reality is that Latino parents very much value the education of their child (Scribner, Young, & Pedroza, 1999; Sosa, 1997). Teachers perceived the limited levels of Latino parent involvement to be a reflection of their immigrant status, lack of knowledge of the U.S. education system, or diminished value for education. A high school teacher from a rural school explained: "The only challenge is the families that have come straight from

Table 10.6. Cross-Tabulation of School Type and School Effort to Schedule Parent Nights/Conferences at Convenient Times for Latino Parents

School Accommodates for Latino Parents	School Type			χ^2	Φ
	Urban	Urban Ring	Rural		
Always	21.7%	22.1%	53.8%	45.47***	.45
	(13)	(21)	(49)		
Most of the time	35.0%	39.0%	37.1%		
	(21)	(30)	(34)		
Sometimes	25.0%	31.2%	7.7%		
	(15)	(24)	(7)		
Rarely	13.3%	7.8%	1.1%		
	(8)	(6)	(1)		
Never	5.0%	0%	0%		
	(3)	(0)	(0)		

Note. *** = $p \leq .001$. Group frequencies appear in parentheses below row percentages. N = 228.

Mexico. There are very few that value an education.... It is not high on their priority list."

Similar sentiments were commonly expressed among the middle and high school math teachers we interviewed. Teachers had also recommended that perhaps Latino parents needed to be educated on the U.S. education system through parent liaisons in the community. Another high school teacher from an urban ring school district explained the dilemma their school faces because of the limited interaction with Latino parents.

> The biggest problem I think on campus is that we don't have very big connections with families ... I feel like we don't, as a school, know very well how to connect with those communities and make sure that they feel like we want them to participate. Maybe I'll meet with one family a year tops, and then we'll talk about how's their kid doing. It is very rare.

Reaching out to parents as collaborators in raising student achievement and engagement, influencing school reform efforts, and creating a college-going culture is documented as a best practice in the literature (Gibson, Gándara, & Koyama, 2004; Lewis-Charp, Yu, & Friedlaender, 2004). The teacher data from this case study of Washington convey the "growing pains" of a state that is not yet up to speed with understanding optimal approaches for working with Latino families and their students.

IMPLICATIONS AND CONCLUSION

The findings from our study raise serious questions about the readiness of Washington State to meet the needs of Latino students. Washington State typifies the New Latino Diaspora, a state that is grappling with addressing the needs of its Latino students but has yet to full comprehend the major demographic shifts occurring through migration, immigration, and birth rates. This chapter, grounded in both qualitative and quantitative data, attempts to explore multiple causes and potential solutions of the persistent opportunity gap for Latino students. Our evidence indicates that the current focus on high-stakes testing and accountability may be creating teaching contexts, which limit the potential of Latino students. Because of the high failure rates in many of the districts we studied, teachers tend to focus on "teaching to the test." We are concerned about the possibility that this type of reductionist curriculum does not help Latino students acquire the 21st century competencies needed to thrive in contemporary society.

Against the backdrop of reductionist teaching, our research revealed troubling patterns in teachers' expectations of Latino students. In both rural and urban contexts our data showed that teachers held substantially less optimistic views about the future potential and educational achievement outcomes of Latino students than parents and students held. Holding high expectations of students is a central aspect of quality teaching for students of color. While not a direct aspect of our study, it is difficult not to see the relationship between the larger negative and paternalistic political discourse surrounding the issue of immigration and its possible relationship in the way teachers approach their work with Latino students. It is important to see these findings not as "blaming teachers," but understanding the larger social and political context in which the work of teaching occurs.

In addition, our work highlights the tremendous impact that immigration and demographic shifts has had on the teaching profession. Latino parents in our study expressed a difficulty navigating the U.S. education system and difficulty engaging school personnel. Unless Latino parents can fully and completely access structures to both assist and advocate for their children, their students' future outcomes will likely be limited. Our research raises questions about the ability of teachers to productively act as cultural brokers in helping students and families best navigate schooling in the United States.

By exploring the practice- and policy-based barriers (state and federal) that exist for Latino students in Washington State, we hope to offer policy makers, teacher educators, teachers, and community members a deeper sense of the challenges and opportunities in constructing educational opportunities for Latino students. Recent demographic shifts in Washington State create a pressing need to create systems-level change to address the needs of Latino students. The future health, well-being, and mobility of Latino communities depends on our ability to respond to these challenges. We contend that a great deal needs to be done to address these unequal opportunities. Efforts to provide an equitable education for Latino students need to be contextually appropriate and must be owned by the people of Washington State.

REFERENCES

Chavez, L. (2004, August). *Access to advanced math for latino high school students: the gatekeeping role of geometry.* Paper presented at the annual meeting of the American Sociological Association, San Francisco, CA.

Coleman, J. (1988) Social capital in the creation of human capital. *American Journal of Sociology, 94,* 95–120.

Contreras, F. (2005). Access, achievement and social capital: Standardized exams and the Latino college bound population. *Journal of Hispanics in Higher Education, 4*(3), 197–214.

Contreras, F. (2011). *Achieving equity for Latino students: Expanding the pathway to higher education through public policy.* New York: Teachers College Press.

Contreras, F., Stritikus, T., Torres, K., O'Reilly-Diaz, K., Esqueda, M., Sanchez, I., Ortega, L., & Sepulveda, A. (2008). Understanding opportunities to learn for Latinos in Washington. Report prepared for the Washington State Commission on Hispanic Affairsand Washington State Legislature under HB 2687.

Cytel Inc. (2005). *StatXact.* Cambridge, MA: Author.

Delgado-Gaitan, C. (1991). Involving parents in the schools: A process of change for involvement parents. *American Journal of Education, 29,* 20–46.

Delgado-Gaitan, C. (2001). *The power of community: Mobilizing for family and schooling.* Lanham, MD: Rowman & Littlefield.

Delpit, L. (1995). *Other people's children: Cultural conflict in the classroom.* New York, NY: The New Press.

Delpit, L. (2001) The politics of teaching literate discourse. In E. Cushman, M. Rose, B. Kroll, &E Kintgen (Eds.), *Literacy: A critical sourcebook* (pp. 545–554). Boston, MA: Bedford/ St. Martin's.

Gamboa, E., (1999). *Mexican labor and World War II: Braceros in the Pacific Northwest, 1942–1947.* Seattle, WA: University of Washington Press.

García, E. (2001). *Hispanics education in the United States: Raíces y Alas.* Boulder, CO: Rowman & Littlefield.

Gándara, P. (1995). *Over the Ivy walls: The educational mobility of low-income Chicanos.* Albany, NY: State University of New York Press.

Gándara, P., & Bial, D. (2001). Paving the way to postsecondary education: K–12 intervention programs for underrepresented youth. Report prepared for the U.S. Department of Education, National Center for Education Statistics. Washington DC.

Gándara, P., & Contreras, F. (2009). *The Latino education crisis: The consequences of failed social policies.* Cambridge, MA: Harvard University Press.

Gándara, P., Maxwell-Jolly, J., & Driscoll, A. (2005). Listening to the teachers of English learners. Report Prepared for Policy Analysis for California Education (PACE).

Gibson, M., Gándara, P., & Koyama, J. (2004) *School connections: U.S. Mexican youth, peers, and school achievement.* New York, NY: Teachers College Press.

Goldenberg, C. (1996). Commentary: The education of language minority children: Where are we and where do we need to go? *The Elementary School Journal, 96,* 353–361.

Hale-Benson, J. (1986). *Black children: Their roots, culture, and learning styles.* Baltimore, Md: Johns Hopkins University Press.

Haycock, K. (1998). Good teaching matters ... a lot. *Thinking K–16, 3*(2), 3–14.

Hamann, E. T., & Harklau, L. (2010). Education in the New Latino Diaspora. In E. G. Murillo (Ed.), *Handbook of Latinos and Education* (pp. 157–169). New York, NY: Routledge.

Hill, N. E., & Torres, K. (2010). Negotiating the American dream: The paradox of aspirations and achievement among Latino students and engagement between their families and schools. *Journal of Social Issues, 66* (1), 95–112.

Jones, T. G. (2003). Contribution of Hispanic parents' perspectives to teacher preparation. *School Community Journal, 13* (2), 73–97.

Ladson-Billings, G. (1995). Toward a theory of culturally relevant pedagogy. *American Educational Research Journal, 32*(3), 465–491.

Lewis-Charp, H., Yu, H., & Friedlaender, D. (2004). The Influence of intergroup relations on school engagement: Two cases. In P. Gándara, M. Gibson, & J. Koyama (Eds.), *School connections: U.S.-Mexican Youth, peers, and school achievement* (pp. 107–128). New York: Teachers College Press.

Lucas, T., Henze, R., & Donato, R. (1990). Promoting the success of Latino language-minority students: An exploratory study of six high schools. *Harvard Education Review 60*(3), 315–340.

McDonough, P. (2004). Counseling matters: Knowledge, assistance, and organizationalcommitment in college preparation. In W. G. Tierney, Z. B. Corwin, & J. E. Colyar (Eds.), Preparing for bollege: Nine elements of effective outreach. Albany, NY: State University of New York Press.

Meier, K., & Stewart, J. (1991). *The politics of Hispanic education: Un paso pa'lante y dos pa'tras.* Albany, NY: State University of New York Press.

Nieto, S. (1992). *Affirming diversity: The sociopolitical context of multicultural education.* New York, NY: Longman.

Nieto, S. (1996). *Affirming diversity: The sociopolitical context of multicultural education.* New York, NY: Longman.

Portes, A., & Rumbaut, R. G. (2006). *Children of immigrants longitudinal study (CILS), 1991–2006* [Computer file]. Ann Arbor, MI: DataSharing for Demographic Research. doi:10.3886/ICPSR20520

Rodríguez, R. F., & López, L. C. (2003). Mexican-American parental involvement with a Texas elementary school. *Psychological Reports, 92*(3), 791–792.

Rousseau, C. K., & Tate, W. F. (2003). No time like the present: Reflecting on equity in school mathematics. *Theory Into Practice, 42*(3), 210–216.

Sosa, A. S. (1997). Involving Hispanic parents in educational activities through collaborative relationships. *Bilingual Research Journal, 21*(2), 1–8.

Scribner, J. D., Young, M. D., & Pedroza, A. (1999). Building collaborative relationships with parents. In P. Reyes, J. D. Scribner, & A. P. Scribner (Eds.), *Lessons from high-performing Hispanic schools: Creating learning communities.* New York, NY: Teachers College Press.

Stanton-Salazar, R. D. & Spina, S. U. (2003). Informational mentors and role models in the lives of urban Mexican-origin adolescents. *Anthropology & Education Quarterly, 34*(3), 231–254.

Suárez-Orozco, C. E., & Suárez-Orozco, M. M. (2001). *Children of immigration.* Cambridge MA: Harvard University Press.

Suárez-Orozco, M., Suárez-Orozco, C., & Todorova, I. (2008). *Learning a New Land.* Cambridge, MA: Harvard University Press.

Swail, W. S., Cabrera, A. F., & Lee, C. (2004). *Latino youth and the pathway to college.* Washington, DC: Pew Hispanic Center.

Tatum, B. D. (1999). *Why are all the black kids sitting together in the cafeteria? And other conversations about race: A psychologist explains the development of racial identity.* (Revised ed.) New York, NY: Basic Books.

Telles E., & Martinez, V. (1999). *Generations of exclusion: Mexican Americans, assimilation, and race.* New York, NY: Russell Sage Foundation.

Tienda, M., & Mitchell, F. (Eds.). (2006a). *Multiple origins, uncertain destinies: Hispanics and the American future.* Washington, DC: National Academy Press.

Tienda, M., & Mitchell, F. (Eds.). (2006b). *Hispanics and the future of America.* Washington, DC: National Academy Press.

Valdés, G. (1996). *Con respeto* [With respect]. New York, NY: Teacher College Press.

Valencia, R. (2002). *Chicano school failure and success.* New York, NY: Routledge-Falmer.

Valenzuela, A. (2005). *Leaving the children behind: How "Texas-style" accountability fails Latino youth.* Albany, NY: State University of New York Press.

Valli, L., & Buese, D. (2007). The changing roles of teachers in an era of high-stakes accountability. *American Educational Research Journal, 44*(3), 519–558.

Wortham, S., Murillo, E. G., & Hamann, E. T. (Eds.). (2002). *Education in the New Latino Diaspora: Policy and the politics of Identity.* Westport, CT: Ablex.

Yan, W., & Lin, Q. (2005). Parent involvement and mathematics achievement: Contrast across racial and ethnic groups. *Journal of Educational Research, 99*(2), 116–127.

CHAPTER 11

EARLY CHILDHOOD EDUCATION AND BARRIERS BETWEEN IMMIGRANT PARENTS AND TEACHERS WITHIN THE NEW LATINA(O) DIASPORA

Jennifer K. Adair

The presence of young children in Latino immigrant families is changing the dynamics of early childhood settings across the United States (Arzubiaga & Adair, 2009; Arzubiaga, Noguerón, & Sullivan, 2009; Garcia, 2005). Early childhood education has a special role within the New Latino Diaspora (NLD) since it is the first institutional experience for many immigrant families (Garcia & Gonzalez, 2006. Early childhood education continues to be an indicator of future school success for children of immigrants (Takanishi, 2004), but we are only beginning to understand the dynamics of immigration and its affect on early childhood settings (Adair & Tobin, 2007; Souto-Manning, 2006). Documenting how teachers and parents navigate early childhood education is critical for educational researchers and practitioners who want to better understand how educational systems

Revisiting Education in the New Latino Diaspora, pp. 207–224

are responding to new Latino immigrant families in rural and urban settings across the NLD.

This chapter uses data from the Children Crossing Borders (CCB) project to describe how preschool teachers are responding to Latino immigration in two emerging gateway cities within the NLD; a rural town referred to here as Farmville, Iowa and Nashville, Tennessee.[1] This chapter describes barriers between Latino immigrant parents and preschool teachers at schools where the Latino presence is new by drawing upon and analyzing focus group interview data from Nashville and Farmville and then comparing it to other CCB data collection sites.

Children Crossing Borders and Multivocal Ethnography

Being able to discuss Farmville and Nashville approaches to early childhood education with recently arrived immigrant families was possible because of the comparative approaches utilized in the larger the CCB project. CCB is an international, multi-sited, multivocal ethnographic study of immigration and early childhood education in five countries: France, Germany, England, Italy and the U.S. The main focus of CCB has been to understand and take seriously the perspectives of immigrant parents and preschool teachers on the education of young children of immigrants. The version of multivocal ethnography used in this study was developed by Joseph Tobin and his colleagues in the books *Preschool and Three Cultures* (1989) and *Preschool and Three Cultures Revisited* (2009) and has been described extensively elsewhere (Adair & Tobin, 2007; Kurban & Tobin, 2009; Tobin, 1999; Tobin & Davidson, 1991; Tobin & Hsueh, 2007).

Multivocal ethnography includes making a film, showing the film to participants in different sites/contexts and then using their reactions to the common film as data. To conduct CCB research in the United States, we chose to film a preschool classroom in Phoenix, AZ that was informally bilingual because the two teachers, as well as at least half of the students, were native Spanish speakers. After spending various weeks in Liliana's classroom in Phoenix and letting the children play with and test out the film cameras, our research team filmed over two days and then worked with both teachers, parents and children to condense the footage into a twenty-minute film that represented a typical day at the school. We held focus groups in and around Phoenix, AZ and then at preschool sites in Nashville (TN), Farmville (IA), San Luis (AZ), and New York City (NY). At each, immigrant parents and preschool teachers watched and responded to the film. Because of scenes involving language, parent/student interactions, discipline, peer conflict, play, group instruction, and parent/teacher communication, participants responded to the film and offered insight into how they believed school *should be* for young children of immigrants.

The responses of parents, teachers, directors, children and community members to the common stimulus film constituted the analyzed data. As participants revealed what they liked or did not like in the film, we could understand better the common values and cross-cultural differences among participants, particularly in what they expected from early childhood settings. Of course the films were not meant to be representative of all U.S. preschools—many of the preschools we visited did not have bilingual teachers. The inclusion of bilingual teachers and an informal bilingual program provoked strong opinions and discussion around language, bilingual children, bilingual classrooms, teacher accents, and whose responsibility it was to help children be multilingual and maintain their home language(s). Even though staff bilingualism was not common across all of the sites, the film resonated with teachers in each of them. The practices, environment, teaching styles, and routine were familiar to them.

Prior to this chapter, the multivocal ethnographic method allowed us to conduct analysis that compared parents and children who were filmed, parents and teachers in the school sites' community, parents and teachers in the same city, and parents and teachers in the same country. We compared immigrant parent and teacher ideas about pedagogy (how participants responded, corrected, detested, applauded the teacher in the film) by city, linguistic background, or country. We also compared immigrant teachers and nonimmigrant teachers (Adair, 2011), national ideas about early childhood education (Adair & Pastori, 2011; Tobin, Arzubiaga, & Mantovani, 2007) as well as immigrant parents and preschool teachers in specific countries (Adair & Tobin, 2007; Arzubiaga & Adair, 2009; Brougère, Guénif-Souilamas, & Rayna, 2008; Kurban & Tobin, 2009). This is the first analysis of the data, however, that compares NLD sites to sites where the presence of Latinos is longstanding.

New to Latino Immigration: Farmville, IA and Nashville, TN

During the comparative analytic process of comparing the perspectives of immigrant parents and preschool teachers in multiple cities and countries within the United States, we noticed that preschool teachers and immigrant parents in places relatively new to Latino immigration struggled in different ways than did teachers and parents in cities with a longer history of immigration. When we collected our data, Farmville and Nashville were both *emerging gateway cities* (see Singer, Hardwick, & Brettell, 2008) because they were new entry points for immigrant communities (although Farmville is not a "city" by most conventional uses of that word). They both were experiencing recent immigration from Mexico and Central America and had significantly different demographic make-ups than they did 10 years earlier (U.S. Census Bureau, 2007; Urban Institute, 2006).

Farmville, Iowa was a small Midwestern town, which was barely kept alive by a fledgling meatpacking industry. Recruited workers from small towns in Southern Mexico had come to the town, repopulated the schools, and energized town businesses by participating in the local economy. The presence of newcomers had doubled the population of the town in about five years and dramatically shifted the demographics of the local school. In 2005, for the first time in the town's history, the elementary school graduated more children of immigrants of Mexican descent than White students. In turn, Nashville, the capital of Tennessee and part of the former Confederacy, had one of the fastest changing populations in the U.S. and was considered a new "destination state" for refugees as well as documented and undocumented immigrants (U.S. Census Bureau, 2006).

Early childhood educators in both Nashville and Farmville particularly struggled with misunderstanding immigrant parents because of language issues or false assumptions (Valdés, 1996; Villenas, 2002). In both cities, teachers reported that they "hardly ever saw the parents" and thought that if they asked, "more parents would help them." This chapter explores in detail why parent and teacher relationships were so troubled in the NLD and what types of barriers need to be removed in order to have effective parent/teacher communication.

Barriers Between Latino Immigrant Parents and Preschool Teachers

In the CCB study, we found a collective set of barriers that made it difficult for immigrant parents to be heard and taken seriously in preschool classrooms. Preschool teachers generally have little preparation or training to work with immigrant families (Arzubiaga & Adair, 2009; Crosnoe, 2006; Karabenick & Noda, 2004). In turn, immigrant parents are often reluctant to share their ideas about education with teachers (De Gaetano, 2007; Good, Masewicz, & Vogel, 2009). Particularly within the two cities considered part of the NLD—that is, Nashville and Farmville—the data we collected included stories of concern *and* gratitude from immigrant parents as well as frustration *and* gratitude from the teachers. Parents appreciated the kind of education their children were receiving, comparing it to the type of early education they themselves received as children in Mexico. Farmville teachers appreciated that the immigrant families' presence in the town afforded them a new school, continued employment, and a new infusion of economic capital into the local economy.

At the same time, in both communities we found parents worried about whether their child's teacher could truly advocate for and comfort their children. We found that immigrant parents had many ideas about preschool education and what types of experiences their children should be having at school. The troubling part and the message of this chapter was that these ideas about what was and was not working seemed to stay within immigrant communities, rarely gaining the attention of teachers and schools. Why is it difficult for immigrant parents to share their opinions or desires for their children's schooling and what prevents teachers from hearing them even when they do communicate?

Trying to understand how parents and teachers can communicate about young children's learning is an important aspect of early childhood education (Arzubiaga, Rueda, & Monzo 2002; Gonzalez-Mena, 2001). While much of the early childhood educational literature insists that parent and teacher collaboration improves student socioemotional health at school as well as their academic achievement (see Hyson, 2008; Riojas-Cortez & Flores, 2009), there is still concern that teachers struggle to hear parents or to include them in their decisions and approaches to children's learning (Adair, 2009; Goodwin, 2002). The barriers discussed here were not only experienced between Latino immigrant parents and preschool teachers but were a specific and contextual version of a larger disconnect between parents and teachers (Adair & Tobin, 2007; see also Lightfoot, 2003; Ramirez, 2003). In other words, immigration did not cause the hierarchical, linguistic, and attitudinal barriers described here but merely illustrated a particularly worrisome version of the longstanding, problematic, parent/teacher dichotomy.

The remainder of this chapter focuses on three areas of concern voiced by Latino immigrant parents in Nashville and Farmville, including power, language, and teacher attitudes. Barriers to parent/teacher mutual understanding were made significantly more obtrusive by characteristics of the NLD. While these examples are situated within early childhood education and made urgent by the presence of young children who are new to school, barriers described here can be applied to pre-K–12 schooling contexts across the NLD struggling to have authentic parent/teacher communication. For clarity in the following examples, parents are denoted by their last name and teachers by their first name.

HIERARCHICAL BARRIERS

A few years before we arrived to begin the research, Farmville elementary school had implemented a transitional bilingual program for the newly arrived Spanish-speaking children. The program was meant to teach children core academic subjects in their native language while introducing English vocabulary. When we arrived to do interviews, teachers and parents were both sorry to tell us that that program had been discontinued. However their perspectives on why were drastically different. Immigrant parents explained that the school had conducted a meeting about whether to keep the bilingual program, but few parents (immigrant or native-born) had attended. At first, the immigrant parents blamed each other for not coming to the meeting. They argued that parents did not take it seriously and so the program was taken away. As one mother explained,

> What happens is that when there is a meeting like this, people don't show up. Because when I was asking to not take away the bilingual, how many came? Ten people, and there's a lot more of us. More than 300 people and nobody came and that's why they got rid of it. We don't support each other amongst ourselves, they got rid of the bilingual because people didn't come.

Other immigrant parents, however, disagreed that the reasons the bilingual program ended was because they, the parents, did not care. One parent spoke up and suggested that the parent meetings be made mandatory so that the factory would let them leave work to attend, saying, "It's that here, for us to be able to come to a meeting, there has to be a mandatory note." Other parents pointed out that even this change wouldn't have worked.

Ms. Garcia: Well I think that a lot of people get off work and they work around here, close to here. But here they don't let you unless it's to go to the hospital. For some school thing, almost never.

Ms. Diaz: I work there in the factory and they only let you go if it's mandatory, and if not, they don't let you.

Ms. Montero: They never let my husband go. Even though she told them she had to go for a meeting or that she had to go, they told her no, that there weren't enough people [workers]. "No" because of this, "no" because of that.

Ms. Sanchez: And sometimes not even for emergencies. Because yesterday I had to call my husband twice for an emergency and they wouldn't pass my call to him.

Ms. Ruida: Me too. They called me that the girl was sick and they took two hours to give me the message there in the factory.

While the parents were extremely frustrated by the insensitivity of the factory that prevented them from attending school affairs, they went on to suggest that the school should have anticipated such a conflict since so many of the immigrant parents worked in the factory. Immigrant parents suggested that the meeting be made later, pointing out that most parents finished work by 8:00 P.M. They also said that Saturdays or Sundays would be better times to meet because most parents would not be working.

They said that many more would have attended the meeting and possibly changed the result if the meeting time had been different. One immigrant parent explained,

> There are people who, who would like to, because I've heard 'Hey how was it? Because [the factory] didn't let me go. Some who work and get off at seven. Why would they come [to the meeting for] half an hour, 15 minutes? Not even.

Immigrant parents in this case saw the problem first as one of personal responsibility—the program was discontinued because they did not attend the meeting—but then they complicated that explanation. Reasons for not attending the meeting ranged from not supporting the community to having an inflexible workplace that would not let them attend. The parents' inability to attend the meeting was not only seen within the group as a failure, but also a symptom of their economic dependence on the jobs within the factory.

When we asked teachers at the same school why the bilingual program was stopped, they explained that it was because of test scores and blamed the district's attention to ratings and accountability measures.

> Angela: I'm just really curious about that, because the parents did mention yesterday the bilingual program as you are confirming, is no longer there. How did that come about?
> Jane: I think it's called No Child Left Behind and test scores.
> Terri: And making sure whatever special programs were around had data to support. It's the support, [seeing] progress or not, and the data wasn't showing really either way.
> Jane: It's the data, the accountability issue, really.

Farmville preschool teachers never blamed the parents for what happened to the bilingual program, yet the parents believed it was their fault for not coming to the district meeting. The teachers also wanted the bilingual program back, but felt hopeless about it because it had not produced the desired test score results necessitated through federal policy. During our time with them in focus groups and informal conversations, we had no evidence that either group knew they had different perspectives on why the bilingual program ended. Both teachers and parents felt somewhat powerless in relation to federal mandates and local factors like district policies and factory working conditions. While it is true that teachers across the U.S. struggle within their own educational spaces to have political voice as well as decision-making autonomy in their classrooms (see Nichols & Berliner, 2007), teachers in the relationship of Latino immigrant parent and teacher are given a high-level cultural status and often deferred to as authority figures. Further, the teachers blamed the district, and the immigrant parents blamed themselves for the disintegration of the bilingual program. The varying perspectives on why the bilingual education program ended for preschoolers indicate a power differential between immigrant parents and preschool teachers. While teachers felt like the decision to end bilingual education was unfortunate, even, shortsighted, they did not blame themselves or each other.

LINGUISTIC BARRIERS

Latino immigrant parents in Nashville and Farmville expressed a great deal of concern about the lack of Spanish at their child's school. Parents did not bring up materials like books or signs. They were mostly concerned with relationships. Their worry about language centered on two main concerns: the relationship between themselves and the teacher and the relationship of the teacher and their young children.

Parent/Teacher Communication

Across the United States, Latino immigrant parents (as well as immigrant parents from other cultural and linguistic groups) wanted bilingual staff. This desire was noticeably more desperate in schools where this was not yet available. Even in traditional immigrant communities like metropolitan Phoenix and New York City, parents from new immigrant groups described being isolated by language. These concerns mirror those described by Latino immigrant parents in Nashville and Farmville. For example, Mixteco parents in Phoenix, Arizona wanted teachers who could communicate with them in Mixtec, instead of relying on a community interpreter who visited the school every so often. Immigrant parents from Ivory Coast who attended a focus group in Harlem wanted teachers who could speak French so that they could talk directly with them. Mexican immigrant parents in Phoenix and Dominican immigrant parents in New York City agreed that having a bilingual teacher was important for them, as parents, to stay connected and involved in the education of their children. The similar concerns in the NLD were not just about communicating logistics. Parents believed that if they could communicate through their first language to teachers and to the school, they would be perceived more positively by the school and by their own children.

In one school site in Phoenix, we interviewed Mexican immigrant mothers who were attending "parent education" classes while their children attended the preschool program. While explaining their embarrassment about not speaking English, they also revealed a problem with English-only approaches in schools.

> Ms. Rodriquez: For example, in the meetings for my daughter's class, I still don't understand what the dinosaur party is or something like that. And there are many times that she has asked, "Come!" until she cries. And we didn't want to go because she told me that the meetings with the teacher are going to be in English. She only speaks English. It's something that frustrates me because I do not understand what she says to me, and there is no translator or anything.
>
> Ms. Villa: Now she has [my daughter] come, she brings Cristal and what does Cristal say? "She says that I am behaving well" and what, what does Cristal say? "I'm doing well."
>
> Interviewer: And you don't believe what she is saying?
>
> Ms. Villa: By herself.
>
> Interviewer: Do you think that your children see this and for them, they do not understand what happens to you because you do not know much English?
>
> Ms. Rodriquez: They are starting to realize.
>
> Ms. Villa: Yes, they do.
>
> Ms. Franquis: As for me, I get embarrassed and so I'm giving myself some space to learn English.
>
> Ms. Rodriquez: Yes because sometimes my son asks me, "Mama?" The stores send papers, and he picks them up and asks me, "Come here, come here Mama, what does this say?" And I tell him, "My son, it is in English and I don't know what it says." "Oh, well then study so that you learn English too." And sometimes it is embarrassing for us because what are they going to think? You already have some time here and you don't know the language here.

Immigrant parents generally, like these mothers, expressed concern and embarrassment when they felt they were being treated like an immigrant, rather than a parent. Parents worried about their ability to help their children at school. Many of the immigrant parents we spoke with were having their first schooling experience in the U.S. and felt unsure about how their children would do in school and even how they would do as parents.

Parents in Nashville and Farmville shared these concerns about being able to communicate with teachers in Spanish. Consider a Nashville parent who centered her concern about Spanish in her own position as a parent:

> In fact, honestly, I think the main problem here is that, the teachers in the majority of the preschools only speak, only speak English. Then, when the children start, I think they become disoriented. I mean, because there's not anybody, I mean, *somebody for us and the children*; there's not anybody who can help us with the translation in the school.

While this mother began speaking about children needing some Spanish, she changed and focused on "anybody who can help us with the translation in the school." Another Latina Nashville mother lamented,

> *The truth is that I don't speak English and she brings homework and I can't help her because, for that reason, because I don't speak English either. And well, sometimes I ask her if they didn't teach her in Spanish or what that means in Spanish and sometimes she doesn't answer, that is, she knows it in English but not in Spanish.*

Parents, most often mothers, who participated in our focus groups in Nashville and Farmville saw bilingual staff as a way to remain connected and be informed about their child's progress in order to help with what happens at school. When parents are unable to communicate with the teacher, they begin to break down as a parent in the eyes of their children and the teacher. They cannot easily fulfill their roles as parent when their child is translating, a note comes home in English or they cannot help out with homework. Parents are concerned that as children realize that they, as parents, are not able to communicate, their ability to act as parents in the schooling life of their children decreases. Recent studies like Orellana's (2009) work on children as language brokers demonstrate that authority between parents and children is complicated as children intervene, translate, and act on their parents behalf because translation is not provided by the school.

TEACHER/CHILD RELATIONSHIP

Latino immigrant parents in Farmville and Nashville took their concern about language one step further than the other cities. They also wanted bilingual teachers who could act as advocates for their preschoolers. One Nashville mother explained her deep concern for how her daughter might be treated as a minority at the school. In her concern, she referenced a scene from our film-clip in which the teacher intervenes in a dispute between two girls. The girls in the film fought over a dress in the dramatic play area.

I have a daughter, who just started here. She comes here to the group. She just started two months ago at the preschool, that they accepted her for me. The problem is that in the previous school there wasn't a Spanish speaking person. Then at the beginning, she cried a lot because, even [here], because all her classmates spoke English very well and she didn't. Sometimes, like, that's why they [classmates] take advantage of them since they don't know how to defend themselves. They don't know how to answer. That's what happened with the girl with the dress, right? They were fighting for the dress. Maybe the teacher should have taken the dress away from them and not giving it back to either of them, right? But at the end, one of them got it. That is, when the two girls were fighting for the dress. Then, it's the same when a child who just enters, who speaks Spanish only, the other children take advantage of them and they don't know how to defend themselves. They don't even know how to tell the teacher that a child hit him, that a child took something from him because he doesn't, the teacher doesn't understand them because she doesn't speak the language; she doesn't speak Spanish. I think that that's the problem for us here in the preschools.

This mother argued that because the teacher did not know Spanish, the child who deserved to have the dress, the child who was wronged, does not end up getting the dress. She blames this injustice on language, explaining that "the teacher doesn't understand them because she does not speak the language." Using the dress argument as a powerful metaphor, the mother worries that her child as a Spanish speaker will be taken advantage of and will always be the one without the dress. Her child may always be on the losing end of such disputes, because children are often unable to explain what is happening in English or because the teacher cannot understand the argument if the argument takes place in Spanish. As another parent pointed out, "Children need to be able to defend themselves." When children, don't know how to defend themselves [with language], they are at risk.

Parents in Farmville and Nashville were not alone in their concerns that Spanish was absent from school even while it was central in their homes. The literature suggests that children of immigrants whose home life is validated at school tend to do better in areas like literacy, science and mathematics (Reese & Gallimore, 2000; Riojas-Cortez, Huerta, Flores, Perez, & Clark, 2008). Studies like Hughes and Greenhough's (2006) work on knowledge exchange activities suggest that as parents and teachers equally share knowledge, classrooms are better able to represent children's lives outside of school in a way that invites more in-depth learning experiences for children of immigrants (see also Riojas-Cortez, 2001). Ginsberg (2007) also argues that knowledge gained from immigrant families can foster respect between teachers and families and lead to a more relevant curriculum for children of immigrants. Language as a means to connect home and school was not something Latino immigrant parents articulated as a pedagogical approach or academic content. Rather, as studies like *Funds of Knowledge* (González, Moll, & Amanti, 2005) find, language is something that can help children of immigrants and their parents feel more connected to the school.

"We Can't Demand More"

So far we have talked about Latino immigrant parents' concerns about having bilingual teachers and staff for their preschoolers, as well as their concerns about how teachers may or may not care and advocate for their children. We have also discussed how perspective differences between Latino immigrant parents and preschool teachers result in varying perspectives that often overemphasize immigrant parent responsibility and negate school or structural decision making. The key to this discussion is not necessarily what concerns immigrant parents but why teachers do not know the concerns or are unable to respond to them effectively. Again, according to research carried out in a variety of settings in early childhood contexts, the parent/teacher partnership is the key to successful transitions (Arzubiaga, Rueda, & Monzo, 2002; Goodwin, 2002; Riojas-Cortez et al., 2008). Yet Latino immigrant parents and preschool teachers in our study struggled to communicate about basic concerns and worries, particularly in Farmville and Nashville. Even in our focus group interviews, Latino immigrant parents often struggled (as did most immigrant parents in our study) to critique the schools their children went to. Often when parents spoke with concern about the (pre)school their child attended, it was either preceded by or followed up with an expression of gratitude. For example, Norma, a mother in Nashville explains,

> Actually here the preschool is 100 times better than in México. I mean, honestly, *we can't demand more*, well, a little bit more of the language, as she said, to introduce the language so the children can cope with it. Because, it even affects them when they can't participate in class, they can't answer and they can't express themselves, right?

The sentiment *we can't demand more* is an understandable position for immigrant parents who feel grateful despite their anxiety about being able to communicate with the teacher. This gratitude is representative of many first-generation immigrants who do not have as much conflict or *cultural dissonance* (Suárez-Orozco & Suárez-Orozco, 2001) as later generations. The danger for many preschool teachers, especially those with little contact or knowledge of immigrant families and communities they work with, is that they may mistake this gratitude or lack of complaint as agreement. For example, Norma says she is grateful and that compared to Mexico the preschool her daughter attends is substantially better. This does not negate, however, that Norma also has some concerns. She is worried about language, how much or how well her child participates, and whether her child can express herself in class. In the set up we witnessed, these concerns remained unaddressed.

Compliance and/or expressing gratitude do not mean parents agree with all that their children are encountering, nor does it deny that parents have sincere and deep concerns about their child's education, as this discussion is illustrating. Preschool teachers or any teacher who takes compliance from an immigrant parent as a sign of successful parent/teacher communication is most likely not asking the right types of questions or is perhaps focusing too much on the gratitude authentically communicated by parents. It is possible that teachers are not taught to listen carefully enough to immigrant parents or that immigrant parents understand that schools and teachers may not take their concerns seriously. Consider a Nashville mother who seems torn between gratitude and concern.

> In spite of everything, the teachers here, I think that they are very good because they understand us, well, even though it's only with signs, but they understand us and try to help us and well, they understand us. Because, honestly, we don't know the school procedures or when they send papers in English. I found a translator who sometimes understands me by signs. They tell me what the papers are for and they are good even despite their language and our language

This mother states that the teacher is good even though the teacher can't communicate very well with her as the mother. She says twice that the teachers "understand us' but follows it with "even though it's only with signs."

This mother makes two important points to teachers who work with children of immigrants within the new Latino Diaspora. First, immigrant parents *are* grateful and try to be positive about an less-than-ideal situation. Teachers can be good teachers of children of immigrants without knowledge of their home language, but only to a point, as these teachers are poorly positioned to know, let alone build upon, their students' and those students' parents funds of knowledge (González, Moll, & Amanti, 2005). Newcomer parents' capacity to see teachers as good despite not being able to communicate with them is evidence of immigrant parents' ability to be *ecologically pragmatic* (Arzubiaga & Adair, 2009). Although the absence of bilingual staff at their child's school is not ideal (nor recognized as such by parents) as evidenced in many of the previous examples, parents still notice and appreciate kind and patient teaching that they believe helps their children academically and socially.

The second point for teachers in the NLD is that even while parents believe their teacher is good, they still have significant concerns about teachers not speaking Spanish. They want teachers who can communicate with them as parents and with their children during inevitable conflicts or misunderstandings. The parents make decisions and set expectations based on local contexts, not necessarily on idealized scenarios or hope and often keep their concerns quiet. If teachers mistake this silence for full agreement, they will miss the opportunity for meaningful engagement in open dialogue with parents whose culture and perspectives they may know little about. Missing such opportunities to hear and address immigrant parents concerns reflects lack of capacity. Farmville and Nashville teachers did not see their own incapacity to hear and respond to immigrant parent concerns as a barrier to creating a strong parent/teacher relationship. It was only when we had parents and teachers watching films and speaking together that such lack of capacity was called into question directly.

In Farmville, after we had met with the preschool teachers and parents separately to watch the U.S. film, we conducted a focus group discussion with a few parents and some of the preschool teachers together. The topic of the discussion was what immigrant parents thought was important about preschool education for their children. It was meant to be an opportunity for the teachers to "listen" and "hear" the concerns and desires of the immigrant parents. Teachers explained how much they wanted to get to know the parents and how important it was to welcome young children into school and help them feel comfortable. Then, teachers listened as a father and two mothers explained in detail some of the difficulties they were having with the school and the town. They gave examples of discrimination as well as economic disparity. The teachers remained quiet until one teacher spoke up and said, seemingly out of exasperation "If it is so hard here, then why are you here? Why are you here? Why don't you go back?" Some parents' responded with silence. The father in the group expressed gratitude about being in Farmville but added, "*Eso no significa que no hay problemas* (That doesn't mean there are no problems.)"

The Farmville teachers' (at least those who spoke up) seemed angry at the parents and resented their critique of the teachers' school and town. The parents, perhaps, were violating the "pro-immigration script" in raising issues they experience in the town and in their new country (see Hamann, 2011; Suarez-Orozco, 1998). The teachers' frustration in the meeting shifted the focus from the perspective of the parents to the needs and defensive stance of the teachers. It was not only the teacher who spoke out who seemed surprised and angry. The other teachers shifted in their chairs as the father explained his struggles living in the U.S. and looked at each other throughout. The discussion became a conflicted space in which the parents had to determine whether to continue being honest or shift to a more grateful discourse, as if reassuring the teachers that the parents' struggles were not the responsibility or fault of the teachers. Farmville teachers admitted that they had little contact with parents and families from the immigrant communities (see Adair, Tobin, & Arzubiaga, 2012). The teachers collectively had taken compliance and silence as agreement and so were surprised and angry when confronted with the realities of immigrant parent lives in their community and school.

CONCLUSION

In early childhood education, where parents are typically encouraged to participate in the classroom and where immigrant parents (like all parents) are learning their role in their child's education, teachers' assumptions or attitudes impact how parents see themselves as part of the school/classroom (Souto-Manning & Swick, 2006). Preschool teachers in the NLD need more knowledge and experience with the Latino immigrant families in their schools. Misconceptions or prejudices that the teachers have about immigrant families cannot be adequately addressed just by loving the immigrant child in their classroom (Sleeter, 2001). As teachers come to know the communities they work with by associating with them outside of school, they can move past a superficial "gratitude phase" with parents and understand on a deeper level the desires and concerns that immigrant parents have for their children. Teachers in the NLD particularly need space, time and practice to get to know the families in their schools and replace suspicions or assumptions with experience. Only by having experience with immigrant families and pursuing opportunities to talk openly with them, can preschool teachers gain insight into the feelings with the parents and to connect with them as equal partners in their child's education.

NOTE

1. Farmville is a pseudonym and all school names are pseudonyms to protect anonymity. Because Nashville is a big metropolitan area, naming it does not jeopardize the anonymity of project participants from that locale.

REFERENCES

Adair, J. K. (2009). *Teaching children of immigrants: A multi-sited ethnographic study of preschool teachers in five U.S. cities* (Unpublished doctoral dissertation). Arizona State University.

Adair, J. K. (2011). Confirming *chanclas*: What early childhood teacher educators can learn from immigrant preschool teachers and their critique of language "modeling" techniques. *Journal of Early Childhood Teacher Education, 32*(1), 55–71.

Adair, J. K., & Pastori, G. (2011). Developing qualitative coding frameworks for educational research: Immigration, education and the Children Crossing Borders project. *International Journal of Research and Method in Education, 34*(1), 31–47.

Adair, J., & Tobin, J. (2007). Listening to the voices of parents. In C. Genishi & A. Goodwin (Eds.), *Diversities in early childhood education: Rethinking and doing* (pp. 137–150). New York: Routledge Falmer.

Adair, J. K., Tobin, J., & Arzubiaga, A. (2012). The dilemma of cultural responsiveness and professionalization: Listening closer to immigrant teachers who teach children of recent immigrants. *Teachers College Record, 144*(12), 1–37.

Arzubiaga A., & Adair, J. K. (2009). Misrepresentations of language and culture, language and culture as proxies for marginalization: Debunking the arguments. In E. G. Murillo (Ed.), *Handbook of Latinos and Education*, (pp. 301–308). New York, NY: Routledge Falmer.

Arzubiaga, A., Noguerón, S. C., & Sullivan, A. L. (2009). The education of children in im/migrant families. *Review of Research in Education, 33*(1), 246–271.

Arzubiaga, A., Rueda, R., & Monzo, L. (2002). Family matters related to the reading engagement of Latino children. *Journal of Latinos and Education, 1*(4), 231–243.

Brougère, G., Guénif-Souilamas, N., & Rayna, S. (2008). Ecole maternelle (preschool) in France: A cross-cultural perspective, *European Early Childhood Education Research Journal, 16*(3), 371–384.

Crosnoe, R. (2006). *Mexican roots, American schools: How children from Mexican immigrant families make the transition into the American educational system.* Stanford, CA: Stanford University Press.

De Gaetano, Y. (2007). The role of culture in engaging Latino parents' involvement in school. *Urban Education, 42*(2), 145–162.

Fortuny, K. (2010). *Children of immigrants: 2008 state trends update (Research Report).* Washington, DC: The Urban Institute

Garcia, E. E. (2005). *Teaching and learning in two languages: Bilingualism & schooling in the United States.* New York, NY: Teachers College Press.

Garcia, E. & Gonzales, D. (2006). *Pre–K and Latinos: The foundation for America's future.* Washington DC: Pre–K Now.

Ginsberg, M. B. (2007). Lessons at the kitchen table. *Educational Leadership, 64*(6), 56–61.

Good, M. E., Masewicz, S., & Vogel, L. (2009). Latino English language learners: Bridging achievement and cultural gaps between schools and families. *Journal of Latinos and Education, 9*(4), 321–339.

Goodwin, A. L. (2002). Teacher preparation and the education of immigrant children. *Education and Urban Society, 34*(2), 156–172.

González, N., Moll, L. C., & Amanti, C. (2005). *Funds of knowledge theorizing practice in households, communities, and classrooms.* Mahwah, NJ: L. Erlbaum Associates.

Gonzalez-Mena, J. (2001). *Foundations: Early childhood education in a diverse society* (2nd ed.). Mountain View, CA: Mayfield.

Goodwin, A. L. (2002). Teacher preparation and the education of immigrant children. *Education and Urban Society, 34*(2), 156–172.

Hamann, E. T. (2011). The Anglo politics of Latino education: The role of immigration scripts. In D. L. Leal & K. J. Meier (Eds.), *The politics of Latino education* (pp. 103–121). New York, NY: Teachers College Press. (Retrieved from http://digitalcommons.unl.edu/teachlearnfacpub/105/)

Hughes, M., & Greenhough, P. (2006). Boxes, bags and videotape: Enhancing home-school communication through knowledge exchange activities. *Educational Review, 58*(4), 471–487.

Hyson, M. (2008). *Enthusiastic and engaged learners: Approaches to learning in the early childhood classroom.* New York, NY: Teachers College Press.

Kurban, F., & Tobin, J. (2009). "They don't like us": Reflections of Turkish children in a German preschool. *Contemporary Issues in Early Childhood Education, 10*(1), 24–34.

Lightfoot, S. L. (2003) *The essential conversation: What parents and teachers can learn from each other.* New York, NY: Random House.

Nichols, S., & Berliner, D. (2007) *Collateral damage how high-stakes testing corrupts America's schools.* Cambridge, MA: Harvard University Press.

Orellana, M. F. (2009). *Translating childhoods: Immigrant youth, language, and culture.* Piscataway, NJ: Rutgers University Press.

Ramirez, A. Y. F. (2003). Dismay and disappointment: Parental involvement of Latino immigrant parents. *Urban Review, 35*(2), 93–110.

Reese, L., & Gallimore, R. (2000). Immigrant Latinos' cultural model of literacy development: An evolving perspective on home-school discontinuities. *American Journal of Education, 108*(2), 103–134.

Riojas-Cortez, M. (2001). It's all about talking: Oral language development in a bilingual classroom. *Dimensions of Early Childhood, 29*(1), 11–15.

Riojas-Cortez, M., Huerta, M. E., Bustos Flores, B., Pérez, B., & Riojas Clark, E. (2008). Using cultural tools to develop scientific literacy of young Mexican American preschoolers. *Early Child Development and Care, 178*(5), 527–536.

Riojas-Cortez, M., & Flores, B. B. (2009) Supporting preschoolers' social development in school through funds of knowledge. *Journal of Early Childhood Research, 7*(2), 185–199.

Singer, A., Hardwick, S. W., & Brettell, C. (2008). *Twenty-first-century gateways: Immigrant incorporation in suburban America.* Washington, DC: Brookings Institution Press.

Sleeter, C. E. (2001). Preparing teachers for culturally diverse schools: Research and the overwhelming presence of whiteness. *Journal of Teacher Education, 52*(2), 94–106.

Souto-Manning, M., & Swick, K. J. (2006). Teachers' beliefs about parent and family involvement: Rethinking our family involvement paradigm. *Early Childhood Education Journal, 34*(2), 187–193.

Suárez-Orozco, M. M. (1998). State terrors: Immigrants and refugees in the postnational space. In Y. Zou & E. T. Trueba (Eds.), *Ethnic identity and power:*

Cultural contexts of political action in school and society (pp. 283–319). Albany, NY: State University of New York Press.

Suárez-Orozco, C., & Suárez-Orozco, M. M. (2001). *Children of immigration*. Cambridge, MA: Harvard University Press.

Takanishi, R. (2004). Leveling the playing field: Supporting immigrant children from birth to eight. *Future of Children, 14*(2), 61–79.

Tobin, J. (1999). Method and meaning in comparative classroom ethnography. In R. Alexander (Ed.), *Learning from comparing: New directions in comparative educational research* (pp. 113–134). Oxford, England: Symposium Books, Oxford University Press.

Tobin, J., & Davidson, D. (1991). The ethics of polyvocal ethnography: Empowering vs. textualizing children and teachers. *International Journal of Qualitative Research in Education, 3*(3), 271–283.

Tobin, J., & Hsueh, Y. (2007). The poetics and pleasures of video ethnography of education. In R. Goldman (Ed.), *Video research in the learning sciences*. New York, NY: Lawrence Erlbaum Associates.

Tobin, J. J., Arzubiaga, A., & Mantovani, S. (2007). Entering dialogue with immigrant parents. *Early Childhood Matters 108*, 34–38.

Tobin, J. J., Hsueh, Y., & Karasawa, M. (2009). *Preschool in three cultures revisited*. Chicago, IL: University of Chicago Press.

Tobin, J. J., Wu, D., & Davidson, D. (1989). *Preschool in three cultures: Japan, China, and the United States*. New Haven, CT: Yale University Press.

Urban Institute. (2006). *Children of immigrants: Facts and figures*. Washington, DC: Urban Institute

U.S. Census Bureau. (2007). *Population finder*. Retrieved January 5, 2009, from http://factfinder.census.gov/servlet/SAFFPopulation?_event=ChangeGeoContext&geo_id=16000US1915420&_geoContext

Valdés, G. (1996). *Con respeto: Bridging the distances between culturally diverse families and schools*. New York, NY: Columbia University, Teachers College Press.

Villenas, S. (2002). Reinventing educación in new Latino communities: Pedagogies of change and continuity in North Carolina. In S. Wortham, E. G. Murillo, & E. Hamann (Eds.), *Education in the New Latino Diaspora* (pp. 17–36). Westport, CT: Ablex Press.

CHAPTER 12

THE 3 Rs

Rhetoric, Recruitment, and Retention

Socorro G. Herrera and Melissa A. Holmes

We have to ask ourselves, is it about one more free tee-shirt, postcard, Cinco de Mayo booth, and translated brochure, or doing an assessment of what Latino families and students need to be recruited and retained in institutions of higher education?

—Melinda Lewis, Advocate

As the nation becomes increasingly aware of the dramatic increase in Latina/o students in the K–16 education pipeline, educators are beginning to consider ramifications of this changing demography for existing systems of practice. Although universities often are part of this national school reform conversation, they generally are not the focus of attention. Indeed, as Hamann and Harklau (2010) noted, none of the chapters in *Education in the New Latino Diaspora* (Wortham, Murillo, & Hamann, 2002), the precursor volume to this book, considered higher education settings as sites of impact/change.

This chapter seeks to attend to this gap by placing universities front and center in an exploration of the efforts of a predominantly White, Midwestern university to recruit and retain Latina/o students. A further impetus

Revisiting Education in the New Latino Diaspora, pp. 225–243
Copyright © 2015 by Information Age Publishing

for this chapter is to examine the discrepancy that often exists between the "please come" rhetoric that defines universities' current responses to recruiting and retaining Latina/o students and the reality of what it takes to recruit Latina/o "non-college bound" students (at least not initially college bound) and to support their successful march to graduation. Yosso, Smith, Ceja, and Solórzano (2009) succinctly articulate the long-standing problem:

> Beyond portraying a racially diverse group of students in recruitment brochures, historically White universities do not necessarily commit to providing equal access and opportunities for Students of Color, let alone promise an inviting, positive campus racial climate. Genuine racial diversity or pluralism refers to underrepresented racial and ethnic groups being physically present *and* treated as equals on the college campus. (p. 664, original emphasis)

The current study is situated within the context of a larger, longitudinal, applied study on the BESITOS (Bilingual/Bicultural Education Students Interacting to Obtain Success) program model (Herrera, Morales, Holmes, & Terry, 2011-2012; Holmes, Morales, Sisley, Herrera, & Murry, 2005) at Kansas State University. While there is a longstanding Latino presence in western Kansas related to meatpacking plants in particular, Manhattan (where Kansas State is located) is in the north central part of the state, an area that historically has been home to few Latinos and is clearly part of the new Latino diaspora. While Latina/o students still represent a very small proportion of the student body (5.8% of the domestic students), Latina/o enrollment at the university has increased by over 400% since 1990.

The BESITOS recruitment and retention model, which is designed to recruit and retain culturally and linguistically diverse (CLD) students, has been implemented since 1999 when the first cohort of students was recruited to the College of Education as participants in the BESITOS Scholarship Program funded by the Office of Bilingual Education and Minority Language Affairs (now OELA). Students are recruited into the BESITOS Program as they transition from high school to college, or from a community college to the university. At times, students have also joined the BESITOS Program after they already have begun their academic program at Kansas State University.

Although the BESITOS program model is specifically designed to address the needs of Latino/a students, students of other underrepresented racial/ethnic groups often are in need of similar types of opportunities and supports. As a result, the BESITOS Program attracts students from a variety of linguistic and cultural backgrounds. White students who demonstrate (through their application materials and during their interview) exceptional cross-cultural understandings and commitment to cross-cultural and cross-linguistic issues within education also may be considered for acceptance in the program. Approximatley 82% of BESITOS students and graduates are Latina/o, and, perhaps reflecting its link with teacher education (which is female dominated), the majority of these individuals are female (81%). Recruitment, retention, and support that students receive in the BESITOS Program are approached by "out of the box" strategies that acknowledge the inequitable landscape often faced by some kinds of students in institutions of higher education. This support continues through graduation and induction in the field and is guided by a deep understanding of the biographies of the students and families the program serves (Herrera, 2010).

INTRODUCTION

The national picture of educational attainment for Latinas/os in higher education is bleak. Traditional college-aged (18–24 year old) Latinas/os are less likely to be enrolled in degree-granting institutions than their Black and White peers. For example, in 2006, only 24% of this Latina/o population was enrolled in such institutions, compared to 33% of similarly aged Black students and 41% of White students (Santiago, 2008). Latino males have been in an especially precarious position. From 1974 to 2003, Latino 18-to 24-year-old males were the only group whose participation in postsecondary education declined, from 27% to 22% (National Center for Education Statistics [NCES], 2005).

The path in postsecondary education that students take to obtain a bachelor's degree also matters. As Nuñez (2009) notes, "Students are more likely to complete bachelor's degrees if they enroll in four-year institutions... yet Latinos are overrepresented in community colleges, while less than half (about 44%) are enrolled in the four-year sector" (p. 23). From 2000 to 2009, the percentage of Latina/o students enrolled in degree granting institutions did increase from 10% to 12% (compared with the percentage increase in Black students from 11% to 14% and the percentage decrease in White students from 68% to 62%) (Snyder, 2011). This increase, though noteworthy, fails to reveal the larger reality: Latinas/os continue to be underrepresented in higher education. In 2009, for example, Latinas/os represented approximately 18% of the U.S. resident population aged 18 to 24 years (NCES, 2009).

Also disconcerting is the reality that while Latina/o students are finding greater *access* to higher education, they are not equally gaining in *attainment*. From 1976–77 through 2007–08, the percentage of total Latina/o students enrolled increased from 3.5% to 11.4%, while the percentage of bachelor's degrees conferred to Latinas/os over the same time period increased only from 2.0% to 7.9% (NCES, 2009). These numbers suggest that while the enrollment of Latina/o students increased by approximately

31%, the persistence of these students to graduation increased only by approximately 25%.

Santiago (2009) differentiates between enrolling and serving Latina/o students, insisting that "Serving Latino students is about intentionality.... It means considering adaptations to curricular design, academic, and support services to increase retention or promote persistence for your Latino students. Serving Latino students means graduating your Latino students" (p. 20). Yet many institutions of higher education (IHEs), especially predominantly White IHEs, continue to use the same strategies and structures to instruct and support students, even as they struggle to make their campuses more diverse. Existing graduation rates of Latinas/os highlight the hazard of simply maintaining the status quo. For example, results from a recent nationwide study that tracked students who began as freshmen in four-year colleges and universities revealed that only 51% of Latina/o students had completed a bachelor's degree wthin six years (Kelly, Schneider, & Carey, 2010). With Latina/o students projected to provide universities with the greatest increases in enrollment in the coming years (Hussar & Bailey, 2008), increased attention must be paid to current recruitment and retention dynamics so that lessons learned can be implemented to ensure greater Latina/o student success.

RECRUITMENT: A CLOUDED LENS ON WHAT REALLY MATTERS

Issues that frequently come to mind when considering the recruitment of Latinas/os into higher education are potential language barriers with native Spanish-speaking families, a need for basic information about the college process for students who are first-generation college students, and financial access for students from low-SES backgrounds. This generally translates to knee-jerk reactions that spur universities to translate brochures and recruitment information into Spanish and to encourage Latina/o students to complete the FAFSA (Free Application for Federal Student Aid). Bilingual learners who are completing applications for admission might also be guided to select options requiring that they take an English proficiency test to determine their eligibility to enroll in general education courses. Some universities might even employ bilingual recruiters to speak with high school students interested in attending college. While all of these efforts can stem from noble intentions to better meet the needs of this student population, they allow universities to continue following the same basic route to student recruitment without any rethinking of the overall process.

In spring 2011 we surveyed Latina/o individuals who either were current participants in the BESITOS program or had participated in BESITOS and had since graduated. We asked about their fears prior to arriving at Kansas State University. The 43 respondents (36 females, 6 males, 1 did not indicate gender) rated issues such as language, completing required forms and paperwork, and finances using a scale of 1–5, with 1 representing "Not Concerned" and 5 representing "Extremely Concerned." With regard to language, only 7% described themselves as extremely concerned, while 77% rated their fears from 1–3. Similarly, completing required forms and paperwork garnered a rating of 4–5 from only 37% of participants, indicating that, though this is an important issue, the majority did not find this issue to be a source of great anxiety. Finances, however, were a source of stress for at least 70% of respondents, who rated their level of concern as a 4 or 5. And yet, what does all this mean for recruitment practices in general? Very little! All of these students came (and were still enrolled or graduated). While it is important to note overarching trends for this group of students, persisting or dropping out is a decision of *individual* students.

Two students in this group were not first-generation college students, 13 students indicated that the primary language spoken in the home during their childhood was English, Spanglish, or "other," rather than Spanish, and nearly half of the participants indicated that they were second-generation immigrants or "other" as opposed to first-generation immigrant students. While it can be easy to make assumptions about the concerns a *typical* Latina/o student might bring to the table, a little digging reveals that there is no such thing as a typical student.

It also can be easy for university recruiters to assume that their primary goal is to win over students to their particular institution. Yet this mindset fails to take into consideration that they first must convince many students that college, in general, is a prospect for them. According to our survey, which for this issue has the real limitation of only including those who matriculated, nearly a quarter of participants (23%) decided that they were college bound *post*-high school. Universities cannot assume, therefore, that all prospective students will be thinking about higher education as a potential pathway while in high school. Assumptions that high school counselors and general university recruiters are sufficient to route students to a given institution are especially problematic. Only two survey respondents indicated that such individuals were most important to their decision to attend Kansas State University. On the other hand, family members, whose role in encouraging the pursuit of higher education is often minimized in the literature, were top on this list, followed by a recruiter for a specific university program (e.g., BESITOS, College Assistance Migrant Program, Kansas Bridges to the Bachelor's Program, Multicultural Engineering Program).

WHERE DO I FIT?
THE UNIVERSITY THROUGH STUDENTS' EYES

Current literature documents many of the realities that Latina/o students encounter in the university setting, especially at predominantly White institutions (the overwhelming norm in the new Latino diaspora). Many challenges relate to the campus racial climate and cultural congruence, both of which play an integral role in students' decision to persist.

Campus Racial Climate

Gurin, Dey, Hurtado, and Gurin (2002) explain that while IHEs tend to focus on *structural diversity*, or the numerical representation of each racial/ethnic group, they tend to neglect *informal interaction diversity* and *classroom diversity*. Informal interaction diversity relates to the frequency and quality of inter-group experiences of students in the daily course of events, such as out-of-classroom discussions and interactions in residence halls or at campus events. Classroom diversity, in turn, involves both learning content knowledge about diverse groups of people and interacting with diverse peers in the formal learning environment of the classroom. IHEs that lack structural diversity will have an even harder time ensuring informal inter-action diversity and classroom diversity for their students, but even with structural diversity informal interaction diversity and classroom diversity are not givens.

Latina/o students often have to contend with negative interactions on campus and in the classroom that hinder informal interaction and class-room diversity. As Yosso et al. (2009) explain, Latinas/os often experience *microaggressions*, which they describe as "incessant, subtle, yet stunning racial assaults" (p. 660). The term was first introduced by Chester Pierce in 1969 and used to refer to offenses aimed at Black individuals. As described by Sue and colleagues (2007), microaggressions can be one of three forms: a *microassault* (a purposeful, explicit, derogatory attack intended to harm the victim through verbal or nonverbal means), a *microinsult* (a subtle, rude, and insensitive verbal or nonverbal communication meant to degrade the victim's identity or racial heritage), or a *microinvalidation* (communications that attempt to negate, diminish, or dismiss the experiences, feelings, or thoughts of the victim). Microaggressions targeting Latina/o students often involve insinuations about immigration status, surname, accent, language, physical appearance, and culture (Yosso et al., 2009). All forms of microag-gressions can lead Latinas/os to feel unwelcomed and undervalued at the university. While IHEs might not be able to eliminate microaggressions aimed at Latina/o students, having institutional supports for students in place can promote their resiliency in the face of them.

Students also are buoyed by seeing people like them reflected in the faculty and administration, as well as in the curriculum (Gurin et al., 2002; Yosso et al., 2009). Akin to Meier and Stewart's (1991) still relevant finding for K–12 education, faculty diversity can provide greater opportunities for students to find mentors that match their racial/ethnic, cultural, and linguistic backgrounds. The findings of Santos and Reigadas (2002), for instance, suggest that Latina/o students benefit most from relationships with a mentor who matches their race/ethnicity. Increasing numbers of culturally and linguistically diverse (CLD) students on campus can spur IHEs to develop and support ethnic studies programs, multicultural courses, diversity-oriented student organizations, and special academic support programs (Hurtado, Milem, Clayton-Pedersen, & Allen, 1998). However, efforts such as these can easily be constructed as "add-ons" or "cxtras" rather than as reflections of integrated attention to and appreciation for diversity within the larger system and curriculum.

Cultural Congruence

Castellanos and Gloria (2007) define cultural congruity as "the fit between students' personal and institutional values, which prompts their interpersonal connectedness and subsequent cultural validation within their university environment" (p. 391). Cultural congruity has an impact on students' ability to adjust to and persist at an institution and influences their psychological health (Castellanos & Gloria, 2007; Gloria, Castellanos, Lopez, & Rosales, 2005). According to Gloria, Castellanos, Scull, and Villegas (2009), increased stress and feelings of isolation, alienation, and hopelessness are common effects of mismatches in values of the home culture (e.g., interpersonal connectedness, collaboration) and the values of the university culture (e.g., individualism, competition). As such, Latina/o students often struggle to see themselves as full members of the university community.

Social support that students receive from others (e.g., family, peers, faculty) can play a key role in helping students cope with or minimize perceptions of the cultural incongruity that many CLD students are negotiating (Constantine, Robinson, Wilton, & Caldwell, 2002; Gloria et al., 2005). Nuñez (2009) notes the importance of students' senses of belonging (Hurtado & Carter, 1997) and social cohesion within the institution. These constructs, which imply multiple avenues for students to form networks and affiliations within the larger community, contrast fundamentally with the idea of social integration, which suggests alignment with dominant norms of the organization. In her study involving 362 Latina/o students, Nuñez (2009) found that student perceptions of faculty taking a sincere interest in their development was one of the strongest positive predictors of their sense of belonging.

Castellanos and Gloria (2007) highlight the need for Latina/o students to feel validated and to have their cultural identities affirmed in higher education. The lack of such basic elements of psychological and cultural grounding can lead students to experience what González (2002) termed *cultural starvation*. Exploring in depth the lived realities of two Latino students in their first two years of attendance at a predominantly White university, González determined that three cultural systems of the larger campus culture were lacking in representations reflective of the students' identities. He labeled these systems the *social world* (i.e., racial/ethnic composition of student body, faculty, and staff; the political power of each group/subgroup; languages spoken), the *physical world* (i.e., campus building architecture, sculptures, artwork, and symbols, such as flyers and posters), and the *epistemological world* (i.e., knowledge that is exchanged and exists on campus in formal and informal learning environments). When students experience a dearth of self-representation within and across these worlds, they find themselves positioned to fight the ultimate cultural challenge: self-preservation (Villalpando, 2003).

To survive threatening university environments, Latina/o students often respond with efforts to build community with others like themselves and to develop critical navigation skills that allow them to move effectively between home and university cultures. As Yosso and colleagues (2009) describe, students develop a sense of family and community by creating social and academic counterspaces that allow them to celebrate and draw on their wealth of cultural and linguistic resources, knowledge, and skills without the pressure of having to look, behave, speak, or think a certain way. In these spaces, they find validation and are themselves sources of validation for peers. Students work to encourage and support each other as they journey together to reach their goal of graduating. They utilize resources provided at the university as well as those derived from their home communities to succeed, despite the obstacles, and to pave the way for future generations of Latina/o students.

SERVING STUDENTS BY RESPONDING TO INDIVIDUAL BIOGRAPHIES

Castellanos and Gloria (2007) recognize the need for universities to deconstruct the idea of success in relation to the recruitment and retention of Latina/o students: "Undoubtedly the numerical representations and data indices can in part provide an overview of success at the institutional level, yet overshadow and render invisible the individual stories of students whose 'success' has come at personal, social, and cultural costs" (p. 381). Increasing graduation numbers means taking a closer look at each student's unique situation and circumstances. As such, Gloria and Rodriguez (2000) introduced the psychosociocultural (PSC) approach, a metatheory for understanding the (non)persistence of CLD students higher education. The PSC approach encompasses interrelated psychological (e.g., self-efficacy, self-esteem), social (e.g., peers, mentors), and cultural dimensions (e.g., ethnic identity, cultural congruity) (Castellanos & Gloria, 2007). Employed with undergraduates from multiple backgrounds (e.g., Gloria & Ho, [2003] and Gloria & Robinson-Kurpius [2001]) and empirically tested as a conceptual framework for the persistence of Latina/o students (Gloria et al., 2005), this approach provides an avenue for exploring the experiences of Latina/o students at IHEs from a holistic perspective.

In our own work with undergraduate Latina/o students in the new Latino diaspora, we, too, have found understanding of these factors (psychological, social, and cultural) to be integral to our efforts to support students to graduation. However, we also find that these are mediated by the deeper history, or biography, of the CLD student. The CLD student biography encompasses the totality of students' experiences and includes the interrelated sociocultural, linguistic, cognitive, and academic dimensions (Herrera, 2010; Herrera et al., 2011–2012; Herrera & Murry, 2005; Holmes, Fanning, Morales, Espinoza, & Herrera, 2012). Experiences in each of these dimensions, especially those throughout the individual's period of K–12 schooling, lay the foundation for the way a student will perceive, interpret, and respond to the climate and culture of the university.

Consider, for example, the *testimonio* (Urrieta, this volume) of a young Latina woman about her own journey to obtaining access to postsecondary education:

Where I come from people who look like me with brown hair, brown eyes, brown skin, tend to be set-aside in schools. We are labeled as problematic and many times as disabled learners. A lot of administrators and teachers at my school didn't bother with us; they let us slip through the cracks and then blamed it on our lack of motivation. They would blame our family, our culture, our language but never reflected on their effectiveness as teachers; they never tried getting to know us.

Things weren't always bad for me in school; as a child I exceeded [excelled] in academics. But when I got to high school I really struggled. As a freshman, I probably flunked more than half of my classes. During sophomore year, I got labeled as a truant and had to attend seminars where they stressed the importance of an education. I just couldn't stand the fact that education was stressed so much, but at the actual schools our future didn't really matter. I played catch-up my junior year; but when I arrived at my senior year, it felt like it was too late. I managed not to give up, but I still only graduated high school with a very low GPA.

I recall that, during my senior year, I started applying at colleges and universities. I still remember meeting with my counselor so she could fill out a counselor's reference letter. Her words still anger me when I think about them. She told me that I would have to come at a later time because she had more important students to meet with that day (referring to the valedictorian and salutatorian; whom both were friends of mine). I managed not to break down and stood my ground demanding she fill out my paper because I too had taken time to make an appointment.

This undergraduate learned early that achieving academic success often meant persevering *in spite of* educators and administrators that she encountered along the way. Having struggled through years of accumulated inequities, students such as this Latina often have to fight their way to and through the university, burdened by histories of oppression and marginalization and K–12 school records that may better index how they were treated than how capable they are. As such, it is critical that university faculty and staff place the biography of individual students at the forefront of their recruitment, advising, mentoring, and retention efforts; indeed, this is the only way to ensure that such efforts are culturally responsive to both the assets and needs of each student.

Attending to Within-Group Differences

The role that a student's individuality within his or her cultural group may play on identity, participation, and persistence in college has not been explored in depth in current literature and discourse on the recruitment and retention of Latina/o students. Nonetheless, key among factors affecting self-identity are the student's immigration history, including country of origin, generational standing, age of immigration (if applicable), and his or her particular funds of knowledge (Moll, Amanti, Neff, & Gonzalez, 1992). Funds of knowledge references ways of being, seeing, thinking, speaking, and interpreting cross-cultural experiences developed through socialization in the family and community (Herrera, 2010). At another level students' identity must be understood from the lens of different points of contact; that is, What have been the results of their living within particular community and public school settings? What role (if any) have experiences of prejudice, discrimination, and exclusion played in the way a Latina/o student responds to denial of access or nonacceptance in new, monocultural and monolingual spaces? By looking deeper into the discourse of Latina/o students as they make sense of their roles and realities in higher education, we can see how their experiences of success and failure frequently are framed within their biographical and historical makeup.

Often arriving from communities that were predominantly Latina/o (even in the new Latino diaspora), students frequently take different paths in determining what a predominantly White, monolingual learning environment means for them. One of our students wrote:

KSU is not a very diverse university; people sometimes can be mean and give you funny looks. As in any university there are good and not so good instructors. Some of them would get to know you, for some others you are just a number, or they just know you because you are the only minority student in his/her class. My experience in KSU has not being [been] the best because, like I said, I come from a town with a big Hispanic population. So coming to KSU was a big cultural shock ... I think that the education at KSU is good, but the population not so much. So I would advise the [hypothetical] student to come to KSU only if I knew he would have the emotional support because, if he does not, it would be really easy for him to just drop out.

This student was a first-generation immigrant from Mexico who had experienced a great deal of adversity due to others' deficit assumptions about her language and culture. She also was newly married and, due to immigration-related complications, was raising their infant without the direct support of the father.

By contrast, the following Latina student, who grew up in the same region of the state as the young woman above, has had little trouble confronting any negativity experienced at the university. She reflected:

The school [university] is predominately White with a monolingual English-speaking population. However, that should not affect the [hypothetical] student if the student has a set mind about his career. I believe that in school you build friendships and long-lasting relationships, but one does not come here for friendship, one comes to the university to obtain a degree. There is nothing wrong with being different; it just makes us unique among others. I personally don't like to be another one in the crowd, I like to stand out and be myself. Being around White people will not change who I am, I will just learn more about them and their culture, their traditions and many more things.... If you have a clear mindset of the goals you want to accomplish and a clear identity of yourself, nothing and no one can stop you from achieving your dreams.

The self-confidence of this second student is evident here. For her, a person's mindset is what distinguishes a person's ability to maneuver through a predominately monocultural setting. She, too, is a first-generation immigrant from Mexico who is recently married. However, beyond having no children to care for, she has spent more time in the United States, she moved from her initial receiving community to attend the predominantly White high school within the same community in which the university is located, and she has benefited from the opportunity to follow the example of her older cousin, a recent graduate from the same program and college within the university. Given the differences in these students' biographies and histories that underlie the superficial similarities, it is easy to understand how they have experienced and responded to the new campus environment from two distinct perspectives.

Students Re-navigating Their Identity

For many Latina/o students, their experiences at a predominantly White university involve, at one point or another, a re-navigating of what it means to be Latina/o in a setting that, to a large extent, does not reflect their own identity. Most frequently, students experience the shock of being different as soon as they arrive and then they gradually come to find a sense of belonging. The perspective of the following student exemplifies this pattern.

> Almost four years after graduating [from high school] I started at K-State and could honestly say I got cultural shock. I was not used to so many *"gueritos"* [little blonde people] being at one place at the same time. I felt like an outsider looking in, never really feeling that I actually belonged. I got stared at, whispered about, I even got pennies thrown at, and I was even called swine flu!! But all these things didn't deter me. I soon found my niche at K-State and got to meet people who believe that our cultural differences are more like assets.

In contrast, other Latino/a students initially do not seem bothered by the lack of diversity at the university. They seem confident about both their identity and their place within the larger context of the campus and student body. Some even feel that, at times, too much emphasis is placed on the effects of race and ethnicity in society. Yet, as they become increasingly immersed in the specific, daily interactional contexts of their learning environment, their feelings of frustration with experiences of alienation and discrimination too can begin to reach overwhelming levels.

The following student painted a vivid picture of his reality as he reached the final semester of his academic preparation to be a secondary teacher.

> I'm currently in block 2 and there are only 2 students that are black, 2 students counting myself that are Hispanic, and the rest of my colleagues are white. This makes it really hard for me to speak up in class because of the vibes I get from my colleagues. I feel like they are scared to be around me because I am Hispanic. When we do group work, they won't listen to me. I believe they think because I'm Hispanic I'm not at their level.... They [university administration, faculty, and staff] talk about being part of the K-State family. What they don't take into consideration is how they are going to help the diverse population feel part of this family. I've taken time to learn about their culture and the way they do things, but when are they going to try to learn about my culture to better meet my needs while attending school here. I've never felt that race mattered until I came to K-State. There has been

times where I've hidden my language, and who I am so that I don't scare or threaten the White, monolingual students. It upsets me that, as soon as they find out I'm Hispanic, that they will start judging negatively. Rather then trying to get to know me for who I am, they see my race and don't even want to get to know me. I've seen it happen in the schools. As soon as I introduce myself as Mr. Salazar [pseudonym], even the teachers won't look at me, or try to get to know me. Rather I'm the one that has to make the first move and introduce myself because they won't do the same thing.

For Latina/o students pushing forward to navigate their own self-realized identity and their interactions within a university climate that they inter- pret as an incongruous "playing field," the disequalibrium they experience can be the turning point that defines the level of support needed for persis- tence to occur in the university setting. All university faculty and personnel who claim to want diversity within the university community must under- stand this multifaceted and complex set of circumstances. As Mr. Salazar put it, "What they don't take into consideration is how they are going to help the diverse population feel part of this family."

PERSISTENCE: *CUESTE LO QUE ME CUESTE*

Analysis of the data from this study revealed that for most students who persisted to graduation, as well as for those who were currently attending the institution, there were multiple layers of coping mechanisms utilized to maintain a "no looking back" attitude about finishing their degree. Students looked both internally and externally for support. For many the internal motivation to succeed was propelled by past experiences of oppres- sion or discrimination and the desire to make family members proud. This internal locus of control led many to overcome or bypass any obstacles that came their way. The following student describes her own inner strength and drive:

In my hometown people like you and I are never really thought of as "college material," but did I ever let that get to me? Uh, heck NO! They see us as maids, housekeepers, nannies, waitresses, and housemothers; the stereotypi- cal Hispanic women. It sucks, doesn't it? Well one thing is a fact; I'm none of the above. Ever since I was a young girl, I knew I would graduate high school and attend college, even after I was looked down on and told many times that my test scores weren't high enough to attend college, or even after I was constantly reminded by our financial problems that I didn't have the money to attend college. See, if you knew me, you would know that I am pretty *cabezona* [stubborn] and I always find a way! ¡Cueste lo que Cueste! [No matter what it costs!] My mother has a big part to do with that. Anyhow, sometimes being a little stubborn is what it takes to pursue your dreams and become successful.

Students attested to the importance of family support, even if many parents were unable to completely understand the realities their children faced at the university. In fact, when responding to a survey question designed to ascertain the factors important to their retention, respondents overwhelmingly indicated that family members were the most crucial to their decision to persist against all odds. The following quote exemplifies what many of the students continue to voice about their families:

> There are many aspects in my life that play a part in my identity and pro-
> fessional life.... My parents' values and customs have helped me with my
> identity and in finding myself and knowing who I am now. Their values and
> beliefs have made me who I am and in believing in my self that I can be a
> successful teacher. My family has been supportive of my decision of being a
> teacher and this support has helped me in my professional life now that I am
> almost done with my [academic] career.

Additional support was found from caring faculty and staff at the university; peers within a student organization, fraternity, or sorority; a center designed to support diverse students; and a special program designed to support students' academic success. The following student indicated that her ability to find a sense of belonging at the university was dependent on her willingness to branch out and get to know others who held perspectives different from her own and her efforts to maintain communication with faculty members that she trusted.

> As to the life experience of the university life, it is entering to a new country;
> you will not know its customs, culture, people, motives, history etc. Until
> you choose to not just live there but to experience these concepts. How?
> Depends how much you want to experience. As for me, I love cultures, there-
> fore I attend activities [and] events where I can meet people that are differ-
> ent from me.... I also have friendships with certain professors, which I keep
> a consistent visit with them to update them on my goals and struggles as a
> student and converse about their goals and struggles as well.

Students frequently commented on the additional importance of developing relationships with faculty who valued and could relate to their cultural and linguistic identities. In providing advice to potential Latino undergraduates, one participant summed up her thoughts with the following suggestion: "Find an adult mentor that mirrors your culture and knows your experience."

Others students find comfort in organizations where there are people who are culturally and linguistically like themselves. This type of involvement provides a sense of belonging that often is not found in the unwelcoming environment of their classes. One Latina student described her experience in the following way:

My experience here at Kansas State University has been quite a journey for me. My freshman year I hated it; I was homesick and hated how it was not diverse at all! After I took the time to look and see if there were other orga- nizations here on campus for multicultural I joined them. After doing that I started to feel a little bit better about Kansas State University. Now as a junior here I would say that, on a scale [of] 1 to 10, I like it about an 8. The two that is missing would probably just be because of my classes. At times I do not feel welcomed in there due to my peers.

For many of the participants, their support system came as a result of being part of a smaller community within the university setting. As one student noted, "Freshman and Sophmore year I was completely isolated from the general [campus] population. After being accepted into the BESITOS program I felt connected and integrated within the group." Students described their participation within the center-based, scholarship program community as one of the only places where they were taught and supported from an asset perspective that challenged them to take control of their learning and their future by building upon their identity. One student described her experience within the community:

So not until I got to BESITOS is when my self esteem started being built—a building block, one block at a time. From my teachers, Socorro [director], [name of past coordinator], from everybody. We were always given so much. Everybody. It was like being with family ... they were building our self-esteem as we went along: "Don't be afraid." "You are who you are and you have to be proud." And while they were building our self-esteem, they were building our academic level. The two went hand in hand.

THE REALITY WITHIN THE RHETORIC

What is evident from this study is the complexity and range of experiences of Latina/o students within our campus communities. New Latino diaspora universities, like ours, have begun to do more to recruit and retain Latina/o students, but will it be enough? How do we define enough? If we believe that the Latino/a students we are recruiting are the same as those we have traditionally recruited, then, "Yes." However, as quantitative studies from across the country documenting Latina/o students' struggles in higher education illustrate, incoming Latino students are not completely like the students that institutions like ours have traditionally served. Our recruitment efforts must begin to move from outdated public relations missions to understanding and building relationships within diverse community settings. Our retention efforts must move from perceiving students from Latino communities as part of a homogenous entity and toward auditing our systems to address the uniqueness and complexity of each student.

Although we are proud of the BESITOS effort, the tasks of recruiting, welcoming, and integrating should not be the remit just of a special program. Rather, preparing all faculty members, advisors, counselors, and the university at large to understand the dynamics of cross-cultural relationships is essential. For example, we must recognize that working from a remediation context (e.g., drill and practice labs often staffed by tutors unprepared to work with Latina/o students) does little to encourage student persistence. Rather, we must recognize the *ganas* [desire] that Latinas/os have in earning a postsecondary degree and develop programs of acceleration that use students' cultural and linguistic knowledge, resources, and skills as a foundation for reading, writing, and math at the university.

CONCLUSION

Even in institutions of higher education that are striving to both recruit and retain culturally and linguistically diverse students, challenges related to a hostile university climate (e.g., Gurin et al., 2002; Yosso et al., 2009) and cultural incongruence (e.g., Castellanos & Gloria, 2007; Gloria et al., 2005; Nuñez, 2009) often limit students' educational access and undermine their academic efforts. Predominantly White universities in particular must make their campuses more welcoming, safe environments in ways that go beyond merely allocating space for CLD student participation. They must create learning environments in which all students can *thrive*. This requires attention to the individual histories and biographies of the students who attend their campuses. Universities also must also ensure that faculty and staff have the perspectives, skills, and resources needed to critically reflect on and make necessary adaptations to their student services, curriculum, and instruction. What is required then is a "deep and pervasive" transformation (Eckel & Kezar, 2003, p. 18). There is much to be done and little time to prepare. Moving beyond the current rhetoric and acting based on what Latinas/os on campus tell us will ensure that we move into the coming years prepared to recruit, serve, and graduate our Latina/o students

As Latino populations in the new Latino diaspora grow, the Latino populations attending the region's large colleges and universities should also grow. Yet the challenge is not just to recruit a previously unserved population to campus, but rather to assure that once recruited, Latino students fare as well as any other student population. This can mean an explicit strategy for Latino student success, but it must also entail differentiation (what helps one student thrive is not the same formula as what helps another) and across-the-institution commitment.

REFERENCES

Castellanos, J., & Gloria, A. M. (2007). Research considerations and theoretical application for best practices in higher education: Latina/os achieving success. *Journal of Hispanic Higher Education, 6*(4), 378–396. doi:10.1177/1538192707305347

Constantine, M. G., Robinson, J. S.,Wilton, L., & Caldwell, L. D. (2002). Collective self-esteem and perceived social support as predictors of cultural congruity among Black and Latina/o college students. *Journal of College Student Development, 43*(3), 307–316.

Gloria, A. M., Castellanos, J., Lopez, A. G., & Rosales, R. (2005). An examination of academic nonpersistence decisions of Latino undergraduates. *Hispanic Journal of Behavioral Sciences, 27*(2), 202–223. doi:10.1177/0739986305275098

Gloria, A. M., Castellanos, J., Scull, N. C., & Villegas, F. J. (2009). Psychological coping and well-being of male Latino undergraduates: Sobreviviendo la universidad. *Hispanic Journal of Behavioral Science, 31*(3), 317–339.

Gloria, A. M., & Ho, T. A. (2003). Environmental, social, and psychological experiences of Asian American undergraduates: Examining issues of academic persistence. *Journal of Counseling and Development, 81*, 93–105.

Gloria, A. M., & Robinson-Kurpius, S. E. (2001). Influences of self-beliefs, social support, and comfort in the university environment on the academic persistence issues for American Indian undergraduates. *Cultural Diversity and Ethnic Minority Psychology, 7*, 88–102.

Gloria, A. M., & Rodriguez, E. R. (2000). Counseling Latino university students: Psychosociocultural issues for consideration. *Journal of Counseling and Development, 78*, 145–154.

Gonzalez, K. P. (2002). Campus culture and the experiences of Chicano students in a predominantly white university. *Urban Education, 27*, 193–218.

Gurin, P., Dey, E. L., Hurtado, S., & Gurin, G. (2002). Diversity and higher education: Theory and impact on educational outcomes. *Harvard Educational Review, 72*(3), 330–366.

Eckel, P. D., & Kezar, A. J. (2003). *Taking the reins: Institutional transformation in higher education*. Westport, CT: American Council on Education and Praeger.

Hamann, E. T., & Harklau, L. (2010). Education in the New Latino Diaspora. In E. G. Murillo (Ed.), *Handbook of Latinos and Education* (pp. 157–169). New York, NY: Routledge.

Herrera, S. (2010). *Biography-driven culturally responsive teaching*. New York, NY: Teachers College Press.

Herrera, S. G., & Murry, K. G. (2005). *Mastering ESL and bilingual methods: Differentiated instruction for culturally and linguistically diverse (CLD) students.* Boston, MA: Allyn & Bacon.

Herrera, S. G., Morales, A. R., Holmes, M. A., & Terry, D. (2011–2012). From remediation to acceleration: Recruiting, retaining, and graduating future culturally and linguistically diverse (CLD) educators. *Journal of College Student Retention: Research, Theory & Practice.*

Holmes, M., Fanning, C., Morales, A., Espinoza, P., & Herrera, S. (2012). Contextualizing the path to academic success: Culturally and linguistically diverse students gaining voice and agency in higher education. In Y. Kanno & L. Harklau (Eds.), *Linguistic minority immigrants go to college: Preparation, access, and persistence* (pp. 201–219). New York, NY: Routledge.

Holmes, M., Morales, A., Sisley, L., Herrera, S., & Murry, K. (2005, January). *Institutionalizing practices for the success of Hispanic/Latino college students: A case study.* Session presented at the annual Hawaii International Conference on Education, Honolulu, HI.

Hurtado, S., & Carter, D. F. (1997). Effects of college transition and perceptions of the campus racial climate on Latino college students' sense of belonging. *Sociology of Education, 70*(4), 324–345.

Hurtado, S., Milem, J. F., Clayton-Pedersen, A. R., & Allen, W. R. (1998). Enhancing campus climates for racial/ethnic diversity: Educational policy and practice. *Review of Higher Education, 21*(3), 279–302.

Hussar, W. J., & Bailey, T. M. (2008). *Projections of education statistics to 2017* (NCES 2008-078). Washington, DC: National Center for Education Statistics.

Kelly, A. P., Schneider, M., & Carey, K. (2010). *Rising to the challenge: Raising Hispanic graduation rates as a national priority.* Washington, DC: American Enterprise Institute.

Meier, K. J., & Stewart, J., Jr. (1991). *The politics of Hispanic education: Un paso pa'lante y dos pa'tras.* Albany, NY: State University of New York Press.

Moll, L. C., Amanti, C., Neff, D., & Gonzalez, N. (1992). Funds of knowledge for teaching: Using a qualitative approach to connect homes and classrooms. *Theory into Practice, 31*(2), 132–141.

Nuñez, A.-M. (2009). Latino students' transitions to college: A social and intercultural capital perspective. *Harvard Educational Review, 79*(1), 22–48.

National Center for Education Statistics. (2005). *Mini-Digest of education statistics, 2003.* Washington, DC: U.S. Department of Education. Retrieved from http://nces.ed.gov/pubsearch/pubsinfo.asp?pubid=2005017

National Center for Education Statistics. (2009). *Digest of education statistics.* (Table 16: Estimates of resident population, by race/ethnicity and age group: Selected years, 1980 through 2009; Table 227: Total fall enrollment in degree-granting institutions, by race/ethnicity of student and type and control of institution: Selected years, 1976 through 2008; Table 285: Bachelor's degrees conferred by degree-granting institutions, by race/ethnicity and sex of student: Selected years, 1976–77 through 2007–08. Washington, DC: U.S. Department of Education.

Santiago, D. A. (2008). *The condition of Latinos in Education: 2008 Factbook.* Washington, DC: Excelencia in Education. Retrieved from www.edexcelencia.org

Santiago, D. (2009). Enrolling vs. serving Latino students. *Diverse Issues in Higher Education, 26*(16), 20.

Santos, S. J., & Reigadas, E. T. (2002). Latinos in higher education: An evaluation of a university faculty mentoring program. *Journal of Hispanic Higher Education, 1,* 40–50.

Snyder, T. D. (2011). *Mini-digest of education statistics, 2010.* Washington, DC: U.S. National Center for Education Statistics.

Sue, D. W., Capodilupo, C. M., Torino, G. C., Bucceri, J. M., Holder, A. M. B., Nadal, K. L., & Esquilin, M. (2007). Racial microaggressions in everyday life: Implications for clinical practice. *American Psychologist, 62*(4), 271–286.

Villalpando, O. (2003). Self-segregation or self-preservation? A critical race theory and Latina/o critical theory analysis of findings from a longitudinal study of Chicana/o college students. *International Journal of Qualitative Studies in Education, 16*(5), 619–646.

Wortham, S., Murillo, E. G., & Hamann, E. T. (Eds.). (2002). *Education in the New Latino Diaspora: Policy and the politics of identity.* Westport, CT: Ablex.

Yosso, T. J., Smith, W. A., Ceja, J., & Solórzano, D. G. (2009). Critical race theory, racial microaggressions, and campus racial climate for Latina/o undergraduates. *Harvard Educational Review, 79*(4), 659–786.

CHAPTER 13

BILINGUAL EDUCATION POLICY IN WISCONSIN'S NEW LATINO DIASPORA

Rebecca Lowenhaupt

INTRODUCTION

As one of several states experiencing rapid growth in their Hispanic population during the first decade of the 21st Century, the case of Wisconsin offers more general insight into the influence of state policy on education in the New Latino Diaspora (NLD). As this volume highlights, many regions of the country are experiencing widespread dispersal of newcomer youth, leading to the diversification of schools (or at least of their enrollments) with little to no tradition of supporting linguistic, cultural, or racial difference. In these locales, schools are asked to adapt their daily practice in order to meet the changing needs of their students and must navigate difficult decisions about how best to respond.

As their numbers grow, immigrant communities and the schools that serve them depend on the enactment of education policies to support their English language learning. While previous NLD research considered the influence of hostile language policies on the implementation of

Revisiting Education in the New Latino Diaspora, pp. 245–261
Copyright © 2015 by Information Age Publishing

effective instructional practices for Spanish-speakers in Georgia (Beck & Allexsaht-Snider, 2002; Hamann, 2003), this case provides a very different illustration of the impact of a bilingual orientation on state policy and local practice.

After an overview of critical issues for practice and policy, I offer a brief description of immigration trends in Wisconsin and analyze state education policy pertaining to the education of immigrant youth (the vast majority of whom were Latino). I then report survey results that highlight the influence of policy on school practice. In so doing, I question the role of state policy in the response to demographic shifts and conclude with a discussion of the implications for the design of supportive state policies and school practice in the context of the NLD.

Issues of Practice

As many newcomer children's first "systematic contact" with the new culture, schools are critical in the lives of many immigrant students and their families (Suárez-Orozco & Suárez-Orozco, 2001). For these youth, schools are often the location where "youth become exposed to the native culture for the first time, interact with immigrant and native children of their same ethnicity, and form beliefs about what society and persons outside of their family expect from them" (Perreira, Chapman, & Stein, 2006, p. 1397). Within these schools, complex issues of immigrant incorporation are contested among administrators, teachers, students, and their families. Both linguistically and racially, Latino newcomer students are noticeable as a distinct cultural presence in the NLD and bring with them a unique set of educational needs that many educators in emerging communities have not been prepared to support. As their proportions grow, these Latino students are having a profound impact on the schools they diversify, which must rapidly adapt to serve these newcomers well.

Concerns about the achievement of newcomer students in school are not new, as debates about how best to support these students have long raged in the field of Latino education (e.g., Gándara, 2005; Valenzuela, 1999). With higher drop-out rates than other immigrant and nonimmigrant groups, lower achievement scores, and lower representation in higher education, Latino students stand out as the least well-served large group of students in our public school system (Van Hook & Stamper Balistreri, 2002).

Prior scholarship in the broad field of immigrant education, and education for the NLD specifically, has highlighted challenges of developing effective instruction for newcomers in a system which often lacks the capacity to do so (Dalla, MoulikGupta, Lopez, & Jones, 2006; Dentler & Hafner, 1997; Wortham, Murillo, & Hamann, 2002). As such, many advocate for efforts to develop more effective programs and instructional support for these students in schools across the country (Bartolomé, 2002; Meskill, 2005).

In the context of the NLD, these concerns are amplified by a lack of access to resources more readily available in traditional gateway locations (Capps et al., 2005; Quiñones-Benitez, 2003). In schools experiencing demographic shifts, the required qualifications and skills of staff also shift, as the instructional needs of a new population require the development of new forms of knowledge (Miramontes, Nadeau, & Commins, 2011). But in their report for the Urban Institute, a group of researchers speculated that "the institutional capacity to teach newcomer and non-English-speaking children may be more limited in new immigrant destinations than in traditional gateway communities that can draw on networks of bilingual and ESL teachers, curricula, and other resources" (Capps et al., 2005, p. 35). Regions of the new immigration are often linguistically isolated and have difficulty attracting bilingual support (Wortham, Murillo, & Hamann, 2002). This isolation means that, unlike staff in traditional immigration gateways, many of the teachers working with new Latino immigrants have had little previous exposure to Latino cultures (Gibson, 2002). Far from the bilingual and cultural resources of established immigrant communities, schools in emerging locations are faced with the challenge of attracting new staff with appropriate qualifications and developing current staff without much access to relevant resources.

Although the importance of schools in the lives of immigrant youth is uncontested, there is little policy consensus about how best to incorporate and support these students in schools. Debates rage about how best to ensure equal access to education for students with limited English proficiency (Capper & Scanlan, 2007). These debates are influenced by powerful language ideologies and contested ideas about what it means to be American occurring outside of the boundaries of education (Beck & Allexsaht-Snider, 2002; Suárez-Orozco, 1998). Strong advocates exist on all sides, supporting the gamut of instruction from dual-language immersion to English-only immersion. Although there is a growing research base about program design for immigrant students, one can find at least limited empirical research to support almost any variety of programming. Navigating decisions about best practice is not only complicated by conflicting messages, but also by the fact that much of the research about best practices for English Language Learners (ELLs) assumes a wealth of resources and capacity; in short, most insight about best practice assumes a particular capacious context unlike that of many schools serving members of the NLD. As such, these schools are left to decide how best to navigate highly politicized decisions about how to serve their growing immigrant communities (Leal & Meier, 2011).

The Role of Education Policy

As schools design responses to demographic change, they do so within a complex policy landscape. As suggested by policy implementation research (e.g., Levinson & Sutton, 2001; Spillane, 2004), policy influences school-level reform efforts, although local interpretations of that policy play a mediating role in determining what schools actually do. In his work on standards-based reform, Spillane (2004) concluded that local actors make sense of and incorporate features of state policy based on prior understanding and local capacity. In the context of the NLD, the enactment of policy in response to demographic shift has been found to be similarly influenced by local politics and interests (Hamann, 2007, 2003). Given this perspective on the role of state policy in decisions about school practice, it is important to consider the policy context, before tracing how local interpretations of that policy have led to local responses to an influx of immigrant youth.

The context during the first decade of the 21st century made successful adaptation to newcomers all the more urgent, as schools responded in an unforgiving policy climate of high-stakes accountability and No Child Left Behind (Valenzuela, 2005). At the same time that many schools were undergoing major demographic shifts, they were also being asked to report on their success to an unprecedented degree (Capps et al., 2005). Additional pressure was exerted by federal and state policies related to the support for ELLs. Some states including California and Massachusetts chose to mandate an immersion model through the adoption of "English-Only" policies (see Gándara [2005] for a discussion of the implications of this), while other states funded a variety of bilingual programs.

The case of Georgia, one of the states experiencing the most rapid growth in Hispanic populations in the "New South" (Hamann, 2003), offers insight into the influence of an English-only state policy on local education practice. Previous research on the incorporation of the NLD has depicted the Georgia case as an instance where a hostile policy climate led to troubling school practices. Researchers described how deficit beliefs led to subtle forms of discrimination in an English-only policy context (Beck & Allexsaht-Snider, 2002; Hamann, 2003; Harklau & Colomer, this volume; Murillo, 2002; Wainer, 2006). Beck and Allexsaht-Snider (2002) described a "lurking atmosphere of intolerance" in several districts in Georgia, resulting in attempts to erase cultural difference. Hamann (2003) explained that although some local policies appeared well-intentioned in writing, their implementation revealed underlying biases. These studies emphasized that these deficit-based perspectives had a profound influence on the schooling of immigrants.

In contrast, at the time of my inquiry, Wisconsin offered a policy context that was bilingual-friendly and generally supportive of school-based efforts to respond proactively to an influx of immigrant students. While previous studies have emphasized the influence of state policies on schools that were unsupportive at best and hostile at worst, there has been much less research on how more supportive state policies influenced the educational experiences of members of the NLD.

Research Site and Methods

With greater than 200% growth in its Latino population between 1980 and 2000, Wisconsin can be classified as an "emerging Hispanic state" scrambling to respond to the needs of growing immigrant communities (Fry & Gonzales, 2008). Driven by economic, political, and legal circumstances, Latino immigration shifted to new rural, suburban, and urban communities in Wisconsin in the 1990s (Marrow, 2005; Singer, 2008). As in other Midwestern states, restructuring in the food processing and agricultural industries has provided opportunities for Latino settlement in rural areas (Marrow, 2005; Striffler, 2005; Stull & Broadway, 2004).

These immigration trends have led to significant changes in public school enrollments in the state, including significant growth in the number of Spanish-speaking ELLs in Wisconsin schools. Although overall numbers remain low in comparison to some 'traditional' states, with 2009–10 data showing that Spanish-speakers made up 3.5% of total enrollment, that percentage was nearly triple that in the 1998–1999 school year (1.4%).

However, while the total percent of ELLs was low, a large percentage of schools across the state served this growing group, with 58% (1,354 schools) enrolling at least a few Spanish-speaking ELLs. (See Bruening [this volume] for more about low-incidence ELL districts.) In 1999, the majority of schools across the state (71%) did not enroll any Spanish-speaking ELLs. Only 5% of them (102 schools) enrolled more than 20 Spanish-speaking ELLs. By 2008, the number of schools without any Spanish-speaking ELLs had become a minority (42%), while the number with 20 or more students had more than doubled to 13% (293 schools). In many of these schools, increasing numbers of ELLs triggered annual yearly progress measures for this category of student under the federal No Child Left Behind Act. These trends highlight that, despite the minority status of Spanish-speaking ELLs in Wisconsin's public schools, this was an increasingly relevant aspect of the educational landscape in the state.

This chapter draws on two data sources to discuss the implications of this demographic trend for early 21st century education policy and practice in Wisconsin. First, I analyze state education policy documents related to immigrant youth to illustrate Wisconsin's policy context. Specifically, I discuss a textual analysis of the Bilingual-Bicultural Education Act (Wis.

Stats. ch. 115 § 95 and PI 13). Then I apply a policy analysis framework defined by Stone (1997) that focuses on the interpretation of various mechanisms by which state education policy functions. Specifically, I identify mechanisms of policy, including mandates, inducements, the orientation or facts put forward by the policy, and the power granted by the policy to local actors.

Second, this chapter uses data from a statewide survey of educators to describe school-level practices as they relate to this state policy context. Using a growth-rate of Spanish-speaking ELL enrollments over the last decade, the study took an attempted census of 384 schools across the state that served members of the NLD (Lowenhaupt & Camburn, 2011). Data included results from 115 principal surveys (30% response rate) and 152 teacher surveys (40% response rate). Sampling analysis suggests that these surveys were generally representative of schools serving members of the NLD, with similar distributions of school types and demographics among participants and the target population (Table 13.1). Although an imperfect check, this sampling analysis indicates that these aspects of school context were not predictors of participation in the study and supports the generalization of findings to school practices across the state. Survey analysis includes descriptive and inferential statistics, as well as textual analysis of open-ended textboxes.

Table 13.1. School Characteristics of Survey Participants

Characteristic	% of 384 Total Sample	% of 115 Principal Responses	% of 152 Teacher Responses
Urban	36.7	31.3	40.4
Suburban	36.5	35.7	31.8
Rural	26.8	33.0	27.8
Elementary School	68.0	67.0	65.4
Middle School	19.5	21.7	19.0
High School	11.7	10.4	15.7

WISCONSIN'S BILINGUAL EDUCATION POLICY

The post-1965 history of immigrant education has been characterized by language debates about the use of bilingual education programs. (U.S. immigration laws were dramatically overhauled in 1965, precipitating a new round of immigration to the U.S. that was substantially higher than the decades that preceded it.) Since the 1974 *Lau v. Nichols* U.S. Supreme Court case mandated identification and educational accommodation of

ELLs, state policies about bilingual education have emerged, often from contested political processes. In Wisconsin, political organizing in Milwaukee and Racine led to the narrow approval of the Wisconsin Bilingual Bicultural Law in the late 1970s (Lowenhaupt & Turner, 2009). At the time of approval, the law applied to only a handful of districts, but by 2000, the number of districts affected by the law had grown to more than 170 districts across the state (Boals, 2001). Under this legislation, federal obligations to provide equitable educational opportunities for immigrant children were guided by state requirements regarding the establishment of particular programs to support these students. While language debates led some states to establish English-only laws prohibiting the use of other languages for instruction, Wisconsin maintained its Bilingual Bicultural Law through the time of this writing (in 2012).

As mandated by Wisconsin statute (Wis. Stats. ch. 115 § 95 and PI 13), schools were obligated to support ELLs by establishing a "Bilingual-Bicultural" program once they met certain enrollment thresholds. Provisions in the statute required that these programs be staffed by bilingual or ESL teachers, with a specific provision that in the context of Spanish language a teacher had to have a bilingual certification (Wis. Stats. ch 115§ 97). These constituted the two basic legislative mandates: that districts had to establish a program and that at least one teacher in the program possess bilingual certification—an add-on license to the general education licenses in the state. In fulfilling these mandates, schools became eligible for additional funding to support their programs.

Inducements in the form of state and federal funding were made available to districts implementing "Bilingual-Bicultural" programs. As the statute declared, "It is the policy of this state to reimburse school districts, in substantial part, for the added costs of providing the programs established under this subchapter" (Wis. Stats. ch. 115 § 95(3)). Under Title III of that law, districts received approximately $120 per pupil of additional federal aide for the 2008–2009 school years for students with identified LEP levels between 1–5. Additional funding tied to the No Child Left Behind Act also generated some discretionary grants to support the design of supplemental services and capacity building efforts in districts serving emerging immigrant communities (DPI, 2010). According to the 2010 call for proposals, these funds were intended, "to pay for activities that provide enhanced instructional opportunities for immigrant children and youth" (WI DPI, p. 2). As such, districts developing after-school tutoring programs and professional development for teachers were eligible to apply for grants of up to $40,000 to support these activities.

While these mandates and inducements supported the formation of bilingual education for newcomers, a close analysis of the language of the statutes reveals a monolingual purpose to the policy. Support for bilingual instruction—conveyed through the titles of the statute and program and through wording in the policy that encouraged the use of home languages—still identified the purpose of bilingual programming as enhancing the learning of English. The statute stated that,

> fundamental courses may be taught in the pupil's non-English language to support the understanding of concepts, while the ultimate objective shall be to provide a proficiency in those courses in the English language in order that the pupil will be able to participate fully in a society whose language is English. (Wis. Stats. ch. 115 § 95(5))

In fact, despite using the language of bilingual education, there is an explicit goal of transitioning students as quickly as possible into English only learning environments, with no mention of the benefits of bilingualism, a monolingual goal in line with the philosophy behind most transitional bilingual programs (Cummins, 1992; Snow & Hakuta, 1992). As such, while bilingualism is permissible under the legislation, there is a clear articulation of a monolingual goal. In other words, bilingual instruction is considered one potential strategy among several to support the acquisition of English. In fact, schools are not required to use languages other than English in their "Bilingual-Bicultural" programs. Importantly, this policy does not advocate for bilingualism or biliteracy, arguably a relevant pursuit in a globalizing and increasingly transnational society (Villenas, 2007). Instead, the "bilingual-ish" orientation of the policy highlights a more conservative use of home languages as a useful tool to support the ultimate goal of English proficiency.

Finally, it is important to note that while the policy contains loose mandates, power (and discretion) were explicitly left in the hands of local decision-makers regarding the ways in which schools and districts implement these mandates. In the context of a strong local-control state, the mandates of this legislation were markedly limited, leaving a significant amount of discretion to districts in deciding how to implement it. The policy made a point of "allowing each school district maximum flexibility in establishing programs suited to its particular needs" (Wis. Stats. ch. 115 § 95(2)), with approved programs ranging from dual-language immersion to English-only support. In many ways, this purposeful provision for local discretion can be viewed as a strength of the policy, given what we know about local policy implementation (Spillane, 2004). In particular, this discretion may be key in the context of emerging immigrant communities where resource and capacity considerations facilitate certain forms of programming over others. Practically speaking, this feature of the policy has supported the use of a range of instructional programs and led to wide variation in the implementation of "Bilingual-Bicultural programs," as I will discuss momentarily.

In sum, state bilingual education policy made use of various policy mechanisms to promote a supportive educational climate for immigrant students. Unlike Georgia and other states that had created hostile environments for bilingual education, Wisconsin policy advocated for it, albeit with limitations. The policy included conflicting philosophies of education and strong assurances that power remained in the hands of local decision-makers to decide how best to serve newcomers. As such, I characterize the state policy as "bilingual-ish," in that it mandated bilingual programming without a bilingual purpose. The characteristics of Wisconsin's policy play a key role in the way its schools develop practices to support members of the NLD, reminding us of the state-to-state heterogeneity of the school experiences learners negotiate. In the sections below, I discuss those school-level responses to Wisconsin's Bilingual Education Act.

Policy to Practice: Bilingual Programs

According to the policy, schools must implement a "Bilingual-bicultural education program," defined as "a program designed to improve the comprehension and the speaking, reading and writing ability of a limited-English proficient pupil in the English language, so that the pupil will be able to perform ordinary classwork in English"(Wis. Stats. ch. 115 § 955(2)). Therefore, despite its name, the mandate does not require the implementation of bilingual programs; only 24% of principals reported using bilingual programs in survey results. Given that districts had discretion in the design and implementation of programs to support ELLs with minimal reporting requirements or oversight from the state, schools implemented a wide range and sometimes multiple programs for ELLs. Indeed, the majority of principals (61%) identified the use of more than one program in response to a survey question about program type.

Table 13.2 highlights the frequencies of particular program labels reported by principals when asked to identify the programs in place in their schools (Table 2). The most common program was "pull-out ESL," with 62% of principals reporting the use of this form of support. As suggested by official program definitions, the programs implemented in schools in the study run the gamut of imaginable responses to second language learners. Many of the programs in place have nothing 'bilingual' about them, although they are all classified as "Bilingual-bicultural programs" by state policy. This program variation illustrates that local interpretations of a discretionary policy have made full use of this discretion to implement programs based on local considerations and context.

Table 13.2.   Program Prevalence and Definitions

Program Label	% of Principals	Definition: *http://www.ncela.gwu.edu*
Pull-out ESL	62%	ELLs are "pulled out" of regular, mainstream classrooms for special instruction in English as a second language. Variation: "push-in."
Content-based ESL	45%	This approach makes use of instruction of content areas as the vehicle for developing language, content, cognitive and skills.
Structured English Immersion	21%	Language minority students receive subject matter instruction in their second language. The teacher uses a simplified form of the second language. Students may use their native language in class; the teacher uses only the second language.
Sheltered English Instruction	17%	English is not taught with a focus on learning the language. Rather, content knowledge and skills are the goals. Use of simplified language & physical activities to teach vocabulary for concept development in content areas.
Transitional Bilingual	14%	Subjects are taught through two languages, and English is taught as a second language. The purpose is to facilitate transition to an all-English environment while receiving content instruction in the native language to the extent necessary.
Developmental Bilingual	10%	Teach content through two languages to develop both languages with the goal of bilingualism and biliteracy.
Dual Language Immersion	12%	Two language groups are put together and instruction is delivered through both languages so both become biliterate and develop cross-cultural understanding.

$n = 115$

In addition to the variety of programs, it is important to note that there was variation within a given program category (e.g., not all pull-outs were implemented the same way). Survey participants were asked to respond to a series of questions about the kinds of instructional support within those programs. Analysis of responses suggested that the meaning of these labels varied widely across schools.

For example, there were several surveys in which teachers marked the presence of some form of "bilingual" program, yet reported little Spanish use, particularly for intermediate and proficient language learners. While the majority of the 26 teachers reporting the presence of bilingual programs indicated some use of Spanish for beginner students (66%), there were ten reports of schools with "bilingual" identification that did not report the use of any Spanish for instruction. Even more common were reports of schools with "bilingual" programs that did not use Spanish to support those language learners not classified as beginners. A small minority reported Spanish use with intermediate students (27%) and only two schools (8%) reported Spanish use with proficient students. Despite a formal definition of "bilingual" program as instruction and content delivered in two languages, in practice, the design of the program was interpreted and implemented differently in different contexts. Across the state, not only were a range of programs implemented, but the design of these programs varied widely within program types.

Despite the bilingual orientation of state policy, in practice, the study found that support for Spanish-speaking ELLs varied widely both within and across schools, with a wide range of programs being implemented. In many cases, schools appeared to mix and match programs, suggesting a lack of resources, strategy, or coherence in the design of educational support for these students, a fairly common characteristic in districts serving ELLs (Dentler & Hafner, 1997). So the presence of a mandate to implement "bilingual-bicultural programs" did not lead to coherent nor consistent implementation of bilingual programming across the state.

Policy to Practice: Staffing

The second mandate of the policy was the requirement to hire at least one bilingual or ESL-certified teacher once a program reached threshold enrollments of ELLs. There were, however, no requirements about the ratio of students to bilingual teachers in bilingual programs, nor were there requirements about the ratio of ESL teachers to serve ELL students in nonbilingual programs. As such, once schools with bilingual programs had hired one bilingual teacher, they had met their policy obligation to serve students. Schools that had not yet reached the required concentration to implement a bilingual program had no state policy requirement to hire staff with particular licensure. Consistent with the prevailing "local control" philosophy, Wisconsin's policy contained minimal mandates, leaving much of the decision-making about staffing to individual districts.

Given the state policy context, it is not surprising that the majority of principals in the study (86%) reported at least one staff member with either bilingual or ESL certification. There were 14 principals (14%) who reported that their schools did not have any bilingual or ESL certified teachers, all of whom were below the threshold in terms of ELL enrollments, but the rest indicated that they have at least one staff member with either bilingual or ESL certification. Thirty nine percent (40 principals) reported that they had only one such teacher. The rest of the schools reported a range from 2 to 9 bilingual or ESL teachers. Of all respondents, 74% reported the presence of 2 or fewer certified teachers.

The prevalence of reports of 0 or 1 teachers in the context of emerging immigrant communities is to be expected, given the low numbers of Spanish-speaking ELLs in many schools in the study. However, a closer analysis of those 54 principals (52%) reporting the presence of 0 or 1 certified bilingual or ESL teacher in their schools revealed that these were not always schools with lowest enrollments of Spanish-speaking ELLs. While 8 of the 14 principals reporting that there was no certified teacher in their school devoted to ELLs had fewer than 10 Spanish-speaking ELLs, the remaining six schools had Spanish-speaking ELL enrollments ranging from 10 to 26. Half of the 40 schools with only one bilingual or ESL certified teacher had more than 20 Spanish-speaking ELLs (and the highest number of Spanish-speaking ELLs in a school reporting just one certified teacher was 88 students).

These findings indicate that while the policy usually seemed to ensure the presence of some expertise in the support of newcomers, staffing was often not sufficient to support actual enrollments. Comments from teachers emphasized the increasing demands on their time. For example, one teacher commented that, "the school district is very understaffed in the area of ESL/Spanish support." Another teacher described her responsibilities in the district as untenable: "I split time between two schools that have over 125 ESL students." It seemed that, while schools in the study initially hired someone to support newcomers, they did not hire additional staff to maintain a reasonable student-to-teacher ratio as numbers grew.

Several surveyed teachers also noted that overwhelming demands on the few ESL or bilingual teachers limited their effectiveness at providing direct support to students. As one teacher wrote, "It seems to me that many teachers are discouraged with the lack of support, resources, and staff appropriate to the needs of this population." Another asserted, "In our small school, support is limited; so it's a "sink or swim" type environment." According to these educators, the lack of more effective support for ELLs exacerbated the challenge of creating effective support for newcomers. In fact, the variation in program development may be attributable to the challenge of creating effective programs without the professional expertise (in terms of number of qualified staff) to support them.

CONCLUSIONS

This chapter has focused on the relationship between state education policy and local decisions about how to respond to the widespread dispersal of Spanish-speakers in Wisconsin. The case of Wisconsin, with a bilingual orientation to its state policy, offers a counterpoint to the Georgia examples described in the literature (including Lynn [this volume] and Harklau and Colomer [this volume]). Unlike Georgia, Wisconsin policy ostensibly encourages bilingual programs while ensuring local control in developing programs to support newcomers based on local context. One might interpret the spirit of the policy as welcoming the language and culture of newcomers, while at the same time accepting the practical and political realities of the state. Yet Wisconsin school practice may not be all that different from Georgia, in the sense of a scarcity of actual affirmation of Spanish skills and a comparative paucity of expertise related to the size of the eligible population.

As evidenced by the implementation of varying levels of support through a range of programs, practices, and the uneven distribution of certified ESL/bilingual teachers, one must conclude that there is a disconnect between the bilingual orientation of the language of the policy and the implementation of that policy. While aspects of the policy appeared to result in bilingual aspects of school programs, there was little bilingual mission in most of the schools in the study, although a few schools did identify themselves as promoting bilingual, biliterate students. Future research might seek to identify whether and how this variation leads to differential educational outcomes for students in these contexts.

In guiding responses in practice to this demographic change, other policy mechanisms appeared to support the widespread variation depicted above. For example, the study found that the two mandates contained within the policy were by and large being met in school practice across the state, with most schools officially implementing "Bilingual-bicultural programs," as defined by the policy and employing at least one ESL or bilingual certified teacher to support those programs. As such, these schools qualified for policy inducements, in the form of financial support, at the same time that the quality and definition of their responses varied widely. One can assume that this variation was at least in part due to the power the policy places in local actors to determine how best to respond.

Given this variation and the usual lack of a strong bilingual mission within the schools, one might interpret the bilingual policy as a failure. Arguably, the degree to which the school practices observed in this study reflect practice in other states with far less progressive language policies is troubling. However, I argue that the policy itself is not fundamentally flawed. Following recent work by Spillane and Coldren (2011), I think it is important to note that a straightforward analysis of policy implementation can fail to acknowledge the key role schools do and should play in the diagnosis and design of school practices. In this sense, the policy itself can be interpreted as a nuanced document that offers direction for schools, while placing authority in the hands of those local practitioners best aware of the specific context. In the context of the NLD, variation in the numbers, ages, and language capabilities of immigrant children, as well as a wide range of staff capacity and resources to respond in schools with little experience working with Spanish-speakers make a one-size-fits-all policy inappropriate.

Rather than critique the policy itself for the ensuing problems of practice observed here, I would like to suggest that the problem lies in the degree to which schools and districts lack guidance, support, and the resources to enact the spirit of the policy. In fact, education laws related to immigrant education have led to the establishment of services in most of the schools in the study. As such, they have effectively established the need for additional support for these students. However, schools have been left on their own to provide that support without sufficient guidance or resources from state and local agencies. While I do not argue for mandated program implementation, I do see a role for the state departments of education, institutions of higher education, and local agencies in offering technical support to schools experiencing demographic shift. Given the growing relevance of this policy in schools across the state, local and state agencies must take a more active role in supporting schools as they interpret the policy and support demographic change in their local contexts. Ultimately, the success of the policy depends on coupling it with the appropriate guidance and resources to influence the design of effective support for the growing number of Spanish-speakers in Wisconsin's schools.

REFERENCES

Bartolomé, L. (2002). Creating an equal playing field: Teachers as advocates, border crossers, and cultural brokers. In Z. Beykont (Ed.), *The power of culture: Teaching across language difference* (p. 167). Cambridge, MA: Harvard Education Publishing Group.

Beck, S., & Allexsaht-Snider, M. (2002). Recent language minority education policy in Georgia: appropriation, assimilation, and Americanization. In S. Wortham, E. Murillo, & E. Hamann (Eds.), *Education in the new Latino diaspora: Policy and the politics of identity* (pp. 37–66). Westport, CT: Ablex.

Boals, T. (2001). *Legal responsibilities when serving limited-English proficient (LEP) students in K–12 public schools.* (Equity Information Update, Bulletin No. 3). Madison, WI: Department of Public Instruction. Retrieved March 30, 2010, from http://www.dpi.state.wi.us/ell/doc/legalrsp.doc

Capper, C., & Scanlan, M. (2007). English Language Learners and ICS. In C. Capper (Ed.), *Leading for social justice: Transforming schools for all learners* (pp. 151–174). Thousand Oaks, CA: Corwin Press.

Capps, R., Fix, M., Murray, J., Ost, J., Passel, J., & Herwantoro, S. (2005). *The new demography of America's schools: Immigration and the No Child Left Behind Act.* Washington DC: The Urban Institute.

Cummins, J. (1992). Bilingual education and English immersion: The Ramirez report in theoretical perspective. *Bilingual Research Journal, 16,* 91–104.

Dalla, R., MoulikGupta, P., Lopez, W., & Jones, V. (2006). "It's a Balancing Act!": Exploring school/work/family interface issues among bilingual, rural Nebraska, paraprofessional educators. *Family Relations, 55,* 390–402.

Dentler, R., & Hafner, A. (1997). *Hosting newcomers: Structuring educational opportunities for immigrant children.* New York, NY: Teachers College Press.

Fry, R., & Gonzales, F. (2008). *One-in-five and growing fast: A profile of Hispanic public school students.* Washington, DC: Pew Hispanic Center.

Gándara, P. (2005). Learning English in California: Guideposts for the nation. In M. Suárez-Orozco, C. Suárez-Orozco, & D. Qin (Eds.), *The new immigration: An interdisciplinary reader* (pp. 219–232). New York, NY: Taylor & Francis Group.

Gibson, M. (2002). The New Latino Diaspora and educational policy. In S. Wortham, E. Murillo, & E. Hamann (Eds.), *Education in the new Latino diaspora: Policy and the politics of identity* (pp. 241–252). Westport, CT: Ablex.

Hamann, E. (2002). ¿Un paso adelante? The politics of bilingual education, Latino student accommodation, and school district management in Southern Appalachia. In S. Wortham, E. Murillo, & E. Hamann (Eds.), *Education in the new Latino diaspora: Policy and the politics of identity* (pp. 67–98). Westport, CT: Ablex.

Hamann, E. (2003). *The educational welcome of Latinos in the new South.* Westport, CT: Praeger.

Leal, D., & Meier, K. (Eds.). (2011). *The Politics of Latino Education.* New York, NY: Teachers College Press.

Levinson, B., & Sutton, M. (2001). Introduction: Policy as/in practice—A sociocultural approach to the study of educational policy. In M. Sutton & B. Levinson, *Policy as practice: Toward a comparative sociocultural analysis of educational policy* (pp. 1–22). Westport, CT: Ablex.

Lowenhaupt, R., & Camburn, E. (2011). *Anatomy of the shift: Changing demographics in Wisconsin public schools.* (WCER Working Paper). University of Wisconsin-Madison, WI: Wisconsin Center for Education Research. http://www.wcer.wisc.edu/publications/workingpapers/Working_Paper_No_2011_04.pdf

Lowenhaupt, R., & Turner, E. O. (2009, October). *State policy implementation and Immigrant acculturation in Wisconsin's new Latino diaspora.* Paper presented at the conference on Latino Education and Immigrant Integration, Athens, GA.

Marrow, H. B. (2005). New destinations and immigrant incorporation. *Perspectives on Politics, 3*(4), 781–799.

Meskill, C. (2005). Infusing English language learner issues throughout professional educator curricula: The Training All Teachers Project. *Teachers College Record, 107*(4), 739–756.

Miramontes, O., Nadeau, A., & Commins, N. (2011). *Restructuring Schools for Cultural and Linguistic Diversity* (2nd ed.). New York, NY: Teachers College Press.

Murillo, E. (2002). How does it feel to be a problem? "Disciplining" the transnational subject in the American South. In S. Wortham, E. Murillo, & E. Hamann (Eds.), *Education in the new Latino diaspora: Policy and the politics of identity* (pp. 215–240). Westport, CT: Ablex.

Perreira, K., Chapman, M., & Stein, G. (2006). Becoming an American parent: Overcoming challenges and finding strength in a new immigrant Latino community. *Journal of Family Issues, 27,* 1383–1414.

Quiñones-Benitez, A. L. (2003). Training teachers of English Language Learners through instructional conversations: A metalogue. *NABE Journal of Research and Practice, 1*(1).

Singer, A. (2008). Twenty-first-century gateways: An introduction. In A. Singer, S. Hardwick, & C. Brettell (Eds.), *Twenty-first century gateways: Immigrant incorporation in suburban America* (pp. 3–31). Washington DC: Brookings Institution.

Snow, C. E., & Hakuta, K. (1992). The costs of monolingualism. In J. Crawford (Ed.), *Language loyalties: A source book on the Official English controversy* (pp. 384–394). Chicago, IL: University of Chicago Press.

Spillane, J. P. (2004). *Standards deviation: How schools misunderstand education policy.* Cambridge, MA: Harvard University Press.

Spillane, J. P., & Coldren, A. F. (2011). *Diagnosis and design for school improvement: Using a distributed perspective to lead and manage change.* New York, NY: Teachers College Press.

Stone, D. (1997). *Policy paradox: The art of political decision making.* New York, NY: W.W. Norton.

Striffler, S. (2005). *Chicken: The dangerous transformation of America's favorite food.* New Haven, CT: Yale University Press.

Stull, D., & Broadway, M. (2004). *Slaughterhouse blues: the meat and poultry industry in North America.* Belmont, CA: Wadsworth/Thomson Learning.

Suárez-Orozco, M. M. (1998). State terrors: Immigrants and refugees in the post-national Space. In Y. Zou & E. T. Trueba (Eds.), *Ethnic Identity and power: cultural contexts of political action in school and society* (pp. 283–319). Albany, NY: State University of New York Press.

Suárez-Orozco, C., & Suárez-Orozco, M. (2001). *Children of immigration.* Cambridge, MA: Harvard University Press.

Valenzuela, A. (1999). *Subtractive schooling: U.S.-Mexican youth and the politics of caring.* Albany, NY: State University of New York Press.

Valenzuela, A. (Ed.). (2005). *Leaving Children Behind: How Texas-Style Accountability Fails Latino Youth.* Albany, NY: State University of New York Press.

Van Hook, J., & Stamper Balistreri, K. (2002). Diversity and change in the institutional context of immigrants adaptation: California Schools 1985–2000. *Demography, 39,* 639–654.

Villenas, S. (2007). Diaspora and the anthropology of Latino education: Challenges, affinities, and intersections. *Anthropology & Education Quarterly, 38*(4), 419–425.

Wainer, A. (2006). The new Latino South and the challenge to American public education. *International Migration, 44*(5), 129–165.

Wisconsin administrative code, ch. PI13. Limited English Proficient Pupils. No. 582 Wis. Adm. Code. 2002, December 1.

Wisconsin Department of Public Instruction. (2010). *Wisconsin's Title III Part A, Immigrant Children and Youth Grant.* Madison, WI: Author. Retrieved March 30, 2010, from http://dpi.wi.gov/ell/doc/immigrantchildrenrfp.doc

Wisconsin Information Network for Successful Schools (WINSS) successful school guide [data analysis files]. Retrieved from http://data.dpi.state.wi.us/data/selschool.asp

Wisconsin state statutes, ch. 115, § 95–966. Bilingual Bicultural Education. Wis. Stats. 2010, March 31.

Wortham, S., Murillo, E. G., & Hamann, E. T. (Eds.). (2002). *Education in the new Latino diaspora: Policy and the politics of identity.* Westport, CT: Ablex.

CHAPTER 14

INCREASING "PARENT INVOLVEMENT" IN THE NEW LATINO DIASPORA

Sarah Gallo, Stanton Wortham, and Ian Bennett

As Mexicans move to areas of the United States that have not historically been home to Latino residents, towns across the country are experiencing rapid and unfamiliar demographic changes. Marshall (a pseudonym), a suburb of about 35,000 in the mid-Atlantic United States, has gone from approximately 100 Mexican-origin residents in 1990 to 8,000 in 2010. At two of the six Marshall elementary schools half of the students are now from Spanish-speaking households, as are two-thirds of the kindergarten students, and 27% of the K–12 student body is now Latino. This rapid growth in the Mexican newcomer population presents practical and symbolic challenges both for longstanding residents and Mexican newcomers, as well as the institutions that serve them. Like any New Latino Diaspora (NLD) community, many long-time residents are now interacting with newcomers from Latin America for the first time. As described in this volume and elsewhere (Hamann & Harklau, 2010; Millard & Chapa, 2004; Wortham, Murillo, & Hamann, 2002; Zuñiga & Hernández-León, 2005), the newness of the immigrant population presents both challenges and opportunities. Hosts and newcomers sometimes forge productive

Revisiting Education in the New Latino Diaspora, pp. 263–281

relationships, and yet the host community also commits symbolic and physical violence against immigrants (Grey & Woodrick, 2005; Murillo, 2002; Rich & Miranda, 2005).

In this chapter we describe Marshall educators' attempts to increase Spanish-speaking parents' involvement in local schools between 2008–2010. As university-based researchers and advocates, we collaborated with local educators in this venture, and we will show how the project achieved some success. But, following Villenas (2002), we argue that the notion of "parent involvement" also makes questionable assumptions. Normally, educators want parents to be "involved" such that they help with the typical activities of schooling, assuming that these activities are universally accepted and optimal for all children—and that "they" (immigrants) should learn to educate like "us" (longstanding residents). We argue instead that different people and different contexts sometimes need different educational practices and that parent involvement requires change both by educators and by immigrant families. We summarize our argument with two terms: "heterogeneity" and "repertoires."

Typical models of parent involvement assume that the host society has a homogeneous and productive way of doing schooling, such that immigrant children should learn to speak "our" language and then do the usual school activities in order to learn the curriculum. Typical models also assume that an immigrant group is homogeneous, having a set of cultural beliefs and practices which probably diverge in some respects from mainstream American ones and thus also from "our" educational ideas and practices. This assumption is false, however, because the immigrant community is quite heterogeneous. In Marshall, for instance, some students were born in Mexico and others in the U.S. Some are working class while others are middle class. Some parents have had many years of education in Mexico, while others have had only a few. Families also come from various parts of Mexico, from the Caribbean to the Pacific coast and from both rural and urban settings—and some have lived for extended periods in various parts of the United States. Some children immigrated as preschoolers, some immigrated as adolescents and others were born in the U.S. Some have immigration documents and others do not. Some live in an intact family, while others have family members still in Mexico and a few have divorced parents. Increasing parent involvement, then, cannot be as simple as making "them" behave like "us," since "they" are heterogeneous and should not all be treated the same.

"We" are not all the same either. Our second key term is "repertoires." As Gumperz (1964), Gutiérrez and Rogoff (2003), and Rymes (2010) argue, members of a speech community do not always speak in the same ways or believe the same things. That is, speaking the "same" language and coming from the "same" culture do not mean that people share a full set of linguistic and cultural concepts, values and practices. A speech community is more like a Venn diagram with many overlapping circles. Most members of a community can do certain things, like order food in a restaurant and make simple declarative statements about everyday phenomena. But some can speak like football announcers, or participate in debates about economic theory, or advise musicians about how to improvise more effectively, while many competent speakers cannot. Failure to speak fluently in any of these ways does not indicate an inability to speak English or lack of American identity. Any English speaker controls only a subset of the speech repertoires that make up American English, and any speaker overlaps only to some extent with others, no matter how fluent. From this perspective, the formal education of children or the assimilation of immigrants means helping them master more repertoires. Any immigrant language learner can already manage some repertoires in English, if only from movies, scripts and stereotypes they have been exposed to in their home country. Any language learner also controls many repertoires in Spanish or a Spanish/English combination that can serve as resources for helping them master English repertoires that will be useful in the U.S. Furthermore, since "we" native speakers do not control all the same repertoires, educators could themselves productively master new repertoires for interacting with Mexican immigrants, or for speaking about topics that they do not normally address in English (perhaps soccer, or Catholic festivals, for example).

We argue that "parent involvement" needs to be reframed. It is certainly the case that Mexican immigrant parents and children can benefit from learning various repertoires in English—how to talk about academic subject matter, how to make requests of educational professionals, how to participate in politics, etc. However, a school may more productively involve immigrant parents if educators themselves master new repertoires for communicating with immigrants, if they recognize that they can build on repertoires in both Spanish and English that immigrant parents and children already control, and if they acknowledge that educational success for any individual student means mastering an overlapping but somewhat heterogeneous set of repertoires.

In this chapter we briefly describe the town of Marshall, the parent involvement initiatives that we created with the Marshall Area School District (MASD), and both traditional and repertoire-based models of parent involvement. Then we describe in more detail the 2 years of parent involvement projects that we undertook in Marshall, drawing on data from four aspects of our work there: creating bilingual resource rooms, launching a Latino parent leadership group, creating a film through which immigrant parents could share their hopes and suggestions with Marshall educators, and creating a directory that reduced barriers to preschool and pediatric services for these families. Over the two years of our parent involvement project, everyone involved—we, Marshall educators and immigrant parents—all shifted from a more traditional approach to parent involvement to a repertoires approach that drew upon individuals' heterogeneous abilities. We propose that a focus on heterogeneous repertoires is especially useful in communities undergoing rapid change, such as those in the NLD.

Marshall

Marshall is a suburb of about 35,000 people that has attracted thousands of Mexican immigrants since the mid-90s. The newcomers work mostly in landscaping, construction, retail and restaurants. The U.S. Census shows dramatic changes in the proportions of racial and ethnic groups in Marshall between 1990 and 2000—going from 71% White, 26% African American, and 3% Latino to 54% White, 35% African American, and 11% Latino. Latino immigration continued over the past decade, and in 2010 the town was 32% White, 35% African American, and 28% Latino. Latino students were 27% of enrolled public school students in 2011. Educational disparities are evident in the MASD. In 2004–2005, the 4-year graduation rate for Latino students was 58%, compared to 82% for African Americans and 87% for Whites. More than half of Latino students score "below basic" on standardized tests, compared with a third of Blacks and 15% of Whites. Marshall schools have struggled with the increase in English Language Learners (ELLs) and the tensions that arise as White and Black residents adjust to newcomers. As in many NLD communities, the growing Latino community has generated mixed reactions in the schools and the town, but the schools, the police, health care providers, the government and other institutions in Marshall are often more welcoming than in other NLD towns (Wortham, Mortimer, & Allard, 2009).

Collaborative Parent Involvement Initiatives

In 2008 we approached MASD with a proposal to work collaboratively on improving education for Spanish-speaking children. District leadership agreed, and they chose to focus on increasing Spanish-speaking parents' involvement with their children's schools. We began the project with two initiatives that presupposed more traditional approaches to parent involvement. First, in response to parents' uncertainty about how to help with their children's homework, we collaborated with teachers at four elementary schools to create weekly Spanish-medium *resource rooms* in which parents and their children could bring topics of concern, clarify questions regarding homework and receive lessons in English. Second, drawing upon Delgado-Gaitan's (2001) work with the "Comité de Padres Latinos," we worked with educators to create a monthly, district-wide, *Spanish-medium parent forum* in which Spanish-speaking parents could discuss their concerns and suggestions about local schools.

As we discuss below, important changes occurred within these two initiatives over the course of the project, leading us to reorganize them in the second phase. Over time the resource rooms shifted from a more traditional site of teacher-centered expertise (phase one) to collaboration among teachers and families (phase two). Through their participation in the resource rooms, some students increased their academic achievement and some teachers and parents developed closer interpersonal relationships than had previously existed, which led to increased comfort and engagement with school-based activities for many immigrant parents. Over time, the more educator-led district-wide parent forum (phase 1) led to the emergence of a Spanish-speaking parent leadership group that met more frequently and eventually secured the participation of the superintendent in monthly meetings (phase 2). Ultimately the meetings developed their own momentum such that our participation was no longer necessary.

We also worked with families from the parent forum to create a 27-minute professional development video that draws on a corpus of video-recorded interviews with a dozen immigrant families who were invited to share their own stories, experiences, and advice with local teachers and schools (the interviews are in Spanish, and subtitled in English). The film (titled *Sobresalir*) was embraced by the parent leadership group and has been adopted by MASD for professional development since its completion in the summer of 2010. Finally, we also worked with immigrant families to identify obstacles they face in utilizing preschool and pediatric services in Marshall. We brought families, preschool service providers, and pediatricians into a joint conversation and created a bilingual guide to pediatric and preschool services that was reviewed and warmly received by the parent leadership group. Our account of these four parent involvement initiatives illustrates the productive work being done by educators and immigrant families in one NLD town, and it shows how the concept of *heterogeneous repertoires* is a useful tool for thought and action in rapidly changing NLD communities.

Models of Parent Involvement

There are three basic approaches to parent involvement, which we call traditional, mismatch, and repertoires. Although each approach can be useful in some contexts, we argue that a repertoires approach is most plausible conceptually and most productive practically. *Traditional* parent involvement models assume that all parents, regardless of their background, should help educators integrate their children into mainstream schooling practices (Epstein & Sanders, 2003). Parents should assist children by helping their children do school-sanctioned tasks (like homework) at home, by supporting school-based events, and by volunteering in school. Parents are viewed as partners, helping educators guide their children to complete school-determined tasks successfully.

As several scholars point out (e.g., Torres-Guzman, 1991; Villenas, 2002), parents who do not do this are often evaluated by educators as not caring about their children's education. The traditional model assumes that parents share the schools' vision for education and that educators, not parents, possess knowledge on how best to educate children (Epstein & Sanders, 2003, p. 413). Family-teacher communication is rarely two-way, with teachers serving as experts who inform parents about school practices, although parents are expected to provide crucial information about their children that the teachers need to know. For Latino and Mexican immigrant families, the traditional model makes the questionable assumption that parents are already familiar with mainstream American educational practices and that they possess the resources (such as fluency and literacy in English) to do them (Arias & Morillo-Campbell, 2008).

The *cultural mismatch* framework argues that differences in nonmainstream families' school involvement are *not* a reflection of indifference or incompetence (Heath, 1983; Mehan, Hubbard, Villanueva, & Lintz, 1996). Instead, families from other cultural backgrounds are familiar with different educational practices and have different educational ideals. No one way of conceptualizing and doing education is superior. "Theirs" and "ours" are simply different and equally valuable. Mismatch-based parent involvement policies often propose bidirectional models, including guidance for parents in navigating U.S. school systems and attempts to infuse school curriculum with what parents know, believe, and practice (Arias & Morillo-Cambell, 2008, p. 11). In this view, parent involvement practices should avoid naturalized assumptions that assume "our" way is best. They should instead clarify differences between mainstream and immigrant approaches to education.

Educators certainly need to recognize the cultural specificity of mainstream approaches and acknowledge the value of immigrants' own ideals and practices. In this sense the mismatch approach improves upon the traditional approach. But the mismatch approach has been criticized on various grounds (Erickson, 1987; Varenne & McDermott, 1998). One central problem is the assumption made by most mismatch theorists that cultures are bounded and homogeneous. As Rampton (1998) argues, especially in this time of global migration, media, transnationalism, and postmodern identities, assumptions about stable speech communities and homogeneous cultures are not accurate. When applied to parent involvement, the mismatch approach implies that all immigrant families have similar ideals and practices about education and parenting—"*this* is the Mexican way, *that* is the American way." Especially in heterogeneous NLD communities like Marshall, this is simply not true.

A third model, which we call *repertoires*, rejects a shared underlying assumption of the first two: instead of treating culture as a homogeneous and bounded set of practices and beliefs that is shared across a group, it focuses on each individual's experiences with cultural practices that may reflect shared histories of engagement but also include divergent capacity and commitment to heterogeneous ideals and repertoires (Gutiérrez & Rogoff, 2003). Such an approach recognizes that there may be some widely shared elements in a group but also claims that each individual member recognizes and accepts only a subset of the total set of practices and ideals. Moreover, there is often substantial overlap with "out-group" members' repertoires, and individuals are often members of multiple communities. A repertoires approach defines a cultural community as "a coordinated group of people with some traditions and understandings in common, extending across several generations, with varied roles and practices and continual change among participants, as well as transformation in the community's practices" (Gutiérrez & Rogoff, 2003, p. 21).

Rymes (2010) makes a similar argument, building on Gumperz (1964), to define *communicative repertoires* as "the collection of ways individuals use language and literacy and other means of communication (gestures, dress, posture, accessories)" to negotiate their participation in various spaces (Rymes, 2010, p. 528). A repertoires approach does not deny that, when longstanding community members begin interacting with newly arrived others, both hosts and newcomers tend to homogenize the other—that is, people themselves tend to adopt either traditional or mismatch models as they make sense of others. But that these theories are commonly invoked does not make them true. As scholars we must do better.

Rymes (2010) highlights four central aspects of a repertoires approach. First, an individual's repertoire is dynamic and contingent upon use. Rather than being composed of static rules or competencies, repertoires are guidelines, deployed improvisationally as people figure out how to make something work in a given context. Repertoires also change over historical time, as skills are applied across varying situations and people learn from experience. Second, Rymes emphasizes that accommodation is inevitable and directionality varies. Because the guidelines that make up repertoires are partial and flexible, and require implementation in context, participants must adjust to others as they communicate or work together in all but the most scripted contexts. Adjustment can be required from various parties to the interaction or practice, and sometimes from everyone involved. Third, Rymes advocates for awareness about our own and others' repertoires. People must critically examine their own norms and beliefs, come to recognize others', and learn how to switch among potential options to achieve understanding in a given situation. Fourth, in a repertoires approach, the learning goal for both children and adults is repertoire expansion.

With respect to parent involvement, a repertoires approach means that immigrant families should not simply internalize educators' repertoires (a traditional approach that Villenas [2002] has shown to be paternalistic). Nor should parents and educators seek to preserve an allegedly pure version of immigrant beliefs and practices (a mismatch approach). Instead the goal is to recognize and adopt some of each other's repertoires, expanding everyone's capacity in the process. In such a scenario, members of neither group are "giving in" (Rymes, 2010, p. 538), because members of each group are developing new repertoires through contact with the other. According to this approach, the ultimate goal for parent involvement initiatives is to design opportunities for educators and families to expand their own repertories through interactions. In many ways NLD communities are ideal spaces to foster this awareness of and (partial) facility in others' repertoires—because such repertoire expansion occurs most easily when individuals cross social boundaries and interact with heterogeneous others.

Facilitating Parent Involvement in Marshall

In this section we provide examples from both phases of Marshall's 2-year experience designing and implementing parent involvement initiatives with Spanish-speaking families. The first phase involved components of both traditional and mismatch approaches, though people did not articulate these assumptions explicitly. The second phase emerged over time—not by explicit intent but of its own accord. In this phase, across our initiatives, academics, educators, and parents all came to presuppose and deploy a repertoires approach. The second phase included a shift in relationships among educators and Latino families, changes in decision-making and collaboration within the different initiatives, creation of a film in which NLD parents took the opportunity to share their individual voices and experiences with local educators, and development of a bilingual guide to local preschool and pediatric services. We did not envision and accomplish the change in models of parent involvement exactly as it occurred, although we did explicitly try to move some educators away from the traditional model of parent involvement that they started with. The change emerged through collective effort as researchers, parents, and educators learned to work together more effectively.

Traditional Parent Involvement

When we began the district-wide parent forum and the after-school resource rooms, MASD educators often established themselves as the experts on the ways schools work and told parents what they thought parents needed to know. This dynamic was particularly visible during one school-wide dinner we held for Latino parents to discuss a potential Spanish-speaking parent forum:

It is a rainy Thursday evening in May as approximately 20 immigrant parents gather in Grant Elementary School's [pseudonym] multipurpose cafeteria and gymnasium for a dinner of tamales and an opportunity to talk about their school-related concerns with the administration. As dozens of young children race around the gym, parents keep a close eye on their behavior and wait quietly for the event to begin. Few families appear to know each other, and they do not converse except for short greetings. Many parents appear nervous and somewhat unsure of the agenda. Teachers speak to one another in English as they busily set up the food on the front table, and then switch to Spanish to encourage families to try the tamales. The one mother from Puerto Rico chooses not to eat, as she does not like spicy Mexican food. Once everyone has finished, the teachers take the children to play board games outside of the cafenasium and Mariana, the coordinator of Migrant Education (who is from Venezuela), welcomes parents. She and the other teachers stand at the front table where they set up the food, and soon the district's ESL Coordinator, John Lichter, goes to the custodial closet for a chair to join the teachers up front. Most of the parents are seated right in front of the teachers at the cafeteria tables, many of them moving so they can face the teachers. This alters the U set-up, intended for a shared conversation among all parents and teachers, to an audience in rows that the teachers proceed to address. Mariana opens the conversation thanking families for coming, and saying this is a chance for them to share their "metas, preocupaciones, o quejas" [goals, worries, and complaints] with them, the school. Through this introduction and set-up, she effectively positions the front of the room, and the school, as those who hold knowledge and expertise, rather than the other parents. John Lichter then gives a lengthy description of the purpose of the meeting, citing the population increase of the Hispanic families in the district, and describing the meetings as "charlas informales" [informal chats, though the more common term in Mexican Spanish would be pláticas] to give the Latino community a voice in the district and help formulate suggestions for the Superintendent. He speaks for 15 minutes, describing his job duties and examples of parent involvement from South America and information he gathered from a conference in Washington, D.C. The length and density of his presentation indicate that he too is setting himself up as an authority figure. For the rest of the meeting parents speak by addressing the educators at the front of the room, and each comment by a parent is responded to by an educator before the next parent is called on to speak. (Gallo FN 05.14.09)

A similar educator-centered format occurred during the early parent forum meetings at the public library in which Maritza—a middle-class Mexican immigrant ESL teacher who had been living in Marshall for many years and took on primary responsibility for the early meetings—facilitated the conversations. She often stood toward the front of the group and would call on different parents to speak, contributing her own comments after each parent, before calling on the next speaker. She also worked with the school administration and those of us from the university to determine the themes of these early forums.

The positioning of teachers as experts also occurred during the school-based resource room sessions in the first year. Each resource room was staffed by two to three bilingual educators, who were either Anglo teachers who spoke Spanish or Latino immigrants from Venezuela, El Salvador, or Mexico who had lived and worked in U.S. schools for many years. When parents spoke, they directed their comments to teachers at the front of the room. Thus the 6 to 12 parents present on any given day would usually speak to teachers rather than one another, at least during the formal part of each meeting. The teachers always responded to parents' questions, rather than parents helping one another. Although this format created opportunities for teachers to become aware of some immigrant parents' concerns and questions, it did not create opportunities for parents to be seen as possessing knowledge themselves. During less-structured interactions, such as when parents arrived, teachers were usually busy preparing the last-minute details and rarely approached parents to welcome them or speak informally about their lives. During the first year of these sessions, teachers tended to sit together, apart from the parents. When teachers spoke to each other, as when they would call across the room to another teacher to pass out materials, they spoke in English—thus creating some distance from parents who did not necessarily understand what they were saying.

These brief examples from the first phase of the resource rooms and the parent forum show educators and parents operating under a traditional model of parent involvement, in which teachers are the experts who decide the topics to cover and help parents understand mainstream schooling practices. Educators explicitly intended to design these initiatives around Latino families' interests, and they did not mean to dominate the sessions. But it was difficult for them to prepare for these extra events in their busy schedules, and it was familiar and comfortable to have teacher-centered events. Latino parents also contributed to the traditional approach taken in these early sessions, as they were timid and hesitated to give explicit direction to educators. We researchers were also familiar with such traditional parent involvement events and did not initially question the organization of the events. All of us were happy to have the events up and running, and busy arranging the details so that the events could continue to happen, so we did not initially reflect on the problems posed by a traditional approach to parent involvement.

A Mismatch Approach

Many of the early resource room sessions stressed overarching differences between schooling in Mexico and the U.S. Thus they also presupposed a mismatch approach and showed that traditional and mismatch framings can co-occur. For example, there was a session held at Grant Elementary to discuss parent-teacher conferences. Using PowerPoint, a fourth grade teacher emphasized how conferences are an important chance for parents and teachers to speak about a child one-on-one and do not mean that the child has done something wrong—which, she said, may be more often the case when parents meet directly with a teacher in Mexico. During this session the teacher had parents write down the questions they had for their child's teacher and asked them to bring these to their conferences, and several parents said this made them feel more prepared to talk with the teacher.

After another session in which teachers presented a detailed explanation of the report cards, parents also said that they appreciated such explanations of how things are done in the U.S. One couple said that if they had not attended the session on report cards, they would have had absolutely no idea what the report cards meant. The father explained how even if they went to someone who knew English and could translate the words for them, they would still not have been able to figure out the meaning of the grades because they were so different stylistically from what is used in Mexico. Several parents were also concerned about how they could figure out if their child was in danger of being held back a grade, a regular occurrence in the early grades in Mexico (in Zúñiga & Hamann's [2009, p. 347] survey of almost 8,000 fourth to ninth grade students in Zacatecas Mexico, almost 9% of students reported having previously repeated a grade.) Others emphasized that the report card format—which does not list subjects such as math, reading, or handwriting, but instead lists dozens of state competencies—made it very difficult for them as parents to figure out what areas to work on with their children.

The early resource room sessions thus assumed overarching differences between U.S. and Mexican school-related topics and offered Latino parents advice about how to navigate these differences. In many cases, the advice was useful. The mismatch approach is not completely wrong, and generalizations about cultural differences can be helpful. But teachers were nonetheless adopting broad generalizations about school practices in Mexico. They had not yet had time to talk with individual parents to learn about their personal experiences and questions. As we will describe below, teachers came to know parents and their more heterogeneous situations better over time, and they were able to tailor their interventions more precisely as time went on.

Repertoires Approach

After about 6–9 months our parent involvement activities changed. Instead of assuming a traditional or mismatch view of cultural difference, we came to presuppose a repertoires view. This happened in fits and starts, at different paces, and did not result in complete transformation. We did not explicitly intend the shift, although the university researchers did encourage educators to give parents more voice as time went on, and several parents took more initiative. The change was nonetheless striking, and it ultimately helped increase the involvement of Latino parents in Marshall schools. We will describe this change initially by focusing on a theme that recurred in the parent forum and the resource rooms: how to help Latino children develop biliteracy in English and Spanish. In this section we provide several examples of how families and educators adapted their beliefs and practices to expand their own repertoires in this area.

In both resource rooms and the parent forum, after several months we observed a shift from teacher-fronted expertise on the topic of Spanish literacy to parents' sharing their own expertise and leadership. Notes from the first resource room meeting at Grant Elementary describe Kassy, a bilingual Anglo teacher, offering advice to parents:

> *In a closing conversation parents bring up reading to children in English and Spanish. Kassy strongly encourages them to read to their kids in Spanish, and strongly advocates for them to speak, write and read in Spanish with their kids so that they don't lose it. Kassy herself developed advanced Spanish repertoires during a university study-abroad program where she met her Chilean husband, and they were raising their son bilingually. Speaking to the parents during this meeting, she is adamant that reading in both languages will not confuse or harm children. She also shares her experiences teaching in a bilingual school in Philadelphia where "gringos" were taught purely in Spanish and by the end of 4th grade could read perfectly in English and Spanish. Many parents speak of older kids they know (some in their own families) who cannot read, write or even speak Spanish anymore, which is negatively evaluated by them. (Gallo FN: 2.19.09)*

Almost all the parents agreed with Kassy. Over time, they began to offer their own experiences and suggestions, which differed across families, instead of simply listening to the teachers. For example, one father explained at a resource room meeting several months into the project that he did not understand why they had to "un-teach" their children Spanish at a young age so that they could excel in English, only to have them try to re-learn Spanish in high school or college. He, and many others, preferred to develop their children's speaking and literacy in Spanish all along. Many parents suggested the creation of an out-of-school Spanish class for Latino children, and some parents offered to help teach it themselves.

As teachers and parents began to talk more in the resource rooms and parent forum about Spanish literacy, both groups became more aware of the issue and reflected on it among themselves, sometimes changing their views on the topic. In a conversation with Sarah Gallo, for example, one family discussed how their beliefs and practices had shifted on the issue because of their participation in the resource rooms and the parent forum:

Seated in their family's living room on a warm Saturday afternoon, Elena's mother Alejandra brings up how one benefit of participating in these Thursday resource rooms has been their thoughts about using Spanish with Elena at home. Alejandra talks about how she lives with some of her own siblings in their house and that when her siblings used to talk to Elena in Spanish, Elena's parents would tell them to stop, to only speak to her in "puro inglés" [solely in English]. Alejandra says they now realize how important it is for her to know Spanish, to know both languages, and it is a good thing to speak Spanish with her. Earlier in the year Elena's father had shared their uncertainty about teaching their children Spanish at a young age. He says that now he understands that it's a good thing and seems very excited about making sure that his daughter is learning to read and write in Spanish. (Gallo FN 03.28.09)

On one hand, these two examples demonstrate the divergent perspectives that Mexican immigrant families had on the topic of Spanish literacy, with one pursuing bilingualism from the start and the other wanting reassurance from experts that this was appropriate. Yet they also illustrate how, over time, opportunities to discuss these topics in a public forum created spaces for reflection and repertoire expansion. For some Mexican immigrant parents this meant re-considering their fears about learning two languages simultaneously. For several teachers who were not as pro-biliteracy as Kassy, it gave them opportunities to learn about Mexican immigrant parents' beliefs on the topic. In more traditional family involvement initiatives parents' knowledge is often overlooked, but in Marshall, as these spaces became open to more heterogeneous repertoires, immigrant parents had opportunities to share their views and even to create educational opportunities to enact their ideas.

During the second year of the resource rooms, parents continually brought up their concerns about biliteracy. The same teachers were running the resource rooms. But two things had changed. The teachers had come to know families personally and they understood better that not everyone had the same knowledge or needs. Thus they relied less on one-size-fits-all lectures about how "we" or "they" do it and when they did lecture they supplemented the lectures with more tailored explanations and interventions. For their part, the parents had become more comfortable with the resource rooms and they now asserted themselves more—asking for specific advice, objecting to unwarranted generalizations, and shaping the agenda themselves.

Parents also asked for help improving their own English repertoires. The teachers responded by restructuring the resource rooms so that students would complete 30 minutes of Spanish literacy lessons with Kassy while parents expanded their English and computer literacy working with the other teachers on a computer-based English instruction program. This is described in the following fieldnote.

> *I help the parents get onto the computers while Christina and Mariana work with them, helping them maneuver through websites and figure out the basics of computer use. I then participate in part of the Spanish literacy lesson that Kassy is doing with students of all ages. Elementary school-aged kids are accompanied by their younger and sometimes older siblings, with the older kids caring for their younger siblings. Kassy first reads a book about "sopa de verduras" [Vegetable Soup] with them, a Spanish-language book explicitly designed to teach vocabulary such as the different tools for the garden and the different names of vegetables. As she reads, she points out these words and says them for students to repeat. After they finish she has everyone draw and label (in Spanish) their favorite vegetable on their individual white board in front of them and talk about it. She then gets some old construction paper and lined paper so they can each design their own book. (Gallo FN 3.17.10)*

This new structure gave teachers more opportunities to get to know parents as individuals, with their unique sets of experiences, beliefs, and abilities. Teachers made space for conversations in which parents could describe their lives as immigrants, their divergent schooling experiences in Mexico, and the realities of living and working in Marshall with differing immigration statuses. Teachers stopped sitting in their own groups and instead mingled with parents and further built relationships with them through informal talk. As one teacher described below, these family-teacher relationships developed during the resource rooms also had positive influences on her teaching as well:

> I was really able to develop a relationship with the parents when we had the after-school program, and the connections I made to those parents during that time are still there ... I got to know the students better. I mean, you have a better knowledge of a student when you know what their parents are like and what's expected of them from their parents; how much support they get; how much support they don't have; family dynamics—I mean, all of that is really important for your knowledge of a student. And then of course that makes you a better teacher. (Interview, 4.11.11)

These new relationships also extended beyond the resource rooms, as parents who participated became more comfortable in other school events and often took on leadership roles.

Parents also began to assert their expertise with respect to developing children's literacy in Spanish. At one session, parents decided to organize Spanish songs and games for kids. Initially, parents were afraid to sing in front of the group, but after Kassy led a few songs that did not include the full version that parents knew from Mexico, even some of the most timid mothers stepped up to teach the group the "correct" version. Kassy drew upon her repertoires in Spanish to sing portions of the songs, but parents clearly had more expansive repertoires in these domains, and this positioned Kassy as a learner. Both parents and teachers also saw the heterogeneous distribution of knowledge about these songs across parents. Some songs were familiar to almost all parents, while others were completely unknown to many families. Parents then became experts to each other and the teachers, sharing what they knew and expanding their own and others' repertoires.

A similar shift occurred in the parent forum at about the same time. For the first six months of the group, families had diligently shown up and expressed their concerns and suggestions, but the discussions were always run by someone from the school district or the university. A transition occurred when several parents began meeting in their own homes, apart from the formal monthly meetings, and formed a leadership group that was subsequently elected by other members. They approached us, the university organizers of the group, and explained—very politely—that they appreciated our work getting the group started and that they could handle it from there. They continued to invite the superintendent, but instead of having the university arrange her visits, the new president of the parent group started to contact her directly.

Features of this Repertoires Approach

The transformation in the resource rooms and the parent forum illustrate important features of a repertoires approach to family-school relationships. As Rymes (2010) argues, repertoires are dynamic, and an individual's development of repertoires depends on their use. In the resource rooms and parent forum, both educators and families began to try out new activities (like teaching each other unfamiliar songs) and their own repertoires expanded as a result. Participants also applied repertoires across situations, as when parents took things they learned in the resource rooms and used them to facilitate their participation in more traditional school-based events like open houses and parent councils. All participants became more willing to try out new ideas and practices and they learned form each other—both across and within "Anglo" and "Latino" groups.

There was thus multidirectionality in the accommodation to others, with families and educators learning to recognize and adopt some of each other's repertoires. Over time, the resource rooms and the forum created spaces for teachers and families to know each other as individuals and to build relationships, and these relationships became important spaces for mutual learning and repertoire expansion. This was visible in some families' decisions to encourage Spanish literacy development with their children and educators' decisions to restructure the resource rooms to more effectively expand both students' repertoires in Spanish and parents' repertoires in English and technology.

As of this writing, the process of building repertoire awareness was ongoing, continuing the 2-year journey of these parent involvement projects. As educators and parents got to know each other, they learned from each other's stories, experiences, and beliefs and came to question some of their own. Both educators and parents came to navigate more flexibly among repertoires. Teachers learned more about individual families' experiences and began to build upon these as they worked with children and planned resource room activities. Parents learned about teachers' expectations and goals and they became more skillful at navigating the U.S. educational system to intervene on behalf of their children. Thus both groups took advantage of contact with others to expand their repertoires.

Of course, such repertoire expansion only happened for teachers and parents who participated in the resource rooms and the leadership forum. In order to reach other educators, we created a documentary film that represents the voices of Latino parents from the forum. This film, titled *Sobresalir*—which was the term one parent used for her hope that her children would get ahead through education—contains excerpts from interviews with a dozen families sharing their experiences, expectations, and hopes for their children's education in Marshall. Themes included the difficulty of abrupt transitions in immigrants' experiences, the difficulty and importance of communication with educators, the challenges of helping children with homework in another language, the importance of respect and moral development, and suggestions about how to improve education for Latino children in Marshall schools. The school district used the film for professional development in 2010–11 and continues to do so. In the first year of its use, almost half of the district teachers and all of the senior administrators saw it. We hope that the film will build awareness of immigrant families' repertoires and concerns.

A final aspect of our project was an effort to help Latino families in Marshall overcome obstacles to accessing pediatric and preschool services. We first interviewed parents, preschool educators, and pediatric health care providers to identify obstacles to the local utilization of preschool and pediatric services. The most important were: limited number of service sites, administrative hurdles, and financial costs. We decided to create a system that provided information about pediatric and preschool services, tailored to the needs of Latino parents. We then surveyed the 51 licensed preschool providers and fourteen pediatric providers in the area and produced a bilingual guide to services. We presented the guide to the parent forum and to providers, seeking their help in planning revisions and dissemination. We have subsequently distributed several hundred copies to schools, agencies, and directly to parents. Throughout the development of the guide, we understood parents as authoritative "experts" about the obstacles that they faced and the information they needed to overcome these barriers. One concrete result has been our attempt to get pediatric and preschool providers to talk to each other about the community that they both serve and to collaborate in reducing unnecessary administrative barriers to services. Through these conversations we hope to help different types of providers learn from each other's repertoires, as well as helping providers learn from parents.

CONCLUSIONS

It turns out that our parent involvement initiatives evolved in the same direction as the theoretical models have been emerging in the literature, from traditional to mismatch to repertoires. At first the resource rooms and parent forum presupposed that host and immigrant cultures were homogeneous, shared across people within the group and incompatible in important ways. Educators mostly tried to instruct parents in "our" way of doing things, although they did recognize that "their" way was valid (although less functional in a traditional school environment). Over time, however, both educators and parents recognized that "Mexican" and "American" cultures are heterogeneous and that individuals have overlapping but distinct and developing repertoires. The resource rooms and parent forum then became sites for expanding all participants' repertoires—as immigrant parents learned from teachers, as teachers learned from parents and as parents learned from each other. Through our subsequent film and guide we are hoping that other Marshall residents can also expand their repertoires, both for their own sake and so that they can interact more productively with newcomers.

One question remains: why were our initiatives mostly successful? Our presence as university researchers made a difference in at least three ways. First, just the fact that we consistently showed up provided an opportunity and some pressure for educators and parents to participate in and plan for the various events. Second, we obtained a small grant that supported participating educators (who were paid at the negotiated rate for after-school work over the 2 years) and provided food for participating families. Third, we provided ideas and some expertise—we knew of the literature on parent leadership groups and suggested that we build one in Marshall—and we had access to technical assistance for producing the film. Marshall itself is also somewhat more open to immigrants than some other NLD towns, as we have described in other work (Wortham, Mortimer, & Allard, 2009, 2011), and this may make educators and immigrant parents more willing to work together. All of these factors made our parent involvement initiatives more likely to succeed, but in the end it was the effort and adaptability of the educators and parents that made it happen.

REFERENCES

Arias, B. M., & Morillo-Campbell, M. (January 2008). *Promoting ELL parental involvement: Challenges in contested times.* Tempe, AZ; Boulder, CO: Education Public Interest Center; Education Policy Research Unit. Retrieved from http://epsl.asu.edu/epru/documents/EPSL-0801-250-EPRU.pdf

Delgado-Gaitan, C. (2001). *The power of community: Mobilizing for family and schooling.* Lanham, MD: Rowman & Littlefield.

Epstein, J. L., & Sanders, M. (2003). Family, school, and community partnerships. In M. Bornstein (Ed.), *Handbook of parenting* (2nd ed., pp. 407–438). Mahwah, NJ: Erlbaum Associates.

Erickson, F. (1987). Transformation and School Success: The Politics and Culture of Educational Achievement. *Anthropology & Education Quarterly, 18,* 335–356.

Grey, M. A., & Woodrick, A. C. (2005). "Latinos have revitalized our community": Mexican migration and Anglo response in Marshalltown, Iowa. In V. Zúniga & R. Hernández-León (Eds.), *New destinations: Mexican immigration in the United States* (pp. 133–152). New York, NY: Russell Sage Foundation.

Gumperz, J. (1964). Linguistic and social interaction in two communities. *American Anthropologist, 66*(6) (part 2), 137–154.

Gutiérrez, K. D., & Rogoff, B. (2003). Cultural ways of learning: Individual traits or repertoires of practice. *Educational Researcher, 32*(5), 19–25.

Hamann, E. T., & Harklau, L. (2010). Education in the New Latino Diaspora. In E. G. Murillo (Ed.), *Handbook of Latinos and education* (pp. 157–169). New York, NY: Routledge.

Heath, S. (1983). *Ways with words: language, life, and work in communities and classrooms.* New York, NY: Cambridge University Press.

Mehan, H., Villanueva, I., Hubbard, L., & Lintz, A. (1996). *Constructing school success. The consequences of untracking low-achieving students.* New York, NY: Cambridge University Press.

Millard, A., & Chapa, J. (Eds.). (2004). *Apple pie and enchiladas: Latino newcomers in the rural Midwest.* Austin, TX: University of Texas Press.

Murillo, E. (2002). How does it feel to be a *problem*?: "Disciplining" the transnational subject in the American south." In S. Wortham, E. Murillo, & E

Hamann (Eds.), *Education in the new Latino diaspora: Policy and the politics of identity.* Westport CT: Ablex Press.

Rampton, B. (1998). Language crossing and the redefinition of reality. In P. Auer (Ed.), *Code-switching in conversation* (pp. 290–317). London, England: Routledge.

Rich, B. L., & Miranda, M. (2005). The sociopolitical dynamics of Mexican migration in Lexington, Kentucky, 1997 to 2002: An ambivalent community responds. In V. Zúñiga & R. Hernández-León (Eds.), *New Destinations: Mexican Immigration in the United States* (pp. 187–219). New York, NY: Russell Sage Foundation.

Rymes, B. (2010). Classroom discourse analysis: A focus on communicative repertoires. In N. Hornberger, & S. L. McKay (Eds.), *Sociolinguistics and language education* (pp. 528–546). Bristol, England: Multilingual Matters.

Torres-Guzmán, M. (1991). Recasting frames: Latino parent involvement. In M. McGroarty & C. Faltis (Eds.), *Languages in school and society: Policy and pedagogy*

Varenne, H., & McDermott, R. (1998). *Successful failure.* Boulder, CO: Westview Press.

Villenas, S. (2002). Reinventing *educación* in new Latino communities: Pedagogies of change and continuity in North Carolina. In S. Wortham, E. Murillo, & E. Hamann (Eds.), *Education in the New Latino Diaspora* (pp. 17–36). Westport, CT: Ablex Press.

Wortham, S., Mortimer, K., & Allard, E. (2009). Mexicans as model minorities in the New Latino Diaspora. *Anthropology & Education Quarterly, 40,* 388–404.

Wortham, S., Mortimer, K., & Allard, E. (2011). Homies in the New Latino Diaspora. *Language & Communication, 31,* 191–202.

Wortham, S., Murillo, E., & Hamann, E. (2002). *Education in the New Latino Diaspora: Policy and the politics of identity.* Westport, CT: Ablex.

Zúñiga, V., & Hamann, E. T. (2009). Sojourners in Mexico with U.S. school experience: A new taxonomy for transnational students. *Comparative Education Review, 53*(3), 329–353.

Zúñiga, V., & Hernández-León, R. (2005). Introduction. In V. Zúñiga & R. Hernández-León (Eds.), *New destinations: Mexican immigration in the United States* (pp. xi–xxix). New York, NY: Russell Sage Foundation.

CHAPTER 15

PROFESSIONAL DEVELOPMENT ACROSS BORDERS

Binational Teacher Exchanges in the New Latino Diaspora

Adam Sawyer

In June of 2006, I accompanied an intrepid group of 11 Nebraska educators and their guides on a 16-day professional development journey to the western Mexican city of Guadalajara. During their stay in Mexico, I joined these in-service and preservice teachers and school support personnel in a structured program of guided school visits, meetings with Mexican educators, Spanish classes, lectures on Mexican culture and immigration, and Mexican family home stays. What compelled this group of educators from the U.S. Heartland to make this voyage to Mexico to immerse themselves in this study abroad course on Mexican schooling, culture, and language? As we will see, Nebraska, like other New Latino Diaspora states, has seen dramatic increases in its Latino population and preparing for/reacting to this shift was one rationale for the travel-study in Guadalajara.

Echoing a pattern found in locales throughout the American Midwest and South, recent immigration had caused Nebraska's Latino population to jump approximately 150% between 1990 and 2000. Standing at just 40,000 in 1990, there were a reported 94,425 Latinos according to the 2000 census, a bit less than 6% of the overall state population, with 75% of Nebraska's Latinos reporting that they were of Mexican origin (U.S. Census Bureau, 2010).

By 2006, the U.S. Census Bureau was estimating that 7.4% of Nebraska's population was Hispanic (Drozd & Deichert, 2007). At the same time, the Nebraska Department of Education identified 18 school districts that were at least 20% Hispanic (including four that were majority Hispanic) and counted 35,107 Hispanic students overall in 2006–07, constituting 12.2% enrollment (Nebraska Department of Education, 2007). By 2012–13, Nebraska's Hispanic public school enrollment had grown to 51,017, constituting 16.8% of total enrollment (Nebraska Department of Education, 2013).

Nonetheless, educators in the state—99% of whom in 2006–07 were not Latino (Nebraska Department of Education, 2007)—had little experience and few cultural and linguistic reference points to guide instructional efforts in meeting the educational needs of this new population. Thus, the rapid influx of a student population with little previous representation in the state's enrollment led to a range of mostly improvisational educational efforts to meet this competency gap (Hamann & Harklau, 2010).

Each of my travel mates on the program was already working with or expecting to work with this burgeoning Mexican immigrant population. This corresponded well with the intended goals of this professional development experience to familiarize these educators with the culture and premigration education institutions and communities of Mexican newcomer students, to better recognize bias and discrimination in their professional and personal lives, and to reflect upon the accommodation of diversity in their future professional practice. The program, known as *Mexican Schools and Communities*, was coordinated as a partnership between a public university in Nebraska and a private religious university in western Mexico and was an example of a growing phenomenon of binational programs loosely grouped together as U.S.→Mexico Binational Teacher Exchanges (Hamann, 2008; see also Richardson Bruna [this volume]).[1]

This chapter tells the story of these program participants, their time in Mexico, and what they felt they gained from this immersion experience in relation to their work as educators in Nebraska. With a special focus on the reflections of three purposively selected teacher participants in the program, I argue that these types of professional development programs possess great potential for developing cross-cultural knowledge, empathy, and an awareness of biases based upon ethnicity and national origin. Nevertheless, it remains unclear if and how they impact future teaching practice and the schooling processes and outcomes of the Mexican-origin students whom they intentionally if indirectly target. Furthermore, as designed, programs like these often have some self-induced limitations to achieving their ambitious objectives.

The results of this study are framed within a larger contextual overview of the persistent underschooling of Mexican-origin students in the New Latino Diaspora and the rising number of U.S.-Mexico travel study efforts (Hamann, 2008). I will also address the state of the knowledge on the impact of teacher belief systems on Latino/a students and the theory of change that guides the work of the Community and Schools in Guadalajara Program.

The Rise of U.S.→Mexico Binational Teacher Exchanges

Mexican-descent students have not been served well by U.S. schools. Throughout their educational trajectory, Latinos (2/3 of whom are of Mexican-origin) have long stood at or near the bottom of the U.S. education system's achievement divide (Carter, 1970; Gándara & Contreras, 2010; Garcia, 2001; Organization for Economic Cooperation and Development, 2003; Valdés, 2001; Valenzuela, 2005). The persistent underschooling of Mexican-origin children has not been lost on education policymakers. Indeed, reform efforts aimed at improving the educational lot of this population have existed for many decades (Blanton, 2004; San Miguel, 2004), and the current era is no different. In fact, No Child Left Behind of 2002 devotes an entire Title to the educational needs of immigrant students and English Language Learners.

Concurrent with the dominant discourse of need and needed action, U.S. →Mexico binational teacher exchanges increasingly sprang up at the turn of the 21st century within traditional Mexican receiving states such as California, Texas, and Arizona and also the newer receiving states of Oregon, Nebraska, Georgia, and Kentucky (Hamann, 2003; Sawyer, 2006). These programs—usually partnerships between U.S. universities, government agencies, private organizations, and a corresponding Mexican partner—send aspiring and in-service U.S. teachers, administrators, and school psychologists to Mexico for first-hand experiences. Within such programs, participants typically take courses in the Spanish language, Mexican culture, migration, and intercultural education while making guided visits to Mexican schools and migrant sending communities. The commonly articulated logic of these programs is that through such experiences U.S. educators will return better able to serve the cultural, linguistic, and academic needs of Mexican and other Latino student populations (Hamann, 2003, 2008; Sawyer, 2006).

Given the relative novelty of widespread U.S.-Mexico binational teacher exchanges, it is not surprising that there is a dearth of academic scholarship that describes them or assesses their impact. One of the first steps in generating this knowledge base occurred during the late 1990s when several programs collected survey data to assess the satisfaction of participants. Within these accounts, many educators reported having experiences that were "life-changing" and "highly satisfying" (L. Cantu, personal communication, January 6, 2006; Licón, 2003; E. Mitchell, personal communication, January 4, 2006), though scant further explication was offered regarding how this specifically was so.

One of the most in-depth studies of the impact of U.S.-Mexico Binational Teacher Exchanges to date is found in Hamann's (2003) account of the *Georgia Project*, a joint venture that ran for a decade between a public-private association in Dalton, Georgia and the University of Monterrey, Mexico. Based upon post-participation questionnaires and observation of 21 teachers upon return from Mexico during the summer of 1997, Hamann found that teacher participants from Georgia nearly universally claimed a greater empathy for the language struggles of their students, increased cultural sensitivity, and a complex set of first-hand impressions of both the positive and negative dimensions of Mexican schools and society. Yet he also noted that the lasting impact of this experience for many participants was hindered by a lack of sustained support.

Another noteworthy recent study was one conducted by two program operators also based in Georgia. McLaughlin and Allexsaht-Snider (2007) focused their qualitative research (based upon participant journal entries) on the *process* of transformation rather than its *content*. They proposed a four-stage transformation continuum for U.S. →Mexico binational teacher exchange participants that progressed in the order of "Discomfort" to "Dissonance" to "Disillusion," and finally to "Discovery."

While this previous literature has yielded some important preliminary insights into the impact of U.S.-Mexico Binational Teacher Exchanges and has made a strong case that such programs are worthy of further empirical study, it is limited in some important ways. For one, none of these studies explored teacher beliefs and understandings *prior* to program participation, thus limiting the analytic possibilities of discerning individual change over time.

Teacher Beliefs and Latino Student Outcomes

In a seminal work, Good (1987) synthesized 2 decades worth of research on teacher beliefs and expectations and their effect on classroom interactions and ultimately student outcomes. He described two types of teacher expectation effects revealed in previous research: *self-fulfilling prophecy effect* and *sustaining expectation effect*. The former effect is the phenomenon by which "an originally erroneous expectation leads to behavior that causes the behavior to become true, while the latter occurs when teachers expect students to sustain previously developed patterns, to the point that teachers take these behavior patterns for granted and fail to see and capitalize on changes in student potential" (Good, 1987, p. 32). Hence, the author concludes based upon the research record that teacher beliefs and expectations have important implications for teacher interaction with students, which in turn affect student outcomes. Good (1987) further notes that minority status can alternately "insulate" or "exacerbate" a student's susceptibility to teacher expectations depending upon teacher beliefs.

Many scholars have found that for Latinos, African American, Native Americans, and some Asian American student populations (e.g., Hmong), teachers have dramatically reduced expectations for these students as compared to middle-class White students, which can be manifest in classroom interactions with learners getting less total instructional attention, being called on less frequently or less often encouraged to continue to develop intellectual thinking less often, being criticized more and praised less, receiving fewer direct responses to their questions and comments, and being disciplined more often and severely than White students (U.S. Civil Rights Commision, 1973, as cited in Gay, 2000). In the case of Latinos, researchers for decades have demonstrated that mainstream educators tend to have very low expectations for and hold negative stereotyped beliefs of this student population (Buriel, 1983; Valenzuela, 1999).

Ashton and Webb (1986 as cited in Gay, 2000) found a strong correlation between teacher self-efficacy and expectations. Ruiz de Velasco and Fix (2000), in their study of secondary teachers serving immigrant students nationwide, found teachers with less knowledge of the cultural and linguistic needs of this population had lower expectations for their academic potential. Thus, the lack of teacher preparation to work with this population could very well lead to a chain reaction of low teacher expectations, poor teacher-student interaction, and ultimately diminished student performance.

A Particular Program's Theory of Change

According to the Nebraska Department of Education (2007), every 5 years since 1990, the proportion of Hispanic (primarily recent immigrant) students in Nebraska's public schools has nearly doubled. According to the creator of the exchange program I studied, schools suddenly serving large number of mostly Mexican Latino immigrant students faced particular challenges. In a published study not cited here to preserve her anonymity, she wrote, "In addition to the obvious language barrier, there are striking differences in cultural expectations that, if unacknowledged, can limit the responsiveness of community services to Hispanic families." She also wrote "for example, children in Mexican schools frequently wear uniforms, carry small notebooks called 'cuadernos' back and forth between school and home with their homework assignments, learn mathematics in a different way, and follow very different academic schedules." So the exchange's leader's diagnosis of the problem of Latino learning in Nebraska schools corroborates with research that speaks to the importance of educators possessing cultural knowledge and competence.

In terms of building educator "cultural competence," the program's theory of change rested on the experiential notion that "cultural competence will emerge more readily from actual cultural experiences than from lecture, reading literature or watching film," and that this will be attained through participants engaging in "cultural encounters with Mexican communities, schools, and families." The program's founding document continues: "We believe that international experiences provide students with unique insights that will be invaluable in their future practice as community service providers, teachers, school psychologists, or administrators in diverse Nebraska communities."

The program, which was conceived in 2002, first enacted in 2004, and in its second iteration when I studied it, was designed primarily for graduate students (9 of the 11 participants were either graduate or post-baccalaureate extension students, although two undergraduates were also accepted under special conditions). Participants enrolled, pending review of their application materials, on a first come, first-serve basis. Cost for the trip was just $1,400 (including airfare, room and board, and transportation), plus tuition. Most of the graduate students had tuition paid for through their assistantships with one receiving a scholarship from the university's International Affairs Office for the entire cost of the trip.

Research Methodology

I collected data for this study over the course my 2-week participation in the "Mexican Schools and Communities" during the summer of 2006 and a 1-week pre-program visit to Nebraska. During my stay in Nebraska, I took daily field notes based upon observations of major Latino receiving communities and when possible, the surrounding communities of the schools where participants worked, as well as informal conversations with both the interview participants and other educators serving the Latino community. In Mexico, I took field notes based upon my experience as a participant in the program, which included observation of structured (classes, fieldtrips) and informal (time with host families, free time in public) program activities as well as informal conversations with program administrators, implementers, Mexican instructors, and host families. The program also administered a survey to all participants at the completion of the 2 weeks, the findings from which I have considered in arriving to my own conclusions. To discern program rationale and main objectives, I have additionally studied official course documents including the syllabus, brochures, and the original project proposal. I had never traveled to Nebraska prior to this research, but I had visited Guadalajara previously for work and as a tourist.

As many scholars have bemoaned, teacher voices are often absent from research and policy reform efforts (Cochran-Smith & Lytle, 2009; Delpit, 1995; González et al., 1995; Latta & Wunder, 2012; Villegas-Reimers & Reimers, 1995). The present case study embeds the stance that teacher descriptions of their experiences and the meanings they ascribe to their changing beliefs and knowledge are crucial to understanding the processes of transformation within professional development programs. For this reason, I selected a sample of three focal teachers whom I shadowed and with whom I conducted three in-depth, semistructured interviews. The first of these interviews was held in Nebraska in late May shortly before the departure to Mexico; the second at roughly the midpoint of the 16-day program; and the third during the last 2 days of the Mexico visit.

Interviews initially focused on biographical information, reasons for program participation, expectations, previous experience working with Mexican immigrant students, and beliefs as to the academic strengths and challenges of this group. Subsequent interviews focused on eliciting teacher description of their participation in program activities and how and if this was shaping or adding to knowledge and beliefs about their Mexican immigrant students. The final interview paid special attention to how participants intended to apply these new insights and understanding to their future teaching practice. One year after participation, the teachers in the focal group were asked to complete a follow up questionnaire in which they were asked to describe their lasting impressions of the program and its impact on their teaching practice.

"The Mexican Schools and Communities Program:" A Description

The Mexican Schools and Communities Program provided an array of formal and informal activities aimed at meeting the program's objectives. All participants in the program (including myself) were provided lodging with host families in the middle class community of Zapopan (part of the sprawling metropolis of Guadalajara, Mexico's second largest city). Classes were held at a private Jesuit university serving a primarily middle-class student body and taught by members of the university's faculty. Every Monday and Wednesday morning, students attended a 2-hour Spanish conversation class followed by a Migration course in the afternoon in which students were provided data on emigration rates from the different states of the Republic as well as the most common hypotheses as to why Mexicans migrated internally and internationally at such high rates (Field Notes, June 4, 2006).

Tuesdays and Thursdays were reserved for visits to an economically marginal Guadalajara suburb. This field site was selected because it was a community known to have a high international migration rate. The first week of excursions to this suburb were devoted to school visits. On the first Tuesday, we visited the community's main primary school and on Thursday, the pre-school. Each of these visits involved a period of classroom observations, in-class interactions with students and teachers, and an informational meeting with school directors. The Tuesday of the second week was spent in discussion with a team of community psychologists serving the neighborhood, and the Thursday in a community tour with a nun who was an ardent advocate for the community (Field notes June 4 and June 11, 2006). Afternoons, evenings, and weekends were devoted to a variety of cultural and recreational activities designed to augment participant appreciation of Mexican culture and heritage and in some instances simply to provide a breather.

Program Impact: Through the Eyes of Three Nebraska Educators

I first got to know Annabelle, Mary, and Jessica (pseudonyms) during my pre-program visit to Nebraska in the spring of 2006. I chose these three women as focal educators because they and one other were the only experienced teachers on the trip who had previously worked with Mexican-origin students.[2] As I was most interested in understanding the impact of U.S.→Mexico teacher exchanges on in-service educators with previously formed impressions of the Mexican-origin students, they were a natural fit. While they varied in terms of background, age, experience, and levels taught, their status as middle-class female educators between the ages of 35 and 56 from different parts of Nebraska meant in some ways they matched most of Nebraska's teaching force, although experience with nontouristic travel abroad, efforts to learn Spanish, and curiosity about Mexico likely made them somewhat atypical when compared to the "average" Nebraskan educator.

Mary

Mary, a 35 year-old high school Spanish teacher with 10 years of service had negotiated a sink-or-swim immersion in Latin America during a two-year Peace Corps placement in Costa Rica in the mid-1990s. Judging by her fluent, well pronounced, and grammatically nearly flawless Spanish, her time in Costa Rica had endowed her with excellent Spanish. This experience also seemed to have inspired an affinity and knowledge of Latinos living in the United States as she spoke enthusiastically and knowledgeably to me of Omaha and eastern Nebraska's different Latino populations, the push and pull factors leading to their migration, and the challenges facing them within the receiving context. Perhaps owing to these language skills and the affinity she gained with the culture during her time in Costa Rica, Mary had also established a special bond with the 6%—and growing—Latino population at her high school on the outskirts of Omaha:

> We have a growing Hispanic population and I've kind of taken the Hispanics under my wing, and started a Latino Leaders group. And so I've been really working with the Latino population trying to get them to understand what opportunities are available to them, that college is available to them.

Mary's involvement with Nebraska's Latino community also extended into her personal life. Through her contacts in Omaha's Mexican immigrant community, she met and eventually married an undocumented construction worker from Veracruz named Hector. She and Hector, despite having been married for 3 years, were separated at the time of my research as they awaited the outcome of the U.S.'s labyrinthine Green Card application process. This experience helped make Mary very aware of the challenges facing Nebraska's Latino immigrant communities and the lives of the families she served at her high school. Since our first meeting in Nebraska in May 2006, I have regularly received e-mails from Mary detailing events in support of immigrant rights.

Mary's high level of personal and professional involvement with Latino communities both in Costa Rica and Nebraska had also infiltrated into her sense of identity. When I asked her whether she identified with her German and Danish-descent past, she responded:

> No, I don't know any ... you know, that's funny. I grew up not knowing anything. I mean I know sauerkraut is something from Germany and I hate ... I can't even stand the smell of it. But yeah, I don't identify with it at all. In fact, to tell you the truth, I think I ... I think I'm Latino in *el corazón*!

Intrigued by this response, I asked Mary what she identified as, ethnically and nationally:

> United Statesian. *Estadounidense*. Yeah. Although ... this is funny ... I mean
> we're laughing about this, but my Latino students made me an honorary
> Latino. And I think my family in Costa Rica made me an honorary Costa
> Rican. And now my family in Vera Cruz, or my husband's family, made me
> an honorary *jarocha*. So ... I guess I'm adopted.

While it is possible that Mary underestimated the impact of her more
distant immigrant past in creating a sense of sympathy and identification
with today's Latino immigrants, what is clear is that Mary had succeeded
in crossing cultural borders. Her goals for the program involved adding
greater depth and complexity to her understanding of Mexican communities and culture:

> Well, I was reading ... that this area where we're going, near Guadalajara, in
> Jalisco, there's a high percentage of migrants or high percentage of people
> leaving that area to go to the States to work ... I thought that was kind of in-
> teresting, that there's a high percentage from that area coming...it sounded
> like to Nebraska or maybe to the Lincoln area. Yeah, and so I guess when
> I'm talking with my kids, if I've actually been from their home state or from
> their ... maybe even their home town, I think that helps provide a connec-
> tion between the kids and the teacher or administrator or whoever it is that's
> going on this trip.... It helps to understand the economic situation in that
> area, what's available as far as farming and work, and what kind of environ-
> ment they grew up in.

Here, Mary displayed an advanced (and pretrip) knowledge of the great
heterogeneity of the group monolithically referred to as "Mexican." She
understood that Mexicans migrate in networks from specific sending contexts to specific receiving communities and that different regions of Mexico
have distinct cultures, circumstances, and ways of life that are transferred
to their U.S. host communities. She was also aware that speaking Spanish
and knowing the superficial—or stereotypical—aspects of Mexican culture
were not enough to profoundly connect with Mexican-origin students in
the United States. As we will see, the program experience, allowed her to
build upon this previous knowledge.

Annabelle

Annabelle was a 46-year-old veteran math teacher from the rural western
panhandle of the state. Though growing up in a largely White environment, Annabelle's multicultural sensibilities were raised during her more
than 20 years teaching high school math on the outskirts of the Pine Ridge
Indian reservation on the Nebraska-South Dakota border and through a
Fulbright Exchange to study schooling in Japan. She described these experiences as instilling in her an awareness of cultural pluralism and a fierce

opposition to what she describes as "one-size-fits-all" educational practices. A doctoral student in math education at the time of the trip, she credited her coursework in Multicultural Education for instilling in her recognition of the necessity of differentiated instruction for diverse learners.

While quite knowledgeable about intricacies of Native American cultures, Annabelle had much less exposure to Latinos. She spoke only rudimentary Spanish and talked about Mexico from the perspective of an outsider, in sharp contrast to Mary. She acknowledged with some shame her first exposure to Latinos came through the pejorative and racially tinged jokes of family members living in close proximity to Mexican migrants:

> A: My aunt lived in Mitchell Nebraska, my aunt and uncle, which is also, you know, like 13 miles from Scottsbluff. And they would make jokes, and I guess ... I'm not, you know, I am so much more cognizant of it now than I probably was then. But you know, about "attention Kmart shoppers," you know, the ... it was always the Hispanics, because of the fact that there was a huge concentration of Hispanics in the Gering, Scottsbluff, Mitchell rural area. And, you know, they would sometimes call them *Beaners*, you know, that was one of the ... I guess slang words for Hispanics at the time.
>
> AS: The "attention KMART shoppers?" I'm not familiar with that.
>
> A: It was just the blue-light special, you know, and stuff. And just because at the time, you know, well, it's like now too, but it's because of prices, low prices. You know, that's ... there were a lot of Hispanics that shopped at Kmart, just like now at Wal-Mart. You know, but that's just the way it is, you know, their lower prices and I just remember some reference to that. I'm not a good joke teller to begin with, but I just remember something on that line, that ... It was a Hispanic reference.

Here, Annabelle's multicultural awareness acquired as an adult comes into tension with the beliefs and actions of her childhood. Even in the present tense, while she expresses very tolerant attitudes towards Latinos, she nevertheless—in contrast to Mary—speaks of them as "the other." Later, she inaccurately stated that undocumented immigrants do not pay taxes and throughout used the terms "Hispanic" and "illegal immigrant" interchangeably.

Here, Annabelle describes her goals in the realm of intercultural competence:

> I think I hope to learn more about the culture ... and how students are addressed. Matter of fact, I got to attend an excellence in education conference

at the end of March and Carmen Tafoya, I think, she gave one of the keynotes and she talked about the mispronunciation of names, you know, like "Tere," and you know, the teacher would say "Terry," you know, and no it's ... you know, "Te-re." And I think that teachers need to be aware of that kind of stuff. It's ... don't try to make them into your mold.

Interestingly, during the Guadalajara experience, Annabelle discovered unexpected levels of commonality between her rural Nebraska roots and the Mexican families she met in Guadalajara—a revelation that opened the door to her developing greater cross-cultural understanding.

Jessica

In her mid-50s, Jessica was the senior member of the focal teacher group. Born and raised in Missouri and having moved to Nebraska as a young adult, Jessica had worked for more than 2 decades as an educator and, at the time of the trip, was a community outreach coordinator and board member for an afterschool program in a rural community in central Nebraska. Of the three educators I profiled, Jessica was by far the one who was serving the largest number of Latino students as the afterschool program's enrollment varied from 40–60% Hispanic depending upon the time of year.

Though speaking only the most rudimentary Spanish, she had spent parts of the past three summers in Mexico on service trips and in language schools. From these visits, she had taken note of harsh poverty that afflicts many parts of rural Mexico:

Well, mainly, I think, succinctly put, they ... Mexicans are a conquered people. They've been conquered and conquered and conquered and conquered. And so the resources have been stripped. I think their hope in government has been stripped. But their pride is in their work ethic, if there is work available. Well, I think that they ... they rely on each other, their families, and they rely on the church. And if they have crisis, or they have need, or whatever, those are the first two places, you know, that they seek help.

Jessica seemed to have a one-dimensional yet sympathetic view of Mexican life. In Nebraska, she saw herself as an advocate for Latino immigrants. In addition to participating in the spring 2006 immigrant marches (that were part of the unsuccessful rallying for President Bush's attempt at comprehensive immigration reform), she criticized what she saw as the rigidity of her fellow educators in meeting the needs of the emergent Latino population:

As an advisory board member of that group, and indeed an early founder of the group, I had been a little dismayed that I cannot get the board to see that you can't run the program, you know, like status quo, how we've always done it, because we have a different clientele. And, you know, they don't necessarily buy into the same things that our kids have bought into before.

Hence, similar to Annabelle, Jessica's views of Nebraska Latinos were tolerant and advocacy-oriented. Also similar to Annabelle, but in contrast to Mary, her views and attitudes of the group still came from an outsider perspective seeking entry into a still mysterious cultural universe. In putting forth what she hoped to gain in terms of cultural competence from the exchange program, she describes the cultural pitfalls she had encountered with the population within the seemingly mundane activity of snack time:

> I looked at the snacks that we provide, a lot of times the Hispanic kids don't eat the snacks. So it kind of got me to getting a group of them together and say "hey, what do you think?" And they said well, you know, like a course … we like chips and salsa. Well, that's pretty messy, you know, for an after school program or whatever, but they don't like Oreos, you know.… But you know, I said okay, so what would you like for a snack. You know, let's work on that. Maybe we'll have soul food one day and you know, we'll call it Cinco de Mayo Day or whatever, you know. And so the kids really kind of liked that idea. But then what I found was they didn't … they meaning the Hispanic kids, really didn't want to be involved in planning it or making it. If it was there, they'd eat it. And so it just … I'm missing some piece here in knowing how to engage these immigrant youth. I don't know where the hook is, you know, for this population

Here we see that Jessica has struggled in her work with Latino youth in her program, and that part of her rationale for participation in the program was a desire to overcome the cultural divide she felt between herself and these students. As we will see, the cultural immersion provided by the Guadalajara program made her both more aware of her commonality with those she meets in Mexico as well as the cultural biases she has held against the group.

Deepened Understanding of the Cultural Background of Mexican-Origin Families

Annabelle and Jessica: Discomfort in a Strange Land

Roommates with the same host family, Annabelle and Jessica spent a great deal of time together during the Guadalajara experience. The two blonde and blue-eyed Nebraskans brought their Midwest friendliness to the streets of Zapopan. As they walked between their host family's home and the university each afternoon, they greeted all passersby with smiles and greetings of *hola, buenos días* and the like. (It is common in Nebraska to greet passersby on the sidewalk, so this likely was continuation of a social habit rather than a new one for a new place.) It was in these interactions—or sometimes lack thereof—that the women's foreignness became painfully apparent to them. According to Annabelle:

> Jessica and I when we'd walk to [the host university] and then we'd walked around after, but anyway, she's friendly, I'm friendly. I mean that's just it. I'll always say, "Buenos dias," "Buenas tardes," "Buenas noches" "Hola," or whatever. But for the most part, the people that are out on the streets, most of them do speak, but some of them would rather, I mean keep their eyes down. And if we speak first, they most generally will speak. But I don't think that they, with the exception of last evening, that they are the ones that initiate the conversation.

Jessica described other incidents in which she and Annabelle felt singled out as foreigners (although the mismatch may well be between big city and small-town experiences, rather than U.S. versus Mexico):

> J: Annabelle and I get the stereotype look quite frequently, you know, dumb gringos.
>
> A.S.: In response to what?
>
> J: Oh, like, if we're at the convenience store, Oxxo, it's hurry up and go. So here we have the gringos standing here going.... And the people are standing there going—you're just handing your money to the cashier, you know, and they're just staring like get out of the way. So, we get that. I really felt segregated last Sunday in Tlaquepaque when we went into the restaurant for lunch and there was kind of an upper patio. And after we'd been there for a little while, I kind of looked around and I said, do you know there are only Americans up here?... And so I thought, well, I wonder if we're going to get to see maria-chis or whatever, so I just went down there and kind of stood and people would kind of look at me like, you know, like I was infringing on their space

Despite the discomfort these encounters brought, it seemed that they also presented opportunities for learning. They both professed—perhaps with some hyperbole given how different their lives still were from minorities in the United States—having gained a sense of empathy for ethnic minorities in the U.S. from having the shoe put on the other foot.

> Annabelle: I think this whole trip has given you a perspective to see

what other people, the minority feel like too.

A.S.: Say more about that.

A: Just the fact that some people will talk to you first. Otherwise, most will ignore you, will look the other way or else will just walk straight ahead, which I've heard that that's the case, you know, with some minorities. Well, [some White people] just not acknowledge the colored people. So. And that's kind of how I felt a little bit. But then I don't know. I'll always try to be happy and be nice. If they don't want to say hello back or whatever, that's their issue.

Despite these uncomfortable encounters in which she felt "othered," Annabelle nevertheless found connection with the unity of Mexican family life, particularly with host mother Lupita and her family:

AS: So I want to talk a little bit more about what the family life has been for you here in Mexico, in Guadalajara, living with the family.

Annabelle: I think it's really been good for me. When I went out to DC too, that was the first thing I missed was being around my family. I couldn't wait to get away. You know, my mom and dad lived in the same town as I did and such. But now I realize how much I missed them, but then here it even amplified that because of the fact that Lupita, her son and her daughter live in Guadalajara, well all three of them live in Guadalajara, and Ernesto I guess lives upstairs still. So there's always been family there with her. And also a couple nights ago she stayed with her daughter's children because her daughter went someplace and so she kind of babysat. And it made me think back again to how important family is. And that's what I really like about this. And all that I have accomplished, I would have never accomplished if it wasn't for my family and having that strong support there.

Having as background a strong and unified family of her own, Annabelle comes to appreciate this facet of her host family's organization, one that she perceived to be common in Mexico. At my prompting, our conversation segued into considering implications of Mexican family unity for educator practice in the U.S. and Annabelle described how middle-school teachers she had interviewed "will say you know there's no family support. They don't have it." Then Annabelle critiqued those teachers' explanations:

Annabelle: I think it's a cop out. I do think it is.

> A.S.: Cop out on the part of whom?
>
> A: Of the seventh and eighth grade [Nebraska] teachers...

Annabelle then critiqued Nebraska teachers misguided equal treatment—"Well, everybody gets the same assignment. Everybody you know has the same expectations rather than thinking of scaffolding or doing things on that and knowing more about their culture"—before returning her attention to parallels between her challenges negotiating Guadalajara and Mexican newcomer parents' challenges negotiating Nebraska schools:

> A: Well, I can see—you know because I've heard again, going back to my little interview that I did, that when parents can't speak the language, they feel uncomfortable trying to communicate with the teachers who are in the other language. I think they feel like, they're perhaps inferior or something, and they shouldn't feel that way. But—but I know that myself as I have had to do hand gestures with (laughing) or who can speak Spanish better than I can. So, I can just kind of put myself in their shoes, I guess.
>
> A.S.: And, could you do that before?
>
> A: No. No. Just because I'm such an experiential learner, you know, you can think about it. But, until you really are immersed in it and have to experience it, then—then it connects from that's how I learn everything, so.

Here, the identification Annabelle felt with Mexican families and her first-hand awareness of the perils of managing language barriers (both from the trip) were directly linked to her experience in Nebraska schools and this led her to make recommendations regarding what better practice in Nebraska might entail.

Mary: "It's kind of like a melting pot here, in Mexico"

Unsurprisingly given her previously attained levels of comfort with Latinos, Mary did not experience as steep a learning curve as Annabelle and Jessica. Nevertheless, she acquired important knowledge from the visit that provided greater complexity and nuance to her pre-existing knowledge set on cultural matters. Mary declined the program's offer of lodging in middle-class Zapopan to stay with her husband's cousin in working-class Lomas de la Primavera. Taking advantage of this insider status and her strong Spanish language skills, Mary learned that the Guadalajara area was a prominent receiving context for internal migrants, which provided her a greater understanding of the complexities of Mexican society:

M: From what I've heard, there are people here from other states that have moved here and, for the same reason that happens in any place, the same reason it happens in Nebraska, you know, Guadalajara is the second largest city, so if there's no work on the farm, you go to the city and, so, where would that city be? Mexico City, Guadalajara, Monterrey, one of the big cities…. [Y]ou have people who aren't necessarily from Guadalajara that come from many different places. For example, you might come to this house and you might get food from Veracruz, you know? And there might be some traditions or music that's listened to there that's traditional from that state, and you might go to the next-door neighbor and have a completely different experience. It might even happen with language. And so, in a school, the teacher might have to deal with that, with different people coming from different places. So, it's kind of like a little melting pot right here, you know, within Mexico.

Reflecting upon how educational practice should accommodate Mexican-origin students, Mary applied some of the lessons on Mexican heterogeneity that she had learned on the trip:

The other thing was talking about students who come to the country and have limited formal education here and how they are different from students who maybe had formal education. They can adapt and learn English much quicker than students who didn't have any education here. So, I think that there needs to be a better process in the U.S. to evaluate those students, and not just throw them in ESL or the wrong Spanish class. Well, let's say this kid comes from the mountains of Mayan country and doesn't even know Spanish very well themselves, they probably need to be in Spanish I. Or, let's say, they've been living in California for 10 years and have never taken a Spanish class in their life. They just speak it on the street and watch movies, they need to start with Spanish I. How about if a student who's in 10th grade and just recently came from Mexico, probably they could be in II or III, you know? We don't want to put them too high because we want them to be able to get the English, too, but there's no reason why they have to be in I and learn *Hola* ... you know what I mean?

It was with this same mindfulness of heterogeneity and complexity that Mary considered the question of having Latino teachers for Latino students:

I think that all students should have teachers from different races. You know, honestly I don't think I had any teachers that weren't Anglo. Where I went to high school, my whole school was white. But yeah, I think it's really important for us to be exposed to other populations. Actually I remember going to Kansas City, we walked into this McDonalds and were the only white family there. And I thought, 'Wow, this is different.' I wasn't freaked out about it; it just felt different. It was different, because that's not what I grew up like in southeast Nebraska at all.

Mary concludes that it is not enough simply to have same-ethnicity teachers; a complex and pluralistic society requires students to be exposed to teachers of multiple backgrounds.

Discussion and Implications

In the fall of 2007, I had the opportunity to follow up with Mary, Annabelle, and Jessica and inquire as to how they thought about their Mexico travel-study more than a year later. With the passage of time, they all seemed to hold on to at least one piece of learning they had acquired during their two-week stay in Mexico and they described varied success in executing plans they had made for applying that experience to their U.S. practice, schools, and lives.

Like with binational exchange teachers described by Hamann (2003), for Mary, the relative resource deprivation of Mexican schools (as compared to those in the United States) and the sacrifices Mexican migrants make to come to the U.S. is what remained most salient:

> Our students should be more appreciative of what they have! I continue to think about families who do everything they can to survive and the sacrifices they make, such as leaving their homes and being separated from their families.

In terms of what she had been able to apply from her Guadalajara experience, she reported:

> I have not been able to do some type of workshop regarding education in Mexico for my colleagues like I'd hoped. I started a new Latino Leaders group. This year I wrote a letter to my colleagues, so they can understand what the group is about. I also gave a letter to each member for their parents in English and Spanish. Hopefully these efforts to reach out will help bridge gaps within the school and between the school and community, as well as promote awareness and cultural understanding.

Annabelle's takeaways related to the reinforcement of the importance of family she had felt in Mexico and the value of multilingualism: "Family and survival are more important than material items. Living in close proximity to your family is more desirous than moving away to make more money. I'll never forget the importance of being bilingual or multilingual."

In terms of how she had applied the Guadalajara experience, she stated:

I often relate the importance of family, which I learned from the trip. In my research with Native Americans this same trend holds true. I think a lot about the European conquerors forcing their "better ways" on the indigenous peoples of North America. Centuries later, some of these mistakes are being rectified, such as native language learning, but is it too late? I joined the mathematics organization *Todos*, which is dedicated to the mathematical learning of all students, particularly English Language Learners. I also have practiced with my Spanish tapes.

For Jessica, the lasting impact of the program tied to recognizing both commonalities and differences between youth in the United States and Mexico:

I reflect upon the fact that kids are kids wherever you go. Some have more, some have less, but they all have spirit and a natural behavior that marks childhood. I look at the level of poverty and make comparisons between U.S. poverty-level families and those in [Guadalajara]. I have told the story repeatedly about children having to go to school only until they are 14 and then the opportunities that don't exist for them if they do leave school at 14.

In terms of applying trip lessons, Jessica reported both triumphs and difficulties in sharing the antibias reflections from the experience:

I have used my knowledge with my Extension Colleagues as a member of the Diversity Team and I am considered as one of the most informed Educators at [university] Extension. I have tried to make people understand why *they* park their cars in the front yard and why they "all live together" and remind people of our own ancestors and how they did the same thing. They always say, but they learned English. I have to say, "Not right away." I have to remind them that the German Reformed Lutheran Church had services in GERMAN of all THINGS until about 7 years ago in our area. We have Danish Days and Scandinavian days and ... but if a Mexican family raises a flag—they are ungrateful!? People don't want to hear it!!! They want to be biased, prejudiced and ignorant! (italics and capitals original)

As we have seen from analysis of the Guadalajara-based data and the follow-up interviews with the three focal educators, the travel-study indeed catalyzed important elements of growth within its participants, some of which remained quite salient more than a year later. The 1-year follow up also provides some cautions about the long-term impact of the program.

Cross-Cultural Awareness

One area in which each of the focal educators claimed growth was in gaining a deepened understanding—albeit in distinct ways—of the cultural background of Mexican-origin families. For Mary, who came to the program with considerably more background knowledge than the other two, this growth added an additional piece to an already intricate puzzle. For Annabelle and Jessica the new impressions gained were preliminary breakthroughs—analogous to laying out the puzzle's frame. Collectively, their learning suggests that teachers with varying knowledge of Mexico and Mexican peoples might all benefit from programs like this.

The activities most useful towards the attainment of these new understandings were the home stays, the migration course, and the visits to the working class community. As we saw, participants learned a great deal about the structure and norms of the Mexican families with whom they resided, while better familiarizing themselves with the complexities of Mexican migration—perhaps most importantly, the push factors and costs behind migration. The importance of such knowledge is twofold: first, borrowing from the Funds of Knowledge theorists (González et al., 1995), a better understanding of family structure and practices helps educators create classroom routines and instruction that build upon what a child already knows and norms to which they are accustomed. Second, knowledge of the migration experience potentially creates empathy for educators of the children and families.

Limitations to how this competency was pursued during the exchange included the fact that home stays were with families of the Mexican middle class—dissimilar in many ways from the working-class backgrounds of most migrants to Nebraska. Also, work by Reese (2002) comparing parenting practices of Mexicans in "el Norte" versus in Mexico demonstrated that migration transforms cultural norms in important ways, while work by Portes and Rumbaut (2001) argues that Mexican migrants are in many ways nonrepresentative of those who stay behind. Thus, one must be careful when comparing Mexicans in Mexico to those who have migrated north. Greater readings on this subject (such as the one just cited) as well as group discussions on the impressions participants had and how they intended to extrapolate them to the United States context would have been beneficial in meeting this competency.

Awareness of Bias

As we saw, especially in the examples of Annabelle and Jessica, the experience of being a foreigner and limited speaker of Spanish in Mexico (even for 2 weeks) raised participants' awareness of biases based upon ethnicity and national origin. Observing Mexican people within the Mexican cultural context also made Jessica more aware of the relativity of cultural values and how educational institutions and practices are infused with values that can be at odds with the funds of knowledge Mexican-origin students bring to school. The implications for the development of such understandings are significant. Educators aware of these biases are more likely to seek ways to bridge home and school culture while attempting to avoid the making of cultural value statements that provide negative social mirroring (Suárez-Orozco & Suárez-Orozco, 2001) to Mexican-origin students. Similarly, teachers with awareness of cultural bias are conceivably more ready to question prejudice in terms of their own beliefs and expectations towards students and how this is conveyed in their practice. As we know from the work of Good (1987), Buriel (1983), and Hamann and Reeves (2012), teacher beliefs and expectations can have important implications for teacher-student interactions as well as for student performance, especially in the case of Latino students.

In terms of bringing needed teaching competencies back to the new Latino diaspora, the exchange program was limited in some important ways. For one, while 2 weeks was sufficient to develop some empathy about biases minorities face in U.S. life, it certainly pales in comparison to being faced with discrimination over many years or a lifetime as Mexican immigrants face in the United States. Despite the discomfort program participants may have felt over the course of the 2 weeks, they were also well aware that they would soon be returning home to the comforts of their American life, both materially and culturally speaking. Another limitation (also cited by Hamann [2003]) was the lack of opportunities to critically reflect on impressions during and particularly after the program. This sometimes left participants with beliefs counter to the goals of the program. For example, while not the case with these focal teachers, I overheard other participants within private chatter voicing highly critical—and unchallenged—views of Mexican culture.

Perceived Application to Future Teaching Practice

Literature on the teaching profession and teacher professional development would suggest that the creation of reflective space for teachers—as the exchange program obviously if imperfectly provided—is desirable in itself, and quite important for the realization of professional development objectives (Cochran-Smith, 2004; Osterman & Kottkamp, 1993). Thinking about accommodating diversity and defending against biases in one's practice are essential for realizing the possibilities of transforming teacher beliefs and practice.

However, limitations to teachers like Mary, Annabelle, and Jessica applying these new principles to their work can be found in the reports they provided a year after program participation. As we saw in the cases of Mary and Jessica, the ability of teachers to implement changes in classroom and school practice can be greatly hindered (or supported) by the professional context in which they work. For example, Jessica may have great ideas for implementing positive change for Latino students in her afterschool program—such as the idea of including Latino parents into the governing board—but if her collaborators are unreceptive to these ideas, she is rendered ineffective and frustrated in her efforts. (It bears mentioning that Hamann (2003) found this type of professional frustration common amongst participants returning to unreceptive professional environment in the Georgia Project program). Furthermore, as the teacher professional development literature warns, the value of one professional development experience is diminished if there are not ongoing structured opportunities to reflect upon and add to this learning (Cochran-Smith, 2004; Ostermand & Kottkamp, 1993). Perhaps Mary, Annabelle, and Jessica deserve credit for attempting to carry forth the exchange-generated ideas they did despite the absence of structured follow up activities to the program.

As Mexican-origin populations continue to grow within the New Latino Diaspora, educators will be increasingly challenged to equip themselves with the skills and sensitivity necessary to provide an excellent education to this underserved population. This case study shows that travel-study efforts have promise (and limitations) in terms of providing teachers of the New Latino Diaspora with useful insights and background knowledge of Mexican schools and Mexican-origin families and students.

NOTES

1. As Richardson Bruna notes (this volume), Mexico's Drug War, which led to the U.S. State Department issuing travel warnings in 2010, led to the suspension of most teacher exchanges to Mexico. As of this writing, both Mexican violence and U.S. institutional postures towards it continue to dramatically curtail exchanges like the one depicted here.
2. I asked the fourth teacher, Samantha, to participate in my study. Without explicitly denying my request, she nevertheless posed numerous roadblocks (such as not returning my initial correspondences and making excuses not to be interviewed while in Mexico) that made it impossible to include her within my interviews. Interestingly, she was the participant who I perceived to have the most negative experience in Mexico. I will comment more on the implications of Samantha's experience in the discussion section.

REFERENCES

Blanton, C. K. (2004). *The strange career of bilingual education in Texas, 1836–1981.* College Station, TX: Texas A&M University Press.

Buriel, R. (1983). Teacher-student interactions and their relationship to student achievement: A comparison of Mexican-American and Anglo-American children. *Journal of School Psychology, 75*(6), 889–897.

Carter, T. P. (1970). *Mexican Americans in school: A history of educational neglect.* New York, NY: College Entrance Examination Board.

Cochran-Smith, M. (2004). *Walking the road: Race, diversity, and social justice in teacher education.* New York, NY: Teachers College Press.

Cochran-Smith, M., & Lytle, S. L. (2009). *Inquiry as stance: Practitioner research for the next generation.* New York, NY: Teachers College Press.

Delpit, L. (1995). *Other people's children: Cultural conflict in the classroom.* New York, NY: The New Press.

Drozd, D., & Deichert, J. (2007). *2006 Nebraska Population Report.* Omaha, NE: The Center for Public Affairs Research, the University of Nebraska-Omaha. Retrieved from http://nlcs1.nlc.state.ne.us/epubs/U8220/B089-2006.pdf

Gándara, P., & Contreras, F. (2010). *The Latino education crisis: The consequences of failed social policies.* Cambridge MA: Harvard University Press.

Garcia, E. E. (2001). *Hispanic education in the United States.* New York, NY: Rowman and Littlefield.

Gay, G. (2000). *Culturally responsive teaching: Theory, research, and practice.* New York, NY: Teachers College Press.

González, N., Moll, L. C., Tenery, M. F., Rivera, A., Rendon, P., González, R., & Amanti, C. (1995). Funds of knowledge for teaching in Latino households. *Urban Education, 29*(4), 443–470.

Good, T. (1987, July–Aug.). Two decades of research on teacher expectations: findings and future directions. *Journal of Teacher Education, 38,* 32–47.

Hamann, E. T. (2003). *The educational welcome of Latinos in the New South.* Westport, CT: Praeger.

Hamann, E. T., (2008). Advice, cautions, and opportunities for the teachers of binational teachers: Learning from teacher training experiences of Georgia and Nebraska teachers in Mexico. In J. González & K. Singh (Eds.), *Second binational symposium resource book.* Tempe, AZ: Southwest Center for Education Equity and Language Diversity, Mary Lou Fulton College of Education, Arizona State University. Retrieved from http://digitalcommons.unl.edu/teachlearnfacpub/76

Hamann, E. T., & Harklau, L. (2010). Education in the New Latino Diaspora. In E. G. Murillo (Ed.), *Handbook of Latinos and education* (pp. 157–169). New York, NY: Routledge. Retrieved from http://digitalcommons.unl.edu/teachlearnfacpub/104/

Hamann, E. T., & Reeves, J. (2012). Accessing high-quality instructional strategies. In T. Timar & J. Maxwell-Jolly (Eds.), *Connecting the dots and closing the gaps* (pp. 95–110). Cambridge, MA: Harvard Education Press. Retrieved from http://digitalcommons.unl.edu/teachlearnfacpub/134

Latta, M. M., & Wunder, S. (Eds.). (2012). *Placing practitioner knowledge at the center of teacher education: Rethinking the policy and practice of the education doctorate.* Charlotte NC: Information Age.

Lee, S. (2005). *Up Against Whiteness: Race, school, and immigrant youth.* New York, NY: Teachers College Press.

Licón, S. (2003). *The teacher exchange program between Mexico and the United States: A case study of the challenge and promise of binational education efforts.* Cambridge, MA: Unpublished Paper, Harvard Graduate School of Education.

McLaughlin, H. J., & Allexsaht-Snyder, M. (2007, April). *Discomfort, dissonance, disillusionment, and discovery: Educators' self-reflections on their experiences in rural Mexico.* Paper presentation at American Educational Research Association annual meeting, Chicago, IL.

Nebraska Department of Education. (2007). *2006–07 State of the schools report.* Lincoln, NE: Author.

Nebraska Department of Education. (2013). *2012-13 State of the schools report.* Lincoln, NE: Author.

No Child Left Behind Act of 2001, Pub. L. No. 107-110, § 115, Stat. 1425 (2002).

Organization for Economic Cooperation and Developoment. (2003). *PISA 2003.* Paris, France.

Osterman, K. F., & Kottkamp, R. B. (1993). *Reflective practice for educators: Improving schooling through professional development.* Newbury Park, CA: Corwin Press.

Portes, A., & Rumbaut, R. G. (2001). *Legacies: The story of the immigrant second generation.* Berkeley, CA: University of California Press.

Reese, L. (2002). Parental strategies in contrasting cultural settings: Families in México and "El Norte." *Anthropology & Education Quarterly, 33*(1), 30–59.

Ruiz-de-Velasco, J., & Fix, M. (2000). *Overlooked and underserved: Immigrant students in U.S. secondary schools.* Washington, DC: Urban Institute.

Villegas-Reimers, E. M., & Reimers, F. (1996). Where are 60 million teachers? The missing voice in educational reforms around the world. *Prospects, 26*(3), 469–492.

San Miguel, G. (2004). *Contested policy: The rise and fall of federal bilingual education in the United States 1960–2001.* Denton, TX: University of North Texas Press.

Sawyer, A., (2006). *Summers in Mexico: A promising professional development innovation for teachers of Latino immigrant students* (Unpublished term paper). Harvard Graduate School of Education.

Suárez-Orozco, C., & Suárez-Orozco, M. (2001). *Children of immigration.* Cambridge, MA: Harvard University Press.

U.S. Census Bureau, (2010). *American community survey.* Washington, DC: Author.

Valdés, G. (2001). *Learning and not learning English: Latino students in American schools.* New York, NY: Teachers College Press.

Valenzuela, A. (1999). *Subtractive schooling.* Albany, NY: SUNY Press.

Valenzuela, A. (Ed.). (2005). *Leaving children behind: How "Texas-style" accountability fails Latino youth.* Albany, NY: State University of New York Press.

CHAPTER 16

THE IOWA ADMINISTRATORS' AND EDUCATORS' IMMERSION EXPERIENCE

Transcultural Sensitivity, Transhumanization, and the Global Soul

Katherine Richardson Bruna

I learned through the experience of sitting in classrooms [in Mexico] where I was the one who didn't speak the language. I think this was a very powerful lesson for me because I experienced classrooms in which the teacher's methodologies kept me informed of what was happening and others in which I didn't have a clue. It's one thing to talk about techniques that are effective for ELL learners [English Language Learners] in a class, but another to directly experience it as another *human* being.

> —A teacher educator at an Iowa university describing
> his cognitive learning (emphasis added)

I think it was the opportunity to sit in someone's living room, someone's kitchen, someone's backyard, to see pictures of families on the walls, treasures of the family's history, and trying to communicate and share bits of lives with each other.... It brought home to me in a very concrete way that people are people, with the same needs, wishes, dreams—possibly in a different shape —but the *human* piece is one we all share.

> —An Iowa Department of Education administrator describing
> her affective learning (emphasis added)

Revisiting Education in the New Latino Diaspora, pp. 307–333
Copyright © 2015 by Information Age Publishing
All rights of reproduction in any form reserved.

I kept thinking about what we do to work with students from rural Mexico and what we could do differently to make it better for them. It made me make mental checklists of the questions I was going to ask our counselors, translators, administrators, and teachers when I got back home. Did we process their registration forms or did we take a few minutes to find out what they really were interested in as kids, people, *humans*?

—An ELL Curriculum Coordinator in a
demographically-transitioned Iowa school
district describing her pedagogical learning (emphasis added)

In her concluding chapter in *Education in the New Latino Diaspora* (2002), Gibson cautions against subtractive acculturation in Latino schooling. Instead of practices that serve, explicitly or not, to pressure Latino youth to assimilate by devaluing their cultural and linguistic identities, Gibson offers a vision of educational policy and practice guided by an understanding of acculturation that is additive. Summarizing the findings of both quantitative and qualitative research indicating that, "[i]n fact, immigrant students who feel they must shed their home cultures and languages may be at greater risk in school," Gibson then describes the need for a "major reorientation" of this country's teacher professionalization programs around the goal of equipping educators with the knowledge, skills, and dispositions to enable Latino youth to "remain securely anchored in their home communities and cultures" (p. 247), while also enjoying academic success. She points to the development of joint U.S.-Mexico programming as a promising means of such educational reorientation.

In this chapter, I share the purpose, structure, and outcome of a Mexican immersion experience that I, a university-based researcher in the United States, designed and facilitated, under the visionary leadership of Carmen Sosa, former Director of ELL Services at the Iowa Department of Education.[1] Specifically, I revisit the technique of transcultural sensitization (Spindler, 1997) as a tool of transhumanization in teacher professionalization. As Hamann and Harklau note in their introduction (this volume), given administrators', teachers', and teacher educators' limited experiences with and training for cultural and linguistic difference, "Latino students in new diaspora communities are encountering improvisational education responses" (p. 5). The Iowa Administrators' and Educators' Immersion Experience (IAEIE) that I was so centrally involved with may be thought of as one such improvisation, an intervention into the experience and training of a small segment of the state's educational force in order to help them make sense of and respond to the New Latino Diaspora in their communities, schools, and classrooms.

Difference and The New Global State: Towards an Additive Acculturation Framework of Educational Policy and Practice

Mexican immigrant families who have come to Iowa at the beginning of the 21st century have done so as a result of economic forces of globalization. At the same time that free trade policies allowed U.S. subsidized corn *from* the Midwest to flood the Mexican market, undermining small farming in that country, meatpacking plants *in* the Midwest, to curb unionization and maximize profits, moved from urban to rural communities (Genoways, 2013; Hackenberg, 1995; Hackenberg & Kukulka, 1995). Their need for a new and cheap source of labor was filled by the left-adrift traditional growers in Mexico who, responding to their economic displacement with physical displacement, came north *to* the Midwest, becoming in the eyes of many just "little brown people without names" working the line (Fink, 1998, p. 113).

This movement of goods and people across national borders is a defining feature of the current globalization era (Coatsworth, 2004), an era that, in turn, is definitively reconfiguring the U.S. Midwest. The number of Latinos in Iowa, for example, grew 96% from 2000 to 2012. This included a 210% increase in Latino school enrollment and 172% increase in Latino ELL enrollment over the same period. Projections indicate that by 2040 the percentage of the Latino population in the state will more than double to 13% (State Data Center of Iowa, 2013).

Yet various data indicate that, overall, Iowa's Latino population fares more poorly on measures of education, employment, and poverty than Iowa's White population (State Data Center of Iowa, 2013). These data underscore the challenge of preparing the state's educators to work with this population in the spirit of additive acculturation, one that provides Latino youth with the cultural and linguistic tools for academic success while, as Gibson suggested, not devaluing the lived practices of their homes and communities.

The stance of respect and affirmation that is required for additive acculturation to take root in schools' policies and practices may be hard to uphold, however, if educators mistake demographic data on the lower socioeconomic well-being of Latinos in Iowa as indicative of some lower intrinsic value of Latino culture and language instead of as indexing the persistent ethnic and class inequity in U.S. society. In order to intervene in this (mis)interpretive process, educators need experience and training in how to shift away from a tendency to view Latino data through a difference-as-deficit lens to, instead, regard such data through a difference-as-disparity lens (Ladson-Billings, 2006) and then from that second stance to act.

How to view and utilize difference in the current era of globalization is one of the "greatest challenges to schooling worldwide" (Suárez-Orozco & Qin-Hilliard, 2004, p. 3). Difference can be seen in various areas "where cultural communication and miscommunication play out" (p. 3) and where people are "challenged to engage and work through competing and contrasting models, such as kinship, gender, language (monolingual and multilingual), and the complicated relationships between race, ethnicity, and inequality" (p. 4). While challenging and complicated, such negotiation taps "a cornerstone of human intelligence: the ability to consider multiple perspectives" (p. 5). Since schools are one area where difference is negotiated (Goode, Schneider, & Blanc, 1992), they are also, as institutions dedicated to learning, an area where it can be leveraged in the service of intellectual expansion. Teachers and other education professionals who work in, around, and with schools have essential roles to play in tapping into the benefits of difference, provided they have had the opportunity to interrupt their own "'thinking as usual'—the taken-for-granted understandings and worldviews" (p. 4) that have shaped their cognition, affect, and pedagogy.

Exploring teachers' beliefs about, practices regarding, and (non) engagement with difference is acknowledged in the multicultural education literature as an important part of professionalization (Banks, 1997; Nieto, 1998; Sleeter & Grant, 1999). One way to create an interruption, or change, in teachers' beliefs is through learning experiences that provide teachers with meaningful knowledge about and interactions with communities that are different than their own. Exploration has typically taken place through (1) university coursework that focuses on the recognition of different perspectives, experiences, and values and on the historical and political issues that shape and surround difference in U.S. schools and society (Brown, 2004; Milner, 2005); (2) field placement in culturally- and linguistically-diverse U.S. schools (Wiggins, Follow, & Eberly, 2007); (3) homestays with culturally- and linguistically-diverse U.S. families (Ference & Bell, 2004), or (4) some combination of the three. Ference and Bell (2004), for example, designed an experience to prepare their preservice teachers for work with Latino students in the demographically-transitioning communities of Georgia that combined coursework, field placement, and home-stay approaches. They reported that students gained insights into the motivations for and adjustments required by immigration, came to understand the importance of ELL-oriented pedagogy for immigrant students, broke through their stereotypes and misconceptions of Latinos, and became sensitized to the experience of being an outsider.

The ultimate objective of the exploration provided by programs such as Ference and Bell's (2004) is to alter teachers' self-concepts when it comes to difference; that is, to change the way they think about their own experiences and behaviors and the degree to which these feel challenged when confronted with difference. Since teachers' own self-concepts are filters through which they perceive and practice with students in the classroom, the purpose of professionalization is to alter teachers' self-concepts "in ways that form the bases of their ability to integrate multicultural tenets into the classroom environment, instruction, and assessment" (Brown, 2004, p. 123).

In her overview of approaches to preparing teachers for diverse schools, Sleeter (2001) described the positive outcomes of immersion experiences where teachers have to "grapple with being in the minority, do not necessarily know how to act, and are temporarily unable to retreat to the comfort of a culturally familiar setting" (p. 97). In this way, immersion experiences lead to "new, firsthand understandings of what it means to be marginalized, to be a victim of stereotypes and prejudice, and how this might affect people" (Cushner, 2007), understandings that enhance potential for effective work with culturally-and linguistically-diverse youth and families. While there is brief reference to experiences abroad (i.e., Merryfield, 2000; Mahan & Stachowski, 1990, as cited in Sleeter, 2001, p. 97), the programs in the research Sleeter reviews overwhelmingly provided teachers experiences with families and youth in culturally-and linguistically-diverse U.S. communities.

Searches for examples of international immersion experiences for educators often turn up programs in European locales such as Rome (Pence & Macgillivray, 2007) or London (Marx & Moss, 2011) and these report similar outcomes related to cross-cultural growth. But, for educators working with Latinos in demographically transitioning schools and classrooms, I believe growth is needed in the particular cross-cultural knowledge, skills, and dispositions that align to the particular histories, needs, and lives associated with Latino immigration. Even immersion programs in Mexico (Willard-Holt, 2001) may not, simply by virtue of being in Mexico, provide educators with understandings of the antecedent conditions that prefigure immigration patterns from one community to another, and the particular nature of family and classroom life that influences how immigrant youth respond to U.S. schooling. The travel-study experience in Mexico needs to be different and more substantive than just an exchange experience, as an emergent literature on teacher travel-study in Mexico (Hamann, 2003, 2008; Sawyer, this volume) is starting to show.

My assessment of the kind of understandings that educators require to work effectively with U.S. Mexican youth is situated at an intersection of my own institutional teaching and research positionings.[2] As a multicultural teacher educator, I am well familiar with the area of education focused on the preparation of culturally responsive teachers. My teaching work involves making relevant to my students (many of whom come from small, rural, homogenous communities) the historicity of the social identity dimensions of race/ethnicity, class, language, and religion, for example, and, around these dimensions, making a compelling case for equity pedagogy (Banks, 2008), for instruction that is modified to enhance educational access for all students. Despite this work in multicultural education—an area that, taken as a whole, relies on relatively modernist (singular, bounded, stable, not-situated) understandings of these social identity categories—I have always come at my teaching from a critical, postmodern (multiple, unbounded, unstable, situated) perspective (McLaren, 1994) and insisted on troubling these dimensions for my students, even as we use them to make sense together of the world we live and learn in (Richardson Bruna, 2007a, 2009).

I brought this critical perspective to my research work as an ethnographer, documenting how the U.S. Mexican identity ascribed to newcomer students from Mexico is best understood not as an *a priori* one but rather as an acquired and performed one, construed within and in response to particular contexts of schooling and classroom practices (Richardson Bruna, 2007b). My own process of discovery with respect to the difference of U.S. Mexican youth as a transnational identity that is dually-linked to both national contexts has been shaped over the years by work on the "sister" communities of Villachuato, Michoacán, Mexico, and Marshall-town, Iowa (Richardson Bruna & Chamberlin, 2008; Richardson Bruna & Lewis, 2009). I have experienced, through my interactions with people and places in that work, how this dual linkage is lived.

It is, as Trueba described it, a way of "becoming *other*" to both the country of origin (Mexico) and the "host" country (the United States), such that reference to either a Mexican social field or an American one is explanatorily insufficient (Trueba, 2004, p. 88, italic added). U.S. Mexican students navigate both social fields simultaneously in that they are neither "in" or "of" one or the other, but always "in" and "of" both together. In their studies of transnational youth in Mexican schools who had schooling histories in the United States, Hamann, Zúñiga, and Sánchez García (2006) have reported similar lived *ambi*-social experiences (Hamann & Zúñiga, 2011; Zúñiga & Hamann, 2009).

Guerra (2004) uses the idea of *transcultural repositioning* to talk about the practices of these *ambi*-social individuals as they "move back and forth with ease and comfort between and among different languages and dialects, different social classes, and different cultural and artistic forms" (p. 8). It follows that, in order for educators to become effective and additively acculturative in working with U.S. Mexican youth and families, they need to be able to recognize, respect, and affirm such transcultural repositioning in their teaching and relationship-building as an inherent part of what working towards academic success also means. They need, in short, a sensory experience of the transnational. It was to accomplish this goal of providing educators with first-hand insight into the transnational reality of Mexican immigrant life that I designed and facilitated the IAEIE.

The Iowa Administrators' and Educators' Immersion Experience (IAEIE)

Thirty Iowa educators traveled to the rural community of Villachuato, Michoacán, Mexico in 2007 or 2008 through the IAEIE. Villachuato is the largest sending community of immigrants to Marshalltown, Iowa. Marshalltown made national news in shortly before the trips when it was one of six meatpacking communities in six states concurrently raided by Immigration and Customs Enforcement (ICE) (see Hamann & Reeves [2012] for more about that raid). The educators' stay in Villachuato was meant to provide these educational professionals with understandings about the kinds of family and schooling experiences that are antecedent to and preconfigure their interactions, in Iowa, with immigrant youth from rural Mexican communities so that they could better advocate for teaching practices and policies that best serve, from an additive stance, their cultural and linguistic differences and related socioacademic interests and needs.

There has been growing recognition of the intimate relationship between Villachuato and Marshalltown in the anthropological and educational literature (Grey, 1997, 2002; Grey & Woodrick, 2005;Meyers, 2009a, 2009b; Richardson Bruna & Chamberlin, 2008; Richardson Bruna, Chamberlin, & López Ceballos, 2007; Richardson Bruna & Lewis, 2009b; Woodrick, 2006). Grey (1997, 2002) was instrumental in first documenting the "sister city" relationship between the communities and, indeed, in facilitating and reporting on an immersion experience he led and designed to foster varied Marshalltown leaders' understanding of the Villachuato context (2002). Because the targeted participating leaders in Grey's immersion experience included representatives of the business, law enforcement, religious, and education segments of the community, the IAEIE was the first immersion experience in Villachuato that focused specifically on enhancing *educator* understandings of the particular differences that immigrants from rural Mexico bring to U.S. schooling.

Due to my professional relationship with the then-ELL Director at the Iowa Department of Education (who was aware of the research I was doing on newcomer Mexican immigrant students in Marshalltown and the contacts it had established with family members and school staff in Villachuato) I received funding to support three trips (in May and September of 2007 and in January of 2008) of approximately 10 participants each.[3] Department of Education staff broadly advertised the experiences, put out a call for participants, and provided me the final roster of travelers. These included, by design, a combination of superintendents, principals, ELL coordinators, teacher educators, and Department of Education administrators. In addition to having all trip expenses covered, participants also received an incentivizing stipend. Because the trips' monies came from federal funds focused on the professionalization of educational leadership, classroom teachers did not have the opportunity to participate. This meant that ways to bring "take-away" insights from the trip into the hands of classroom teachers was a prevailing theme of participant discussion on each trip.

Each of the three trips had the same overall structure: one three-hour predeparture orientation session held at an airport hotel the evening prior to take-off; 5 days in Villachuato that included family homestays, school visitation experiences at Villachuato's elementary and middle schools (there is no high school in the community), and daily, guided, reflective conversations; and one 3-hour postreturn debrief session held at the airport hotel the morning after arrival. Most of the data shared here comes from the predeparture orientation and the postreturn debrief exercises, as well as information about cognitive, affective, and pedagogical learning obtained via phone and e-mail interviews 6 months after participation. The nature of the in-community immersion experience itself was, as one might imagine, immensely rich and could be the topic of a chapter itself. Instead, what I aim to do here is to document and describe the pre- and posttrip debriefings with an eye to illuminating the enduring value of the transcultural sensitivity technique as a tool in the anthropology of education. This proposes to be an addition of New Latino Diaspora research to the larger discipline.

As someone exposed to educational anthropology early in her doctoral training, the objective I wanted to accomplish through the IAEIE was influenced by Spindler's (1997) technique of transcultural sensitization. This technique concerns itself with "the ways common errors in transcultural observation and interpretation can be anticipated and how sensitivity concerning them can be acquired" (Spindler, 1997, p. 498). Spindler designed the technique to use with Stanford undergraduates studying in Germany to get at their "perceptual distortions" (p. 498) because "[h]uman beings tend to interpret new experience in the light of past experience unless there is a decisive intervention in the interpretive process" (p. 499).

I had the opportunity to work with Spindler as his Teaching Assistant when he guest-taught at the University of California, Davis, and to watch him introduce the technique to undergraduates there. The meaning he intended of "transcultural" is admittedly different than how I use it here. He used it to refer more broadly, and more neutrally, to the idea of simply moving across two distinctly defined cultures. My adaptation here, more narrowly, more politically, and more in keeping with the postmodern turn in cultural study (Denzin & Lincoln, 2011), updates Spindler by infusing "transcultural" with the meaning associated with the transnational framework required by globalization—that of moving across cultural fields that, rather than being distinctly-defined, are always indistinct because of the ways that they are overlaid and intertwined; today's globalizing transcultural fields cannot be understood in isolation from each other. Developing this kind of transcultural sensitivity to the education of U.S. Mexican youth, as it relates to four specific layers, or aspects of experience that prefigure these youth's immigrant identities—that is, place, family, schools, and society—was my goal.

The focal exercise of the predeparture orientation session was the beginning of a KWL activity that, first, asked participants what they Knew (K) about Villachuato with respect to these four specific aspects: place, family, schools, and society. Each participant was provided a worksheet on which to record his/her information in table form. After completing the "What Do You Know?" column for each of these four aspects, participants watched a 20-minute silent slideshow of images from Villachuato. These images were from my own personal library of photos, taken during my previous research trips to the community. Following this viewing, I facilitated discussion around the images. Participants were asked to identify and share what they thought the images told them about Villachuato, and why. The purpose of this discussion was to lead them to feel how they, already, were making assumptions based on limited information, to get them to pose challenges to what they thought they knew. The purpose was to not to affirm or negate the information that participants had identified as prior knowledge; it was, instead, to focus them on the fact that they, indeed, held beliefs, that they held those beliefs because of particular interpretive lenses, and that those beliefs would be, throughout the trip, up for continual re-examination; the purpose was, then, to allow them to see what Delpit (1993) calls the "worlds in [their] heads."

> We all carry worlds in our heads, and those worlds are decidedly different. We educators set out to teach, but how can we reach the worlds of others when we don't even know they exist? Indeed, many of us don't even realize that our own worlds exist only in our heads and in the cultural institutions we have built to support them. (p. xiv)

In this way, IAEIE participants' early understandings were deemed as tentative cultural claims around which experiences accrued during the trip would give them cause to either retain or dismiss their previously-held "worlds."

After discussion, participants then returned to the KWL table and filled out the "What Do You Want to Know?"/(W) column. This information was then shared and used to transition to a discussion about the cognitive, affective, and pedagogical learning goals of the trip. Participants were asked to tune in to what they were learning at the level of the head, as well as the heart, and always think about connections to educational practice. The KWL tables were collected and held for participants during their experience in the community.

The morning after arrival back from Villachuato, after 5 days of homestay and school observation experiences, participants attended a post-return debriefing session. They were given back their KWL tables and asked to review them. They were then shown the same silent slideshow as in the predeparture orientation session and asked to revisit their initial information. I facilitated discussion around which cultural claims, which "worlds," they could now, with more assurance, retain or dismiss. This discussion culminated in having participants identify, individually, what they Learned (L) about Villachuato and, as groups, articulate as essential understandings insights they would be sure to share with colleagues. Table 16.1 summarizes the central themes of these KWL discussions:

Table 16.1. Summary of Key Themes From Pre- and Post-trip KWL Discussions

	What Do We Know?	*What Do we Want to Know?*	*What Did We Learn?*
About the **Place** of Villachuato	Villachuato is ... *rural *traditional *simple *poor *immigrant-sending	What is Villachuato's ... *agriculture *economy	Villachuato is a small, rural, historically agrarian community severely affected by free-trade economic policy. The town's development is supported by money sent back from family members in the United States, like those who work at the meatpacking plant in Marshalltown, Iowa. It is a place of complex economic and cultural developments and intersections.
About the **Families** of Villachuato	The families of Villachuato are ... *close-knit *multi-generational *not well-educated	How do Villachuato families ... *feel about members leaving to work in the U.S. *perceive the importance of education	Migration to the U.S. is an expected and respected form of family contribution. Its benefits— assurance of family survival— outweigh the challenges—family separation and generational disconnection. Families' views of education have been affected by this concern for survival; it has often been a luxury that many could not afford.

(Table continues on next page)

Table 16.1. (Continued)

	What Do We Know?	What Do we Want to Know?	What Did We Learn?
About the **Schools** of Villachuato	Schools in Villachuato are ... *limited by a lack of resources *affected by the transiency of a migrant population	How are schools in Villachuato ... * similar to and and different from U.S. schools *addressing the needs of students educated in the United States.	Schools in Villachuato, in general, have fewer resources than Iowa schools and this affects all aspects of education. They do have access to technology. Meeting the needs of students educated in the U.S. poses an institutional, curricular, and instructional challenge.
About the **Society** of Villachuato	As a society, Villachuato is ... *affected by migration *religious *unstable	How has Villachuato society ... *been shaped by its economic history *been affected by migration	As a supplier of workers to European landholders, Villachuato has, historically, been a site of labor exploitation. Its existence as a transnational community today is just an extension of this. Its deep and enduring ties to labor markets in the north are visible everywhere. Migration is the norm, so families affected by migration are not abnormal; they are in many respects happy families facing challenges unique to their own social and economic contexts. Abiding religious beliefs and practices provide continuity amidst change.

In what follows, I illuminate what the "re-worlding" of IAEIE participants' ideas around U.S. Mexican youth looked like, as emergent from the
transcultural sensitization technique. Since this is a chapter in a book about
the New Latino Diaspora and, as such, central to its considerations is the
migration of (Latino) peoples from their home lands to their host lands, I
will take participants' emergent insights as related to the first of the four
focal aspects, *place*, as my illuminative example of the technique's power.
To enhance the explanation of transcultural sensitization as an interpretive
process, I additionally include a few of the images around which the pre-
and posttrip discussions of Villachuato-as-place revolved.

Transcultural Sensitivization: (Re)Interpreting Place

In the pretrip orientation, when asked what IAEIE participants knew
about Villachuato as a "place," the shared descriptors were that it was

"rural," "simple," "poor," and "immigrant-sending." When shown the slide show, they pointed to pictures like the one below (Figure 16.1) as confirmation of Villachuato's rural poverty and the materially "simple" lifestyle to which it must lead.

Figure 16.1.   A house in Villachuato

Participants also referenced the following image (Figure 16.2) of a woman making tortillas, as supporting their preconceptions about Villachuato. It connoted for these Iowan educators, a life lived "off the land", a life fed with the "simple" and "traditional" staple of the Mexican diet.

Additionally, the image in Figure 16.2 supported IAEIE participants' understanding that corn was a crop likely to be grown in Villachuato, as a rural, agrarian community. But they found it hard to reconcile with the following image (Figure 16.3), which led them to believe that there must be a leisure economy in Villachuato as well.

It was with this image— seeing the presence of gaming technology— that IAEIE participants, already in the pretrip orientation, began to re-think or "re-world" their original ideas of Villachuato's "traditional" "simplicity." It made them want to know more about the extent of Villachuato's agricultural activity and the viability of other economic avenues, including small businesses like this one.

Figure 16.2.   A woman making tortillas.

Figure 16.3.   A video game arcade.

Upon return, participants' discussion of these same images in the post-trip debriefing reflected altered understandings of Villachuato as a place. Revisiting the image of the house in Figure 16.1, participants noted that they now comprehended the significance of the newer house, under construction (in the background of Figure 16.1), adjoining the first one. They noted that this second house, in the background, had been overlooked and/or undervalued in the pretrip viewing. They realized that they "saw" it now because, after spending time in the community, they had seen how numerous were such examples of newer homes being built right next to the older homes, or as additions to them. Indeed, the small kitchen in which all participants ate their meals during the immersion experience was, at one time, the entire home of the host family. Seven children were born and raised in what was now just one room in a larger structure that had been built around it to encompass a living room, two bedrooms, and a bathroom. In this way, participants tuned in to how common it was for many families in Villachuato to live amidst reminders of their previous poverty. It was frequently pointed out to them that the construction activity going on—the sound of hammering as routine ambient noise from morning until evening every day—was only possible because of funds sent back from family members who were working in the United States (and, often, in Iowa).

Learning about the community's economic dependence on resources from the U.S. underscored for participants how affected the community was by free trade policy that had undermined the value of a traditionally grown crop, such as corn. Thus, upon return, Figure 16.2 of the woman making tortillas had changed in meaning for them as well: the corn she was using was likely not corn grown locally by small farmers in Villachuato, as it once surely would have been, but, instead, was corn either imported from the United States—which, due to its subsidization *here* can be sold at lower prices *there*—or was corn brought in from a large-scale grower in a surrounding community. Further, it was even noted that the clothing worn by the woman making the tortillas was likely to have been brought from or sent from the United States; several participants, in the second viewing, made comments that they now recognized her sweater as one they had seen at big-box retailers in their home Iowa communities.

Understanding, in this way, the economic interrelationship of Villachuato to U.S. labor, agriculture, and retail markets brought new meaning to Figure 16.3 of the video game arcade. After having been in the community, participants better understood how this small business fit. It was not, as they had originally wondered in the pretrip session, evidence of thriving commercial activity; indeed, it was the only gaming arcade to be found in Villachuato. The community did not have what one would recognize as an entertainment or leisure industry: there were no hotels, movie theaters, discos, nor large bars and restaurants. What it had were a pharmacy, a couple of *tortillerias*, stationary and clothing stores, and several corner markets. Locally purchasable goods in Villachuato consisted mainly of what people needed to meet the daily demands of their lives and not much more. This, participants commented, made the video arcade somewhat anomalous. From the understanding they took away from their visit to the community, participants reasoned the arcade was likely a venture funded by money from the U.S. and one that highlighted the change that Villachuato was in the process of undergoing, from a traditionally poor yet self-sustaining agrarian community to a more prosperous one dependent on resources from the United States.

The presence of these resources in the community meant development—the building up of homes, the paving of roads, the upkeep of the church, and the creation of businesses, like the video game arcade, that moved beyond stereotypical impressions of a "poor" and "simple" life. Participants came to understand that the economic reason for the existence of the arcade was far from "simple" and its presence 'technologized' the kinds of experiences children in Villachuato had access to. For them, Figure 16.3 became a snapshot of a moment in time in a change process where leisure businesses like this one, through the experiences they provide youth in the community, were transforming "simple" "traditional" cultural identity and activity.

IAEIE Participants' Cognitive and Affective "Re-Worlding"

Interviews performed with participants 6-months after the trip documented the enduring nature of this understanding that Villachuato was, economically, a transnational place. Reporting on the cognitive aspects of their learning, the following comments indicate awareness of the economic dependency of Villachuatans on U.S. labor markets (and, of course, of U.S. labor markets on Villachuatans):

> I learned that much of both the individual family dwellings and community improvements in Villachuato are possible because of the money sent from the North.

> I learned how money is sent continuously back to Villachuato by those in Iowa and other Midwest states and how, without it, the town and others like it would most likely have dried up by now.

> The trip provided me with a better understanding of why some immigrants are coming to Iowa and the economic forces behind it. It seemed to me that small farmers in Mexico are squeezed by the same economic forces that

affect small farmers in Iowa. Corporate agriculture has affected children and families in both countries.

I couldn't believe the number of people we ran into that had lived in Marshalltown or other places in Iowa, or Nebraska, or California! I learned that families up North supply Villachuato family members with their clothes and almost everything. All their clothes looked familiar, and their microwaves, stereos, bikes, etc.

Many of the people of Villachuato are poor, but it didn't seem like any of them were desperate. Most of them seemed to have their basic needs met (food, clothing, shelter). Those who had family members working in American seemed to be living well with new home additions, TVs, and the like.

Some participants went further, noting how awareness of the economic interdependency of Villachuato and the U.S. had hit them at an affective level. It had compelled them to reflect on their own economic and political positions and (in)activities. Referring to our discussions of this topic in our daily debriefing meetings in Villachuato, one woman stated, "When we talked as a group, I got some emotional learning experiences as I sat and analyzed how little I do politically to express my views on issues related to immigration and U.S. economic policies." Another participant reported that he "felt guilty of being a rich *gringo* from a culture of riches and waste that uses the labor of immigrants to support our bubble of decadent wealth." Moving beyond an examination of his own positionality, this participant also commented on the tension he perceived between Villachuatans' reaction to his visit to their community and the reaction a newcomer from Villachuato would likely get in his own (in Iowa):

The warmth and welcoming of people everywhere we went was very impactful. For example, one person we met at random in the village asked where we were from, recounted all the places in Iowa he had worked, and welcomed us with "*mi casa es su casa*" [my house is your house] generosity. I reflected on how the reception given to migrants by some in our Iowa communities and by our immigration policies seem a stark contrast. We don't treat them with the same *humanity* (emphasis added).

Transcultural Sensitivization as Transhumanization: Towards New Pedagogical Worlds

The summary I have provided above is an example of how I worked with participants in the IAEIE, adapting Spindler's (1997) transcultural sensitization technique to examine, challenge, refine, and build understandings related to the antecedent conditions that prefigure the experiences of U.S. Mexican youth and families in demographically-transitioning Iowa schools and communities. Thinking about Villachuato from the vantage points of place, family, schools, and society helped participants arrive at *enhanced*— that is, more complicated and thus more accurate—understandings of the immigrant experience as a transnational, transcultural one. This accomplished the goal of transhumanization, of bringing to participants' full and living attention their shared humanity with Mexican immigrants (see also Murillo [2002]). The quotes I used to open the chapter, excerpted from their 6-month-post-trip interviews, reveal how participants developed enduring understandings of how this humanity is often obscured by practices in schools and our own ethnocentric blinders.

Specifically, the first and third of these quotes illustrate how, through the IAEIE, participants began to re-think educational practices through the lens of immigrant students' experiences. In the first, a teacher educator begins to truly grasp, by virtue of him having had the opportunity to sit in a classroom in which he didn't speak the language of instruction, the importance of the teaching methods for ELLs that he introduces to his teacher education students. In the third, an ELL Curriculum Coordinator re-sees her school's intake process and how little it allows the school to know about immigrant students. Having participants come to realizations like these about practice and to use those to be change-agents in their New Latino Diaspora school settings, was the overarching goal of the IAEIE.

Spindler (1997), in describing the technique of transcultural sensitization, identifies how the intervention works to reveal the effects of stereotypes on thinking about cultures other than one's own. Three of his explanations are especially relevant for the changes in participants' thinking that I've described here. One way that the transcultural sensitization intervention works is to illuminate how "there is a stereotype of experience related to the event, object, or situation patterned in the observer's culture" (p. 510). One major insight of IAEIE learning was the need to reconceptualize culture in terms of multiplicity. As members of the dominant racial/ethnic class (only two IAEIE travelers out of the 30 were not White), the majority of participants had never explored the idea of a monolithic cultural identity as normative and hegemonic—that is, as reflective of a privileged social location. Members of nondominant racial/ethnic communities grow up learning to navigate between the subjugated knowledges and experiences of their home lives and the kinds of knowledges and experiences, reflective of the dominant class, that are valued in school and the larger society (Nieto, 1998). Members of dominant communities do not need to depend on such daily cultural crossings for their survival, so they are more likely to be oblivious of them.

So IAEIE participants were awakened, in transnational and transcultural Villachuato, to how their conception of culture as singular and stable was, in fact, a trace of their own privilege and not to be taken as a universal truth. Their prior understanding was, in fact, out-of-step with the globalizing reality of the current historical moment. What one participant described as "the cyclical patterns of leaving and coming back that the families experience in their lifetimes, the moving back and forth between two worlds, the paradox of instability and stability, that in order to keep the home one must leave it" constituted ordinary parts of the culture of many U.S. Mexican families in the New Latino Diaspora.

Another way the intervention works, according to Spindler (1997), is to illuminate how "there is a stereotype of the experience of meaning of the event, object, or situation as it is presumed to exist in another culture" (p. 51). For the IAEIE participants, the question about the value of education in Villachuato was pressing. Many of them worked with teachers who held the belief that Mexican immigrant families didn't care about education. This belief was formed out of their teacher colleagues' impressions from working with Mexican immigrant families in U.S. schools—these families were uneducated and uninvolved, to their colleagues' way of thinking, in making schooling decisions. Time in Villachuato allowed participants to interrogate the frames of reference through which such claims were made and expose them, again, as culturally-biased. Coming to understand how the historical context of poverty (current-day Villachuatans are the descendants of peasant laborers whose work for European landowners was consistently exploitive) has structured access to education and has shaped the community's regard for schooling's relevance to their lives allowed participants to reframe their thinking about immigrant families' backgrounds and involvement. They came to understand that what is mistaken in the U.S. as the difference of "not caring" is, instead, an indication of long-standing social and economic disparity; until recently, for these families, education had been a luxury few could afford. Some participants noted this realization as follows:

> Meeting the daily life demands is very difficult. Thus, families have placed an extremely high value on survival and family. Therefore, educators in the U.S. must be aware of this situation and not jump to the conclusion that they do not value their education. What I have come to realize is that the reason for missing school is not necessarily that education is not valued; rather, family and economic necessity has historically, so culturally, [been] valued more.

> We need to try to limit our judgments about the family's priorities and try to work with the families to help their children. We need to share awareness that families may not have the resources or the education to be able to assist their children in the way we would assume they should.

Coming to the realization that the difference they had noted in Mexican immigrant families' participation in schooling was, in fact, a reflection of larger socioeconomic disparity allowed IAEIE participants to fully appreciate how, in coming to the United States, immigrant families were, despite their own lack of access, providing important educational opportunities for their children (especially since there is still not a high school in the community). On a personal note, I have had the pleasure of attending the college graduation of a Villachuato family's grandaughter who was, because of her parents' immigration to California and, subsequently, Marshalltown, educated in the United States. Watching her walk across the stage and receive her diploma, the very first in her family, knowing the context that prefigured that experience and, indeed, the supreme value her family placed on that accomplishment, was one of the most moving experiences I have had the pleasure to enjoy in association with my work.

A third way that transcultural sensitivization works, according to Spindler (1997), is to illuminate that, "there is a projection of emotional states ascribed to subjects in another culture" (p. 511). IAEIE participants came to understand that they had associated the poverty they expected to see in Villachuato with ideas about deficiency or unhappiness. They realized it surprised them that the individuals and families they had the opportunity to interact with seemed happy. This made them question the importance they placed on the acquisition of material goods as a means to fulfillment and as an indicator of success. As one participant said, "It made me realize that many Americans would look at their slow, less modern lifestyle as a deficit when in reality their family connections made the traditional two-parent working family look deficit in the amount of quality time they spend with their children." In this same vein, another participant stated:

> I think the thing that struck me the most was that these people (at least the ones I encountered) seemed HAPPY. Even though many missed family members "up north" and have survived some very difficult hardships, there seems to be a joy in life—a joy in relationship—that for some reason caught me by surprise. It made me think that "poverty" addresses the lack of resources, but the people seemed to be rich in so many other ways. (emphasis original)

Transhumanizing Teaching for the Global Soul

Because of these and other ways in which the process of transcultural sensitivization serves to interrupt deeply held and previously unexamined systems of belief, Spindler (1997) suggests that the technique "be a part of all teacher-training programs" (p. 512). In order for it to be as effective as possible in enabling educators to work with U.S. Mexican youth and families and to facilitate the additive acculturation that Gibson (2002) urges, the technique would need to be, as Sleeter (2001) advises, coupled with longer immersion experiences than was possible with the IAEIE, with ongoing teacher education and professional development that continues long after the immersion experience itself has ended, and with more extensive data collection efforts that strongly document the long-term outcome of the experience on routine aspects of school and classroom practice. Indeed, IAEIE participants, at the posttrip debriefing session, outlined ambitious action plans for transformed teaching.[4] The IAEIE participants described the design of prospective slideshow presentations that could be used in classrooms with students and in staff development with teachers, the development of Spanish-for-Teachers courses to help take advantage of the home language in the classroom, the creation of newcomer-orientation sessions to forge new relationships with families, the implementation of dual language programs, and possible acts of "giving witness" through newspaper editorials and legislative hearings.

As I was writing this chapter, I took the opportunity to e-mail participants and invite them to share the activities they had been involved with since completing the IAEIE. One of these, a superintendent, began by noting that, "The Villachuato experience was one of best educational experiences I've had in 20+ years in education." The rest of his response is revealing for how it exemplifies the living spirit of transcultural sensitivity as an important intervention in teachers' interpretive processes:

> Most important is the way the Villachuato experience helped to reshape the way I think about children coming to America ... I finally understood why they did certain things, such as not putting toilet paper in the stool. Out of ignorance I always thought they were being dissonant by doing this but in their village if someone place toilet paper in the system it could clog up the whole village. I remember often teachers making comments like, "They are too stupid to flush the paper?" It's only by understanding where they come from that I understand the things they do or don't do. I understand how important it is for me as an administrator to educate my staff on these issues so that these children have a fair chance in our public schools without being labeled or being placed at a disadvantage.

While this toilet paper example may strike us as basic, and even base, in the way it indexes a deficiency orientation toward U.S. Mexican youth, what is important is the way this participant was able to use the example to identify what he himself describes as his "ignorance" and, from that, to envision himself, instead, as an informed advocate of far-from-basic bold reforms. He goes on to explain that, as a result of the trip, he started a

K–12 bilingual education program in his predominantly white rural Iowa district. He explains:

> I believe that by embracing the native language and teaching all children the importance of bilingual education we create two-way understanding. This benefited the school because more Hispanic children opened-enrolled into our school because of this program, but more importantly it helped to break down barriers of prejudice and misunderstanding. The White children gained an understanding of how difficult it is to learn another language. It was a real eye-opener for teachers who were required to take part in the program. They found the learning process very difficult. With the positives came a few negatives. In rural Iowa many people do not understand the importance of such programs, so I found myself having to defend the program.

This participant closed by adding that, as a result of the trip, he replaced an "ineffective" ELL Director with a more effective Spanish-speaking individual and had developed ELL Teams in schools to discuss ways they could better meet the needs of these children and to participate in book studies to broaden their understandings. The book they were reading when we exchanged e-mails was Helen Thorpe's (2011) *Just Like Us*. The administrator explained that it describes four Mexican girls growing up in Denver. "Two of them are legal, two are not. The two who are illegal have no options for college/postsecondary education because of our laws. The book takes you through their struggles and the limits our 'close the border' policies are having on them."

Developing an affirming attitude toward culturally- and linguistically-diverse students, a stance achieved through the gaining of sociocultural consciousness, is an essential part, as Villegas and Lucas (2002) explain, of becoming a culturally responsive teacher. This superintendent's remarks, several years after his participation in the IAEIE, provide intriguing evidence of how the experience provided him with enduring understandings that led to concrete changes in his and others' practices.

If imitation is the sincerest form of flattery, then perhaps the biggest recommendation for the experience comes with the following participant's comments. Describing her own transcultural sensitization work with a colleague who also participated in the IAEIE, this participant, an ELL Consultant at one of Iowa's Area Educational Agencies (which provide support services to teachers), wrote:

> I am attaching a sheet that we have used at trainings. We made a Powerpoint, which included our pictures from Villachuato and other locations. We ask participants to write down their impressions under the headings of: geography, financial, religion, and education. The discussion that follows is worth a million dollars. In some classes where I may have educators of

only Hispanic students (especially in the Marshalltown area), I use only the Villachuato pictures and the 'realness' that these were actually taken in their "hometowns" creates a whole new perspective for many educators who do not have a clear understanding of what life is like there and creates a whole new discussion about the movement to the U.S., prior schooling of their students, education and income of parents, and family life.

This participant estimated she had co-facilitated presentations, using a version of transcultural sensitivitization, with approximately 250 Iowa educators.

What makes *trans*humanization different than other ways of talking about humanization in education? Discussions of humanizing pedagogy (Bartolomé, 1994) already emphasize the need to understand and leverage, through culturally responsive approaches to curriculum, instruction, and assessment, the experiences that historically oppressed students bring with them into the classroom. Transhumanization offers us a way of naming how the experiences that constitute the "difference" of U.S.-Mexican students are transnational and transcultural in nature, reflective of a particular historically constructed social field emergent from the cultural, linguistic, and economic interconnection of the United States and Mexico. "The ability to formulate an identity," as Suárez-Orozco (2004) writes, "that allows comfortable movement between worlds will be at the heart of achieving a 'global soul'" (p. 173). Helping U.S.-Mexico students understand, negotiate, and affirm their transnational and transcultural identities in a way that allows such "comfortable movement" needs to be an essential theme in the work of teacher professionalization (Zúñiga & Hamann, 2009). Through the IAEIE, education professionals in Iowa began the work of understanding what it would mean to take seriously their responsibility of helping U.S. Mexican youth achieve a global soul and, in the process, began to achieve global souls of their own.

NOTES

1. This chapter is dedicated to the memory of Carmen and her tireless work to enhance the education of ELL students in the state of Iowa through innovative teacher education and professional development efforts. Carmen, you touched so many lives with your vision, leadership, and passion. And I dedicate it too in celebration of Miriam Sánchez and the lives of so many other talented and ambitious U.S. Mexican youth in Iowa and elsewhere. Miriam, with your persistence and success, you make your families proud.
2. Given the sheer size of the U.S. Mexican population as an ethnic subcategory, the contextual information surrounding their schooling takes on particular significance. Rubén Rumbaut (2006) noting that, in 2000, U.S. Mexicans

constituted 63% of the larger Hispano-Latino population, wrote, "[I]t should be underscored that aggregate statistics for the total Hispanic population reflect the predominate weight of the characteristics of the Mexican-origin population" (p. 33).Taking up this argument, and further noting the National Science Foundation's goal that broadening educational attainment of underrepresented groups is not advanced by the aggregation of data without regard to ethnic subgroup (National Science Foundation, 2004), my work (notably Richardson Bruna, 2012) attends to the U.S. Mexican experience as a particular one, necessary to be accounted for as such.

3. As this chapter goes to press, it is worth noting that innovative professional development experiences, like the IAEIE, involving immersion in Mexican communities for U.S. students, educators and other leaders, have been eliminated or severely restricted due to the escalation of drug violence in Mexico and the real or perceived danger to participants as assessed by U.S. agencies and by institutions of higher education. For example, at my home institution, Iowa State University, all study abroad programs in Mexico were cancelled when the State Department, in 2011, issued its widest-ever Mexico Travel Warning. The nature of violence in Mexico, its root causes, and the reaction of U.S. policymakers, other stakeholders, and the general public has now become part of the need for "transcultural sensitization," for intervention into the interpretive process, in a way that was not as strongly felt at the time of my IAEIE facilitation. When, perhaps, we most need these tools to counter some educators' media-fueled, deficiency-driven perceptions of Mexico and Mexicans, we are less likely, in fact, to be able to use them.

4. This stance echoes that of the Georgia teachers who studied in Mexico who were described by Hamann (2003). The Georgia teachers' enthusiasm, however, to do something different did not mean their U.S. working environments were readily amenable for change.

REFERENCES

Banks, J. A. (1997). *Teaching strategies for ethnic studies* (6th ed.). Needham Heights, MA: Allyn and Bacon.

Banks, J. A. (2008). *An introduction to multicultural education* (4th ed.). Boston, MA: Pearson/ Allyn and Bacon.

Bartolomé, L. (1994). Beyond the methods fetish: Toward a humanizing pedagogy. *Harvard Educational Review, 64*(2), 173–195.

Brown, E. L. (2004). The relationship of self-concepts to changes in cultural diversity awareness: Implications for urban teacher educators. *Urban Review 36*(2), 119–145.

Coatsworth, J. H. (2004). Globalization, growth, and welfare in history. In M. M. Suárez-Orozco & D. B. Qin-Hilliard (Eds.), *Globalization: Culture and education in the new millennium* (pp. 38–55). Berkeley, CA: University of California Press.

Cushner, K. (2007, Winter). The role of experience in the making of internationally-minded teachers. *Teacher Education Quarterly, 34*(1), 27–40.

Denzin, N. K., & Y.S. Lincoln (2011). *The Sage handbook of qualitative research.* Thousand Oaks, CA: Sage.

Ference, R. A. & Bell, S. (2004). A cross-cultural immersion in the U.S.: Changing preservice teacher attitudes toward Latino ESOL students. *Equity & Excellence in Education 37,* 343–350.

Fink, D. (1998). *Cutting into the meatpacking line: Workers and change in the rural midwest.* Chapel Hill, NC: University of North Carolina Press.

Genoways, T. (2013). This land is not your land: Deciding who belongs in America. *Harpers* (February). Retrieved February 1, 2014, from http://harpers.org/archive/2013/02/this-land-is-not-your-land/

Gibson, M. A. (2002). The New Latino Diaspora and educational policy. In S. Wortham, E. G. Murillo, Jr., & E. T. Hamann (Eds.), *Education in the New Latino Diaspora: Policy and the politics of identity* (pp. 241–252). Westport, CT: Ablex.

Goode, J. G., Schneider, J., & Blanc, S., (1992). Transcending boundaries and closing ranks: How schools shape inter-relations. In L. Lamphere (Ed.), *Structuring diversity: Ethnographic perspectives on the new immigration* (pp. 173–213). Chicago, IL: University of Chicago Press.

Grey, M. A. (1997). Secondary labor in the meatpacking industry: Demographic change and student mobility in rural Iowa schools. *Journal of Research in Rural Education, 13*(3), 153–164.

Grey, M. A. (2002). Unofficial sister cities: Meatpacking labor migration between Villachuato, Mexico and Marshalltown, Iowa. *Human Organization 61*(4), 364–376.

Grey, M. A., & Woodrick, A. C. (2005). "Latinos have revitalized our community": Mexican migration and Anglo responses in Marshalltown, Iowa. In V. Zúniga & R. Hernández-León (Eds.), *New destinations: Mexican immigration in the United States* (pp. 133–154). New York, NY: Russell Sage Foundation.

Guerra, J. C. (2004). Emerging representations, situated literacies, and the practice of transcultural repositioning. In M. H. Kells, V. Balester, & V. Villanueva (Eds.), *Latino/a discourses: On language, identity, and literacy in education* (pp. 7–23). Portsmouth, NH: Heinemann.

Hackenberg, R. A. (1995). Joe Hill died for your sins. In D. D. Stull, M. J. Broadway, & D. Griffith (Eds.), *Any way you cut it: Meat-processing and small-town America* (pp. 232–264). Lawrence, KS: University Press of Kansas.

Hackenberg, R. A., & Kukulka, G. (1995). Industries, immigrants, and illness in the New Midwest. In D. D. Stull, M. J. Broadway, & D. Griffith (Eds.), *Any way you cut it: Meat-processing and small-town America* (pp. 187–211). Lawrence, KS: University Press of Kansas.

Hamann, E. T. (2003). *The educational welcome of Latinos in the New South.* Westport, CT: Praeger.

Hamann, E. T., (2008). Advice, cautions, and opportunities for the teachers of binational teachers: Learning from teacher training experiences of Georgia and Nebraska teachers in Mexico. In J. González & K. Singh (Eds.), *Second binational symposium resource book.* Tempe, AZ: Southwest Center for Education Equity and Language Diversity, Mary Lou Fulton College of Education,

Arizona State University. Retrieved from http://digitalcommons.unl.edu/teachlearnfacpub/76

Hamann, E. T., & Reeves, J. (2012). ICE raids, children, media and making sense of Latino newcomers in flyover country. *Anthropology & Education Quarterly, 43*(1), 24–40. Retrieved from http://digitalcommons.unl.edu/teachlearnfacpub/127

Hamann, E. T., Zúñiga, V., & Sánchez García, J. (2006). Pensando en Cynthia y su hermana: Educational implications of U.S./Mexico transnationalism for children. *Journal of Latinos and Education, 5*(4), 253–274.

Hamann, E. T., & Zúñiga, V. (2011). Schooling, national affinity(ies), and transnational students in Mexico. In S. Vandeyar (Ed.), *Hyphenated selves: Immigrant identities within education contexts* (pp. 57–72). The Netherlands: Rozenburg.

Ladson-Billings, G. (2006). It's not the culture of poverty, it's the poverty of culture:The problem with teacher education. *Anthropology and Education Quarterly, 37*(2), 104–109.

Mahan, J. M., & Stachowski, L. (1990). New horizons: Student teaching abroad to enrich understanding of diversity. *Action in Teacher Education 12*(3), 13–21.

Marx, H., & Moss, D. M. (2011). Please mind the culture gap: Intercultural development during a teacher education study abroad program. *Journal of Teacher Education, 62*(1), 35–47.

Merryfield, M. M. (2000). Why aren't teachers being prepared to teach for diversity, equity, and global interconnectedness? A study of lived experiences in the making of multicultural and global education. *Teaching and Teacher Education 16*, 429–443.

Meyers, S. (2009a). So you don't get tricked: Counter-narratives of literacy in a rural Mexican community. *The Community Literacy Journal, 3*(2), 19–35.

Meyers, S. (2009b). Calling the shots: The value of literacy in rural Mexico. *Decision: Expertise for Action in Adult Education, Spring*, 55–58.

McLaren, P. (1994). White terror and oppositional agency: Towards a critical multiculturalism. In D. T. Goldberg (Ed.), *Multiculturalism: A critical reader* (pp. 45–74). Oxford, England: Blackwell.

Milner, H. R. (2005). Stability and change in US prospective teachers' beliefs and decisions about diversity and learning to teach. *Teaching and Teacher Education, 21*(7), 767–786.

Murillo, E. G. (2002). How does it feel to be a *problem?* "Disciplining" the transnational subject in the New South. In S. Wortham, E. G. Murillo, & E. T. Hamann (Eds.), *Education in the New Latino Diaspora: Policy and the politics of identity* (pp. 215–240). Westport, CT: Ablex.

National Science Foundation, Committee on Equal Opportunities in Science and Engineering. (2004). *Broadening participation in America's science and engineering workforce: The 1994–2003 decennial and 2004 biennial reports to Congress.* Washington, DC: Author. Retrieved January 1, 2009, from http://www.nsf.gov/of/oia/activities/ceose/reports/ceose2004report.pdf

Nieto, S. (1998). From claiming hegemony to sharing space: Creating community in multicultural courses. In R. Chavez & J. O'Donnell (Eds.), *Speaking the unpleasant: The politics of (non)engagement in the multicultural education terrain* (pp. 16–31). Albany, NY: State University of New York Press.

Pence, H. M., & Macgillivray, I. K. (2007). The impact of an international field experience on preservice teachers. *Teaching and Teacher Education 24*, 14–25.

Richardson Bruna, K. (2007a). Manufacturing dissent: The new economy of power relations in multicultural teacher education. *The International Journal of Multicultural Education 9*(1). Retrieved from http://ijme-journal.org/index.php/ijme

Richardson Bruna, K. (2007b). Traveling tags: The informal literacies of Mexican newcomers in and out of the classroom. *Linguistics and Education, 18*, 232–257.

Richardson Bruna, K., Chamberlin, D., Lewis, H., & Ceballos, E. (2007). Teaching science to students from rural Mexico: What educators need to know. *The Science Teacher, 74*(8), 36–40.

Richardson Bruna, K. & Chamberlin, D. (2008). Illuminated by the shadow: US-Mexico schooling and pedagogies of place. *Multicultural Perspectives, 10*(3), 123–132.

Richardson Bruna, K. (2009a). Materializing multiculturalism: Deconstruction and cumulation in teaching language, culture, and non(identity). *Mind, Culture, & Activity, 16*(2), 183–190.

Richardson Bruna, K.& Lewis, H. (2009b). Sister city, sister science: Science for sustainable rural living in the new borderlands. In W.-M. Roth (Ed.), *Taking a stand(point): Science education from people for people* (pp. 90–114). New York, NY: Routledge.

Richardson Bruna, K. (2012). On knowing and US Mexican youth: Bordering science education research, practice, and policy. In B. J. Fraser, K. G. Tobin, & C. J. McRobbie (Eds.), *Second international handbook of science education* (Vol. 2, pp. 555–568). New York, NY: Springer.

Rumbaut, R. G. (2006).The making of a people.In M. Tienda & F. Mitchell (Eds.), *Hispanics and the future of America* (pp. 16–65). Washington, DC: The National Academies Press.

Sleeter, C. E. (2001). Preparing teachers for culturally diverse schools: Research and the overwhelming presence of whiteness. *Journal of Teacher Education 52*(2), 94–106.

Sleeter, C. E., & Grant, C. A. (1999). *Making choices for multicultural education: Five approaches to race, class, and gender* (3rd ed.). Upper Saddle River, NJ: Macmillan.

Spindler, G. D. (1997). Transcultural sensitization. In G. D. Spindler (Ed.), *Education and cultural process: Anthropological approaches* (pp. 498–512). Prospect Heights, IL: Waveland Press.

State Data Center of Iowa. (2013). Online resource. Retrieved from March 19, 2014 at http://www.iowadatacenter.org/Publications/latinos2013.pdf

Suárez-Orozco, C. (2004). Formulating identity in a globalized world. In M. M. Suarez-Orozco & D. B. Qin-Hilliard (Eds.), *Globalization: Culture and education in the new millennium* (pp. 173–202). Berkele, CA: University of California Press.

Suárez-Orozco, M. M., & Qin-Hilliard, D. B. (2004). Globalization: Culture and education in the new millennium. In M. M. Suarez-Orozco & D. B. Qin-Hilliard (Eds.), *Globalization: Culture and education in the new millennium* (pp. 1–37). Berkeley, CA: University of California Press.

Thorpe, H. (2011). *Just like us: The true story of four Mexican girls coming of age in America*. New York, NY: Scribner.

Trueba, E. T. (2004). *The new Americans: Immigrants and transnationals at work*. New York, NY: Rowman & Littlefield.

Villegas, A. M., & Lucas, T (2002). *Educating culturally responsive teachers: A coherent approach*. Albany, NY: State University of New York Press.

Wiggins, R. A., Follo, E. J., & Eberly, M. B. (2007). The impact of a field immersion program on pre-service teachers' attitudes toward teaching in culturally diverse classrooms. *Teaching and Teacher Education, 23*, 653–663.

Willard-Holt, C. (2001). The impact of a short-term international experience for preservice teachers. *Teaching and Teacher Education 17*, 505–517.

Woodrick, A. C. (2006). Preparing the way: Hispanic ministry and community transformation in Marshalltown, Iowa. *Urban Anthropology, 35*(2-3), 265–294.

Zúñiga, V., & Hamann, E. T. (2009). Sojourners in Mexico with U.S. school experience: A new taxonomy for transnational students. *Comparative Education Review, 53*(3), 329–353.

CHAPTER 17

EDUCATION POLICY IMPLEMENTATION IN THE NEW LATINO DIASPORA

Jennifer Stacy, Edmund T. Hamann, and Enrique G. Murillo, Jr.

Villages, towns, and cities throughout the United States, including the 41 states of the New Latino Diaspora (NLD), continue to host/receive heterogeneous populations of Latinos who transform the physical and cultural landscape in ways that require social institutions, like schools and universities, to respond. Increasingly, this transformation includes newcomer parents starting families. Thirty-three percent of the U.S. Hispanic population is age 18 or younger, while that age profile is true of slightly below 20% of non-Hispanic Whites (Pew Hispanic Center, 2012). While voter rolls and retirement community residents may remain much Whiter than the U.S. population as a whole for a number of decades, school enrollment will be increasingly Latino.

Table 17.1 (next page) shows the 22 NLD states where Latinos constitute at least 10% of the age 18 or younger population (as of 2011). It also highlights that in only one of those states, Maryland, is more than half of the Latino population (51%) foreign-born, although in seven more than 40% of the Latino population was not U.S.-born. We share these numbers

Revisiting Education in the New Latino Diaspora, pp. 335–347
Copyright © 2015 by Information Age Publishing

because they clarify the underlying demography, including demographic shifts, that compels educational institutions to respond to this portion of their enrollment.

Table 17.1.   New Latino Diaspora States With Hispanics Constituting at Least 10% of the 18-and-Under Population (Also Shows Total Hispanic Population and Portion of Hispanic Population That Was Foreign-Born), 2011

State	Total Hispanic Population	Percentage of 18-and-Under Population That is Hispanic	Percentage of Hispanic Population That is Foreign-Born
Nevada	738,000	40%	41%
Oregon	466,000	21%	37%
Rhode Island	135,000	21%	41%
Washington	790,000	20%	35%
Utah	373,000	17%	40%
Kansas	307,000	17%	34%
Idaho	182,000	17%	31%
Nebraska	174,000	16%	39%
Massachusetts	650,000	15%	31%
Oklahoma	347,000	15%	33%
Hawaii	126,000	15%	9%
Wyoming	52,000	15%	19%
North Carolina	828,000	14%	47%
Connecticut	494,000	14%	26%
Delaware	76,000	14%	32%
Georgia	880,000	13%	47%
Maryland	489,000	12%	51%
Virginia	649,000	11%	47%
Arkansas	190,000	11%	42%
Pennsylvania	750,000	10%	23%
Indiana	397,000	10%	34%
Wisconsin	344,000	10%	30%

The seven preceding chapters all illustrate how various educational institutions in the NLD have addressed various goals for various Latino populations. Each response, whether a formal policy (like that addressed by Lowenhaupt), a partnership (like those described by Gallo, Wortham, and Bennett and Richardson Bruna), an inquiry into how the accumulation of policies have shaped teacher beliefs (as in Contreras, Stritikus, Torres, & O'Reilly Diaz and Adair), or something as modest as a university course with a travel study component (Sawyer) embeds and transmits varying ideologies about who Latinos are, how we/they are or are not imagined as part of the community, and what we/they are assumed to need. These responses are all, on varying scales, policies that seek to reform a certain aspect of the educational experience in the NLD. In practically all of these cases although Latinos are the objects of policy implementation, they are not key architects of it. The BESITOS program described by Herrera and Holmes stands out as an exception on this account.

The authors of these seven chapters remind us that community responses to Latinos are neither unilateral nor unidirectional. Nor are they ever fully implemented in accordance with the ideals by which they were conceived. Rather, actual responses—the praxis of education in the NLD—depends on the comprehension and conviction of those who mediate the conversion of policies into practice. With cases spanning the country from Washington State to Tennessee, collectively the authors of this section of the book illuminate both the range and nuance of educational policy implementation within the NLD.

Levinson and Sutton (2001) write that policy is always appropriated by practitioners and intermediaries; it is the creative way through which, "agents 'take in' elements of policy, thereby incorporating these discursive and institutional resources into their own schemes of interest, motivation, and action" (p. 3). The myriad voices that are captured by the authors of this section, ranging from students and parents to teachers, administrators, and state policymakers (as well as the chapter authors themselves), remind us that policy appropriation happens by many means simultaneously. The dialogic nature of policy is exponential and interconnected: it is appropriated individually by stakeholders on a microlevel, but as it is executed these appropriations come into dialogues with each other and construct a complex interplay of conceptions and action, each in varying degrees of accordance (or fidelity) to the original ideas. The authors in this section invite us to enter into the dialogic space of policy appropriation within the context of the NLD.

Our summation/reaction looks at the dialogues that are happening in each of the seven chapters within this section. Then, we put the chapters in dialogue with each other to shed light on emergent themes. It is this intersection of dialogues in which readers are invited to engage in order to convert findings into educational practices, policies, research, and/or cautionary tales. Table 17.1 showed how numerous and geographically widespread is the rising generation of Latinos in the NLD, but on their own numbers do not illuminate the heterogeneity—by age, origin, (im) permanence, community history, and so forth—that frames the varying experiences of NLD Latinos in educational settings. As Hamann and Harklau (2010) insisted in the *Handbook on Latinos and Education* chapter that was adapted to start this volume, the time for surprise and improvisational response to Latinos in NLD educational settings is over. Latino students constitute a large and growing proportion of enrollments from New England to the Great Plains, from the Deep South to the Pacific Northwest. Collectively, they are not being served as well by schools as the population they are replacing. The chapters analyzed not only shed varying insights into why or how this has been so, they collectively offer an insistent voice: From now on, it needs to be better. Fortunately, a cross-chapter analysis suggests some ways for this to become so.

The Dialogues of Different Stakeholders

Throughout these seven chapters, we are reminded that educational institutions encompass and configure multiple stakeholders of various backgrounds who interact with policies, practices, and each other, resulting in a complex and intriguing dialogue that shapes the cultural context of the educational space. Inevitably, the heterogeneity (Wortham & Rhodes, this volume) of the NLD and of these accounts (ranging from early childhood to higher education) is both a starting point and a caution; while there may be a shared imperative for "getting education right" for Latinos in the NLD; there is not a single pathway for realizing this goal. The authors of these seven chapters have presented research that highlights how different stakeholders within these communities co-construct and interact with the educational infrastructure. They shed light on what different stakeholders deem to be an appropriate educational response to meet the needs and aspirations of Latino students and their families. This is exhibited through the policies that are drawn up by Departments of Education and school administrators and through the process by which these policies are understood, adapted or ignored, and acted upon.

Loewenhaupt's chapter on the Bilingual Education Policy in Wisconsin is the most straightforward analysis in this collection of a statewide policy being put into practice. She follows up on Wisconsin's mandate for schools to establish "Bilingual-Bicultural" programs by surveying principals statewide to illustrate how the policy has been appropriated (Hamann & Rosen, 2011; Levinson & Sutton, 2001). The policy's title about bilingual education was misleading; the content of the mandate privileged English immersion and as a result, the majority of schools in the state (76%) decided to forego the bilingual education component of the mandate and implement pullout English as a Second Language (ESL) programs. While most schools complied with the mandate's call for bilingual or ESL-certified teachers, Loewenhaupt reports that staffing was not sufficient to support actual enrollments, resulting in high student-to-teacher ratios at the schools with the most Spanish-speaking students. Aware of the dialogue between principals and state policy, Loewenhaupt cautions against blaming the mandate for the shortcomings of implementing actual bilingual supports for the Spanish-speaking students. Rather, she suggests that state and local agencies must provide the support, guidance, and resources to facilitate local school's discussions with policies.

Herrera and Holmes present the only dialogue in this section that directly includes the voices of students (although there are many such examples in Chapters 2 through 9 of this volume). Findings from a survey of students, the majority Latino, participating in the BESITOS program at Kansas State University revealed that these students' experiences were diverse and that sculpting an experience in higher education that is congruent with students' backgrounds requires much more than simply recruiting more Latino students. They show that an increase in structural diversity (in this case, the recruitment of more Latino students) across campus did not guarantee cross-group informal interactions nor classroom diversity; as a result, "Latina/o students often struggle to see themselves as members of the university community" (p. 231, this volume). Herrera and Holmes argue that the university's recruitment and retention efforts must respond to these students by expanding efforts to incorporate students' biographies into all aspects of the university and offering genuine support not only through special programs.

Two studies in this section focused on the dialogue between educational policy and parents. Adair used multivocal ethnography to involve parents in a conversation about preschool, the inclusion of bilingual teachers, and an informal bilingual program. Parents in towns in Iowa and Tennessee watched a video of an informal bilingual preschool classroom in Arizona and discussed it in focus groups. The parents' children were not enrolled in a bilingual preschool program, yet the video spurred conversations about their beliefs of how school *should* be for their children in their own districts. The discussions illuminated a power differential between parents and teachers that resulted in barriers to communication and authentic relationships between parents and teachers as well as students and teachers. Although parents complied with school practices, they did not always agree with them; they felt that bilingual teachers would help the school perceive them more positively *as parents* and not just *as immigrants*, and help their children have better and more just learning experiences. The most poignant finding from this study, though, was not the concerns of the parents per se, but rather that the teachers did not know these concerns or did not know how to respond to them effectively. The parents, though grateful for this educational experience for their children, did not feel comfortable expressing their concerns to the teachers (even though Adair was able to elicit them). When there was an opportunity to discuss parent concerns during a focus group session, the teachers resented the criticisms (illustrating the parents' correct assumption that their feedback would not be welcome). This structural barrier indicates that the manner in which and the extent to which the parents are invited to engage in the dialogue about Latino students in schools is determined by the school (Adair suggests that the school expects parents to abide by a proimmigrant script [Hamann, 2002; Súarez-Orozco, 1998]) and is, as a result, limited.

Gallo and her co-researchers studied a collaborative effort between a school district and a university to increase Spanish-speaking parents' involvement in a school in the mid-Atlantic town of Marshall. (See also Wortham & Rhodes, this volume.) That project facilitated parent involvement through parent meetings with school administrators and through the use of after-school resource rooms. Over time, the project shifted from using a *traditional approach* to working with parents, which was educator-centered and included the school telling the parents what they should to, to a *repertoire approach* that recognizes individuals' experiences with cultural practices that may or may not reflect the shared histories of a group. The latter approach had a "divergent capacity and commitment to heterogeneous ideals and repertoires" (Gutierrez & Rogoff in Gallo et al., p. 269, this volume). In regard to parent involvement, this approach adopts some of the repertoires of everyone involved, expanding everyone's capacity in the process. The project organically transitioned from a traditional approach as the teachers and parents formed more personal relationships and the teachers responded to parents' requests for language instruction in the resource rooms. Parents also asked to take over organizing the parent meetings with the administration, advancing the shift toward a repertoire approach. Perhaps because this was a long-term project or perhaps because of sustained third-party involvement, the parents, teachers, school officials, and researchers were able to move past the structural power imbalance that Adair had noted in her study and generate a more equitable dialogue amongst participants.

Four of the seven chapters in this section looked more intently at teachers, including the just-discussed Adair chapter. Another chapter (Contreras et al.) accounted for teachers' responses to the changing demographics at their schools in the Pacific Northwest and posited how these perceptions could contribute to the educational experiences of Latinos. The two other studies (Sawyer & Richardson Bruna) looked at travel-study programs constructed for teachers to help them learn critical intercultural skills to be better prepared to work with Latino students and families, although in Richardson Bruna's example the educator participants were no longer in the classroom, but instead educational administrators. All four studies, demonstrate the centrality of educators in shaping the institutional response to Latino families.

Contreras and her research team used a mixed methods approach to learn about teachers' perceptions of and interactions with Latino students and their families at eight different school districts (urban, rural, urban ring) in Washington State. Through survey data, they found that while all schools were concerned with accountability for Latino student learning measured via state testing, rural schools were more concerned than urban. Interview data found that teachers placed a degree of blame on Latino students for preventing the school from meeting their goals. The majority of teachers surveyed felt that less than a quarter of their Latino students were bound for college, and while it was not made clear how these attitudes translated into practice, in the interviews, a general deficit view of how these students prepared for the future was articulated and concerns for college readiness were deflected to a special program to help students prepare for higher education. Echoing the findings of Adair (this volume), Washington teachers cited the limitations of the language barrier when working with parents, yet few discussed how they actively worked to engage parents. Contreras et al. pointed to the integral role that teachers play in forming the educational landscape for Latino students and determining the degree to which students and families are included in the dialogues that shaped their educational experience.

Both Sawyer and Richardson Bruna presented participant-observation studies of programs that were aimed at better preparing teachers and administrators to work with students and families within the NLD through short-term travel abroad experiences in Mexico. Sawyer focused on three practicing teachers from Nebraska during their visit to Guadalajara. All of the teachers were working in towns that had experienced increases in Latino students and were also involved in school initiatives that aimed to support Latino students. Although the teachers had varying degrees of cultural immersion experiences prior to the trip, all three teachers attributed a growing sense of cross-cultural awareness, and an awareness of their own personal biases to their time spent in Mexico. Furthermore, the teachers also indicated how their experience could apply to their teaching practices, such as utilizing greater rigor when placing Mexican-origin students in language and intervention programs and reaching out to Latino parents while expressing a genuine empathy. Such insights suggest that teachers are more apt to think critically about school policies in a way that is empathetic to Latino students and families after participating in such trip, but Sawyer also finds (echoing Hamann [2003]) that the individual transformation the teachers claimed was not reciprocated by a larger response from their educational workplaces. That is, the teachers felt like they knew more and could be more responsive to Latino students and parents, but also that the systems they were part of were not necessarily responsive to or interested in their new capacities.

Richardson Bruna reports on the even briefer experiences of about thirty superintendents, principals, ELL coordinators, teacher educators, and Iowa Department of Education administrators who participated in state-sponsored trips to Villachuato, Mexico. Instead of individual graduate students enrolling in coursework that includes travel-study (which is what Sawyer describes), a key point here is that there was systemic (i.e., state department of education) approval of the learning opportunity. This is even more impressive when one realizes that Iowa's Latino population was not quite big enough, proportionally to even qualify it for Table 17.1 (which counted the NLD states where at least 10% of the 18-and-under population in 2011 was Latino), although at 9% it almost made that table's admittedly arbitrary threshold.

The described trip visited the Mexican community of Villachuato, which, although only a small town of just over 3000 inhabitants, was the largest sending community to Marshalltown, Iowa (population 27,500), a meat-packing community with a sizeable Latino newcomer contingent. The Villachuato visits were intended to "provide these educational professionals with understandings about the kinds of family and schooling experiences that are antecedent to and preconfigure their interactions, in Iowa, with immigrant youth from rural Mexican communities so that they could better advocate for teaching practices and policies that would best serve, from an additive stance, their cultural and linguistic differences and related socio-academic interests and needs" (Richardson Bruna, this volume, p. 313).

Richardson Bruna demonstrates how the participants came to acknowledge and reexamine the "worlds in [their] heads" (Delpit, 1993, as cited in Richardson Bruna, this volume), that is, the beliefs, based on particular interpretive lenses, that they held about the Latino students in Iowa's schools. Participants' post-trip reflections about photographs that they had also viewed before departing included more intricate insights to the globalized and transnational characteristics of Villachuato, such as the recognition of that community's economic dependence on resources from the U.S. (remittances) used to upgrade and upkeep houses and the related recognition that the U.S. subsidizing corn production (including in Iowa) meant traditional corn growing in Villachuato was no longer economically competitive. Trip participants reported integrating their experiences into their worksites and their relations with Latino students and their families; one participant even replicated the "worlds in their heads" experience by using Richardson Bruna's techniques of examining photographs in professional development sessions. The changes in the participants' "worlds" based on this experience potentially changed how they participated in the dialogue concerning Latino students.

Looking Across Chapters

By clustering these seven chapters together, an underlying conversation between the authors can be made explicit and used to identify at least two topics that deserve further recognition and pondering. First, is the notion of space, belonging, and possibility. The second is educational decisions concerning Latino students in the NLD.

The Concept of Space in the New Latino Diaspora

The concept of space can be looked at several ways. In the simplest regard, space can reference the geographical location in which something occurs, in these cases where a policy is conceived and where it is appropriated. The spaces of the educational infrastructure in these seven studies physically expanded beyond the walls of the schools, crossing into homes, communities, and even into different countries. For example, of the studies depicted how policies reach into students' families' lives in attempts to be more inclusive. Loewenhaupt's analysis of Wisconsin's bilingual-bicultural policy showed state leaders' acknowledgement of the linguistic and cultural dynamics of Latino students' home and their acknowledgement that these children were developing language and cultural practices that transcend traditional conceptions of group culture and language, but the space where this understanding exists (or, more accurately existed) was different from where its observation in practice was to occur. When put into conversation with Adair's and Gallo et al.'s studies, it seems likely that parents would support bilingual and bicultural approaches that would permit students and families the opportunity to develop language skills in both English and Spanish. However, Contreras et al. and Adair demonstrate how the perceptions and preconceptions of teachers can thwart efforts to be more accommodating and accepting of different cultural and linguistic backgrounds. In other words, what seemed advisable and welcome in the domestic spaces of Latino households and, at least in Wisconsin, in the spaces of state-level policymakers did not seem to translate into the classrooms negotiated by Latino children.

Sawyer and Richardson Bruna, however, show that the worlds that educators hold in their heads are not fixed; they can develop and change. The curricular and pedagogical geography of school can physically include the space of Latino students' (multiple) country(ies) of origin through educators' visits to those places. Holding the dialogue in this space permits educators to physically experience a piece of students' and families' lives and learn/appropriate the implications of a structural response, or policy, in a personal manner.

Still, Herrera and Holmes remind us that Latino students' backgrounds stem not only from possible sending communities, but also from the contexts in the United States in which most grew up, partially or completely. Educators need not go as far as Mexico to learn more about students' lives: a more authentic and empathetic understanding of the U.S.-based communities could be integrated into Euro-American-dominated schools and universities. The geo-cultural space of the NLD connects sending sites and receiving sites in transnational communities in which the community has a plural, transnational physical geography that is incompletely defined as *here* or *there* (Guerra, 1998).

As the term "geo-cultural" hints, space can be conceptualized in additional ways than just physical geography. As individuals—parents, students, teachers, administrators, policymakers—enter into dialogue with each other, a "third space" develops between them (Gutierrez, Baquedano-Lopez, Tejeda, 1999). Instead of merely focusing on the back and forth interplay between the initial utterance (the policy or practice in this case) and the other's reply, Bakhtin included the relation between the two as a third dialogic space (Holquist, 1990). This thirdness is a manner to capture the "event of being" as it happens in dialogue, a concept that Bakhtin refers to as addressivity (Holquist, 1990). The dialogues that occur within and across chapters in this section, then, capture the educational addressivity in the contemporary NLD.

Through their analyses of policy implementations, Lowenhaupt, Herrera and Holmes, and Gallo et al. voice the need for support at the different levels of implementation that mirrors the realities of the populations they serve, but that are flexible enough to change over time to be reflective of the dialogue that is unfolding. Contreras et al. and Adair capture the role that teachers sometimes actively play in constructing barriers that hinder Latino students' and families' access to and involvement with educative resources. Yet even as these obstructions are revealed, efforts in Iowa (Richardson Bruna) and Nebraska (Sawyer) to foster intercultural competence suggest that educators can become cognizant of the barriers they are constructing (at that are socially extant) and actively work to abolish them and/or counteract them. For example, they can recognize and build on Latino families' "funds of knowledge"—the means families and social networks deploy to respond to various daily challenges (González, Moll, & Amanti, 2005).

Together, these chapters create a dialogue about educational responses *as they are* and *as they could be* within the NLD. In this space, policies must be implemented in a way that permits them to be molded in order to reflect the heterogeneity (Wortham, this volume) of Latinos in the United

States. Structural responses must include enough support, economic and otherwise, throughout the implementation process. And this support must also be flexible and responsive to the dialogic nature of policy.

Looking Forward: Education Decision Making in the New Latino Diaspora.

Dialogue is generative of ideas and it is hoped that the research presented in this section will encourage educators, researchers, and policymakers to think about the next steps in ways beyond our own imagining. However, we can offer our insight concerning the next steps that this conversation might take in order to continue and to be fruitful. The premise of future conversations must include the understanding that formal responses (which are conventionally called policies) are actually dialogic in nature (Levinson & Sutton, 2001). It is on this principle that we encourage readers to think about possible dialogic "next turns." Whose turn is next? Which voices have been included? Excluded? Who still needs to respond?

It is easy to jump to the conclusion that, knowing what we know now from various stakeholders, that policies should be turned back to their creators in order to be reconsidered and readjusted. However, that leaves intact the privilege of the initiator. We must recognize that there are several stakeholders who have not yet contributed to these conversations or who have only been able to react (not pro-act). Some studies have incorporated the voices of teachers, but not of students or parents. Some have focused on parents and teachers, but not on local or state administrators. Only one of the studies (Herrera and Holmes) actively included students' responses to a policy, but even in this study there is a need to hear from the faculty and staff to complete the dialogic portrait of the BESITOS program.

We do not intend this is criticism, but rather as a jumping off point. Thanks to these authors for capturing what they have captured and depicting what they have depicted, but what next? As these chapters illustrate (even when they include some "good news") the challenges of educationally serving Latinos well in the NLD still is far from full realization. The challenge then is to amplify the dialogue while actively molding and shaping policies to better address students' and families educational needs. Putting these seven chapters in dialogue with the introduction and other eight chapters of the book does offer some amplification. With that gesture we capture the *testimonios* recorded by Urrieta, Kolano, and O. Jo and Raible and Irizarry. We consider the fate of students and families who are not just Latino, not just Mexican, but Purépecha (Leco Tomas, this volume). We consider what it means when there are few other students like you, whether because of adoption (Flores-Koulish) or your district's very preliminary participation in the NLD (Bruening). These help us see that students' input in the dialogue of policy is arguably the most important: their response to the infrastructure informs us as to whether or not the changes we anticipated are manifested into reality.

David Labaree (2010) wrote that students are often the last rung on the ladder of educational reform, but the most important in regard to considering whether or not the reform "worked." Traditionally, efforts need to pass through many hands before they reach the students, yet how students interact with an initiative is the ultimate measure as to how well it served them. As states and towns respond to growth in their Latino populations, an effort is needed to pull students into the dialogue sooner. Imagine K–12 or college students reading the chapters about the changes they noted in their teachers and administrators after they visited their hometown in Mexico. Or reading the chapters about teachers in their states de facto erecting barriers rather than ameliorating opportunity.

The purpose here is not to argue that students as stakeholders should have a louder voice in how institutions respond to demographic changes. Rather, it is to raise awareness about the dialogue that happens inevitably when an institution crafts a policy to put into practice and to challenge educators to think about the presence and absence of stakeholders in that dialogue. The seven studies presented in this section have reminded us that there is a rich dialogue concerning Latino students happening within states and across research that entails multiple voices, but these dialogues and wise practices that could follow remain incomplete. The next step must be to expand the conversation to generate ideas that are authentic to the communities from which they emerge and that seek to best serve students and families in the New Latino Diaspora. Look again at Table 17.1 to remember just how many students, families, and communities this all matters to.

REFERENCES

González, N., Moll, L. C., & Amanti, C. 2005. *Funds of knowledge: Theorizing practices in households, communities, and classrooms.* Mahwah, NJ: Lawrence Erlbaum Associates.

Guerra, J. (1998). *Close to home: Oral and literate practices in a transnational Mexicano community.* New York, NY: Teachers College Press.

Gutierrez, K., Baquedano-Lopez, & P., Tejeda, C. (1999). Rethinking diversity: Hybridity and hybrid language practices in the third space. *Mind, Culture, & Activity, 6*(4), 286–303.

Hamann, E. T., (2002). ¿Un paso adelante? The politics of bilingual education, latino student accommodation, and school district management in southern Appalachia. In S. Wortham, E. G. Murillo, & E. T. Hamann (Eds.), *Education in the New Latino Diaspora: Policy and the politics of identity* (pp. 67–97). Westport, CT: Ablex.

Hamann, E. T. (2003). *The educational welcome of Latinos in the New South.* Westport, CT: Praeger.

Hamann, E. T., & Harklau, L. (2010). Education in the New Latino Diaspora. In E. G. Murillo (Ed.), *Handbook of Latinos and education* (pp. 157–169). New York, NY: Routledge. Retrieved from http://digitalcommons.unl.edu/teachlearnfacpub/104/

Hamann, E. T., & Rosen, L. (2011). What makes the anthropology of educational policy implementation "anthropological"? In B. Levinson & M. Pollock (Eds.), *Companion to the anthropology of education* (pp. 461–477). New York, NY: Wiley Blackwell.

Holquist, M. (1990). *Dialogism: Bakhtin and his world* (2nd ed.). New York, NY: Routledge

Labaree, D. (2010). *Someone has to fail: The zero-sum game of public schooling.* Cambridge, MA: Harvard University Press.

Levinson, B., & Sutton, M. (2001). Introduction: policy as/in practice—A sociocultural approach to the study of educational policy. In M. Sutton & B. Levinson (Eds.), *Policy as practice: Toward a comparative sociocultural analysis educational policy* (pp. 1–22). Westport, CT: Ablex.

Pew Research Center. (2012). Table 8: Statistical Portrait of Hispanics in the United States, 2012: Race and Ethnicity, by Sex and Age, 2012. Washington, DC: Author. Retrieved from http://www.pewhispanic.org/2014/04/29/statistical-portrait-of-hispanics-in-the-united-states-2012/-hispanic-population-by-nativity-2000-and-2012

Suárez-Orozco, M. M. (1998). State terrors: Immigrants and refugees in the postnational space. In Y. Zou & E. T. Trueba (Eds.), *Ethnic identity and power: Cultural contexts of political action in school and society* (pp. 283–319). Albany, NY: State University of New York Press.

ABOUT THE AUTHORS

Jennifer Keys Adair is an assistant professor in the Department of Curriculum and Instruction at The University of Texas at Austin where she studies the role of agency in transforming the learning experiences of young children, particularly children of immigrants attending low-income schools. Trained as a cultural anthropologist, Jennifer's work is concerned with racial, cultural and cross-cultural understandings of early childhood education. Jennifer has published in journals such as *Teachers College Record, Harvard Educational Review and Race, Ethnicity and Education* and recently co-authored the book *Children Crossing Borders*. In 2011, Jennifer was awarded the Outstanding Article of the Year award for her article "Confirming Chanclas: What Early Childhood Teacher Educators Can Learn From Immigrant Preschool Teachers" and in 2012 the Emerging Scholar Award from the Critical Perspectives in Early Childhood Education AERA special interest group.

Ian Bennett is Associate Professor at the Perelman School of Medicine of the University of Pennsylvania. A family physician and researcher focused on disparities in health seen among low income and race/ethnic minority populations, Dr. Bennett has carried out research on the health of mothers and children from the Latino Diaspora community in the Philadelphia region. He has published extensively in this area with more than 70 research papers and book chapters addressing health services for vulnerable populations.

Erika Bruening is a Visiting Instructor at Nebraska Wesleyan University. Her teaching focuses on the development of culturally responsive pedagogy with preservice and practicing educators in low-incidence contexts (e.g., schools with just a few identified ELLs). Her research emphasizes the development of pedagogical content knowledge and the role of teachers in policy implementation at the classroom level. She earned her EdD at the University of Nebraska-Lincoln and continues to serve as a high school reading instructor in Nebraska public schools.

Frances Contreras is an Associate Professor in the Department of Education Studies and Co-Director of the Joint Doctoral Program at the University of California San Diego. She researches issues of equity and access for Latina/o and underrepresented students in the education pipeline—the transition to college, community college transfer, affirmative action in higher education, and the role of the public policy arena in ensuring student equity across the P-20 continuum. Her most recent books include: *Achieving Equity for Latino Students: Expanding the Pathway to Higher Education through Public Policy* (Teachers College Press, 2011) and *The Latino Education Crisis* with P. Gandara (Harvard University Press, 2009). Her work has been published in leading education journals such as the *Harvard Educational Review, Educational Policy, Journal of Hispanics in Higher Education*, and the *Bilingual Research Journal. Diverse Magazine* has honored her as an "Emerging Scholar" and "Top 25 to Watch" among academicians in the United States.

Sarah Gallo is an Assistant Professor in the Department of Teaching and Learning at The Ohio State University. Her research focuses on bilingual and immigrant education, and draws up ethnographic and linguistic anthropological tools to explore the multilingual language and literacy resources that Latino immigrant children deploy and develop across contexts. Her work has appeared in journals such as *American Educational Researcher Journal, International Multilingual Research Journal,* and *Journal of Language, Identity, and Education.*

Edmund T. Hamann is a Professor in the Department of Teaching, Learning, & Teacher Education at the University of Nebraska-Lincoln. An anthropologist of education, he earned his MA in anthropology from the University of Kansas and his PhD in education from the University of Pennsylvania. He has authored more than 60 peer reviewed journal articles, book chapters, and books on the topics of education and migration, education policy implementation, and school reform, including *The Educational Welcome of Latinos in the New South* (2003) and *Alumnos Transnacionales: Las Escuelas Mexicanas Frente a la Globalización* (2008). In 2002 he co-edited *Education in the New Latino Diaspora* (Ablex Press) with the other two editors of this new volume.

Socorro Herrera is a Professor in the Department of Curriculum and Instruction in the College of Education at Kansas State University and directs the Center for Intercultural and Multilingual Advocacy (CIMA). Her K–12 teaching experience includes an emphasis on literacy development, and her research focuses on culturally responsive teaching, strategies for academic language development, and teacher preparation for diversity in the classroom. She has authored six textbooks and numerous articles for publication in journals such as the *Bilingual Research Journal, Journal of Hispanic Higher Education*, and *Journal of Latinos and Education*. She conducts multistate and international professional development on issues related to teacher preparation, biography-driven instruction, and classroom accommodations for culturally and linguistically diverse (CLD) students.

Melissa Holmes serves as Associate Director for Adult Education and Study Abroad in the Center for Intercultural and Multilingual Advocacy (CIMA) in the College of Education at Kansas State University. Her teaching experience focuses on the development of academic language and advocacy skills among culturally and linguistically diverse (CLD) students in higher education. Her research emphasizes the differential learning needs of CLD students and biography-driven instructional strategies for culturally responsive teaching. She coauthored *Crossing the Vocabulary Bridge: Differentiated Strategies for Diverse Secondary Classrooms* (2011). Her work has been featured in a book chapter and has appeared in journals such as *International Journal of Multicultural Education, Journal of College Student Retention, Multicultural Learning and Teaching*, and *Teaching Education*.

Jason G. Irizarry is Director of Urban Education and an Associate Professor in the College of Education at the University of Massachusetts-Amherst. His research focuses on urban teacher recruitment, preparation, and retention with an emphasis on increasing the number of teachers of color, culturally responsive pedagogy, youth participatory action research, and Latino students in U.S. schools. A central focus of his work involves promoting the academic achievement of youth in urban schools by addressing issues associated with teacher education. He is also the author of the award-winning book, *The Latinization of U.S. Schools: Successful Teaching and Learning in Shifting Cultural Contexts* (Paradigm Publishers, 2011) and Co-Editor of *Diaspora Studies in Education: Toward a Framework for Understanding the Experiences of Transnational Communities* (Peter Lang, 2014).

Ji-Yeon O. Jo is the Korea Foundation Assistant Professor and the Kenan Junior Faculty Fellow in the Department of Asian Studies at the University of North Carolina at Chapel Hill. She earned her PhD from the School of Education at the University of North Carolina at Chapel Hill. Her research interests center around issues of language, culture, race/ethnicity, and identity, specifically in relation to sense of belonging, citizenship, and cultural capital in transnational migration contexts. She has published book chapters and several articles in peer-reviewed academic journals. Her current research explores the interactions and intersections among language, law, and family life of ethnic Korean return migrants in South Korea who grew up in the three major regions of the Korean Diaspora—China, the Commonwealth of Independent States, and the United States.

Lan Quach Kolano is an Associate Professor and the Graduate Director of the Teaching English as a Second Language (TESL) programs at the University of North Carolina at Charlotte. She completed her PhD at the University of North Carolina at Chapel Hill in 2004 after working as a public elementary school teacher in Virginia and North Carolina. She has published broadly with a research agenda focused on the educational experiences of learners from diverse immigrant communities and in the development of multicultural teacher efficacy. She is currently leading a 2-year ethnographic project examining the role of community outreach and advocacy on Southeast Asian immigrant youth.

Casimiro Leco Tomás is professor in the Instituto de Investigaciones Económicas y Empresariales (Institute of Economic and Business Studies) of the Universidad Michoacana de San Nicolás de Hidalgo. Recognized as a Level 2 researcher in Mexico's national system of scholars, his research focuses on the migration of Mexican indigenous populations to the United States and migration policy.

Rebecca Lowenhaupt is an Assistant Professor in the Educational Leadership department of the Lynch School of Education at Boston College. She earned an EdM in School Leadership from Harvard University and a PhD in Educational Leadership and Policy Analysis from the University of Wisconsin-Madison. She completed a postdoctoral fellowship with the Distributed Leadership Study at Northwestern University. Her research focuses on leadership and school reform in the context of immigration. Her work has appeared in several academic journals, including *Education & Urban Society* and the *Journal of Educational Administration*. She has received funding for her research from the Spencer Foundation and the National Science Foundation.

C. Allen Lynn: After serving in the Peace Corps (Honduras 1999-2001), Dr. Lynn earned an M.A. at Teachers College, Columbia University and a PhD from the University of Georgia. He is currently an assistant professor in the Watson College of Education at the University of North Carolina Wilmington where his research interests focus on marginalized English language learner populations.

Amanda R. Morales is an Assistant Professor of Foundations and Multicultural Education in the Department of Curriculum and Instruction as well as the Diversity Coordinator for the College of Education at Kansas State University. Her research foci include education foundations, issues of equity and social justice in education, recruitment and retention of Latino/ as in higher education, and underrepresented minorities in science. Morales was the recipient of two national awards for her dissertation work at Kansas State University; one from the American Educational Research Association, Division K in 2012 and one from the American Association of Colleges for Teacher Education in 2013. She is the author of twelve peer-reviewed journal articles and book chapters and has collaborated with three of the authors and one of the editors of this new volume.

Enrique G. Murillo, Jr. is a Professor in the Teacher Education and Foundations Department of the College of Education at California State University, San Bernardino. He earned his Ph.D. from the University of North Carolina-Chapel Hill. He is the Founding Editor of the *Journal of Latinos and Education* and the editor of the *Handbook on Latinos and Education* (2010). He is the founder of the National Latino Education Network (NLEN). He currently serves as Executive Director and founder of the LEAD organization (Latino Education & Advocacy Days). And he was recently elected President of the Southern California Consortium of Hispanic-Serving Institutions. In 2002 he co-edited *Education in the New Latino Diaspora* (Ablex Press) with the other two editors of this new volume.

Karen O'Reilly-Diaz is a PhD candidate in Curriculum and Instruction at the University of Washington. Her research focuses on the relationships between schools and nondominant families, and communities. Her current work seeks to understand collective efforts of Latino/immigrant families and public schools and their potential to create more equitable educational opportunities for Latino/a students.

John Raible is Associate Professor of Diversity & Curriculum Studies and Women's & Gender Studies at the University of Nebraska-Lincoln. He has been interviewed on television and documentaries for his work on transracial adoption, and in the *Los Angeles Times*, the *Wall Street Journal*, *Essence*

Magazine, and the BBC Radio World Service. His scholarly publications include chapters in *Adolescents At School: Perspectives on Youth, Identity, and Education;* the *Handbook of Adoption; Sage Handbook of Curriculum and Instruction;* and *Empowering Teachers for Equity and Diversity: Progressive Perspectives on Research, Theory, and Practice* and articles in *Race, Ethnicity and Education; Teaching & Teacher Education;* the *Journal of LGBT Youth;* and the *Journal of Latinos and Education,* among others.

Catherine R. Rhodes is a joint PhD candidate in Education, Culture, and Society in the Graduate School of Education and Linguistic Anthropology in the Anthropology Department at the University of Pennsylvania. She holds in M.A. in Social Sciences (specialization in Linguistic Anthropology) from the University of Chicago and has a BA with highest honors in Latin American Studies from the University of North Carolina at Chapel Hill. Her Fulbright-Hayes-funded dissertation research—situated in Yucatán Mexico—explores the relationship between the production of scientific knowledge and models of personhood. She has published on topics including scale, narrative, social identification, and the New Latino Diaspora and co-produced the ethnographic film *Adelante.*

Katherine Richardson Bruna is an Associate Professor of Multicultural Education in the School of Education at Iowa State University (ISU). Trained in the tools of educational anthropology, she has produced ethnographic accounts of schooling, particularly as related to the science learning experiences of newcomer Mexican immigrant youth in Iowa's demographically transitioning communities. She has published on this work in journals such as *Linguistics & Education* and *Cultural Studies of Science Education* as well as in her edited volume *Talking Science, Writing Science: The Work of Language in Multicultural Classrooms.* Dr. Richardson Bruna currently serves as the Project Lead for ISU's new promise program partnership with two demographically transitioning elementary schools in urban Des Moines neighborhoods. The goal of the Pathways to College Initiative is to enhance college access and affordability for youth historically-excluded from higher education as well as the diversity of the ISU student body.

Adam Sawyer is an assistant professor for the Bard College Master of Arts in Teaching Program. He has written extensively on schooling within rural and urban contexts of Mexican migration in the United States and Mexico as well as the development of culturally responsive teaching practices within these locales. His work has been published by such outlets as *International Migration Review, Teachers College Press, Teacher Education Quarterly* and *Migration Policy Institute.* Prior to his academic career, Adam worked as a Spanish bilingual teacher in California and as a consultant to the Mexican Ministry of Education.

Jennifer Stacy is a PhD candidate at the University of Nebraska-Lincoln who previously taught elementary and high school in Monterrey Mexico. Her research looks at school-based family literacy programs as a way to learn about how educational institutions perceive Latino families and how this perception influences formal and informal familial outreach initiatives. Through ethnography, she explores how family literacy serves as a nexus where literacy and language learning meet adult and elementary education and how this space influences the roles that newcomer parents take on in their children's schooling.

Tom Stritikus is the deputy director of the College Ready program at the Bill and Melinda Gates Foundation. From 2010 to 2014 he was Dean of the University of Washington's College of Education and before that was a professor there, starting in 2000. His work focuses on the context and process of adjustment for immigrant students and the educational opportunities—from a policy and practice perspective—that schools and districts make available to them. He has taught English in Mexico and, with Teach for America, elementary school in Baltimore. He earned his PhD from the University of California Berkeley.

Kathryn Torres is a PhD candidate in Educational Leadership and Policy Studies at the University of Washington and an Institute of Education Sciences Pre-Doctoral Fellow. Her work has focused on the intersection of accountability and school context within district and school-level implementation responses, the role of leadership for NCLB implementation within context, building district and school capacity to serve diverse student needs, parent involvement, and educational reform.

Luis Urrieta is an Associate Professor and Program Director for the Cultural Studies in Education Program in the Department of Curriculum & Instruction of the College of Education at the University of Texas at Austin. He has by courtesy appointments in Mexican American and Latino Studies, Native American & Indigenous Studies, and Latin American Studies. He earned his Ph.D. at the University of North Carolina at Chapel Hill. His research focuses on processes of identity formation, agency as social and cultural practice, and learning in family and community contexts, in particular in U.S. Latin@ and indigenous communities of Latin America. He is the author of numerous juried publications, including *Working from Within: Chicana and Chicano Activist Educators in Whitestream Schools* (2009, University of Arizona Press).

Stanton E. F. Wortham is the Judy & Howard Berkowitz Professor and an Associate Dean at the University of Pennsylvania's Graduate School of Education. Dr. Wortham has pursued interdisciplinary studies that stretch across anthropology, education, linguistics, philosophy, and psychology. As a graduate student, he continued his interdisciplinary training in the Committee on Human Development at the University of Chicago. He has published broadly and been recognized as American Educational Research Association Cattell Early Career Award for Programmatic Research (2001), W.T. Grant Foundation Distinguished Fellow (2008), and an American Educational Research Association Fellow (2009). In 2002 he co-edited *Education in the New Latino Diaspora* (Ablex Press) with the other two editors of this new volume.

CPSIA information can be obtained at www.ICGtesting.com
Printed in the USA
LVOW07s0258250815

451419LV00021B/322/P